THE REVIVAL OF RIGHT-WING
EXTREMISM IN THE NINETIES

CASS SERIES ON POLITICAL VIOLENCE

series Editors:
DAVID C. RAPOPORT, University of California, Los Angeles
PAUL WILKINSON, University of St Andrews, Scotland

THE REVIVAL OF RIGHT-WING EXTREMISM IN THE NINETIES

Edited by

PETER H. MERKL

Professor Emeritus of Political Science,
University of California, Santa Barbara

and

LEONARD WEINBERG

Professor of Political Science, University of Nevada, Reno

FRANK CASS
LONDON • PORTLAND, OR.

Published in 1997 in Great Britain by
FRANK CASS & CO. LTD.
Newbury House,
900 Eastern Avenue, London IG2 7HH

and in the United States of America by
FRANK CASS
c/o ISBS
5804 N.E. Hassalo Street, Portland, Oregon 97213-3644

British Library Cataloguing in Publication Data
A catalogue record for this book is available
from the British Library

ISBN 0 7146 4676 8 (hardback)
ISBN 0 7146 4207 X (paper)

Library of Congress Cataloging-in-Publication Data
A catalog record for this book is available from the
Library of Congress

Printed in Great Britain by
Bookcraft (Bath) Ltd, Midsomer Norton, Avon

Contents

Preface

Peter Merkl and Leonard Weinberg's *The Revival of Right Wing Extremism in the Nineties* is a thoughtful, scholarly and welcome addition to the Frank Cass Series on Political Violence. Its predecessors, Tore Bjorgo's *Terror from the Extreme Right* (1995) and Michael Barkun's *Millennialism and Violence* (1996), were originally special issues of *The Journal of Terrorism and Political Violence* (TPV). But this volume was planned independently of the editors of TPV.

Each volume so far focuses on violence generated by the right, and that is surprising because, when the series was first discussed, no one thought the original emphasis would be so pronounced. The collapse of Marxism simply made right-wing activities much more obvious and significant.

New themes treated in this volume are related to the activities of the right in Eastern Europe, often led by former Communists. The troubling question of how the circumstances of contemporary Russia compare with those of the Weimar Republic is examined too. When countries are revisited, the emphasis is on right-wing fortunes in the electoral arena and/or on recent remarkable developments like the fall of the Apartheid regime in South Africa and the efforts to conclude a peace in Northern Ireland.

David Rapoport and Paul Wilkinson

Introduction

Peter H. Merkl

This symposium is a follow-up to our earlier *Encounters with the Contemporary Radical Right* (1993) which described the new radical right movements and activities in Europe, Israel, and America, country by country, and according to a common list of important aspects. Each of the contributors was to discuss the ideology, antecedents, political history, and popular support of the relevant movements in his or her country, and the editors rounded out these accounts with particular attention to the question of definitions, continuity with earlier (especially inter-war) movements, and the relation of radical right parties to social movements and individual 'crazies' of the same persuasion. The book 'covered' Britain, Germany, France, Italy, Israel, post-communist Russia, Romania, and the United States. By the time it appeared, the rapidly evolving radical right scene was undergoing dramatic changes which seemed to call for revisions before the printer's ink had dried. Across Western Europe, rising waves of migrants and political asylum-seekers had encountered violent reactions, especially in post-unification Germany. The radical right vote in numbers of countries began to rise to alarming levels, for instance in Austria where Jörg Haider's Freedom Party (FPO) eventually polled 22.6 per cent, in Italy where the neo-fascist Italian Social Movement (MSI) metamorphosed into the National Alliance (AN) after receiving 13.4 per cent of the popular vote and entering the coalition government of Silvio Berlusconi,[1] and Jean-Marie Le Pen's *Front National* (FN) was reinforced by a second large radical right movement – that of Philippe de Villiers, now organized as a party, the Movement for France (MPF).[2] With these countries showing twice the number of extreme right-wing adherents, rumours that the German radical right might do as well in 1994 seemed plausible at first.[3] The Belgian radical right vote has also been rising, especially in the city of Antwerp.

A New Wave of Right-wing Extremism

The anti-foreign violence of the years 1991–93 in Germany, in particular, had loosed an avalanche of media alarms at home and abroad which tended to see in it a revival of national socialism – from Warsaw to Los Angeles, newspapers thought they saw the Nazi stormtroopers on the march again[4] – and excoriated the Kohl government for failing to stem the tide. Only later did it become obvious that such anti-foreign and xenophobic violence had arisen simultaneously in many other Western countries from Poland to Portugal, and in some, such as Britain and France, had long been known to exist in massive proportions, by the police and general public. The severe economic recession in the Western world,[5] moreover, had infused the great debates over immigration and asylum policies from Rome and Bonn to Sacramento, California, with sufficient expressions of ethnocentric prejudice to encourage radical right organization and violent action by 'crazies', skinheads, and others on four continents.[6] Many a politician of the moderate right was seen to jump on the bandwagon and try to use these sentiments to political advantage. De Villiers, for example, and many of his original supporters were from Giscard d'Estaing's Union for a Democratic France (UDF) or the Gaullist party (RPR), while California's Governor Pete Wilson used to be considered a 'liberal' Republican before he 'discovered' these new issues.

The rapidly evolving politics of post-communist Eastern Europe matched the thunder on the right in the West in dramatic ways. With the collapse of communist belief systems, for example, there had been social and cultural movements of nativist beliefs such as *Pamyat* in Russia and the Romanian *Vatra Româneasca*,[7] often dating back before the declining days of communist dictatorship. Vatra actually helped to found a right radical party, PUNR, whereas *Pamyat* still views parties and politicians like Vladimir Zhirinovsky with the distaste of the believers towards the political manipulators.[8] Both Russia and Romania, as well as the other East European states, by now have a whole spectrum of ultranationalistic and xenophobic parties that generally oppose the establishment and completion of liberal democracy in their countries.[9] Many of them came directly out of the old communist establishment like the Greek goddess of war and peace, Pallas Athena, from the forehead of Zeus. There is overwhelming evidence that the old communist regimes had always harboured sentiments of inherent nationalism, and even xenophobic prejudices barely hidden under the cloak of Marxist internationalism. It should not surprise us that many of today's ultranationalist parties are led by ex-communist or neo-communist politicians.[10] Romania's symbiosis of Iliescu's neo-communist government with the ultranationalist parties and leaders is perhaps an extreme case but there are shadings of it throughout the post-communist world, including in East Germany where the neo-communist Party of Democratic Socialism (PDS) has been moderately successful in appealing to a sense of humiliated East German patriotism against the alleged colonization of East Germany by West German business and government.[11]

A New Approach

The lessons drawn by the editors of *Encounters* from the explosive developments on the extreme right in the years 1992–94 were clear. The sudden and dramatic upsurge of the radical right vote in some but not in other countries, the shocking waves of xenophobic violence that were at first attributed only to Germany, and the differences among right extremist movements clearly called for a comparative approach, for which our country-by-country method of *Encounters* had already set out a basis. A number of novel features – or features that now struck us as new – also suggested lines along which such comparisons should be pursued. What was the difference between the old inter-war radical right and the contemporary phenomenon? Were there new social settings, new international compulsions, new conflicts in these societies – for example over the ubiquitous presence of foreign residents or the flow of immigration – that could explain why radical right movements had become so strong in the eighties and nineties? With the enormous changes in the family, in gender relations, and the role of the individual, was the right-winger of today motivated by different psychological forces from those, that Wilhelm Reich, for example, had tried to analyze as a product of his family and relationships?

What really are the differences between the West and East European radical right, and what seems to account for them and for their dramatic evolution in the few years since the fall of communism?[12] Only yesterday, Zhirinovsky's writings and the propaganda of his Liberal Democrats suggested that the greatest menace of their possible success might lie in their manifested desire to reconquer the 'near-abroad', the now independent former union republics of the Soviet Union, and to re-establish the imperial prestige of the former Soviets in the World. The Greater Romania party (and its equivalents in Hungary and Eastern Europe) threatens to use military force to reconquer Bessarabia and to defend Transylvania from alleged Hungarian designs of aggression or takeover from within. Eastern Europe and especially the former Soviet Union is full of the makings of the irredentist scenario of the early German Third Reich. The Nazis could point to pockets of 'oppressed' German ethnic minorities all over the once German or Hapsburg successor states – the Sudeten Germans in Czechoslovakia and similar German settlements in Poland, Yugoslavia, Hungary, and Romania – as an excuse for an imperialistic drive for their 'liberation'. Today it is Russian minorities in the Baltic states, the Ukraine, Moldova, and so on, who seem threatened by the oppression of the new native majorities. Yet the more immediate political appeal of Zhirinovsky – already evident in his successful election campaign of late 1993 – was not for war and empire but for law and order against the crime and anarchy threatening Russians at home. Dictatorship is the first card that will be played by the Russian radical right – and would be the first arrow in the Romanian radical quiver, if the Iliescu government did not already hold quasi-dictatorial sway – against the economic and social disruptions under which ordinary Russians have to live.

Economic reforms and market forces are common bugbears for both ex-communist state employees and right-wing demagogues who often link them with foreign investors and the International Monetary Fund. Once radical right demagogues are given dictatorial power, of course, what would keep them from using this power in acting on their known prejudices, persecuting minorities within and attacking neighbours in pursuit of the re-establishment of a Russian, Romanian, Hungarian, or Serbian empire? Given the power and military might, why would they refrain from horrendous campaigns of ethnic cleansing such as were carried out by the Nazis in conquered Eastern Europe and have been in progress in Bosnia today?[13]

A Look at the Chapters Ahead

Following the clues of the most recent development in right-wing extremism, we approached our subject from several angles at once. In the opening chapter, 'Why Are They So Strong Now', one of the editors addresses the subject of the newness of the contemporary movements of the radical right and their glaring differences from inter-war fascist movements. We follow the traditional distinction between the pre-power *movements* and fascist *regimes* which tend to differ from the movements by 1) adaptation to the political realities of the time, likely coalition partners and special opportunities, and 2) co-optation of groups and entire classes of opportunists, especially members of the previous establishment. This chapter particularly deals with the differences in the political and social settings of contemporary and pre-1945 right-wing extremism – also their very different international environments – and points to the role of immigration, education, and gender issues in the make-up of the current 'white male revolt' and its parallels in different societies. Today's 'post-industrial' radical right in the West and even the post-communist movements of a similar type in Eastern Europe are the product of their respective settings and contemporary problems. It would be astounding if they resembled earlier antecedents in much more than the labels given to them by both their partisans and their antagonists. Having said this, we have to add, however, that the continuities in the East are still stronger than in the West where the linkage between nationalism and territorial control, not to mention war or empire, has faded from the public mind. No Westerners, even of the radical right, would advocate military solutions any more to rightist ethnic grievances.

The next chapter, by Piero Ignazi, takes its departure from ideological commonalities among contemporary radical right groups which gives it a solid base in the traditional definitions of inter-war fascist movements and a standard from which to gauge the varieties of today. Ignazi's distinction between traditional and post-industrial radical right parties marks the dividing line that the first chapter addresses from the angle of different historical and social settings, and from the evolving gender roles.

The third chapter, by Michael Minkenberg, argues somewhat the opposite of our thesis that today's extreme right is very different from that of the inter-war period. He speaks of the danger of a 'Weimarization' of contemporary European politics and of strains of modernization that strike him as quite similar to those that produced the historical fascist movements. Comparing the 'New Right' movements of France and Germany – not to be confused with the intellectual *nouvelle droite* and its related German equivalent which are also discussed at length – yields a populist neo-conservative radicalism on the one hand that rejects the New Left of 1968 and the seventies; it also opposes all social and cultural change and defends social entitlements. On the other hand, there is the militant anti-democratic right-wing extremism of the extreme right parties. These parties, he writes, 'are extreme not in terms of being against or outside the existing constitutional order but... extreme within that order.... In fact, they provide a crucial link between established conservatism (and neoconservatism) and the openly antidemocratic extremists on the right by radicalizing (neo-) conservative positions on the one hand, and legitimizing extreme right positions on the other.' Viewed from this angle, public perception of at least the more populist French LePenist *Front National* and the German *Republikaner* may indeed seem to confuse our Left–Right terms of reference as did Mussolini's blackshirts and Hitler's brownshirts in another age. Were they then an extreme right-wing threat, an extreme left-wing threat, or just zealous if misguided patriots?

Lauri Karvonen tackles the phenomenon in Western Europe from still another perspective, that of attitude changes of the eighties as they were ascertained by the *European Values Study* polls between 1981 and 1991. Karvonen sets the stage for the resurgence of the radical right in some notable attitude changes of the entire population that seem to favour the right's intolerance towards other races and foreign workers and the radical left. But at the same time, he found great ambiguity and unevenness among the West European countries under investigation. The statistical smallness of the radical right and the *ad hoc* protest nature of both voting surges and waves of right-wing violence, for example against foreign asylum-seekers, still make it difficult to link macro-trends of opinion with their specific behaviour. In Germany, for example, anti-foreign sentiment reported in public opinion polls has actually declined since the early eighties and has shown no dramatic resurgence in the nineties (except in some regions), while the radical right experienced a sudden surge in early (pre-unification) 1989 and, in some regions, in 1991/1992. During the latter period, also, anti-foreign skinhead violence – presumably with linkages to the parties of the extreme right – escalated to shocking levels.[14] We need to learn to understand the complexities of these evidently autonomous trends beyond the misled and misleading conclusions drawn by hasty pudding journalism. The nature of protest voting alone deserves far more careful analysis than it has so far received.[15]

The East European Radical Right

In comparison to the complications and open questions about the continuities of the contemporary radical right with its antecedents in Western Europe, their equivalents in Eastern Europe seem at once simpler and more straightforward, but also astounding in their post-communist habitats. After nearly half a century of communist internationalism and deliberate repression of nationalist politics, ultra-nationalist feelings and movements are back with a vengeance, like genies from the bottles in which they were long confined. In the midst of the giddy economic transformations and unstable party systems even the old state communist parties have made a comeback, albeit under new names and programmes. There are once again nationalist, even neo-fascist groups and parties which do indeed resemble their inter-war predecessors even though their class-specific context has changed profoundly. There are no more plotting monarchists or aristocrats, except perhaps 'red barons',[16] and even the military conspiracies are more likely to be at the beck and call of old communist élites and security networks than of feudal lords and landholders.

Other inter-war factors, however, are as live and potent as ever, such as the ethnic rivalries and hatreds that, after deliberate instigation, are setting neighbour upon neighbour in former Yugoslavia for example. Poland still has its minorities, including a German one that sometimes looks to Germany for support.[17] It also has a dozen or so radical right groups held together loosely by their anti-German, anti-Russian, anti-Semitic, and anti-government feelings – especially about privatization and market reforms, or foreign 'conspiracies' ranging from the IMF and EU to foreign investors. Some hark back to the integral Catholic nationalism of Roman Dmowski, and rely on violent skinheads to do their bidding. Some are radical populists, such as Stanislaw Tyminski's Party X or rural self-defence. Czechoslovakia has already been torn in two by the centrifugal pulls of different nationalities, even though what is left of the old Sudeten Germans has been careful not to offend the Czech majority of Bohemia and Moravia – the Sudeten refugees of the immediate post-war period in West Germany are making noise enough for both those who fled or were expelled, and those who stayed behind. Here, too, there are xenophobic and populist movements such as the Republicans and their anti-gypsy, skinhead clientele. Hungary has not only its memories of dismemberment under the 1919 Peace Treaty of Trianon, but large numbers of ethnic fellow Hungarians oppressed in Romania and elsewhere since those days, through the many decades of right-wing and communist dictatorships as well as the Second World War. Hungary also has its anti-semitic and anti-Slav movements and politicians, such as Istvan Csurka. Small wonder, then, as Thomas Szayna relates in Chapter 5, that more or less fascistic nationalist movements have been rearing their heads throughout this northern tier of post-communist Eastern Europe. Some of them consciously relate themselves to such inter-war precedents as Poland's Pilsudski regime, Hungarian nativist writers of the thirties and forties, and aggressive plans to win back ethnic territory and populations that were lost some 70 years ago or since. Domestic ethnic conflicts and rivalries are inextricably bound up with international tensions and the threat of war, as Thomas Szayna explains in his contribution.

Few post-communist countries exemplify the problems better than Romania which is today farther from democracy than most of the new East European regimes. The political opposition in Romania even claims that a kind of 'velvet restoration' has taken place as many of the politicians of the former regime have reappeared in key posts under the re-elected Ion Iliescu and his Romanian Social Democrats (or reform communists). Most interesting to us, and symptomatic of the post-communist evolution in many Eastern European states, is the close co-operation between the ruling Social Democrats and various ultranationalist parties. The Romanian National Union party occupies four ministerial portfolios and the Greater Romania party – *nomen est omen* – has taken over the culture and health ministries. These parties were originally billed as satellite parties of the Social Democrats for 'exploring' sensitive issues such as xenophobia and nationalism, but have long exacted their price for supporting the Iliescu government. Recent actions suspending dozens of mayors and threatening imprisonment for 'slandering the country' and using foreign flags are provocations aimed at the large Hungarian minority in Romania. There are several other minorities, most prominently the gypsies (Roma), who have been fleeing from pogroms and showing up as far away as in Southern France and West Germany, ever since the fall of Nicolae Ceauşescu. As Henry Carey explains in Chapter 6, this is only the beginning of the unholy alliance between neo-communists – the government also relies on the silent support of the Socialist Labour party, the direct successor of the old Communist party – and ultranationalist groups throughout Eastern Europe.

Resurfacing communist leaders themselves quite often exhibit a degree of ultranationalist prejudice we would never have expected from such past paragons of communist internationalism. Among the plethora of Russian ultranationalist and cryptofascist groups, as Vera Tolz relates in Chapter 7 moreover, there is plenty of common ground to be found with nostalgic communists in reconquering the old Soviet empire from the Balts, Ukrainians, Georgians, and other newly empowered national groups. As Sergei Karaganov has warned the West, we cannot even take for granted that the government of Boris Yeltsin and his successors will maintain a conciliatory course of policy towards the other post-Soviet republics forever, given the new Russian *irredenta* there.[18] Perhaps we have tended to misjudge the communist élites of yesterday and failed to notice their latent nationalism all along. Watching the Yeltsin government[19] and its out-of-control military rage against the long-persecuted Chechens – who sought independence from within the Russian Federation itself – should give us a taste of the underlying nationalistic fury that may await the challengers to Russian pride elsewhere. In Ukraine, fortunately, the representation of the Russian minority and avoidance of an ethnically-based citizenship has facilitated compromises between Ukrainian interests and Russian power and, up to now, has denied a focus for agitation to the fragmented, radical right. A major conflict with neighbouring Russia would greatly invigorate and unite the right in their quest for national strength. There may also be another side to right-wing revisionism, as Taras Kuzio explains in his contribution with regard to Belarus, where Pan-Slavs advocate an *Anschluss* with Russia, not unlike that which the Austrian Nazis and Pan Germans of another generation had proposed for Austria and Germany.

Comparing Post-Communist Russia with Weimar

Underneath the valiant struggle for democracy in Russia, not unlike that of the Weimar Republic, there are ultranationalist sentiments of imperial pride and revenge waiting to be released in an explosive fashion. To make the Weimar parallel even more compelling, severe economic crisis and anarchy are widely blamed on the government and its capitalistic market reforms – a boon to both neo-communist propaganda and cryptofascist calls for 'law and order', or actual dictatorship. If the calls for imperialistic solutions to the wounded national pride seem to be in competition with current calls for dictatorial authority – at present the latter seems to have pushed aside the former in the appeals of the radical right – again we should not forget the collapse of the Weimar Republic into the arms of national socialism. Even if the one-third of German voters who voted for Hitler in 1932 did so mostly because they wanted a strong hand to curb violence in the streets (largely initiated by his stormtroopers) and an end to economic misery, how were they to keep him from ultimately using his dictatorial power to renew the national struggle of the First World War and to perpetrate genocide at the most massive level ever known?

The right-wing appeal of nostalgic imperialism and economic misery to functionaries of the old communist regimes also had its parallels among the professional soldiers, civil servants, young students, and business and professional people associated with the German and Hapsburg empires before 1918. The collapsing state structures and socio-economic careers of these old empires, as of the disintegrating communist state societies from 1989 to 1991, left behind large numbers of persons who lost their livelihood and function in the system. Even the less political of the self-declared 'unpolitical' soldiers, security staff, and civil servants, but also young careerists whose opportunity structure had fallen apart, suddenly discovered a fierce loyalty to the old regime and a visceral hatred for its presumable destroyers and successors.[20] Just as many of the disappointed German or Austrian career officers (especially colonial officers) of this description eventually developed a right-wing extremist identity that led them into the Nazi party, many communist ex-officers, ex-KGB men, or their equivalent, but also party and civil administrators, and state farm or factory managers became neo-communist or ultranationalist activists, or a combination of both.[21]

For the older Second World War veterans and lifelong CP (USSR) members who had learned to identify with their function in the old system, there were German imperial precedents – for example, German First World War officers whose insignia were torn off their uniforms by mobs as they returned in defeat in late 1918 from the front to face a pacifist and revolutionized nation and sweeping reforms of their system.[22] We could see their equivalent in the grey heads in the counter-demonstrations against Yeltsin in the last two years. The younger communist careerists had seen their world of values collapse and their educational or professional careers go up in smoke. Neither of them could 'understand' or accept the new values and, therefore, they adopted an extremely defensive oppositional stance, whether neo-communist or stridently nationalist.[23] Some became violent in their outrage, for example the squads that tried to storm communications centres during Yeltsin's standoff with the rebellious parliament in 1993. Others were content to demonstrate with red flags or to vote, anonymously, for Zhirinovsky's Liberal Democrats or one of the smaller ultranationalist groups.

Paranoia, Racism, and Religion

There are other settings for right-wing extremism, especially in countries of the Anglo-American diaspora, which enhance our comparative understanding of the phenomena under consideration. The legacy of racism and apartheid in the United States and the Republic of South Africa, so recently subdued in both countries, still plays a considerable role on the extremist margins of politics and in the form of a threatening backlash – for example in the current assault on American 'affirmative action' programmes.[24] In the current turbulent climate of American politics, moreover, the dividing lines between moderate and extreme right-wing politics have become so blurred, especially with the insurgency of the religious right, that it is often impossible to tell whether a particular politician in national politics is only appealing to exclusionary or racial prejudices or expressing his own. American neo-Nazi and racist organizations, for example the Ku Klux Klan, also have established branches in Europe in some instances and have supplied European neo-fascists with funds and propaganda materials in others.[25] Before 1945, both South African and American apartheid thinking already had a profound influence on European racists and national socialists.

Next to racism, often with a religious angle, American radical right groups have frequently based their appeal on anti-communism, or fears of a threatening communist conspiracy during the Cold War, as Leonard Weinberg, one of the editors of this volume,[26] points out in his comparative chapter on the American extreme right wing. At the height of the civil rights movement and of official anti-communist hysteria, it was very common to accuse civil rights advocates of racial integration, such as Martin Luther King, of being communists. One kind of alleged conspiracy, especially concerning opposition to racism, was easily recoined into another, less dubious one. Largely in the absence of a credible internal communist threat, this recent manifestation of the 'paranoid style' in American history (Richard Hofstadter) has lacked an obvious enemy since the fall of communism and the end of the Cold War. American political paranoia, however, is far from dead, having found new conspiracies and popular targets right and left. Prominent among the targets are the new waves of immigrants, various minorities, and welfare recipients, especially unwed teenage or welfare mothers. The favourite conspiracies-of-the-month of the American right-wing groups include old familiars such as the Jews, North Eastern bankers, the Trilateral Commission, the Council on Foreign Relations and the United Nations, and newer ones – such as Japanese economic power, NAFTA and, with a vengeance, the agents of the federal government. The propaganda of this radical right spews forth in particular from radio talk shows ranging from rural and small town stations to nationally distributed messages from convicted Watergate conspirator, H. Gordon Liddy, and Rush Limbaugh, but also, on appropriate subjects such as women's freedom of choice, from figures of the religious right.[27] This extremist propaganda has been readily picked up and exploited by a tabloidized press and by prominent members of the post-1992 Republican opposition and (since late 1994) new majority in Congress.

The moderate right wing, as I said earlier, is no longer easy to separate in its paranoid expressions from the American radical right. The extreme behaviour, on the other hand, especially the violent actions and a readiness for violence, of American right-wing extremism is clearly still a world apart from the demagogues of radio, pulpit, the tabloid

press, and the campaign circuits. Its activists may feel encouraged by the
torrents of partisan invective and personal hatred, pouring forth from
many quarters, but it is only they – and perhaps a few unbalanced loners
– who have been planning and committing acts of extreme violence,
bombings, arson, and assassination attempts. Among the rapidly
changing scene of groups of the American radical right, the most
prominent now (1995) are some 224 militia groups in 39 of the 50 states.
Of these, 45 in 22 states are known to have ties to neo-Nazi or white
supremacist organizations and there can be little doubt that many of the
new members of the burgeoning militia movement used to be with older
extremist groups of the right, including the now declining racist
skinhead groups in the USA. The car bombing that destroyed the federal
centre in Oklahoma City in spring, 1995, has been widely attributed to
members of the Michigan militia and possibly to others. The chief
suspect, Timothy McVeigh, shares with other extreme rightists – and to
a lesser degree, with the American New Right – a burning hatred of
federal agents[28] and a regular diet of the paranoid newsletters and books
of the radical right, such as *The Turner Diaries* by William Pierce.[29]

The third category of the American radical right, libertarian tax
protesters and survivalists, seems at first glance more peripheral to the
violent core. However, theirs is a significant key role that brings together
many strands of right-wing agitation, a certain kind of religious
fundamentalism,[30] resistance to bureaucrats, defence of wilderness
property rights against federal environmental regulation – or more often,
of inexpensive grazing and mineral exploitation rights on public land in
the West – with a moderate political right in Congress that is motivated
by a profound hostility to federal management and regulation and bent
on cutting taxes and devolving federal power on to the states. Except for
the first category of racism and national socialism, and the direct
organizational linkages to the extreme right in Europe, it is not always
easy to compare the American and European right-wing extremes. Even
anti-communism in its day was rather different in Europe, since there
were (and are) sizeable communist parties and efforts at espionage and
infiltration all over the continent. Tax protest without the paranoia, the
survivalists, and the religious fringe, however, can command a
following in Western Europe.

Our final comparison brings in the extreme right in South Africa and
in Northern Ireland, two areas where long-standing patterns of
domination – whites over South African blacks and Northern Irish
Protestants over the Catholic minority – have come to an end very
recently and, relatively speaking, without paroxysms of right-wing
violence. To be sure, some violence was involved in both cases[31] but, as

Adrian Guelke points out in the final chapter, the changing realities finally won the day. Most significantly in the South African case, a series of democratically elected white governments were in the forefront of the great compromises which ended apartheid. The takeover of control by the British army in Northern Ireland in 1973, by contrast, took away self-determination from the Protestants whose frustration clearly gave the Ulster Defence Forces a broadly-based excuse for resorting to terrorism in response to IRA terror. On the other hand, we have to remember that in Northern Ireland the Protestants had an ample majority over the Catholics and that this majority had shown little inclination to follow a path of compromise similar to that of the South African whites. The roots of the right-wing defence of apartheid in the Afrikaner community and the Dutch Reformed Church, as compared to other ethnic and religious traditions in South Africa, also made for a different situation from that in Northern Ireland.

Notes

1. Along with Berlusconi's *Forza Italia*, a brand-new and unusual party, and the *Lega Nord*, a regional protest movement. The leader of the MSI, Gianfranco Fini, proclaimed the transformation of his party – an outward sign of its new path of moderation and respectability – and, despite the difficulties of his coalition partners and the eventual demise of the government, has enjoyed great personal popularity in Italy. The Berlusconi government lasted less than a year.
2. In the European elections of 1994, de Villiers' anti-Maastricht movement, called The Other Europe (LAE), polled 12.4 per cent and Le Pen's FN (billed as the List Against Maastricht) 10.5 per cent of the popular vote which had a turnout rate of 55.0 per cent of the eligible population. The Italian NA won 12.5 per cent in the same election. Le Pen received 15 per cent of the first presidential ballot in April, 1995.
3. In reality, the German *Republikaner* polled only 3.9 per cent in the European and 1.9 per cent in the German parliamentary elections of 1994, although they had reached much higher levels in some state and local elections in 1992 and 1993.
4. For examples, see Merkl, 'Are the Old Nazis Really Coming Back?' in Merkl (ed.), *The Federal Republic at Forty-Five* (London: Macmillan, 1995).
5. In Germany, for example, the global recession hit home in 1992 and by early 1993, produced an unemployment level of three million. The year of 1992 also saw the highest level of new asylum-seekers, nearly half a million, and the most violent reactions towards them.
6. In addition to Western Europe and North America (where the mean-spirited prejudices of the immigration debates were further encouraged by the passage of Proposition 187 in California and by Republican national plans to deny social benefits to legal as well as illegal aliens), Australia and Japan were similarly stricken by ethnocentric reactions to foreigners.
7. For descriptions, see the essays by V. Krasnov and T. Gilberg in *Encounters*, pp. 95–131 and the chapters by Vera Tolz and Henry F. Carey.

8. The wrath of *Pamyat* was no doubt aggravated by the spectacular success of the Liberal Democrats in the 1993 parliamentary elections. *Pamyat* members also questioned Zhirinovsky's background because his father is rumoured to have been Jewish. For a German reading of Zhirinovsky's imperialistic writings, see P. Roth, 'Schirinowskis Geopolitik', *Die politische Meinung 39*, Oct. 1994, pp. 15–26.

9. See also the chapters by Thomas S. Szayna and Taras Kuzio.

10. The only clue to separating ethnocentric movements and communist revivals in the post-communist states seems to be the reform label. Whether as a slogan, as in Russia, or as a prefix – as in reform communists – the word reform clearly stands opposed to both kinds of collectivism, old-line communism and ultranationalism.

11. It is no accident that certain East German local neo-fascist leaders and many youthful followers have been dubbed the 'brown sons of red fathers' (meaning former communist (SED) functionaries) in a clever reversal of the label of 'red sons of brown fathers' that used to be applied to many of the 1968 rebels in those days in the West where generational conflict often underlay the political dissension in many conservative West German families. For an insider analysis of the difficulties of neo-communism after the collapse, see also M. Brie, M. Herzig, and T. Koch (eds), *Die PDS* (Cologne: Pappy Rossa, 1995). The PDS, incidentally, doubled its percentage of the national vote between the 1990 and 1994 national elections, although most of its 1994 voters may already have voted for it in March 1990, in the first free election in East Germany.

12. See also the survey by P. Hockenos, *Free to Hate: The Rise of the Right in Post-Communist Eastern Europe* (London: Routledge, 1992) where East Germany, Poland, and the Czech, Hungarian, and Romanian radical right movements are discussed at length. Hockenos also sees a clear continuity in the values and political cultures of the right-wing and the antecedent communist regimes.

13. We could also have examined the impact of the enormous changes brought by the Middle Eastern peace process upon the Israeli radical right in the last two years since Israel was 'covered' in *Encounters*, pp. 132–61. Since the Israeli situation is rather different from that of most Western countries, and the religious emphasis also gives the extreme right a different dynamic, we decided not to pursue this investigation further.

14. See especially the findings of H. Willems, *Fremdenfeindliche Gewalt. Einstellungen, Täter, Konflikteskalation* (Opladen: Leske & Budrich, 1993), pp. 33–59, 66–7.

15. Typical German examples are the regional surges of the *Republikaner* (REP) vote in the state elections in West Berlin 1989 (7.1 per cent), Bavaria 1989 and 1990 (14.6 per cent in the European and 4.9 per cent in the *Landtag* elections, respectively), and Baden-Württemberg 1992 (10.9 per cent). In all of these state elections, the sudden surge of the REPs resulted mostly from recent local, regional, or federal decisions or policies which caused CDU/CSU, SPD, and FDP voters to briefly bolster the right-wing vote in order to 'send a signal' to whomsoever was in charge. Having done so, the REP vote usually dropped promptly to its real core of rightists who, for example in Baden-Württemberg, were estimated to be no more than two per cent of the adult population. See P.H. Merkl, 'Protest Voting German Style', in *Newsletter of the Conference Group on German Politics*, April 1995, pp. 5–7.

16. In some post-communist societies, old party apparatchiks and state factory managers have turned out to be almost the only native entrepreneurs, both because they have the connections and managerial skills and because they may possess some capital – often of dubious origins. These new/old élites have been dubbed the

'red barons' by the people and by their detractors.

17. See also P. H. Merkl, *German Unification in the European Context* (Penn State Press, 1993) pp. 6–7, 36–9, and 335–46 where the German minority relations with the Polish government and the Kohl administration before and after 1989 are discussed at some length.

18. See Karaganov, 'Russia and the Other Independent Republics in Asia', *Adelphi Paper 276* (London: IISS, 1992). See also the survey of W.C. Bodie, 'The Threat to America from the Former USSR', *Orbis 37* (Fall 1993), pp. 509–25.

19. The authoritarian position of the president in the new constitution of December 1993 (not unlike that of the Weimar president after 1930) places almost exclusive reliance on the flawed judgement of this one person – who frequently absents himself from the command post granted to him – and on parts of his executive and military apparatus that are responsible to no one. Parliament (which largely opposed the bloody clampdown on Chechnya) was given very little authority to interfere with the president's power.

20. See Merkl, *Political Violence under the Swastika: 581 Early Nazis* (Princeton University Press, 1975), pp. 51n, 56–9.

21. See the paper by Merkl, Collapsing Imperial German Structures and Extremist Identity, 1918–1923, presented at the XIII World Congress of the International Sociological Association in Bielefeld, 18–23 July 1994.

22. See, for example, *Political Violence under the Swastika*, pp. 145, 500–2, 514–16.

23. It is much harder to account for the younger cohorts that might join neo-fascist or right-wing skinhead groups without ever having been in the old career structures. Their old-world values were, of course, destroyed at home and at school, and their parents and teachers may reflect some of the dynamics of older cohorts. Finally, there is the direct attraction of new, dynamic youth movements that may well rope in disoriented youngsters by the dozen. See also the comparable evidence of the recruitment of Nazi stormtroopers in Merkl, *The Making of a Stormtrooper* (Princeton University Press, 1980), Part 2 and *Political Violence under the Swastika*, (Princeton University Press, 1975), Parts 3 and 4, which stress the presence of an autonomous youth culture.

24. The breadth of affirmative action, which has included the role of women and a number of minorities other than Afro-Americans, makes it more difficult to see in its abolition a simple relapse to the pre-civil rights days of black segregation. However, the various rights of women in American society and employment have also been under virulent and vituperative right-wing attack in recent years.

25. One such source of Nazi propaganda materials for German neo-Nazi groups which are not allowed to produce the material themselves has been Gary Laucks of Lincoln, Nebraska whom the Danish police have finally arrested and threatened with extradition to Germany. See also the essays by T. Björge and H. Lööw in Björge and Witte, *Racist Violence in Europe*, Chs. 3 and 5.

26. See also his chapter in *Encounters ...*, pp. 185–203.

27. Typical examples are the campaigns of personal vituperation against Hillary Rodham Clinton, President Clinton, and some of his appointees, for instance the well-organized drive of the Rev. Jerry Falwell to depict the suicide of Vincent Foster, a legal adviser to the president, as a murder carried out on behalf of Clinton to cover up other alleged wrongdoings.

28. In recent years, this hatred particularly focused on the 1993 storming of the Branch Davidian compound in Waco, Texas, by agents of the Bureau of Alcohol, Tobacco and Firearms and the 1992 Idaho shootout involving 'survivalist' Randy Weaver and the FBI. The Waco incident resulted in the fiery death of most of the cultists,

the second event in the death of Mrs Weaver and her son. For the statistics on the militias, see *Klanwatch Intelligence Report*, June 1995, No. 78 and *SPLC Report*, June 1995.

29. *The Turner Diaries* tell a story of a group of self-styled 'patriots' who go underground to escape and combat a tyranny of federal bureaucrats. The book is believed to have inspired the racist group that called itself The Order to embark on a 14-month crime spree to finance their role in an anticipated race war; the author is a notable figure of the American neo-Nazi scene.

30. Implausible though it may seem, there are some linkages between the Christian identity groups and stalwart figures of the religous right whose fulminations against a New World Order have a suspicious, paranoid ring.

31. The largest excesses of violence in the South African transition occurred not between whites and blacks, but between Inkatha's Zulus and ANC's Xhosa tribesmen. And even though there may have been some collusion with the white security forces, this black-on-black slaughter would hardly have escalated without the pronounced hostility between the tribes and their struggle for power after the transition.

1

Why Are They So Strong Now? Comparative Reflections on the Revival of the Radical Right in Europe

Peter H. Merkl

'This is exactly the way things began the last time, in Hitler's time. First you hear speeches full of hate, then come the firebombs, and then suddenly it's out of control,' a *New York Times* correspondent quoted a German schoolgirl on the occasion of the 1992 killing of three Turkish women at Moelln, near Hamburg, by right-wing skinheads. The German press and the opposition Social Democrats and Greens likewise linked the anti-foreign violence of that *annus horribilis* to visions of the old stormtroopers on the march and, for a touch of contemporary realities, to the immigration and asylum policies of the ruling Christian Democrats, specifically their desire to modify the constitutional article (Basic Law article 16) promising political asylum to all comers.[1] In the bitter partisan controversies – the amending of article 16 in mid-May of 1993 led to a veritable siege of the Bonn parliament – and with the supercharged media campaigns in Germany and the United States, everyone was so concerned with making a point that they forgot that schoolgirls do not always make good historians or detached social scientists.[2]

In the meantime, it has become obvious that this 'German disease' has not only long spread to other countries of Western Europe and North America, but was present all along in many of them, in particular in France, Great Britain, the Netherlands, Sweden, and of course in the United States. Everywhere in the West, there are movements of the extreme right and, by now, also manifestations of pronounced prejudice and violence against visible and imagined foreigners. At this point it becomes absolutely necessary to define our terms of reference clearly and carefully. What and whom exactly are we referring to as radical right or extreme rightist? How do organized movements or parties and violent young groups and their outrages relate to one another? Are we describing here a set of beliefs, an organizational history, or the continuities of right-wing personnel or family socialization, or current extremist activities, or all of the above?

In this volume we will argue that the current resurgence of extreme right movements and activities is largely new and *sui generis*, and should be investigated accordingly, as a largely new and disturbing phenomenon related to and largely caused by recent conditions and circumstances. It is not enough to point to the inter-war French fascists of the 'revolutionary right' (Zeev Sternhell) of different colours, Oswald Mosley's British Union of Fascists, the Spanish Falange, Mussolini's blackshirts, or Hitler's brownshirts to shed much light on the present radical right in these countries. The misuse of the old labels both by the right-wing radicals themselves and their pejorative use in partisan debates or by today's media has prevented us from recognizing the newness and the profound changes in the situation of today as compared to the inter-war 'fascist epoch', as Ernst Nolte called the twenties and thirties.

Defining the Radical Right

There is little reason to make a great mystery of who and what belongs to the extreme right today. As the term makes clear, the definition is first and foremost a situational one: To the extent that we still place political parties, movements, and activities on a Right–Left scale – and some people question the validity of such a universal measuring stick – extreme right means just that.[3] Given a particular issue of importance to them, for example immigration, or the rights of asylum, a radical right position is likely to be more hostile or punitive than those advanced by all the other parties, movements, or persons. It may threaten extreme, even cruel measures against illegal immigrants and question the rights of foreign-born legal citizens, as has become common verbiage from the French *Front National* throughout anti-foreign movements all over Western Europe and, last but not least, in Canada and the United States. Extreme measures and violations of the rights of immigrants have also appeared in the form of hostile police or immigration officer treatment of aliens and even of legal residents and citizens associated with them, as for example in the massive police attack ordered by the Paris Prefect of Police, Maurice Papon, on a 1961 demonstration of Algerians, most of them French citizens who were peacefully protesting a curfew imposed on French Algerians.[4]

This last example also hints at the racism, prejudices, and, in some cases, genocidal tendencies we associate with the extreme right. However, our insistence on a situational definition rather than the usual search for a quasi-Platonic 'essence of fascism' avoids the pitfalls of partisan finger-pointing and personal polemics that so often obscure the nature of a particular movement. Calling a candidate or movement 'fascist', 'neo-', 'crypto-', or 'quasi'-fascist sheds no more light on the matter than did the old charges of 'communist', crypto-, quasi-communist, or 'communist sympathizer' in the not too distant past.[5] On the other hand, a situational definition leads to other difficulties. Not only is it perfectly possible for a party or movement that is at the right-most end of the political spectrum on one important issue to be moderate on other issues that it may make it more difficult to classify it. An extreme right position may also pertain to the space available within a moderate or even an extreme left-wing party or movement. When, for example, reborn communist parties in the successor states of the former Soviet Union – a frequent source of confusion of right and left in our accepted sense of the terms – adopt stridently nationalistic policies and threaten the use of the old army and secret police against the challenge of systematic reform, they obviously are no longer on the extreme left and, frequently, close to an extreme right course.

Extreme right movements, as Leonard Weinberg has pointed out, furthermore, differ strikingly from conservative parties both in aims and particularly in their uninhibited use of any means to their ends – 'dirty tricks', subversion, and violence.[6] But we may also find on the extreme right of moderate conservative parties, and particularly of very conservative parties, such as the French Gaullists (RPR), groups and persons of radical right views. For years the tough-minded present Interior Minister of France, Charles Pasqua (RPR), authorized police actions of great severity and 'covered' them when casualties resulted, for example among Islamic youths. His much-quoted statement in 1988, that the Gaullists shared most of the values of Jean-Marie Le Pen's *Front National* (FN), on the other hand, needs to be taken with a grain of salt. It is true that the RPR made him a leading figure and continues to support him, but it has evidently shied away from openly endorsing all of his views and methods.[7] His high-handed actions and strong statements have also caused other RPR leaders such as Premier Edouard Balladur, at times, to distance themselves from him.

Extremist politics, to quote Weinberg again, also tends to be intolerant of a plurality of opinions, and disdainful of those who come up with 'complicated answers to simple questions', as the American populist presidential candidate George C. Wallace reportedly said in the 1964 campaign. To them there is only one answer, *the truth*, and, to paraphrase right-wingers from Mussolini to Pierre Poujade, 'in your hearts you know we [alone] are right'.[8] With such certainty of the truth, naturally the extreme right feels entitled to impose it in the most authoritarian fashion on whomsoever does not believe it, and, if necessary, by brute force. It sees no point in parliamentary or other political discussion of *the truth* and rejects the concept of a democratic market-place of competing ideas in which decisions are made by majority rule.

Some writers on the subject, for example Roger Eatwell,[9] have also drawn attention to the fact that, since the French Revolution, right-wing movements seem to have been principally preoccupied with resisting or even reversing the tides of social change that have come over Western societies, but this only explains a part of a many-sided phenomenon. To be sure, the extreme right often shares with the moderate right an aversion to change. But it also tends to envision the 'good old days' in wildly unrealistic ways, a social world without conflict over class exploitation, gender and environmental issues, or racial discrimination – the way we never were. The Germans call it the image of the *heile Welt* (a world intact) and, as compared to it, the world today and in the immediate past is always found wanting or *kaputt* (broken). People who remind us of the imperfections in our world by fighting them, for example advocates of working-class interests or the homeless, feminists, environmentalists, and advocates of minority interests often arouse a tremendous hatred among the members of the radical right. The unrealistic expectations of many a rightist, however, tend to make extreme rightism a utopian ideology at least as often as it may be a reactionary one. It postulates a social order that (contrary to its own claims) never really existed in the past or present[10] and, in frustration over the alleged imperfections of real society, threatens to impose its utopia by force. The determination to impose its 'order' is at least as much the hallmark of the extreme right as may be the nature of the utopia in the minds of these zealots.[11]

Attempts at Substantive Definition

There is another dimension to the radical right which is usually ignored by accounts written in the spirit of political liberalism because it is so antithetical to liberal thinking about politics. Rather than explaining the appeal of a right-wing leader, programme, or movement in the customary terms of the material interests of the followers, this dimension emphasizes 'spirituality', idealism, and imponderables of 'style' as the great attractions of right-wing charisma. Well-known to fascist leaders of the inter-war period in various guises, this aspect has reached a new prominence in the age of television and sophisticated advertisement and public relations, far beyond the uses of the radical right. To give examples, a skilful demagogue like Adolf Hitler always knew that appealing to the longing of young Germans for heroic idealism, self-sacrifice, and even a hero's death was infinitely more powerful than promising them material rewards. Visions of an ideal, or 'spiritual' *Reich* won hands-down over the rationalistic notions of democracy and democratic representation. He and Mussolini were veritable magicians at the art of manipulating symbols and elements of style – including the brown or black uniforms of their stormtroopers and the dramaturgy of their huge rallies and demonstrations[12] – in order to appeal to the hidden fears and longings of their audiences.

In our age of media-wise politics and professional political 'handlers' and hucksters, this symbolic and style dimension of politics has been appropriated with unlimited campaign chests and conspicuous success by conservative politicians from Ronald Reagan to Silvio Berlusconi, the Italian television mogul and, briefly, prime minister. By comparison, contemporary movements of the radical right, for lack of money and talent, seem less adept at their old art of cultivating charisma. A closer look, however, suggests that here again lies a subtle dividing line between the conservative and the radical right clientele, though not always of their leadership.[13] Though they may value the art of political salesmanship as a welcome means to an end – usually the control of governmental intervention in the economy – moderate conservatives never see in it a purpose in itself. The radical right tends to identify the style of leadership and of their leaders with their distinctive aesthetized view of political reality. It has always been their alternative to 'politics as usual' – politics as the grand, heroic spectacle.

There is merit to the attempts to map out a 'core' of extreme right beliefs as, for example, Piero Ignazi has done in his survey in this work. Some analysts even strive for a model of 'generic fascism'[14] that would include all the historic inter-war fascist movements and regimes as well as serving as a touchstone of true rightwing extremist character today. Such a core of beliefs for the movements originating 1917–23 would have included 1) the Great War (the First World War) as an opportunity for national and individual greatness (regardless of casualties); 2) upper- and middle-class revulsion at the Russian Revolution and its domestic followers; 3) ethnic hatred (including anti-Semitism) and cultural xenophobia; 4) rebellion against Western parliamentary democracy, liberalism, and capitalism; and 5) identification with such rebels against the victorious West and its peace treaties (Versailles, etc.) as Mussolini, Ataturk and others. However, we must not forget that most historians are quite sceptical already that the inter-war fascist movements and regimes had much in common besides rather superficial patterns of imitation – often including some communist movements and the Soviet Union as well – and a label of identification attached by themselves or their enemies after the fact. What most of them did have in common was their times, that is the cataclysmic impacts of the First World War, the Russian Revolution, and the crisis of the pre-war order among the social classes and on the economies, social life, and culture throughout Europe.

None of these major commonalities, of course, apply after 1945, but there are now a few new commonalities that might unite the far right of the various countries: nostalgic memories of the fascist hegemony that was whipsawed between the Eastern and Western victors of the Second World War, 40 years of the Cold War, the provocations of the 1968 generation, and the immigrant and refugee question. Fascist nostalgia probably faded with the passing of the generations by the end of the sixties with the exception of the sizable fascist subculture underlying the Italian successor party MSI and other groups where families and youth organizations may have continued socializing the young.[15] The anti-communism of the Cold War years is fading along with the last vestiges of communist power in the East. The challenges of the New Left of the late sixties, for example in the form of student rebellion, feminism, the post-industrial 'new individualism', and the environmental and life-style social movements of the seventies will be discussed below. The immigrant and refugee streams, especially of the eighties and nineties are the other common preoccupation that seems to bring together radical right movements from California to Saxony.

Mislabelling Radical Right Movements

The ghosts of the fascist era of half a century and more ago continue to becloud our analysis of the phenomena of the most recent past. It is not just tabloid journalism that prefers the stereotypical old label to exploring the complex and often embarrassing reality before us – Americans hardly need to go to Europe to find immigrant-bashing, racism, and violent youth – but there are plenty of academics who are slow to address the obvious. In politics, the polemical use of the old historical labels has always been widespread in partisan controversy, and it is not unusual to find such amusing juxtapositions as in the battles over abortion where both sides have called each other fascist in inspiration.[16] In the case of taxpayer protest movements from the Lega Lombarda/Lega Nord and other European anti-tax parties to the Ross Perot movement of the United States and the Progress party of Western

Canada, established major parties and hostile journalists often conspired to marginalize these new challengers by pillorying them as somehow illegitimate and far right in inspiration. For a while, at least, even academic observers fell for this label, for example, for the *leghisti* of Northern Italy.

More interesting if hardly surprising is the readiness with which many young right-wing activists, and even politically unconnected neighbourhood skinhead gangs – and, in some cases, soccer hooligan groups – have reached for the old Nazi or fascist label and some of their flags and symbols. On the one hand, adopting the political taboo of the Nazi label, for example in present-day Germany, is a surefire way for a young rebel without a cause to set off waves of ardently desired public alarm and hostility: *épater le bourgeois*. When a rebellious youngster in a German classroom shouts 'Sieg Heil' or 'Heil Hitler', or 'Ausländer raus' within earshot of a teacher (who is likely to belong to the New Leftish '68 generation), the desired shock result is predictable, regardless of whether or not the juvenile means or knows what he is saying. On the other hand, many of these youths, especially in post-Communist areas (including East Germany) are growing up in such a painful state of confusion, in a vacuum of collapsing political and social values that they are eager to seize upon ready-made images of ethnic identity, especially in an extreme form that appeals to a young person.[17] For reasons probably related to gender (I will return to this subject below), young right-wingers in Italy, Germany, France, and Scandinavia have particularly identified with the supermacho images of black- or brown-shirted bullies, the Spanish Falange, the Romanian Iron Guard or Hungarian Arrow Cross, the warriors of foreign units of the German *Waffen-SS* of the Second World War, and even the heroes of fables and fantasies such as J.R. Tolkien's *The Hobbit* whose name was adopted by the Hobbit youth camps of late seventies' Italy. The question has to be raised, however, whether the eager self-identification with an old and often poorly understood label – and under completely different circumstances – really resurrects the old identities.

If the labelling and self-labelling process over half a century of profound social and political change and successive generations[18] seems to have little explanatory power, shorter spans of time in some cases may be quite different. There may still be a Franquista subculture in existence in parts of Spain, for example, since Generalissimo Franco only died in 1975. Today's American Christian Right and the Ku Klux Klan in some cases may also spring from intact subcultures that tie their present attitudes to the days of segregation and discrimination that were barely overcome in the seventies. In today's South Africa where racial apartheid ended only yesterday, there are obvious social settings from where both white and black racist movements may spring (see the chapter by Adrian Guelke). And in Eastern Europe where 'alien' communist rule suppressed nationalism and feelings of ethnic identity for so long, its effect seems to have preserved, even bottled up, native nationalisms, which are now resurfacing and irritating one another wherever multiethnic settings encourage them (see the contributions by Vera Tolz and Taras Kuzio). If anything, the communist efforts at placing Russians in great numbers in non-Russian union republics or Serbs in non-Serb Yugoslav member states have aggravated the problems of nationalism and potentiated the support for radical right movements. Unlike in Western Europe today, moreover, East European nationalisms appear to be strongly attached to their respective territories and jealous territorial claims, which lend them an explosive potential and the threat of armed conflict (see also the contributions by Thomas S. Szayna and Henry Carey), if not 'ethnic cleansing'.

The Inter-war Setting

If we cannot really explain the motivation of today's radical right with continuities from the old radical right, what can explain it better? Perhaps we first need to call to mind 'the dog that did not bark', the major factors that determined the mind-set of the old right and that are absent today.[19] There is first of all the absence of the grand international conflicts of the First World War and its aftermath: Most of the big old fascist movements of the inter-war period, such as those of Germany, Austria, Hungary, Turkey, and even Italy – the 'stolen victory' – grew from the terrible struggle, the defeat, and the territorial losses of the war. The peace treaties of Versailles, St. Germain-en-Laye, Sèvres, Trianon and so on, created the mass sentiments of wounded nationalism and the military or quasi-military support behind the Nazi and black-shirt movements, as well as Eastern Europe's fascist movements and the Turkish nationalist movement. There are no significant parallels to this except in today's post-communist states, such as Russia, where some rightists and many old communists would like to reconquer the entire lost empire, or at least the Soviet Union (for example Vladimir Zhirinovsky, *Pamyat* and others).

Some of the old fascist support also resulted from nationalist rivalries and friction in the successor states of the Hapsburg empire, such as Czechoslovakia, Poland, Hungary, and Yugoslavia, where the irredentist national groups (especially Germans, Hungarians, and Slovaks) often sought allies abroad, such as the new Italian, German, or Austrian fascist or authoritarian regimes. The presence of ethnic Germans from Eastern Europe in the Nazi party remained significant from its beginnings in 1919 into the Eastern campaigns and genocidal activities of the Second World War until their expulsion. Among post-war movements, there are weak parallels among British and French ex-colonials and stronger ones, today, among the Russians of the 'near abroad', especially in the Baltic States, Moldova, and the Ukraine.

Some of the support for the inter-war fascist movements also came from the struggle and the defeat of the Russian 'whites' by the Bolsheviks, which touched off 'red' revolutionary stirrings and white-fascist resistance in many countries near the Russian civil war and the resulting Russian Bolshevik regime, for example in Hungary, Austria, Germany, Finland, and the Baltic States. Just as the irredentist minorities in the Hapsburg successor states often sought to ally themselves with fascist Italy, Austria, or Germany, other nationalities identified with the new Bolshevik regime, sometimes on the basis of old notions of Panslavism. Again, there is no post-1945 parallel to the impact of the Russian Revolution.

There is a similar absence today of the grand domestic struggles of the 1920s and 30s that pitted the labour movements and socialist and communist parties against semi-traditional and capitalist élites. The class struggles between rising labour, and in some cases also the peasants, and the owners of industry and productive land played a big role in the genesis and support for the old fascist movements in Italy, Germany, and Austria, as well as in France and Spain.[20] Could Mussolini or Hitler have succeeded if the Italian and German socialist movements had not scared the bourgeoisie and old élites of their respective countries into the arms of the fascists? Can we conceive of Franco's rise to power without accounting for the fright of the church and the old Spanish élites before their duly elected socialist and communist government and its supporters? Today, the only parallels seem to be in the struggle for land in Central and Latin America where crypto-fascist conditions and regimes have abounded, often with military support. Except perhaps for the 'black terrorism' of Italian neo-fascists, no contemporary movement of the radical right seriously looks upon their respective socialist or communist parties as the harbingers of a Bolshevik revolution. Unlike the feudal and bourgeois antecedents of yesterday's right, their followers appear to be mostly blue-collar workers themselves.

Another major element in German, Austrian, Italian, and French fascist movements of the 1920s were the masses of unemployed and underemployed military veterans of the Great War, who often organized as violent and threatening veterans' pressure groups and were available for Freecorps or other massive paramilitary and vigilante action, sometimes under civil-war-like conditions. Austria had its *Heimwehr* and Germany and France their militant veterans associations, not to mention plotting ex-officers. Italy was awash with demobilized veterans unwilling to go back to the miserable life of rural or industrial peonage. Furthermore, the collapsing imperial structures of Germany, the Hapsburgs, Russia, and Turkey after the First World War generally created large numbers of unemployed imperial functionaries, such as military and civil servants, as well as other people who developed a fascist identity because the opportunity structures of their lives had been destroyed.[21]

New Social Conflicts

There are, of course, new social problems and tensions today – this is the dog that does bark although only a few people pay any attention – which generate protest attitudes on the right although they are not always organized in a political fashion. Prominent among them is the 'communications revolution' of the 1980s and the people it has left behind, a new unskilled and undereducated underclass. Among young skinheads and right-wing radicals in particular, this element of the lower third of the 'two-thirds society' appears to be prominent. Much depends on formulations here: Empirical data derived from German arrest records for violent assaults on foreigners have not shown unemployment or membership in socially marginal groups to supply disproportionate numbers of right-wing activists – even current (1991) unemployment increased resentment of foreigners only a little, but a low educational status turned out to be highly related to ethnocentric violence.[22] People feel trapped by their lack of relevant skills. Subjectively, moreover, indignation over allegedly discriminatory treatment of Germans *vis-à-vis* foreigners, especially asylum-seekers living at public expense seems typical of the self-justification of violence or tolerance for the ethnocentric violence of others.

The offenders also seem to be getting younger all the time. Not only does family life in the eighties and nineties fail youngsters at a much earlier age than 50 or 60 years ago. The entire biological and social process of growing up appears to have speeded up considerably since the 1920s and 30s. Even though such violent movements have always favoured the young over older adherents (if not the leaders), the ages of known German ethnocentric offenders are astonishingly low. Over 75 per cent of Helmut Willems' 1400 cases are under 21, half of these even under 18, and about 90 per cent are under 25. This is much younger than the Nazi stormtroopers were.[23] In East Germany, in particular, today's 16- to 17-year-olds are said to have been in the historic conjuncture of their passage into puberty and the breakdown of communist authoritarianism in 1990. In surveys, 14- to 17-year-old East German males have been found to be 'most ready' for settling human conflicts by violence.[24] The extreme youth of the known offenders – the few females among them are even younger – makes them also particularly vulnerable to the effect of alcohol consumption, anti-foreign rock music, media hype and sensationalism, and the rumours of local conflict. It also directs attention once more to the failure of family guidance at an extremely volatile age. Not just post-communist parents, but most German and many other countries' families simply fail to socialize their young to the most elementary standards of human, non-violent, coexistence. This is a major structural change to which we shall come back a little later.

The lack of skills and education, as well as the extreme youth of the perpetrators of ethnocentric violence in Germany may also explain the rather inchoate nature of much of their activities. They appear not to have received much help, or would not accept it, from adult organizations such as the Republicans (Reps) or the German People's Union (DVU). Comparative evidence, for example on similar ethnocentric offenders in France, the Netherlands, Italy, and Scandinavia is still rather incomplete, although we have learned that in Sweden and the Netherlands too, there was little organization behind the high levels of ethnocentric violence.[25]

Foreigners and Immigrants

In France, England and the Netherlands, decolonization in the fifties and sixties brought large numbers of refugees – for example Indians from East Africa after Idi Amin's takeover – immigrants, *pieds noirs,* and their British and Dutch equivalents to the imperial mother countries, causing some economic dislocation, and triggering considerable ethnic hostility and right-wing extremist agitation.[26] In Germany, the hub of inter-war fascism, post-war immigration did not at first evoke any right-wing reactions, neither to the displaced persons of 1945–47, nor to the ten million ethnic German refugees and expellees from Eastern Europe and two million East German refugees to West Germany, who were successfully integrated in society and the economy. Even the millions of non-German 'guestworkers' who were brought in on government-sanctioned contracts in the sixties to work in the West German economy raised little political animosity until the energy crises of the seventies when non-oil-producing Germany suddenly had to face the limits of its once meteoric economic growth.

In 1973, the West German government ceased recruiting foreign workers, but still permitted those already in the country to bring in their families rather than go home. From that time on, with more than four million Turks, Yugoslavs, and Common Market nationals still in the country, West German attitudes began to change. The neo-Nazi National Democratic Party (NPD) was the first to try to halt its own electoral demise from the late sixties with election slogans of *Ausländer raus* (out with the foreigners), though at first with little success.[27] The vote and membership of the radical right went into a tailspin until the next wave, in the late eighties.

In the meantime, however, the relations between natives and foreigners, especially in big cities and between German and foreign youth in schools and neighbourhood gangs, began to deteriorate.[28] In public opinion polls, a wave of anti-foreign prejudices began to build – as high as 13.8 per cent of the adult population in 1980 – and then declined again to 5.7 per cent in 1990 when the German public had at least learned to distinguish between different groups of foreigners and asylum-seekers. At the same time, mounting unemployment had reached levels approaching and exceeding ten per cent of the workforce, especially among the young, and remained this high until the short-lived West German boom accompanying German unification, in 1989–91.[29] The scarcity of jobs in the eighties was aggravated by severe housing shortages at the very moment that a new, dramatic influx of immigrants had begun. Hundreds of thousands of ethnic German resettlers from the Soviet Union, Poland, Romania, and other East European countries came in the eighties and their numbers mushroomed into the millions with the flight of East Germans from mid-1989 into the nineties. Unlike the East German refugees, most of the resettlers had neither a command of German nor did they strike West German natives as German in other ways. Fuelled by the natives' *Wohlstandspatriotismus* (chauvinism of prosperity), popular opinion soon turned against the resettlers and, after a brief period of euphoria over the fall of the Berlin Wall, against the East German refugees as well with whom the natives did not want to share their scarce jobs and affordable housing.[30]

Eurobarometer survey no. 30 of 1988 shows how common the anti-immigrant sentiments were in the major industrial nations of Western Europe. When asked if they thought 'there were too many immigrants of another nationality' in the country, 11.9 per cent of British, 7.4 per cent of French, and 5.6 per cent of West German respondents said yes. In all three countries there were majorities that agreed that the immigrants were 'too many' or 'a lot'. Curiously, changing the question to 'too many immigrants of another race' increased the British response to 12.5 per cent, the French to 9.3 per cent, and the West German numbers to an astounding 20.5 per cent – perhaps they believed the Turks to be of that description. These high levels of anti-immigrant feelings of the eighties, at least in Germany, seem to have declined considerably during the years to follow. While hundreds of thousands of East European (ethnic German) and East German resettlers annually continued to arrive in West Germany, the hitherto modest numbers of seekers of political asylum under article 16 of the German constitution also rose above a level of a hundred thousand a year in the late eighties and finally crested at nearly half a million in 1992. Germany's ultra-liberal asylum regulations had permitted claimants – who came mostly from South Asia, the Middle East, and Africa and, since 1990, from post-communist Eastern Europe – to receive food and shelter at government expense for years before the justification of their political refugee status could be approved or rejected.[31] They were usually housed in more or less temporary shelters and asylum hostels all over the country and the local citizenry often protested their disorderly presence but found its complaints ignored by both Christian Democratic and Social Democratic officialdom.[32]

The Rise of the German Republicans

In the meantime, a new right-wing party, the Republicans (Rep), had been founded on the strength of pre-existing neo-Nazi activists and a substantial defection of Christian Democratic (CSU) dissidents in Bavaria. It immediately latched on to the anti-immigrant issue in its various manifestations. Founded in 1986 by a prominent television host, Franz Schönhuber, who was suddenly revealed to have been in the war-time Waffen-SS, the Reps were named after the American Republicans under Ronald Reagan whose populist appeals[33] evidently struck a chord with the German radical right. The new party opposed not only the presence of 'old foreigners' such as the Turks and the 'new' foreign asylum-seekers, but showed pronounced hostility to the ethnic German resettlers and even to the East German refugees of 1989/90. It was a stunning reversal of the old Nazi and Pan-German attitudes which for more than 50 years had generated calls either to incorporate the ethnic German diaspora in Eastern Europe within an expanded Pan-German

Reich or to summon the ethnics *heim ins Reich* (back home to the German Reich).

The Republicans, of course, questioned the ethnic authenticity of the German resettlers, and rejected the government rationale, that these ethnics had suffered greatly under Stalinist oppression and native persecution after the collapse of the German effort to conquer Eastern Europe and should be given a chance in a prosperous and secure West Germany. The new party was apprehensive of further millions of ethnics who might be tempted to follow the present resettlers. Considering that a major cause of the Second World War and its immeasurable suffering had been the Pan-German nationalistic aim to 'liberate' the ethnic German diaspora throughout Eastern Europe, especially the Sudeten Germans of Czechoslovakia and the Polish Germans left in the wake of the collapsing Hapsburg, Prussian-German, and Russian empires – and considering the flight and expulsion of some 16 million German ethnics from post-war Eastern Europe to West and East Germany, a gigantic and violent drama of 'ethnic cleansing' in reverse, – this was perhaps the final demise of any rationale for German eastward expansion. The ethnocentric perspective of the German radical right, of course, was no monopoly of the Republicans, or of the NPD before them. Ethnocentricity has been a chief motive for the British, American, French, Danish radical right, and even the blue-collar element of the Italian neo-fascists (MSI) throughout the eighties and earlier.

The major German parties, the CDU/CSU, SPD, FDP, and the Greens were deadlocked on immigration policy and were preoccupied with other problems, especially German unification and its enormous economic and legal problems. The deadlock involved, in particular, CDU/CSU and FDP attempts to change the asylum article no. 16, and make entry for the asylum-seekers more difficult. The SPD and the Greens had made commendable if unsuccessful efforts to enfranchise at least the 'old foreigners' at the local level, though the SPD's reaction to the arrival of the German ethnics and the asylum-seekers was rather ambivalent. The more left-wing elements among the SPD and Greens bitterly assailed the government for attempting to rewrite the constitutional article on political asylum and, even at the local level, tended to identify any mention of inter-ethnic tensions with racism and neo-Nazism. The rising tide of anti-foreign violence of 1991–93 at first intensified this deadlock amid mutual recriminations.[34] In late 1992, finally, a compromise was struck between the major parties, and, half a year later, the constitutional article on asylum was modified. A new agreed-upon procedure now compels all seekers of political asylum who are headed for Germany by land routes to remain in one of the non-dictatorial countries they traverse en route. With the co-operation of friendly neighbours, Germany has thus created a *cordon sanitaire* to keep the invasion at bay. There are striking similarities between this and American policy to keep Cuban and Haitian boat people from their shores. The numbers of asylum-seekers in Germany, indeed, have dropped from nearly half a million in 1992 to a third of a million in 1993, and 54,000 by May 1994.[35] Even the resettlers from the German ethnic diaspora, who were not affected by these changes but benefited from the efforts of Bonn to ease their plight back home, in 1994, dropped to half their post-unification level. The goal now is zero immigration except for the German ethnic settlers and 'true' claimants of political asylum (rather than 'economic refugees').

Did the parties of the German extreme right succeed in taking advantage of the post-unification crisis of German immigration policy? In the early half of 1989, the right-wing vote suddenly rose to 7.5 per cent for the Republicans in West Berlin and to a sensational 7.1 per cent in the European parliament elections of 1989 when the party demonstrated its ability to break through the minimal hurdle of 5 per cent nationwide in Hamburg (6 per cent), Hesse (6.5 per cent), Baden-Württemberg (8.7 per cent), and Bavaria (14.6 per cent). This was the first nationwide test of the Republican potential and it seemed likely that it might score a similar breakthrough the following year and win representation in the *Bundestag* in Bonn. The turnout in the European elections, however, had been only 62.4 per cent of those eligible to vote, a far cry from the usual 85 per cent and higher turnout in West German federal elections. Determined minorities, such as the two million Republican voters of the European elections of 1989, can achieve a bigger percentage at such low turnout levels (also in state elections) than in the national elections.[36]

The dramatic breach of the Berlin Wall and the accelerating process towards unification apparently did not help the German radical right at the polls. They were barred from participating in the first free election (18 March 1990) in the former communist German Democratic Republic and unable to attract more than around one per cent of the vote there in the state elections of October 1990. In the West German state elections of that year in Bavaria (4.9 per cent), unified Berlin (3.1 per cent), and the Saar (3.4 per cent), the Rep could not maintain their promising levels of the previous year. The following year in Hamburg (4.8 per cent plus 2.8 per cent for the DVU) and Hesse (1.7 per cent), they were similarly disappointed.[37] Only in Baden-Württemberg did the Reps score significantly with 10.9 per cent in 1992, and in Schleswig-Holstein (6.3 per cent) and Bremen (6.2 per cent), the DVU made its entry into the state diet. The federal elections of 2 December 1990 gave the Republicans only 2.1 per cent of the popular vote in the West and 1.3 per cent in the East. Except for some spotty gains,[38] in other words, the German radical right was unable to take advantage of the popular discontent with the government's immigration and asylum policy.

This was all the more remarkable since, from mid-1991 through 1993, the first post-unification problems brought renewed agitation. A wave of violent anti-foreign incidents convulsed the country, and, in the end, triggered massive counter-demonstrations estimated at several millions against the anti-foreign skinheads and neo-Nazis. Had the Republicans and other right-wing groups missed the boat and become associated only with anti-foreign sentiments? At the very moment that the German and much of the foreign press, especially in the United States, thought that they saw the old Nazi stormtroopers on the rampage again, the real neo-Nazis went into a fatal decline at the polls. Public opinion polls also showed the anti-foreign sentiment cresting in mid-1992 and dropping rapidly in reaction to the counter-demonstrations of the winter of 1992/93, and to the violent outrages themselves. The Republicans and other radical right parties were blamed and made to pay for what they had been quite unable to do, that is to command the violent rabble of skinheads and local anti-foreign groups.[39] Perhaps this was a demonstration of what the Germans have called their *streitbare Demokratie* (militant democracy), their closing of ranks against threats to German democracy from the two extremes of the political spectrum.

By the time of the 1994 *Bundestag* elections, the Republicans, DVU, and NPD – the fragmentation alone of the German radical right has been a major cause of its weakness – had already been struck out in a number of state elections. In the European elections of that year, the Republicans fell short of their triumph four years earlier and no longer will be represented in the European parliament. In the *Bundestag* elections, they scored 1.9 per cent of the popular vote,[40] even less than the 2.1 per cent of the last federal elections, and again did not qualify for representation. Thus ended the quest that had been viewed with such alarm by the media and other notables as recently as in early 1994.[41]

There were several explanations for their defeat, at least with the benefit of hindsight. The amendment of the asylum law and dramatic reduction in the volume of asylum-seekers was a major factor. Other reasons were the economic upturn before the 1994 elections and the internal problems of the German radical right. In an attempt to counteract the competition between DVU and the Reps, for example, in mid-1994 the two parties agreed to co-operate, but this was widely interpreted as an admission that the Reps – who had cultivated more of a populist image, somewhat like the French *Front National* – were openly supporting the neo-Nazi programme of the DVU.[42] Just before the elections, finally, Republican founder Franz Schönhuber announced his resignation as the party leader, in the most recent instalment of the leadership and succession struggles within the party. In the end, the German Christian Democrats had succeeded once more, as used to be the policy under Konrad Adenauer and F. J. Strauss, to keep most right-wing voters under their wide umbrella and not to give a radical right party a chance to establish itself. Thus, in 1994, the Germans joined the Swedes and Britons in marginalizing their respective radical right parties, even while the Austrian Haider movement, the reborn Italian MSI/AN,[43] and the French *Front National* and Struggle for Values movements were at levels between 12 and 25 per cent of the national vote. At the same time, the debates over reforming immigration and asylum laws and policies in France, Germany, Austria, Italy, and the United States and Canada have continued to agitate the minds.[44] Western societies, as the long-ignored North–South tensions have taken on the form of immigration pressures upon the North everywhere, are under the disturbing challenge of questions of multiculturalism and immigration policy as never before.

Different Societies From the Inter-war Period

But the big changes from the 1920s and 1930s are not just coming from the outside; Western societies have been in profound internal transformation, since then, and since the beginning of this century. As the determining factors of the inter-war period have faded, we need to look closely at the crucial social changes and how they have affected the roles and self-images of young males – the principal clientele of European radical right movements in the eighties and nineties of this century. As compared to the twenties and thirties in fascist Europe, since 1945 an enormous amount of destratification and democratization has occurred in the societies under discussion, including those long under communism and communist equality. Not only has the old class struggle of the first half of the century long ended, but the clear reference point of the old class order has become lost in the midst of decades of relative social equality. Now everybody demands a voice and some respect, and the mechanisms of advancing social equality, which Alexis de Tocqueville described so trenchantly a century and a half ago,[45] are asserting themselves throughout Europe. Without the authoritarian guideposts of the past, silent primal sentiments and prejudices surface and assert themselves, and this occurs especially in reaction to dramatic changes and massive waves of mobilization, as, for example, in 1989–91 in Eastern Europe.

The coming of post-industrial society in the seventies and eighties, with a politics no longer driven by the class dynamics of the industrial revolution[46] – owners and managers vs. workers and dependent (white-collar) employees, not to mention older rural dependencies – also triggered major changes in the family roles and structures of most industrialized Western societies. To give an example, West German family households at the turn of the century consisted of two-thirds of families with four or more persons and of only 7.1 per cent single-person households. By the year 1950, after the Second World War, the households of four or more persons were already down to about one-third of the total and the single person households stood at almost one-fifth, a tally that many people still attributed to the carnage and disruptions of the war.[47] By 1990, however, the single person households had become more than a third of the total while the four-and-more persons in a family unit were less than a fifth.

All along, the household composition of East German society, as in other communist states, where over 90 per cent of adult women were gainfully employed[48] had been close to the most recent West German status: one fourth were single person households. In terms of family structure, the prevalence of the smallest German units (one-third in the early nineties), translated to 22 per cent of households of women living alone, 11 per cent of men living alone, and 6 per cent households consisting of single parents raising children (ten per cent in East Germany). Only 30 per cent of the households now involve married couples raising one or more children, which was once presumably the traditional learning situation in which the young men were socialized to the ways and values of preceding generations.[49] We need to bear these German statistics in mind when we contemplate statements about the neglect of youth, the increasing failure of socialization in the families of today's industrialized societies, or about fathers rarely teaching their sons anymore about responsible male adulthood.

Changing Primary Relationships

The changing role of the family environment over the last few decades with regard to size, parental nurturance, siblings, and a stable and protected setting is only one of the co-ordinates of present primary relationships of adolescent males. Another is the changing role of women as a result of the redefinitions and emancipation occurring since the 1960s in most industrialized countries. We are not concerned here with the goals and perceptions themselves of new generations of women who, more significantly than other groups, have followed the trend towards individualization and greater freedom from their traditional roles in the patriarchal societies of the West. Instead the focus here should be on how the young males of the 1980s and 1990s are coping (or otherwise) with these new female roles and images which differ so drastically from those the young men may remember from their mothers or grandparents. Their fathers, to the extent that they try to teach their sons by example or with actual advice, are little help in this process of coping with the new woman.

To continue with the example of ex-communist East and conservative West Germany, the most striking difference between the pre-emancipation era (for instance the 1950s) in the West and the last two decades has been the sharp drop in the birth-rate. Widely attributed to the advent of birth-control pills in the sixties, it really reflects a widespread and deliberate refusal of both married and unmarried young women to be prematurely confined by bearing and raising children. The continuing struggle over abortion rights and, in some European countries, access to birth-control devices, further underlines the serious nature of these changes from the patriarchal past. It should come as no surprise that in a 1979 comparative survey of activists of radical right parties such as the Front National, Progress (Denmark), the MSI, and the German NPD, strong opposition to a woman's right to abortion and equal job opportunities stood out as the most prevalent characteristic that set them off from the activists of middle-of-the-road and left-wing parties.

Behind the recent changes, again, are long-range statistical transformations in European societies that lend them meaning and significance. At the beginning of this century, for example, more than 30 per cent of the German population were under 15 years of age, a percentage that has declined by now to 15 per cent in West Germany and 19 per cent in the East. The steepest drop, however, occurred between the strong birth cohorts of the early sixties and the nineties, for West Germans a period of negative population growth. The somewhat higher birthrates of East Germany – despite the much higher percentage of employment among married East German women – relate to the ubiquitous availability of child care and abortion on demand in the former GDR.[50] Essentially, East German women were constrained to seek careers by the low wage levels of both men and women. But before 1989, they were also philosophically persuaded to a greater extent than their West German sisters that having a career and a family with children was feasible and, in fact, highly desirable. In a 1991 Allbus poll, furthermore, they matched their considerably higher marriage rate (70 per cent as compared to 61 per cent in the West) with a substantially greater commitment (84 per cent vs. 69 per cent) to the institution of marriage as a factor of personal happiness.[51] Increasingly in recent years, however, West German women also have had to emphasize careers and employment more than before because it may take two salaries to support a young couple in the style they prefer, and without financial support from their parents.

We have concentrated on this rather narrow range of issues not because the great change in women's attitudes is limited to the pursuit of careers over family obligations. It would be no exaggeration to describe the attitudinal changes as all-encompassing. With the rise of the New Left, in the seventies, in fact, women's movements became prominent in nearly all the industrialized societies, and their impact on legislation, female representation in parties and parliaments, and on the professional advancement of women throughout the economy and public administration has been extraordinary.[52] Some polls in West Germany tell the story well: Asked in 1953, and again in 1979, on what subjects their husband or wife might disagree, married respondents showed a dramatic change from 1953 to 1979 on the subject of 'political matters', the wives even more than the husbands. The percentage claiming 'we agree on everything' declined from 11 per cent to one per cent. The days of the submissive *Hausfrau*, it seems, ended in the 1970s when three-quarters of the women questioned (barely over half the men) said they approved of the 'increased independence and self-assurance' of women and their readiness to have opinions of their own. By 1979, only one per cent of the adult female sample 'disapproved' of such forwardness, while 7–8 per cent of the married males did and another 25–30 per cent demurred with expressions such as 'It is hard to say' or 'You can't say that'. Among those over 55, no less than 57 per cent particularly criticized in a 1979 poll 'that many women take their occupation more seriously nowadays than they do their marriage and their family.'[53] It is no exaggeration to say that the gender struggle has taken the place of the old class struggle.

There is little doubt that the vast majority of new recruits to the various European radical right groups is male, lower class, and very young. Being a radical right-winger seems to be highly related to the difficulties of growing-up – and the extraordinary physical and psychological changes of adolescence are hard for anyone – combined with being a lower class male in the decades of the eighties and nineties. Unfortunately, we have few hard data on the response of male adolescents and young men to the new female assertiveness in everyday life. Enough is known, however, to speculate that it has had an enormously disorienting impact on them, especially on right-wing youngsters – young left-wing activists show a completely different pattern of acceptance, tolerance, even championship of the new role of the women in their midst. There are many signs of the deeply disturbing impact of female assertiveness on the young men of the radical right. To begin with, they have few women among their members – mostly girl-friends, it seems – and they are not at all comfortable with any public or non-traditional display on their part. It is hard being one of the few committed female activists among male right-wing militants who seem embarrassed by their presence and make every effort to keep them from the media. When interviewers from polling organizations came to interview 'their women', right-wing radicals have been known to intervene and abort the interview, insisting on telling the interviewer what 'she' thinks, or at least never leaving 'their women' alone with the interviewers.

Right-wing skinheads and soccer hooligans often present a particularly repellent environment to young women because of their heavy drinking and involvement in violence.[54] How indeed can a woman put up with such behaviour? On the other hand, as far as we can generalize, from the point of view of the young males, they are growing up in a frighteningly hostile, and thoroughly confusing world.[55] Though many seem to come from authoritarian families, they have often already severed their umbilical cord to them mentally, and indeed physically as well. Even when they still live at home, it seems, they find themselves ignored by parents and siblings and by other adults, except for punishments for unruly behaviour.[56] Whether still at school, outside school, or after graduation, they grow up among youthful gangs and in the midst of numerous gang fights – right- and left-wing skinheads and gangs of young foreigners – and domestic violence. All this is hardly new to observers of America's youth scene, where the lethal violence and high mortality of young urban males in gangs is commonplace, as is their evident fatherlessness. Conservative authors blame the decline of 'family values' and 'feminist' redefinition of standards of young masculine behaviour for the resulting tragedies,[57] rather than the well-known backlash of 'angry white males' or the social cutbacks of conservative governments.

Violence between the parents or within the family, in Europe and America, often accompanied by heavy drinking, not only seems to be a common background of young right-wingers, but it may well be a major example set by fathers and older male siblings for the young male as 'the only masculine way' to put women and children in their place. The devastating impact of domestic abuse on growing children is reflected in later difficulties in social adjustment reported about many of these young men, and in conflicts with the law, or with the authority of teachers, bosses, and other persons of authority. It may also help to explain the deep sense of social isolation, distrust, and pessimism noted by Nonna Mayer and others among Le Pen's voters, especially among the 'unwealthy and uneducated' of the French radical right.[58] Social disconnectedness and isolation as a result of an extraordinary deficit in family and intergenerational socialization seem to characterize the young right-wing male, who is, more often than not, the product of a cruel and non-comprehending world of domestic violence and of the '400 blows', as François Truffaut called his movie about a boy growing up in this kind of setting.

Myths and Heroes

Among the many sub-varieties of the skinhead scene in Britain, Germany, and other West European countries – there are also anti-racist (SHARP) and even gay (GS) skins – the right-wingers stand out with a masculine hero complex. Listening closely to their rock music we can hardly fail to notice the heroic self-images in their rock lyrics and 'fanzines' (informal magazines). In Norway and Sweden, for example, fantasy images of themselves as fighting Vikings or of mythical warriors of Odin fighting rival gods in a final Götterdämmerung draw as much following among the radical right as do American imports such as the heroic images of White Aryan Resistance (WAR) and other racist groups. J.R. Tolkien's Lord of the Rings and other escapist yarns are popular with young Italian neo-fascists and Scandinavian neo-Nazis. German skins like to think of themselves as 'fighters for Doitschland'[59] and to sing along with the Böhse Onkelz, one of their rock bands:

> The saviours of Germany, that's what we are
> I fight like a wild beast for my homeland
> Loyalty, Blood and Honour keep our pride
> for we are hard like German oakwood.

Other images of self-identification by young right-wing males hark back to the Second World War, such as to the foreign units of the German Waffen-SS in the Russian campaign, veterans of the winter war, and other images far from contemporary adversaries such as today's anarchists, left-wing activists, the rising crime rate, and the police. They live in a world of fantasized raids, imagined glorious deeds, and nostalgic *machismo* that could hardly be farther from the real threats to them or to anyone else.[60]

The distance between their heroic dreams and their real world, it would appear, suggests how many of their actions – usually carried out under the influence of alcohol and other drugs – are rather disconnected from their modest lives on the fringes of society. Even where they have attempted to carry out the will of a prejudiced community such as *Hoyerswerda* or *Rostock-Lichtenhagen* to intimidate and expel foreign asylum-seekers, their connection to their 'supporters' has been extremely tenuous. For the neighbourhood skinheads and brawlers are usually looked down upon with disdain by mainstream society and their ethnocentric violence rarely earns them lasting respect. In their everyday lives they share views on foreigners and women that are close to some of the male, blue-collar prison inmates, whose racist and sociopathic attitudes have been studied in various Western countries, including Germany, the United States, Japan, and Australia in the midst of the decline of the stereotypical roles of men as brawny providers.[61] Low-skill jobs, unemployment, or the threat of it in a widespread recession clearly involve the traditional male role of the provider. Physical strength also has long been eclipsed by training and intelligence in a modern economy. Much as these prison inmates, whom many of the skinheads may join some day, the violent young right-wing radicals view male foreigners as dangerous rivals and enemies, and unclean 'parasites' – they take a dim view of what they consider alternatives to 'real masculine work', including work outside one's country – but also as sexual predators capable of rape and all manner of perversion. In the midst of societies still largely dominated by the social order of male hegemonies – men over women, and older men over younger men – their low status and education generally bar them from playing the hegemonic games observed from the alpha males in movies, television, and perhaps even personal acquaintance. They tend to respond to this frustration with hypersensitivity to real and imagined slights ('being dissed', or disrespected), paranoid displacements, and dreams of heroism on their part. They also turn with fury and frustration – it is supposed to be an egalitarian society, is it not? – on male achievers, and even more so on female achievers and on feminists or advocates of opportunities and benefits for women, minorities, and foreigners.

There ensues not only a desperate search for scapegoats to blame, intellectuals, bureaucrats, politicians, 'liberal do-gooders', but violent action against helpless refugees and foreigners – on a graded hit list beginning with gypsies and Turks, black Africans and South or

Southeast Asians, Arabs, Jews, and East Europeans – but also gays, the homeless, handicapped persons, and a long list of *ad hoc* victims. In particular at night, when alcohol and sometimes drugs may obscure the line between reality and heroic delusions, gangs turn into self-styled warriors who defend society in lieu of 'what the police ought to do'. Against the violent lyrics of racist rock, their daytime social marginality seeks nocturnal communion with self-styled patriotism, national symbols, and even a pretend Aryan identity, in the midst of drunken 'group-think'.[62] With the high contemporary level of youthful violence at school and in working-class neighbourhoods dominated by turf fights among youth gangs, it is small wonder that their actions involve degrees of violence to persons that we cannot ignore. It has become a different world indeed from the twenties and thirties, a world in which many young people no longer receive their primary socialization from parents, family or school. They learn from their violent peers, from the thrill-oriented video-culture and exploitationist commercial advertisements surrounding them like substitute parents, and from their music – as did other cults before them. And, like the violent soccer hooligans battling each other before and after the game, and at the 'curve' at half-time, they have their violent games and spectacles at which human beings do get hurt. Unlike the politicized inter-war period when fascists and Nazis were actually struggling for power, much of the violent right-wing 'happenings' of today are not very political.

Notes

1. As the argument of the opposition parties went, the government let the popular reactions to the increased flow of asylum-seekers from Eastern Europe and developing countries escalate to the point where opposition resistance to restricting the granting of asylum could no longer hold out. The government countered with the argument that opposition refusal to co-operate in regulating the increased flow of refugees had in fact brought on the crisis of 1991–93.

2. At one time, the *New York Times* even invented a kind of skinhead origin of the old Nazi party 'in 1922' – actually on page 1 – while other US media expressed their alarm in more guarded terms. See my concluding chapter to Merkl (ed.), *The Federal Republic at Forty-Five* (London: Macmillan, 1995), pp. 429–30 for quotations. The German Minister of Women and Youth, Angela Merkl, recently entitled her introduction to a scholarly book on anti-foreign violence '*Unheilbar deutsch? Sozialfall? Oder was sonst?*' (Incurably German? Failed Social Policy? Or what else?) in H. Willems, *Fremdenfeindliche Gewalt: Einstellungen, Täter, Konfliktseskalation* (Opladen: Leske & Budrich, 1993), pp. 9–15 to characterize the tenor of the heated debates over the wave of anti-foreign violence in Germany.

3. This determination is actually easier today than it was with many inter-war fascist movements which frequently showed little respect for private property – especially that of their enemies – or free enterprise when those had to be subordinated to their

pursuit of aggressive war. In fact, their warlikeness was often a better Cains' mark than most other attributes.

4. S.M. Slitinsky, *L Affaire Papon* (Paris: Moreau, 1983). The attack resulted in over 200 deaths and 10,000 arrests. There are many other examples.

5. The polemical use of either set of terms, of course, has to be distinguished from actual membership in fascist, neo-fascist, or communist parties or networks at the time, as the case may be.

6. Merkl and Weinberg (eds), *Encounters with the Contemporary Radical Right* (Boulder, CO: Westview, 1993) pp. 4–5.

7. See Paul Webster in the *Manchester Guardian*, weekly edition, 28 Aug. 1994, p. 13. Pasqua's comment on the *Front National*, moreover, was obviously intended to keep the RPR voters from straying to the FN rather than as an expression of RPR or even his own views. According to French opinion polls, a majority of French voters support Pasqua's policies on immigration, and RPR adherents do so with huge majorities.

8. In some cases, as with the Christian right in America, this certainty may derive from religious beliefs, or rather from a fanatic conviction that one's own religious insights alone are true and those of other believers false. More often the certainty stems from a limitless faith in an infallible secular leader. *'Il duce ha sempre ragione'* (The duce is always right).

9. See Eatwell in Eatwell and N. O'Sullivan, 'Neo-Fascism and the Right: Conceptual Conundrums?' at the 1991 Conference on the Radical Right in Western Europe (University of Minnesota).

10. Typical examples are the obsession with racial or national purity, wholesome family values, and social harmony among the social classes, within families, or at places of work.

11. Aside from the long list of 'anti-affects' of right-wing extremist movements (e.g., anti-pluralist or anti-egalitarian), some of their positive ideals such as social (class) harmony or national pride may not in themselves be extremist but they become so in the process of being mandated or violently imposed upon society.

12. Some of their approach was actually copied from militant organizations of the left and from the young Soviet Union and the radical right and left were eager to learn from each other in the 1920s and 1930s. Much of Hitler's and Mussolini's (but also that of the communists) appeal was also pitched at their audiences' feelings of being victimized and exploited, and their deep-seated longing for being accepted in the bosom of a solidaristic community. For telling examples, see G.L. Mosse (ed.), *Nazi Culture* (New York: Grosset & Dunlap, 1966), and forthcoming work on the aesthetics of Italian fascism by Simonetta Falasca Zamponi of the University of California, Santa Barbara.

13. Considering the varying size of the camps of followers, and the variety of conservative leadership, admittedly, we should really distinguish the less richly plumed garden variety of conservative politicians, men like Robert A. Taft or Dwight Eisenhower, from media magicians like the Reagan team or Berlusconi.

14. See also R. Griffin, *The Nature of Fascism* (London: Pinter, 1991) and R. Eatwell, 'Towards a New Model of Generic Fascism', *Journal of Theoretical Politics*, 4, 1. Further, W. Laqueur (ed.), *Fascism: A Reader's Guide*, (Berkeley and Los Angeles: University of California Press, 1976), H.A. Turner, Jr. (ed.), *Reappraisals of Fascism* (New York: New Viewpoints (F. Watts), 1975), and Stanley Payne's magisterial *Fascism: Comparison and Definition* (Madison, WI: University of Wisconsin Press, 1980). But see also the rather different or modified questions used by J. Falter and S. Schumann, 'Affinity Towards Right-wing

Extremism in Western Europe', *West European Politics II*, April 1988, pp. 96–110, especially p. 109 for the contemporary extreme right.

15. See especially P. Ignazi, 'The Changing Profile of the Italian Social Movement' in *Encounters* , pp. 75–92 for a description of the complex and heterogeneous changes that have taken place in the half century since the Fascists' last stand.

16. Catholic anti-abortionists have likened state efforts to protect the rights of women to make their own choice to the oppression of the church by the fascist state while the religious zealotry of self-styled pro-life activists and their harassment of staff and women customers at family planning centres has been likened to the bullying of the blackshirts of yesterday.

17. See also my description of the process by which communist and post-communist East Germany fostered the development of neo-Nazi youth in a variety of ways, *Encounters*, pp. 210–14.

18. Socializing influences may reach from parents to their children and, under exceptional circumstances such as broken families, from grandparents to grandchildren. Unusual links such as from bitter old foreign *Waffen-SS* veterans raising neo-fascist grandsons in Sweden are probably the farthest stretch in time of family socialization patterns in a rapidly changing world. After 40 or 50 years this transmission obviously runs out.

19. See also the contributions to S.U. Larsen *et al.* (eds), *Who Were the Fascists? Social Roots of European Fascist Movements* (Oslo: Norwegian University Presses, 1980) for the subtle changes from the at first more military, war-related emphasis to social revolutionary elements. Also this writer's *The Making of a Stormtrooper* (Princeton University Press, 1980) for the German case and for some comparisons in Ch. 6.

20. There is already the huge literature about socialist and communist movements in the 1920s and 1930s, as well as on the old fascist movements themselves. See also Larsen, *op. cit.* and *Stormtrooper*, Ch. 2.

21. See also my paper 'Collapsing German Imperial Structures and Extremist Identity' for RC 34, Sociology of Youth, at the World Congress of the International Sociological Association in Bielefeld, Germany, July 1994.

22. See the report on 1400 arrests (not convictions) in Germany reported by H. Willems, *op. cit.*, p. 89 and Ch. 6. Unlike the left-wing cases of politically violent offenders of the 1970s and early 1980s who had substantially more educational training than the average – even though some of them did not complete their university education or did not follow it up with the usual professional careers – the violent right of the 1990s is substantially below the popular levels.

23. See this writer's *Stormtrooper*, pp. 185–90, and Willems, *op. cit.*, pp. 110–12. In the last years, however, there has been an influx of some older offenders as well, sometimes described as 'old Nazis' but mostly under 60 which would have made them only about ten years old in 1945.

24. *Ibid.* pp. 88–9. There has been an extraordinary increase in German readiness to protest and engage in violent confrontations between the 1980s and 1990s, even though German general enthnocentric hostility seems to have declined in the polls. Willems, *op.cit.*, pp. 25–92. The vote for right-wing parties in the East also has remained very low (1–3 per cent) and voters under 25 have been just as prominent among the neo-communist PDS and the Greens/Alliance 90 as among the Republicans.

25. See especially the accounts by T. Björge, J. van Donselaar, and H. Lööw in Björgo and R. Witte (eds), *Racist Violence in Europe* (London: Macmillan, 1993).

26. See, for example, C. Lloyd in *ibid.*, pp. 211–18, S. Taylor, 'The Radical Right in

Britain', in *Encounters* pp. 168–71, and P. Hainsworth and R. Eatwell, in Hainsworth, *op. cit.*, pp. 32–8, 46–51 and 176–84. On the Dutch, see C. Husbands, *ibid.*, pp. 96–100 and J. van Donselaar in Björgo and Witte, *op. cit.*, pp. 50–7. Husbands also described the role of the immigrant issue in Belgium (in Hainsworth, *op.cit.*, pp. 132–3, 137–8) where the radical right otherwise feeds upon earlier fascist traditions and hostility between the nationalities.

27. The NPD had its best period in 1966–68 when its vote vaulted above the five per cent minimum for representation in Bavaria (7.4 per cent), Hesse (9.9 per cent), Schleswig-Holstein (5.8 per cent), Rhineland-Palatinate (6.9 per cent), Lower Saxony (7 per cent), Bremen (8.8 per cent), and Baden-Württemberg (9.8 per cent), seven of the 11 states. By the time of the next *Bundestag* elections, in 1969, however, the right-wing wave was beginning to ebb and they only received 4.3 per cent and no national representation. See E. Zimmermann and T. Saalfeld in *Encounters*, pp. 60–9.

28. See, for example, K. Farin and E. Seidel-Pielen *Krieg in den Städten: Jugendgangs in Deutschland* (Berlin: Rotbuch, 1991), pp. 18–123, especially pp. 20–54, and, by the same authors, *Skinheads* (Munich: Beck, 1993). Also Merkl, 'Are the Old Nazis Coming Back?' in Merkl (ed.), *The Federal Republic of Germany at 45* (London: Macmillan, 1995).

29. The 1990/91 boom soon faded and unemployment figures in the West rose to 8.3 per cent in 1993 while in East Germany, double-digit unemployment (15.3 per cent in 1993) from the difficult economic restructuring process added to West German figures.

30. J. Sperling, '(Im)migration and German Security in Post-Yalta Europe' *German Studies Review* (17 Oct. 1994), pp. 537–58. See E. Kolinsky, 'A Future for Right Extremism in Germany?' in Hainsworth, *op.cit.*, pp. 82–9 and Merkl, *German Unification in the European Context* (Pennsylvania State Press, 1993), pp. 128–9. The resettlers and refugees were constitutionally entitled to German citizenship and help with finding suitable housing and jobs by state and local authorities.

31. Over the years, ever smaller percentages of the asylum applications were actually approved (three per cent in 1990), but sometimes, the applicants simply escaped deportation by going into hiding.

32. For an account of how official deafness to local complaints about the asylum-seekers' personal cleanliness and probity – in particular toilet habits and petty property offences – in some cases led to local support for skinhead violence against asylum hostels, see Willems, *op.cit.*, Ch. 8.

33. The surprising resonance seems to have involved such themes as the perception of hostility to feminism and resistance to affirmative action, and quite likely an echo to the Bitburg Affair of 1985 which made President Reagan very popular with the right wing of the CDU/CSU and no doubt with German veterans such as Schönhuber.

34. The left accused the government of 'bagatellization' of the violence and of tolerating (if not fanning) disturbances in the hope the urgency of the situation would browbeat the opposition into support for the constitutional amendment. The government instead blamed the opposition for blocking any solution. The final debate on changing article 16 in May 1993 escalated to a virtual siege of the *Bundestag* by anti-amendment forces, trying to keep deputies from arriving and voting on the bill.

35. See Sperling, *op.cit.*, pp. 546–52. A full report on the practices and consequences of the change of policy will have to await a greater lapse of time.

36. Local elections, for example in Frankfurt the same year, demonstrated that, in the

absence of a full set of Republican candidates, the NPD or other neo-Nazi parties could do equally well. The spectacular Republican success in the European elections in Bavaria, 1989, owed much to the defection of substantial numbers of CSU voters and some well-known CSU dissidents to the Reps.

37. In the 1990 state elections in Lower Saxony (1.5 per cent) and North Rhine Westphalia (1.8 per cent) where their vote had approached the five per cent level in the 1989 European elections, the Republicans fell far short of this level, and all this even though the turnout in state elections (65–80 per cent) was not much higher than in the European elections.

38. In 1992 there were radical right deputies in three state diets: 15 Reps in Baden-Württemberg and six and seven DVU representatives, respectively, in Bremen and Schleswig-Holstein. They also did well in the Hessian local election of March 1993 where they won 8.3 per cent statewide, and 9.3 per cent in the Frankfurt area alone. The federal elections of 1990 (turnout 77.8 per cent) had also produced a Rep vote under three per cent in all the states except Bavaria (five per cent) and Baden-Württemberg (3.2 per cent), and West Berlin (3 per cent).

39. On the anti-foreign incidents in Germany, see this writer's essay, 'Are the Old Nazis Coming Back?' in Merkl (ed.), *The Federal Republic at Forty-Five.*

40. In none of the states was the Republican vote anywhere near five per cent and even in Baden-Württemberg it was only 3.3 per cent, in Bavaria 2.8 per cent, and in Hesse 2.4 per cent. As the absolute figures show, moreover, they could not blame their showing on the higher turnout either; their voting support in the various states shows only losses from recent levels, no gains.

41. Polls were still giving the Reps 4–5 per cent at the beginning of 1994. This writer remembers being warned by several highly placed politicians and business leaders during a trip in May, 1993, that the Republicans surely would enter the *Bundestag* and might win 15 per cent, perhaps even 25 per cent (!) of the popular vote.

42. The German *Verfassungsschutz* (Constitutional Protection Service) also took this as a signal to include the Reps among the extremist organizations under its surveillance. It had not done so before.

43. In late October 1994, MSI/AN leader Gianfranco Fini brought about the renaming of his party, dropping the neo-fascist label MSI and sticking only with the name National Alliance. It remains to be seen how deep this change of name without a departure of the nostalgic old fascists or the young neo-fascist militants really goes.

44. The 1994 passage by a margin of 59 per cent of Proposition 187 in California, a measure denying public education and health care to illegal aliens, is another landmark in the sweep of anti-foreign sentiments in the United States. American right-wing politicians are currently debating the elimination of welfare benefits to legal aliens as well as illegal ones.

45. See, for example, his warnings about the 'irresistible' strength of majority opinions in the United States of the 1830s, in *Democracy in America*, Vol. 1, pp. 270–7, or in the sudden passions of multitudes of half-educated people, *ibid.*, pp. 54–5, and of the power of an irresponsible press in such a society, pp. 190–5.

46. Of the large and rather diversified literature, let us mention only the writings of Ronald Inglehart, for example his *Silent Revolution* (Princeton University Press, 1977), which have striven to pinpoint the rise of a new 'postmaterialist' consciousness that traverses the old class-specific alignments of political opinion. Since the early eighties some public opinion institutes, for example, Sinus in Heidelberg or the Stanford Research Institute in California, have attempted to base their surveys on life-style groups rather than on the familiar socioeconomic status

groups of class-specific opinion.
47. The acute housing shortage of those days, if anything, should have made for larger households. It is true, however, that the impact of the First World War, too, had reduced the share of four and more persons in a household from two-thirds (61.2 per cent) to 53.0 per cent in 1925. See Statistisches Bundesamt, *Datenreport 1992* (Bonn, 1992), pp. 49–50.
48. Among West German women over 14 years the share of gainfully employed women had risen dramatically from less than a third in the sixties to over 40 per cent by the 1990s. Other important differences between East and West were the higher divorce rate and higher frequency and earlier age of marriage in the East.
49. Another 23 per cent of households are married couples without children and eight per cent include non-traditional living situations and multigenerational families. The average household sizes, according to UN and German statistics, vary significantly between developing societies such as Iraq (7.8 persons) or the Philippines (5.6) and developed ones such as Sweden (2.2), the United States (2.7), the former Soviet Union (3) or Germany (2.3). Since 1900, when Germany had an average of 4.5 persons per household, it has travelled from the equivalent of today's Egypt (4.9), past China (4.2) to Swedish conditions.
50. See *Datenreport 1992*, pp. 46–8. Even the maturing of the strong pre-1965 birth cohorts into the parentage age from about the mid-80s onwards has not significantly raised the West German birthrate. In East Germany, on the other hand, the birth-rate never dipped quite as low as in West Germany. German unification, finally, seems to have raised the West German rate at least temporarily while depressing the East German rate.
51. *Ibid.*, p. 595–601. However, West German women felt just as strongly that 'one ought to get married' if a couple was permanently living together, and more strongly, 'if there was a child'. When the desire for a career and a family was in conflict, finally, the West Germans more often opted for staying home and leaving the career to the husband, while the East Germans, both men and women, emphasized partnership in contributing to the livelihood of the family.
52. There are a number of careful analyses of whether the resurgent radical right of the seventies and eighties is, perhaps, a 'backlash' to the New Left emancipations of the '68 generation. See, for example, Herbert Kitschelt's writings, such as his 1991 paper, 'Left-Libertarians and Right-Authoritarians: Is the New Right a Response to the New Left in European Politics?', Western European Studies Center, University of Minnesota, 7–9 Nov. 1991. It is indeed a backlash of the 'angry white male', although the concept of a backlash may require clarification. On the women's movement, see the range of contributions on various developed societies in L. Iglitzin and R. Ross (eds), *Women in the World, 1975–1985, The Women's Decade*, Revised ed. (Santa Barbara: ABC: Clio Press, 1986), Chs. 1–4.
53. E. Noelle-Neumann (ed), *The Germans: Public Opinion Polls, 1967–1980* (Westport, CT: Greenwood Press, 1981), pp. 243, 248, and 261.
54. See also my description of German soccer hooligans in Merkl (ed.), *Political Violence and Terror: Motifs and Motivations* (Berkeley and Los Angeles: University of California Press, 1986), pp. 229–32.
55. The following is a composite picture, based on little hard and representative evidence, a considerable amount of impressionistic accounts by experts, and with the gaps filled by my social-psychological imagination. It may serve as a beginning of discussions until proven invalid.
56. Of the 1400 suspects in German ethnoviolence offences in Willems study, one-half had a (non-political) criminal record, 95.5 per cent were single, three-fourths under

20 years old (more than a third under 18), and 90 per cent under 25. Willems, *op.cit.*, pp. 110, 115 and 131–2. Less than four per cent involved women and none of these for assault against persons.

57. In the United States, the ethnic nature of much of the youthful violence is rarely acknowledged, although anyone can see the interethnic school and gang violence all around us. See also D. Blankenhorn *Fatherless America*, (New York: Basic Books, 1995).

58. See her paper 'Explaining the Electoral Rightwing Extremism: The Case of the Le Pen vote in the French Presidential Elections' (pp. 5–6) at the annual meeting of the American Political Science Association, Washington, 2–5 Sept. 1993. Also Mayer and P. Perrineau (eds) *Le Front National à découvert*, (Paris: Fondation Nationale des sciences politiques, 1989), and by both authors, 'Why Do They Vote for Le Pen', *European Journal of Political Research*, 22, pp. 123–41. The two authors present a highly differentiated picture of the LePenists and emphasize also their fear of natural and technological risks, health risks (Aids, drugs), and fear of crime, as well as their limited associative behaviour and predominant concentration on family and neighbourhood.

59. The use of the letters 'oi' in place of 'eu' is an allusion to oi music, one of the musical cults that, along with reggae and ska, are popular with skinhead groups. See also my description in 'Are the Old Nazis Coming Back?' in Merkl (ed.), *The Federal Republic at Forty-Five*.

60. See K. Farin and E. Seidel-Pielen, *Skinheads* (Munich: Beck, 1993), p. 97 and *passim*.

61. See, for example, J. Kersten in *Psychologie Heute*, Sept. 1993, pp. 50–7 and by the same author, 'Crime and Masculinities in Australia, Germany, and Japan', *International Sociology 8*, Dec. 1993, pp. 461–78. See also his *'Männlichkeitsdarstellungen in Jugendgangs'* in H.V. Otto and R. Mertens (eds), *Rechtsradikale Gewalt im wiedervereinigten Deutschland – Jugend im Umbruch* (Bonn: BZPB, 1993). On American society, see also S. Craig (ed.) *Men, Masculinity, and the Media*, (Beverly Hills: Sage, 1992) and J.W. Dower, *War Without Mercy* (New York: Pantheon Books, 1986).

62. Studies such as Willems' investigation of 1400 German youths charged with anti-foreign violence have found most of the culpable acts to be committed by young hangers-on of informal neighbourhood or after-work groups of young males, evidently the result of the desire of the perpetrator to belong to the groups and to validate and show-off claims to toughness. Willems, *op. cit.*, pp. 246–7.

2

The Extreme Right in Europe: A Survey

Piero Ignazi

What is the Extreme Right?

The first problem facing the analysis of the extreme right is a definitional one. What does extreme right mean? Which parties belong to the extreme right? Which common traits must they share in order to be considered members of the same (extreme right) family?

The virtual absence of any effort at definition up to very recent times might be explained by the weak political influence of the parties that were included impressionistically in the extreme right family. Neo-fascist, populist, common man protest, poujadist were some of the labels used to define parties of the right that did not fit into the conservative political family. In reality, the fascism catchword identified quite clearly the ideological reference of this family but such reference was not used as a discriminant filter. In fact, on the one hand, non-fascist parties gravitated toward the extreme right political family, and, on the other, there was no consensus even on the profile of the fascist-type of party. As Klaus von Beyme[1] lamented a few years ago, one cannot find a common ground for the same fascist movements: the variation in the historic references, issues, policies, leadership style, is so high that it is somewhat problematic to assign all of these movements to the same category. Von Beyme's pessimistic outlook seems a little excessive as he deliberately looks for differences rather than similarities. In other words, von Beyme employs a denotative approach more than a connotative one.

The approach to the study of extreme-right parties (hereafter ERPs) that is proposed here is connotative, because, if we descend too far down the ladder of abstraction, no party is similar to another. A classification by political families should clearly stipulate what the elements are that identify a political family. In this respect, a parsimonious strategy, as far as the number of a party's properties is concerned, should be pursued. In our opinion, variables such as organizational structure, or the leadership style, or the electorate (the typical American bias in the study of a party) must be left out in favour of the ideology. This approach revives Duverger's[2] suggestion when he assessed the existence of *'familles spirituelles'*, identified on the basis of the ideological reference of the party.

Ideology is thus the starting point for classifying parties but it is not the only one. As many scholars have suggested – from Deutsch *et al.*[3] to Henig[4], from Seiler[5] to Lane and Ersson[6] – ideology should be linked to other variables: our intention is to integrate ideology with spatial location and attitude towards the system.

The Ideology(ies) of the Extreme Right

The extreme right's ideology is provided by fascism. But having stated this, we know that fascism is an ideological labyrinth and von Beyme's uneasiness comes back again. Therefore, what is fascism? This momentous question extends beyond the scope of the present work; nevertheless we have to stipulate, the 'fascist minimum', that is, according to Sternhell, those common traits that are 'shared not only by the different political movements and ideologies which claim to be fascist, but also by those which reject the description yet nevertheless belong to the same family'.[7] The search for a common denominator can be pursued following a recent, provocative and solidly argued work by Roger Griffin.[8] In his book, Griffin looks for a 'generic ideological core'[9] of fascism that could identify it as an ideal type. This approach tries to define in positive terms what Stanley Payne has highlighted as the fascist negations: 'antiliberalism, anticommunism, anticonservatism'.[10] Proceeding in this way one can avoid the problem of the vastness and contradiction of the historic fascist ideology which utilized so many different inputs that it has been defined as a 'synthesis of organic nationalism and anti-Marxist socialism.'[11]

But, whatever the difference sources and influences are, the 'mythic core' of fascism lies in 'a palingenetic form of populist ultranationalism':[12] fascist ideology points to a kind of resurgence, or 'rebirth', intended to create a new revolutionary order, a new society and, even, a new man. Before and after fascism there must be (for the fascists) a gap, a watershed: the new order has nothing in common with the old, rotten, decadent regime. But this goal cannot be achieved other than through a general, collective, unitary effort by the whole nation: therefore all the nation's energy should be mobilized and channelled to the achievement of its new (and revived) greatness. And this aim is pursued through the active participation of the masses, mobilized by partisan organizations; and also by the leader's appeal to the masses for a popular confirmation of the regime's politics. Therefore the idea of resurgence from a dark period, the emphasis of the nation as a collective, organic body, the projection into a glorious and beaming future, the mass mobilization mainly through the leader's charismatic appeal, constitute the 'ideal type of fascism'.

The brilliant formula of the 'fascist minimum' might be integrated, in terms of the history of ideas, by Sternhell's definition that fascist 'political culture is communitarian, anti-individualist and anti-rationalist, and it is founded, first on the rejection of the Enlightenment and of the French revolutionary heritage, and then on the elaboration of a total overthrowing'.[13] In consequence, the keys of fascist ideology are: (a) belief in the authority of the state over the individual; an emphasis on natural community; distrust for individual representation and parliamentary arrangements; limitations on personal and collective freedoms; collective identification in a great national destiny, against class or ethnic or religious divisions; and acceptance of the hierarchical principle for social organization.

Of course not everyone will agree with this approach of limiting the extreme right's ideology just to fascism. Others would add more beliefs such as traditionalism, Catholic integralism and national populism,[14] or would distinguish among a conservative moderate right, a reactionary right, a radical right, a post-war extreme right and a new right.[15] However by introducing more ideological references we would simply revive the initial difficulty of finding a common trait in this political family. Therefore, we remain wedded to the fascist ideology and we stipulate that *by extreme right we mean that political/ideological space where fascism is the key reference.*

The Members of the Extreme Right

Having stated *what* it is let's turn our attention now to the components of the extreme right. In other words, *who belongs to* the extreme-right? The party family classification, as we have seen, has run across some difficulties in general and more specifically regarding the extreme right parties. After a long period of neglect, researchers have more recently devoted some attention to the extreme right. Elbers and Fennema[16] have defined the ERPs in terms of their opposition to democracy and their racist and nationalist attitudes. Backes and Moreau[17] have identified as a common trait of the ERPs rejection of egalitarianism and the centrality of

an ethno-biological or spiritual 'community'. Griffin[18] has proposed quite
a complex taxonomy including nostalgic fascism, mimetic fascism and
neo-fascism (which is further divided into four sub-categories:
revolutionary nationalism, crypto-fascism, revisionism, conservative
revolution). Betz[19] has introduced the category of extreme right populism
on the basis of four elements: a) the radical opposition to the cultural and
sociopolitical system, without an overt attack to the system as such; b)
the rejection of individual and social equality; c) the defence of the
'common man'; and d) the emphasis on 'common sense'. Also, these
populist parties have racist, authoritarian, anti-women, and law and
order attitudes. Pfahl-Traughber[20] utilizes the category of populism in
order to define those 'modernizing right-wing parties' which appeal to
resentments, prejudices, traditional values and offer simplistic and
unrealistic solutions to sociopolitical problems.

All these classifications are based on the party's doctrine. Therefore
they follow our emphasis on the primacy of the ideological elements in
classifying parties. However, while the ideological element is the crucial
element in classification, its sole use would limit our political family to
neo-fascist parties. But our use of the label *extreme right* instead of *neo-
fascism* has a logic behind it. In fact, when one descends from the
heights of ideology to the realities of partisan politics, one is confronted
with more difficulties. In order to produce a more accurate classification
we propose to combine the ideological criterion with a spatial one. *The
location in the political space along the left–right continuum is essential
for identifying linkage to a political area.*

The expression of faith in the spatial measurement is based on the
assumption that left and right, contrary to many analysts, still maintains
a strong connotative power. The importance of the spatial terminology,
ably argued by Laponce,[21] and Fuchs and Klingemann,[22] is validated by
survey research. Numerous public opinion surveys disclose the
continuing importance the left–right distinction has for western publics
(see for example Mayer).[23] More precisely, we do not adopt the
definition of 'right' but the one of 'extreme right'. The term 'extreme'
in this context does not mean simply a more 'radical' or 'extreme'
ideology. If so, the ERPs would not constitute an autonomous political
family, but simply a variant – more extreme – of the conservative
parties. At the same time we do not use the term extremism in the same
way as the German tradition of studies on the *Extremismus*[24], where this
term refers more to individual characteristics rather than to the relations
among parties (that is systemic property). Our definition states that the
specificity of the extreme right parties is given by *their location in the
left-right continuum and by their ideology.*

In consequence, the way to proceed in the analysis consists in testing the parties' placement in the political spectrum and their relationship to fascist ideology. Following this path we are confronted by some puzzles: parties which are clearly located at the extreme right of the continuum are not heir to the fascist tradition. Looking at the European countries only the Italian MSI, the German NPD and DVU, the Dutch CP '86, the British BNP and, in a problematic way, the Belgian *Vlaams Blok* are linked to fascist ideology: the newer parties such as the French *Front National* and the German *Republikaner* do not fit the 'fascist minimum' requirements because they deny any heritage from, or affiliation with, fascism. Nevertheless, they are part of the extreme right political family because they display, *better than an ideology, attitudes and values opposite to the democratic system.* Therefore, a third criterion for membership in the family of extreme right-wing parties involves the role of opposition parties in democratic regimes.

The basic issue concerns the degree and mode of opposition: when does an opposition cease to be democratic and become anti-democratic? A tentative solution to this problem is suggested by two classical references: Kirchheimer[25] and Sartori.[26] Kirchheimer identifies a typology of opposition:[27] an opposition of principle, where 'goal displacement is incompatible with the constitutional requirements of a given system'; and a loyal opposition, which implies just a 'goal differentiation' . Sartori has introduced the concept of an anti-system party: such a party is characterized by an activity that undermines the legitimacy of the democratic regime, and 'a belief system that does not share the values of the political order within which it operates'.[28] More recently, Gordon Smith has proposed a typology which combines 'compatibility of aims and acceptability of behavior' and has underlined the existence of a 'grey zone of acceptability' according to different time and context; in other terms, what is considered 'incompatible with the system in one era may be accommodated in another'.[29] The evolution of the socialist parties illustrates very well how parties can progressively accommodate themselves to the system's rules.

Summing up, the extreme-right parties should exhibit an 'opposition of principle' and/or should express an ideology which undermines the constitutional rules of the democratic regime. If we refer to fascism as the extreme-right ideology, this ideology is, by any standard, alien and extraneous to liberal-democracy. But, where such reference to such a well-structured ideology does not exist, we have to look for the presence of anti-system political attitudes and beliefs. Many right-wing (non-fascist) parties share some common features which are clearly anti-system. These characteristics include anti-parliamentarism, anti-pluralism and anti-partyism. Even if such parties do not openly advocate authoritarianism, they nevertheless undermine democratic legitimacy by expressing distrust for the parliamentary system and politics in general, and by stressing the weakness of the state, the disruption of traditional communities, and the 'unnatural' equality and excessive freedom that democracy promotes.

In sum, while most ERPs do not share any nostalgia for the inter-war fascist experience, they nevertheless express anti-democratic values throughout their political discourse. Their criticism is expressed by a hostility to modernity, a hatred of divisions and a search for harmony, an exaltation of natural community and a hostility towards foreigners, a faith in hierarchical structures and a distrust of democratic individual representation.

On the basis of these criteria, we can use a typology where parties more on the right of the political spectrum are categorized according to the presence or absence of a fascist heritage and to their acceptance of, or opposition to, the political system. In order to be included in the ERP family, right-wing parties should either fulfil the (historic-ideological) fascist criterion, or exhibit a delegitimizing impact through a series of issues, values, and attitudes which undermines system legitimacy. If a party fits the historic-ideological fascist criterion as well as the systemic one, we can think of it as belonging to the old or traditional or neo-fascist type. If a party is not linked to fascism but has an anti-system profile, we can think of it as belonging to the new or post-industrial type.

Traditional and Post-Industrial ERPs

At the end of this long tour around the problem we can finally provide a classification of ERPs (see Table 2.1). In the category of traditional, old right-wing parties we can include the Italian MSI (even if some change is in progress), the German NPD and DVU, the Dutch CP '86, the British BNP and, for certain aspects, the Belgian *Vlaams Blok*; in the category of the post-industrial new right-wing parties we have the French FN, the German *Republikaner*, the Dutch CD, the Belgian FN, the Austrian Freedom Party, the Danish Progress party and its Norwegian homologue.[30]

The first group constitutes remnants of the conflicts of the first half of the twentieth century activated by the industrial revolution when social groups clashed violently against one another.

TABLE 2.1
CLASSIFICATION OF ERPs

A. The Old Traditional Extreme Right-Wing Parties

Italy	MSI (*Movimento Sociale Italiano* – Italian Social Movement
Germany	NPD (*Nationaldemokratische Partei Deutschlands* – German National Democratic Party
Great Britain	BNP (British National Party)
Netherlands	CP'86 (*Centrumpartij'86* – Centre Party '86

B. The New, Post-Industrial Extreme Right Parties

Austria	FPO (*Freiheitliche Partei Österreichs* – Austrian Liberal Party)
Belgium	VB (*Vlaams Blok* – Flemish Bloc); FNB (*Front National Belge* – Belgian National Front)
Denmark	FRPd (*Fremskridtspartiet* – Progress Party)
France	FN (*Front National* – National Front)
Germany	REP (*Die Republikaner* – The Republicans)
Netherlands	CD (*Centrumdemocraten* – Centre Democrats)
Norway	FRPn (*Fremskrittspartiet* – Progress Party)

The second group is alien to the fascist tradition. These parties are the by-product of the conflicts of post-industrial society where material interests are no longer so central and the bourgeoisie and working class can neither be so neatly defined nor so radically opposed to one another. The post-war economic and cultural transformations have blurred the class identification and loosened the traditional loyalties linked to precise social groups. The development of the service sector, the decline in the ability of labour relations to predict social relations, the process of atomization and secularization and have nurtured different cleavages and aggregations. Parts of the traditional working class and of the not highly educated middle class now face the new middle class and a unionized working class in a conflict over values more than material interests. The conflict on the distribution of resources leaves the room open to that on values allocation. The passage to post-industrial society promotes post-materialist values which emphasize such non-material issues as self-realization and personal identity while loosening and even breaking up traditional societal and political ties and loyalties.[31] The traditional parties tried to find answers to such changes but, inevitably, new actors respond better than old ones to new challenges. In fact, in the eighties, two kinds of parties have emerged on the opposite sides of the political spectrum, the ecologist-libertarian on the left and the (new) extreme-right parties: both are the offspring of the silent revolution and of post-industrial society. Therefore the extreme right-wing parties that have developed in recent years offer an answer to those demands and needs created by post-industrialism and not satisfied by traditional parties: they do not revive the 'palingenetic' myth of fascism. These demands and needs concern the defence of the natural community from foreigners (hence racism and xenophobia), the desire for more law and order, the search for a 'charismatic' leader, and the irritation with democratic representative mechanisms and procedures, and express a desire for an authoritative guide in a society where self-achievement and individualism have disrupted the protective network of traditional social bonds. And finally, there is the demand for a return to rigid moral standards, the counterpart of the post-materialist left-libertarianism.

In sum, the newly born ERPs are not old, disguised neo-fascist parties. Instead, they represent a response to the new post-industrial era and to the new post-material values it has created.

The Traditional Extreme Right

This type of extreme right class is led by the oldest and strongest party of the whole political family, the Italian MSI, *Movimento Sociale Italiano* (Italian Social Movement).[32] The MSI was founded at the end of 1946 by a group of young ex-fascists (backed in the shadows by a group of more experienced members of the old fascist establishment) in order to keep alive the 'idea' of fascism. The party never rejected its direct linkage with fascism either in ideological terms or in party recruitment practices: all the MSI national and local leaders had belonged to the fascist party or the fascist army during the 1943–45 civil war. This fidelity has characterized the MSI up to the present and even the recent adoption of the electoral label of *Alleanza Nazionale* (National Alliance) has not implied a radical ideological transformation. The spectacular rise in electoral support experienced by the MSI in the 1994 election (13.4 per cent) and its participation in government (an absolute novelty for an ERP in Europe) has made MSI leaders more cautious, but no serious debate on the acceptance of the fundamentals of liberal-democracy has started yet.

In West Germany many nostalgic parties appeared immediately after the war and won some seats either at the Land level or the federal level. Up to 1953, parties of 'traditional and new nationalism'[33] got significant support only from among German refugees from the East. After a long period of irrelevance, the extreme right underwent a revival coincident with Germany's first post-war economic crisis. A new party appeared, the NPD, *Nationaldemokratische Partei Deutschlands* (German National Democratic Party), which sought to exploit the situation. In the sixties the NPD passed the electoral threshold of five per cent in almost all the Land elections and seemed on the edge of entering the Bundestag. However, in the 1969 election the NPD only won 4.3 per cent and failed to achieve parliamentary representation. Shortly afterwards the party collapsed organizationally. In more recent years the NPD has reorganized and joined with a new nostalgic party, the DVU *Deutsche Volksunion* (German People's Union); it has surfaced again in Bremen (1991) and in Schleswig-Holstein (1992). However, the chances of an NPD and DVU revival are limited by the appearance of another, more successful German ERP, the *Republikaner*, which belongs to the post-industrial type.[34]

The other parties which constitute the traditional extreme right are much more feeble and on the edge of irrelevance. Some of these have disappeared from the political system, as is true in the cases of Spain, Greece and Portugal.

The Spanish *Frente Nacional* (National Front) – formerly *Fuerza Nueva* (New Force) and the *Falange de la Jons* (the national-syndicalist Phalanx) after having accumulated a series of electoral fiascos dissolved themselves and did not participate in the latest 1993 elections. These two parties represented the Spanish extreme-right tradition in its two distinctive wings, the Francoist tradition, represented by Blas Pinar's FN, and the revolutionary-syndicalist tendency of Primo de Rivera, represented by the tiny *Falange de la Jons*.[35] The extreme right in Spain has now practically disappeared.

The same is true for the Portuguese system where the minor *Partido do Democracia Cristà* (Christian Democratic Party) could be considered a sort of traditional Catholic integralist party, somewhat nostalgic for Salazar's *Estado Novo* (Costa Pinto, 1990). This party was present in parliament with one deputy from 1979 to 1982 when it reached one per cent of the votes, but later declined and disappeared a few years ago without contesting the 1991 general elections. Even a new movement, the *Partido Força National* (National Force Party), founded in 1989 by the merging of two youth groups – *Força National* and *Nova Monarquia*, with the aim of representing the Portuguese corporatist tradition modernized by some *nouvelle droite* ideological contribution, has also failed.

In Greece the neo-fascist movement EPEN, *Ethniki Politiki Enosis* (National Political Union), last incarnation of a long series of extreme right parties before and after the colonels' dictatorship (1967–74), disappeared after having achieved parliamentary representation in the mid-eighties; it has disappeared in the nineties, and no other such movement has arisen in Greece.[36]

In Great Britain, like the Mediterranean countries, the ERPs have experienced a trend towards irrelevance. Even if Great Britain, unlike those countries, is a bastion of uninterrupted democracy, nevertheless, the British extreme right has a clear fascist character beginning with Oswald Mosley's British Union of Fascists in the thirties and ending with the National Front and the British National Party in recent years. The history of the post-war British extreme right is a story of marginal and quarrelling factions where self-promoting leaders fight each other to gain control of their sects.[37] The most conspicuous efforts to build up a sizeable extreme right party was made in the seventies with the foundation of the National Front. The NF achieved some minor electoral success but clashed with the new leadership of the Conservative party led by Margaret Thatcher and against the constraint of the majority single-ballot system. The numerous studies of the NF have underlined the presence of fascist and especially nazi elements, anti-Semitic and anti-immigrant racism, white supremacy (with an emphasis on Anglo-saxonism) and imperialist nostalgia. In the late eighties the NF collapsed, splitting into two factions, one heavily influenced by Julius Evola's traditionalist ideology with some Strasserite sentiments, the other pointing to a third way between capitalism and socialism. Both factions however are now practically irrelevant. The only remaining extreme-right presence is provided by the BNP which has inherited the classical racist and anti-semitic issues of the first NF and has quite recently received some modest support in the 1992 and 1993 city council elections in London. In September 1993 for the first time a BNP candidate was elected in the district of the Isle of Dogs in London. Aside from this rather exceptional event the presence of the extreme right in Britain remains quite marginal.

The last example of the traditional extreme right is the Dutch Centrumpartij '86, CP86 (Centre Party '86).[38] This party is the descendent of the former Centrumpartij which tried to merge a classical neo-fascist outlook with a more moderate and conservative appeal. However, the internal tension between the radical fringe, overtly racist with neo-nazi traits, and the more conservative one led to the break-up of the party: CP86 reflected the fascist component which aimed at a 'national revolution' and a 'New European Order'. This component, however, has been less relevant than the other more moderate faction which retained the name of CD.

Finally another party might be included in this analysis even if its classification is more difficult: the Belgian *Vlaams Blok* (Flemish Bloc).[39] At its beginning the *Vlaams Blok* (founded in 1978) followed the path of Flemish nationalism (more autonomy for Flanders) but with the new leadership of Karel Dillen it acquired a xenophobic stance: Flanders must be freed not only from the francophone Belgians but from all foreign presence. Racism and white supremacism characterize the *Vlaams Blok* but even if the reference to a 'superior race' (sometimes identified as the Flemish one) can tie this party to the fascist tradition there is no linkage to the historic fascist movements of the thirties. Therefore the Vlaams Blok is somewhat in between the two types of ERP.

The New Post-Industrial Extreme Right

The French *Front National* is the prototype of post-industrial extreme-right parties. Although the FN was founded in 1972 by the fusion of small sects of the extreme right, it never achieved political relevance before 1983.[40] Only in that year, did the FN win a significant level of voter support at local elections and attention by the mass media. The presence of a high profile personality such as Jean-Marie Le Pen as party leader then provided immediate visibility for the FN. The *Front National* reached 11 per cent of the vote at the European elections in 1984 and has remained afterwards more or less at the same level. This success was not based on the revival of the fascist tradition. While many old fascists, members of the many post-war right-extremist groups, occupied prominent positions within the party, no nostalgia for the *pétainiste* experience was exhibited. On the contrary, the new problems of contemporary French society were put at the top of the agenda: and as these problems were not treated by the established parties (even the conservative ones) the FN was able to attract a sizeable electorate, underlining, at the same time, how far from the concerns of the common man the other parties were. The crisis of representation of established parties and the general distrust of politics and the democratic system in general, further fuelled the FN's appeal.

The growing salience of new or neglected issues, such as immigration and law and order, together with a more general anti-party and anti-system outlook are at the base of FN's success, as well as that of all the other post-industrial ERPs. The question of immigration represents a clear difference between those parties and the traditional ERPs because the former do not emphasize biological superiority. Their hostility towards foreigners is expressed in terms of national identity and cultural traditions. The discourse about racism developed by the FN suggests that it is not in the interests of the immigrants themselves to leave their country of origin and lose their cultural and affective bonds: everyone has his place. The presence of foreigners is acceptable only in limited numbers and when linked to strictly economic necessities. Therefore, it is not surprising that the post-industrial ERPs support a policy of more aid to the third world, to keep the immigrants away. In particular, the Scandinavian parties – the FRP *Fremskridtsparti* (Progess party) in Norway and Denmark (and the brand new *NY Demockrati* (New Democracy in Sweden) are very attentive to this point.

The French *Front National*, the most successful party of the new generation of extreme-right parties, has paved the way for the others. The Belgian *Front National* is a perfect example of this process of imitation.[41] In fact when it was founded in 1985 it not only adopted the same name but took overt inspiration from its French counterpart. The Belgian FN has followed all the French FN's suggestions up to the point that some planks of its platform (for example, the 'proposition on immigration') are directly drawn from the French ones. This party, which has recently gained more and more influence in the Francophone area of Belgium – especially in Brussels, won in 1991 5.7 per cent of the votes and a seat in Parliament. The Belgian *Front National* is clearly anti-system but it fiercely denies any linkage to fascism, a tendency that was represented instead by the former PFN, *Parti des Forces Nouvelles* (New Forces Party), dissolved after its failure at the 1991 elections.

In a less direct way the impulse of Le Pen's party is present in other countries. The German *Republikaner* has adopted some of the arguments and the reasoning of the *Front National*, especially after their common experience in the Euroright group in the European Parliament. The Republikaners differentiate themselves from the DVU and NPD by denying any overt nostalgia for Nazism and for the linkage they established between the question of national identity and immigration. The dramatic increase in asylum-seekers, refugees and resettlers, together with the traditional quota of foreign workers (*Gastarbeiter*), has offered the opportunity for the Republikaners to find an easily accessible scapegoat for sociopolitical anxieties: the foreigners are responsible not only for the increase in crime but for the enfeeblement of German national identity. After their sudden surge in the 1989 Berlin and European elections (7.5 per cent and 7.1 per cent respectively) the Republikaners have experienced a series of successes and setbacks before their recent failure at the 1994 Euroelection (3.9 per cent). However their presence in some *Land* parliaments and their force of attraction in the urban areas and the economically weak eastern regions leave them a strong potentiality for development.

Quite close to the *Republikaner* because of the emphasis on the *völkisch* element of the nation and of the German *Kulturnation* is the Austrian FPOE *Freiheitliche Partei Österreichs* (Austrian Liberal

Party).[42] This party is the heir of the old VdU, a nostalgic party composed mainly of old nazi supporters purged in the aftermath of the war. The liberal tendency within the FPOE had difficulties in emerging because of this neo-fascist presence. When the liberal wing finally took power in the early eighties the FPOE departed from its electoral ghetto and was accepted as a coalition partner even by the social-democrats. However, this moderation did not last long and, quite surprisingly, in 1986, the leadership changed again and the new party secretary, Jorg Haider, offered a totally different party outlook. Anti-establishment, anti-partyism, anti-politics were the key issues of Haider policy; this opposition to the system did not limit itself to the procedure and outcomes of the democratic government, but even to its fundamentals. In fact, Haider introduced (and partially revitalized) latent themes such as the nostalgia for the German *Kulturnation* and the defence of national identity against foreign presence, including the Jews. The xenophobic and anti-Semitic positions were accompanied by a certain glossing over of the nazi past. Haider's leadership led the FPOE to double and even triple its votes at the regional and national level (1990:16.6 per cent) but also caused its domestic marginalization and its expulsion from the Liberal International.

A peculiar example of the post-industrial ERPs is provided by both the Progress parties in Denmark and Norway.[43] Both parties were founded in the early seventies on the basis of an anti-tax and anti-socialist sentiment. Their appeal was mainly against the high costs of the welfare state system and, by consequence, against the establishment which supported it. The anti-welfare attitude led to a deeper critique of the system as a whole and to the role of the political parties as such. Later on, new themes such as immigration and law and order became part of the Progress parties' agendas. The peculiarity of these parties lies in their emphasis on the free market and capitalist economy coupled with opposition to cutting the welfare benefits for the poorest citizens (but not the immigrants). Their inclusion in the extreme-right family is questionable but it is based mainly on their 'opposition of principle', on their constant activity to undermine the system's legitimacy and on their negation of the equality of man expressed in their xenophobic statements.

Conclusion

The 1980s represent a watershed in the history of the post-war extreme right. Up to that decade the extreme right was represented only by the Italian MSI, the sole party which had gained parliamentary representation with sizeable percentages (around five per cent) since 1948. Other parties had some flash appearances but they neither got parliamentary seats at the national level nor lasted for long. The German nationalist-nostalgic parties in the early fifties and the Austrian VdU were partial exceptions. In the mid-eighties the political landscape of the right wing changed. The French FN emerged 'from a decade of darkness and sarcasm', as Le Pen expressed it after the 1984 European elections, and became a prominent party in the French political system: in a few years such newly-born parties as the Belgian FN and the German *Republikaner*, or pre-existing ones such as the *Vlaams Blok* and the CD, followed the French example. With national variants, all pointed to an appeal against the welfare state, against democratic institutions, and against the establishment, the traditional parties and the politicians. But, contrary to the traditional ERPs, they did not recover any 'socialist' element in their political discourse. The new parties reject any reference to socialism whatsoever and accept the neo-liberal (in economic terms) tendency that emerged at the eve of the eighties, first in the Anglo-Saxon countries and later all over Europe. The Free Market is exalted by the new ERPs, while the traditional, neo-fascist parties have always manifested hostility towards it and envisaged a corporatist solution where the state plays a crucial role. The success of these new parties, contrary to the decline and even disappearance of the traditional ERPs, is linked to their different origins. The new ERPs are the offspring of the post-industrial society. This identity and material achievement are meshed together, but these parties place special emphasis on traditional moral values, respect for hierarchy, patriotism and so on: issues that are related to post-modern politics. In short, these parties offer a new agenda for a new era.

Notes

1. K. von Beyme (1988), Right-Wing Extremism in Post-War Europe, *West European Politics*, 11: 1–18.
2. M. Duverger (1951), *Les Partis Politiques* (Paris: Armand Colin).
3. E. Deutsch., D. Lindon and P. Weil (1966) *Les familles politiques* (Paris: Edition du Minuit).
4. S. Henig (ed.) (1969), *Political Parties in the European Community*. London: Allen & Unwin.
5. D.L. Seiler (1980), *Partis et Familles Politiques* (Paris: PUF).
6. J.E. Lane and S.O. Ersson. (1987), *Politics and Society in Western Europe* (London: Sage).
7. Z. Sternhell (1987), *Ni Droite ni Gauche. L'Idéologie Fasciste en France* (Paris: Editions Complexes).
8. R. Griffin (1993), *The Nature of Fascism* (London/New York: Routledge).

9. Ibid., p. 13.
10. S.G. Payne (1980), 'The Concept of Fascism', pp. 14–25 in: Larsen, S.U., Hagtvet, B. and Mykelbust, J.P. (eds.) *Who Were the Fascists* (Oslo: Universitetsforlaget).
11. Z. Sternhell (1987), *Ni Droite ni Gauche. L'Idéologie Fasciste en France*, p. 56 (Paris: Editions Complexes).
12. R. Griffin (1993), *The Nature of Fascism* (London/New York: Routledge).
13. Z. Sternhell (1989), p. 15. *Naissance de l'idéologie Fasciste* (Paris: Fayard).
14. A.M. Duranton-Crabol (1991), pp. 24–7. *L'Europe de l'extrême droite* (Paris: Editions Complexes).
15. R. Eatwell (1989), The Nature of the Right, 2: The Right as a Variety of Style of Thought, pp. 62–76, in Eatwell, R. and O Sullivan, N. (eds.) *The Nature of the Right* (London: Pinter).
16. F. Elbers and M. Fennema (1993), *Racistische partijien in West Europa* (Leiden: Burgershapskunde).
17. U. Backes and P. Moreau (1993), *Die Extreme Rechte in Deutschland* (München: Akademischer Verlag).
18. R. Griffin (1993), *The Nature of Fascism* (London/New York: Routledge).
19. H. G. Betz (1993), 'The New Politics of Resentment. Radical Right Wing Parties in Western Europe', *Comparative Politics*, 16:413–27.
20. A. Pfahl-Traughber (1993), 'Rechtspopulistische Parteien in Westeuropa', pp. 39–56, in Jesse, E. (ed.) *Politischer Extremismus in Deutschland und Europa* (München: Bayerische Landzentrale für Politische Bildungsarbeit).
21. J.A. Laponce (1981), *Left and Right. The Topography of Political Perception* (Toronto: University of Toronto Press).
22. D. Fuchs and H.D. Klingemann (1990), 'The Left-Right Schema' pp 203–34 in Jennings, M.K. et al. *Continuities in Political Action* (Berlin and New York: De Gruyter).
23. N. Mayer (1993), *Explaining Electoral Right Wing Extremism: the Case of the Le Pen Vote in the 1988 French Presidential Elections.* Paper presented at the APSA Annual Meeting, Washington.
24. U. Backes and E. Jesse (1993), *Politischer Extremismus in der Bundesrepublik Deutschland* (Bonn: Bundzentrale für politische Bildung).
25. O. Kirchheimer (1966), 'The Vanishing Opposition', pp. 237–59 in: Dahl, R. (ed.) *Political Opposition in Western Democracies* (New Haven and London: Yale University Press).
26. G. Sartori (1976), *Parties and Party Systems* (Cambridge: Cambridge University Press).
27. O. Kirchheimer (1966), 'The Vanishing Opposition', pp. 237–59 in Dahl, R. (ed.), *Political Opposition in Western Democracies* (New Haven and London: Yale University Press).
28. G. Sartori (1976), *Parties and Party Systems* (p. 133) (Cambridge: Cambridge University Press).
29. G. Smith (1987), 'Party and Protest: The Two Faces of Opposition in Western Europe', pp. 63–4 in Kolinsky, E. (Ed.) *Opposition in Western Europe* (London: Croom Helm).
30. P. Ignazi (1994), *L'estrema destra in Europa* (Bologna: Il Mulino).
31. D. Bell (1980), *The Winding Passage* (Cambridge, MA: ABT Books).
32. P. Ignazi (1989a), *Il Polo Escluso. Profilo del Movimento Sociale Italiano* (Bologna: Il Mulino); (1989b), 'Un Nouvel Acteur Politique', pp. 63–81 in: Mayer, N. and Perrineau, P. *Le Front National à Découvert* (Paris: Presses de la Fondation Nationale des Sciences Politiques.

33. R. Stöss (1991), *Politics against Democracy. Right-Wing Extremism in West Germany* (New York and Oxford: Berg).
34. M. Minkenberg (1993), 'The Far Right in Unified Germany'. Paper presented at the APSA Annual Meeting, Washington.
35. J. Gilmour (1992), 'The Extreme Right in Spain: Blas Pinar and the Spirit of the Nationalist Uprising', pp. 206–31 in Hainsworth, P. (ed.) *The Extreme Right in Europe and the USA* (London: Pinter).
36. P.E. Dimitras (1992), 'Greece: The Virtual Absence of an Extreme Right', pp. 246–68 in Hainsworth, P. (ed.), *The Extreme Right in Europe and the USA* (London: Pinter); van Doonselaar, J. (1991), *Fout na de Oorloq. Fascistische en racistische organisaties in Nederland 1950–1990* (Amsterdam: Uitgeverij Bert Bakker).
37. C.T. Husbands (1988), 'Extreme Right-wing Politics in Great Britain: The Recent Marginalization of the National Front', *West European Politics* 11:65–79. R. Eatwell (1992) 'Why has the Extreme Right failed in Britain?' pp. 175–92 in Hainsworth, P. (ed.) *The Extreme Right in Europe and the USA* (London: Pinter Eatwell 1992).
38. J. van Doonselaar (1991), *Fout na de Oorloq. Fascistische en racistische organisaties in Nederland 1950-1990* (Amsterdam: Uitgeverij Bert Bakker). G. Voerman and P. Lucardie (1990), The Extreme Right in the Netherlands: The Centrists and Their Radical Rivals, *European Journal of Political Research*, 22:35–54.
39. H. Gijsels (1992), *Het Vlaams Blok* (Leuven: Uitgeverij Kritak).
40. G. Birenbaum (1992), *Le Front National en Politique* (Paris: Ballard); P. Ignazi, (1989a), *Il Polo Escluso. Profilo del Movimento Sociale Italiano* (Bologna: Il Mulino). P. Ignazi (1989b), 'Un Nouvel Acteur Politique', pp. 63–81 in: Mayer, N. and Perrineau, P., *Le Front National à Découvert* (Paris: Presses de la Fondation Nationale des Sciences Politiques); P. Perrineau (1993), 'Le Front National: 1972–92', pp. 243–97 in Winock, M. *Histoire de l' extrême droite en France* (Paris: Sueil).
41. G. Breës (1992), *L'Affront National. Le nouveau visage de l'extrême droite en Belgique* (Bruxelles: EPO).
42. K. R. Luther. (1988). 'The Freiheitliche Partei Österreichs: Protest Party or Governing Party?' pp. 213–51 in: Kirchner, E.J. (ed.) *Liberal Parties in Western Europe* (Cambridge: Cambridge University Press); M. Steger (1993), 'The New Austria', the 'New Europe' and the 'New Nationalism', paper presented at the APSA Annual Meeting, Washington.
43. J.G. Andersen (1992), Denmark. The Progress Party: Populist, Neo-liberalism and Welfare State Chauvism, pp. 193–205 in Harmsworth, P. (ed.), *The Extreme Right in Postwar Europe and USA* (London: Francis Pinter).

Bibliography

Andersen, J. G. (1992), 'Denmark. The Progress Party: Populist, Neoliberalism and Welfare State Chauvinism', pp. 193–205 in Harmsworth, P. (ed.), *The Extreme Right in Postwar Europe and USA* (London: Francis Pinter).
Anderson, J. G. and Bjørklund, T. (1990), 'Structural Changes and New Cleavages: The Progress Parties in Denmark and Norway', *Acta Sociologica* 33: 195–217.
Backes, U. and Jesse, E. (1993), *Politischer Extremismus in der Bundersrepublik Deutschland* (Bonn: Bundzentrale für politische Bildung).

Backes, U. and Moreau, P. (1993), *Die Extreme Rechte in Deutschland* (München: Akademischer Verlag).

Bell, D. (1980), *The Winding Passage* (Cambridge, MA: ABT Books).

Betz, H. G. (1993), 'The New Politics of Resentment. Radical Right Wing Parties in Western Europe', *Comparative Politics*, 16:413–27.

Beyme, K. von (1988), 'Right-Wing Extremism in Post-War Europe', *West European Politics*, 11:1–18.

Birenbaum, G. (1992), *Le Front National en Politique* (Paris: Ballard).

Breës, G. (1992), *L'Affront National. Le nouveau visage de l'extrême droite en Belgique* (Bruxelles: EPO).

Costa Pinto, A. (1990), 'The Radical Right in Contemporary Portugal: An Introduction', paper delivered at the ECPR Joint Session of Workshops, Bochum.

Deutsch, E., Lindon, D. and Weil, P. (1996), *Les familles politiques* (Paris: Editions du Minuit).

Dimitras, P. E. (1992), 'Greece: The Virtual Absence of an Extreme Right', pp. 246–68 in Hainsworth, P. (ed.), *The Extreme Right in Europe and the USA* (London: Pinter).

van Donselaar, J. (1991). *Fout na de Oorloq. Fascistische en racistische organisaties in Nederland 1950–1990* (Amsterdam: Uitgeverij Bert Bakker).

Duranton-Crabol, A. M. (1991), *L'Europe de l'extrême droite* (Paris: Editions Complexes).

Duverger, M. (1951), *Les Partis Politiques* (Paris: Armand Colin).

Eatwell, R. (1989), 'The Nature of the Right, 2: The Rights as a Variety of 'Style of Thought', pp. 62–76, in Eatwell, R. and O'Sullivan, N. (eds), *The Nature of the Right* (London: Pinter).

Eatwell, R. (1992) 'Why Has the Extreme Right Failed in Britain? pp. 175–92 in Hainsworth, P. (ed.) *The Extreme Right in Europe and the USA* (London: Pinter).

Elbers, F. and Fennema M. (1993), *Racistische partijen in West Europa* (Leiden: Burgershapskunde).

Ferraresi, F. (1988), 'Julius Evola: Tradition, Reaction and the Radical Right', *European Journal of Sociology*, 28: 107–51.

Fuchs, D. and Klingemann, H.D. (1990), 'The Left-Right Schema', pp. 203–34 in Jennings, M.K. *et al.*, *Continuities in Political Action* (Berlin and New York: De Gruyter).

Gijsels, H. (1992) *Het Vlaams Blok* (Leuven: Uitgeverij Kritak).

Gilmour, J. (1992) 'The Extreme Right in Spain: Blas Pinar and the Spirit of the Nationalist Uprising', pp. 206–31 in Hainsworth, P. (ed.) *The Extreme Right in Europe and the USA* (London: Pinter).

Griffin, R. (1993), *The Nature of Fascism* (London/New York: Routledge).

Henig, S. (ed.) (1969), *Political Parties in the European Community* (London: Allen & Unwin).

Husbands, C. T. (1981), 'Contemporary Right-Wing Extremism in Western European Democracies: A Review Article', *European Journal of Political Research*, 9: 75–100.

Husbands, C. T. (1988), 'Extreme Right-wing Politics in Great Britain: The Recent Marginilization of the National Front', *West European Politics*, 11: 65–79.

Ignazi, P. (1989a), *Il Polo Escluso. Profilo del Movimento Sociale Italiano* (Bologna: Il Mulino).

Ignazi, P. (1989b), 'Un Nouvel Acteur Politique', pp. 63–81 in: Mayer, N. and Perrineau, P., *Le Front National à Découvert* (Paris: Presses de la Fondation Nationale des Sciences Politiques).

Ignazi, P. (1992), 'The Silent Counter-Revolution. Hypotheses on the Emergence of Extreme Right-Wing Parties', *European Journal of Political Research*, 22: 3–34.

Ignazi, P. (1994), *L'estrema destra in Europa* (Bologna: Il Mulino).

Kirchheimer, O. (1966). 'The Vanishing Opposition', pp. 237–59 in: Dahl, R. (ed.), *Political Opposition in Western Democracies* (New Haven and London: Yale University Press).

Lane, J. E. and Ersson, S. O. (1987), *Politics and Society in Western Europe* (London: Sage).

Laponce, J. A. (1981), *Left and Right. The Topography of Political Perception* (Toronto: University of Toronto Press).

Luther, K. R. (1988), 'The Freiheitliche Partei Österreichs: Protest Party or Government Party? pp. 213–51 in: Kirchner, E. J. (ed.), *Liberal Parties in Western Europe* (Cambridge: Cambridge University Press).

Mayer, N. (1993), *Explaining Electoral Right-Wing Extremism: the Case of the Le Pen Vote in the 1988 French Presidential Elections*. Paper presented at the APSA Annual Meeting, Washington.

Minkenberg, M. (1993), 'The Far Right in Unified Germany'. Paper presented at the APSA Annual Meeting, Washington.

Payne, S. G. (1980), 'The Concept of Fascism', pp. 14–25 in: Larsen, S. U., Hagtvet, B. and Mykelbust, J. P. (eds), *Who Were the Fascists* (Oslo: Universitetsforlaget).

Perrineau, P. (1993), 'Le Front National: 1972–92', pp. 243–97 in Winock M. (dir.), *Histoire de l'extrême droite en France* (Paris, Seuil).

Pfahl-Traughber, A. (1993) 'Rechtspopulistische Parteien in Westeuropa', pp. 39–56, in Jesse, E. (ed.), *Politischer Extremismus in Deutschland und Europa* (München: Bayerische Landzentrale für Politische Bildungsarbeit).

Sartori, G. (1976), *Parties and Party Systems* (Cambridge: Cambridge University Press).

Seiler, D. L. (1980), *Partis et Familles Politiques* (Paris: PUF).

Smith, G. (1987) 'Party and Protest: The Two Faces of Opposition in Western Europe', pp. 55–76 in Kolinsky, E. (ed.), *Opposition in Western Europe* (London: Croom Helm).

Steger, M. (1993), 'The 'New Austria', the 'New Europe' and the 'New Nationalism'. Paper presented at the APSA Annual Meeting, Washington.

Sternhell, Z. (1987). *Ni Droite ni Gauche. L'Idéologie Fasciste en France* (Paris: Editions Complexes).

Sternhell, Z. (1989). *Naissance de l'Idéologie Fasciste* (Paris: Fayard).

Stöss, R. (1991), *Politics against Democracy. Right-Wing Extremism in West Germany* (New York and Oxford: Berg).

Voerman, G. and Lucardie, P. (1990) 'The Extreme Right in the Netherlands: The Centrists and Their Radical Rivals', *European Journal of Political Research*, 22: 35–54.

Ysmal, C. (1990), 'The Browning of Europe. Extreme Right Parties in the 1989 European Election'. Paper presented at the APSA Annual Meeting, San Francisco.

3

The New Right in France and Germany: *Nouvelle Droite, Neue Rechte,* and the New Right Radical Parties

Michael Minkenberg

Western Democracies in the 1990s have undoubtedly entered a new era. In Europe, the collapse of communist regimes, the Soviet empire and the Cold War order, new conflicts and massive population movements, German unification and the altered process of European integration have shifted the political parameters significantly. In particular, the erosion of hitherto rather stable political orders in East *and* West recalls the turbulences of the inter-war period and raises the spectre of a Weimarization of European politics – including the threat of a new right-wing extremist attack on democracies (in the West) and democratization (in the East).

In this chapter, I want to elaborate the role and impact of the New Right in Western democracies. My basic argument is that the shift to the right precedes the recent international changes, that they are, rather, a reaction to 1968 than to 1989, although the consequences of 1989 have accelerated and exacerbated these shifts. More specifically, New Right here is understood as a counter-movement and reaction to fundamental social and cultural change in Western societies at two distinct but not unrelated levels. At the level of intellectual and political élites, the (European) New Right advocates anti-modern, anti-liberal and anti-Western views, which implicitly or explicitly put into question the concept of Western democracies and their realization in the most recent democratization shifts, often coupled with a recourse to themes of the Weimar conservative revolution. At the level of movements, parties and elections, the New Right vulgarizes central positions of the intellectual New Right and presents a populist-neo-conservative radicalism in rejection of social and cultural changes and in defence of social entitlements. As a *Wohlstandschauvinismus* in the context of established democracies under stress, it is neither a traditional conservatism of establishment politics, nor is it a militant anti-democratic right-wing extremism, although it serves as a link or 'hinge'[1] between the two.

The argument of this chapter will be structured into three parts. First, a theoretically informed outline of the argument will be presented including definitions of right-wing extremism, Old and New Politics, and New Right in particular. Second, the intellectual movements of the New Right will be discussed with regard to ideological and organizational aspects. Finally, evidence from the two countries (France and Germany) will be provided for the New Right parties concerning ideologies, voting patterns and the question of historical continuities.

Concepts: The New Right in Western Democracies

In this chapter, I will argue that the New Right does not simply represent 'modernization losers' since most of their supporters are not 'losers' in any objective sense. Although a correlation between mass unemployment and the emergence of a significant radical right exists in various parts of modern European history, it is not primarily the unemployed or those facing immediate lay-offs who support the New Right. Moreover, the New Right cannot be reduced to the revival of anti-democratic extremism, because in rhetoric and in behaviour they are as much pro- as they are anti-system. Finally, a perspective which focuses on economic changes and variables overlooks the aspects of individual-level and cultural change, which have contributed significantly to the reconfiguration of the political spectrum in Western societies.

Instead, the New Right is conceptualized as a radical reaction to fundamental social and cultural changes in Western societies. The vast literature on political ideologies suggests that the left–right or liberal–conservative schema reflects fundamental orientations towards politics and society and that the underlying dividing line is to be found in attitudes towards change. Karl Mannheim has emphasized that conservative and progressive thought were established as the two socially based and mutually related *Weltanschauungen* in the modern world. They are a result of the differentiation of the traditional feudal order into diverse classes, interests, and ideologies and the emergence of bourgeois society.[2] Only this challenge to the established order and its hitherto unquestioned underlying norms and beliefs could bring about a 'conservative' consciousness that 'discovered' its interests in defending or even restoring these norms and the order, that is, that transformed them from an unpolitical traditionalism of 'eternal' values and institutions into objects of political conflict.

Following Mannheim's approach, conservatism is defined not simply as an anti-modern movement but as the dialectical counterpart to political modernization (democratization, emancipation, self-government, equal rights, and so on), which becomes mobilized in processes of differentiation and accelerated change. In consequence, conservatism cannot be reduced to so-called eternal conservative values but, like all other political ideologies, must be specified within historical conflict constellations. With the nationalist revolutions of the nineteenth century, conservatism involved the upper classes against the liberalism of the rising bourgeoisie. With the Industrial Revolution a new cleavage emerged in which the conservative bourgeoisie and remnants of the old order united against the workers' movement and its claim for participation and economic redistribution.[3] 'Left' became associated with the lower classes and allied élites which strove to change society in a more self-governing, egalitarian direction, whereas 'Right' was associated with maintaining and defending the *status quo* of the liberal bourgeois order.

Definitions of right-wing extremism usually start from this basic concept and differentiate between conservatives and the extreme right by arguing that the former seek to preserve the *status quo*, while the latter attempt to restore some *status quo ante*, often by the use of 'illegitimate' means, that is, force. But the examples of the 'conservative revolution' in Weimar Germany and the ideology and policies of the National Socialists show that this criterion is questionable: neither of them sought to restore the traditional social ideas or structures of the German past.[4] An analytically more promising distinction between conservatives or the moderate right and the extreme right can be derived from Sartori's discussion of anti-system parties. Such a party is defined as one which 'abides by a belief system that does not share the values of the political order within which it operates'.[5] The values of the political order can be identified by the Constitution, insofar as its underlying logic and values are concerned, or, more broadly, the political culture of a nation feeding into its political order of which the Constitution is only one part. In order to differentiate the right-wing extreme from other anti-system parties, the particular ideology, especially the use of a country's (pre-democratic) past, and public support patterns must be taken into account.

Here, a useful approach, combining aspects of both Adorno's and Lipset's models is provided by Erwin Scheuch and Hans-Dieter Klingemann who sought to put the NPD's sudden electoral success in West Germany in the 1960s into a comparative, cross-national perspective.[6] Their theory is based on the assumption that the potential for right-wing movements exists in all industrial societies and should be understood as a 'normal' pathological condition. In all fast-growing modernizing countries there will be some people or whole social groups that cannot cope with economic and cultural development in their society and that react to the pressures of readjustment with rigidity or closed-mindedness. These reactions can be mobilized by extremist movements or parties offering political philosophies that promise an elimination of pressures and a simpler, better society, usually an image of a romaticized past of the country.[7] More specifically, in terms of ideology, right-wing extremism comprises the totality of anti-democratic attitudes and behaviour patterns, in particular the rejection of the democratic *Rechtsstaat* and its fundamental values and principles in favour of an organic view of society, an ethnically/racially based concept of nation and an authoritarian view of politics and political leadership, often coupled with an anti-liberal and anti-communist bias.[8] It develops strength in times of accelerated social and cultural change and perceived failure of all available political philosophies.

Such fundamental and challenging changes were provided by the transition of Western capitalism into a phase of advanced industrial capitalism, or 'post-industrialism', the exhaustion of the welfare state, and a cultural shift which challenged established social values, life-styles and institutions. They brought about a new dynamism in Western politics that resulted in new conservative responses and opened up opportunities for new parties on the left and right with the latter mobilizing the 'normal pathological' right-wing potential. The decline of blue-collar and agrarian occupations in a continuously shrinking productionist sector of the economy along with the rise of white-collar occupations and the service sector resulted in a weakening of the class cleavage.

Social class-based voting patterns and corresponding partisan conflicts between left and right were further neutralized by an intergenerational value change. Considerable parts of younger, better educated cohorts developed so-called 'post-materialist' value priorities defined as personal freedom, democratization of political and community life, a less impersonal society over 'materialist' values of general economic growth, wealth and the maintaining of political order.[9] Progressive, largely post-materialist new social movements and new parties emerged, defined here as a 'New Left', which opposed the Vietnam war, struggled for women's and minority rights and new life-styles and promoted environmentalism and grass-roots democracy.[10] Particular effects of the emerging new value-based cleavage on party politics included a weakening of voter loyalties and an increase in issue-based voting and voter volatility, especially among younger, post-materialist voters.[11]

The year 1968 stands out as a symbolic date marking both the general shift of political paradigms in Western democracies, especially the emergence of the New Left and the resulting challenges to the political order, and more country-specific features of this shift. For example, in the context of French political culture, 1968 was just the latest of a long series of upheavals and street revolutions since 1789. As such it reconfirmed the traditional dichotomy of left versus right, of revolutionary versus anti-revolutionary positions and forces.[12] Thus, whereas in France, 1968 symbolizes a confirmation of key elements of French political culture as well as a reformulation of the project of the left, the same year stands for a transformation of German political culture. In the context of post-war West German society, the student protest was both narrower and broader than in other countries. It was narrower because it did not involve workers and mass strikes and was largely confined to universities and student groups.[13] It was broader, however, since it raised more fundamental questions of national identity. It provided for the long-needed public debate on the role of the average German's involvement in the Nazi regime and his or her historical responsibilities, the so-called *Vergangenheitsbewältigung* or 'coming to terms with the past'. And it brought up demands for more democracy and new forms of citizen involvements such as sit-ins, civil disobedience and other variants of 'unconventional political behaviour'[14] contrary to the common law-and-order mentality in Germany and its 'subject culture'.

As a response to the rise of post-materialism and the New Left, influential élites and a large proportion of Western publics have 'turned' to the right in a Mannheimian sense. They 'rediscovered' as their political philosophy traditional and materialist values and the Old Politics agenda of economic growth, technological progress and a stable order. The novelty of this mounting conservative response does not lie in the issues or the underlying philosophy itself but in the fact that it is an alliance of traditionally left-of-centre groups, both at the élite level and at the mass level, with traditionally conservative groups against the new challenge on the new, value-based conflict axis, that is, the New Politics dimension. Thus, neo-conservatism reflects the materialist end of the new cleavage. It is not simply the revival of traditional conservatism in the Old Politics sense – that is, opposition to the welfare state and to the redistribution of income, or the return of church-based religious traditionalism – but a new coalition of forces which see their common enemy in the post-materialist New Left and its political agenda.

The parties of the New Right radicalize this neo-conservative reaction and fuse its tenets with a populist, anti-establishment and anti-

party thrust. Thus, the New Right is not simply the extension of
conservatism towards the extreme right but the product of a
restructuring of the political spectrum and a regrouping of the party
system. Constituencies of established parties tend to realign according to
the New Politics cleavage rather than the Old Politics cleavage. In the
context of European politics, a sense of political crisis in the 1980s and
the immigration issue have fed this radicalization process and related
dealignment and realignment trends in the electorate.[15]

The crisis phenomena (a growing split in the economy and rising
unemployment, and political scandals involving government and
opposition parties) have considerably damaged the public support for
the established parties and governments. In Germany since unification,
both major parties have suffered a continuous loss of confidence in both
parts of the country, while at the same time increasing numbers of
Germans voice their discontent with the present state of society,
particularly with regard to crime and the economy.[16] A sense of crisis is
equally prevalent in France as growing fears of unemployment,
especially in the private sector, increase discontent with the shape of
French society – in 1993, 45 per cent of the French considered it
necessary to change society completely – as low levels of trust in the
government indicate.[17]

In both countries, popular feelings against the presence of foreigners
– especially from non-EC countries – have been strong for some time. In
1990, 46 per cent of the French preferred the return of 'a large number
of immigrants' to their countries of origin whereas 42 per cent favoured
their integration.[18] In the same year, 13 per cent of West Germans were
completely against an influx of labour migrants from EC countries
(thereby rejecting the official EC policy of EC-wide employment
opportunities) but 34 per cent were against immigration of labourers
from non-EC countries and 30 per cent rejected the settlement of asylum-
seekers.[19] A direct comparison of public attitudes in France and Germany
shows that those who think there are too many non-EC foreigners in the
country (35 per cent in each country in 1992) or those who feel disturbed
by the presence of other nationalities (France: 16 per cent, Western
Germany 18 per cent in 1992) are roughly equivalent in number.[20]

In sum, the challenge of a New Left with its political agenda of
egalitarianism, feminism, multi-culturalism and environmentalism, as a
result of sociostructural and value changes and the symptoms of a crisis,
provide the input into a further fragmentation of the political spectrum
in France and Germany. At the other end of the New Politics dimension,
the race and immigration issue – as a sign of an uncertain sense of
national identity and personal insecurities – becomes a defining element

of groups and parties of the New Right which stand as the negation of 1968 and the New Left's agenda.

The Intellectual New Right: Nouvelle Droite and Neue Rechte

In the wake of 1968, European politics witnessed an increasingly visible role of New Right intellectual groups with a strong emphasis on ethnic and European identity and organizational and personal links across national boundaries.[21] Their political impact is difficult to measure because of various ideological adjustments and their strategy. Rather than trying to directly influence electoral and party politics or governments, the New Right intellectuals pursued a 'metapolitical' approach largely inspired by Antonio Gramsci's concept of 'cultural hegemony'. According to Gramsci cultural hegemony, that is the power over the minds of people and their constructing of social reality, facilitates or even leads to the seizure of political power. Thus the strategy of the New Right, in an obvious attempt to 'learn' from the left and the New Left in particular, focused on spreading their ideas through infiltration of the education system, the mass media and other 'metapolitical' spheres of the public.[22] Consequently, new think-tanks, or écoles de pensée, newspapers and magazines were established, and existing ones became the target of the New Right's personnel placement strategy.

Among the key groups of the Nouvelle Droite in France during the 1970s were the Groupement de Recherche et d'Études pour la Civilisation Européenne (GRECE), or Study and Research Group for the European Civilization, and the Club de l'Horloge. GRECE was founded by Alain de Bénoist, Roger Lemoine and others in 1968, in part responding to May 1968 and the French intellectual New Left.[23] Hierarchically organized and attracting (in the 1980s) about 3,000 members in 30 local and regional groups, especially students, teachers and the academic middle class, GRECE held seminars and workshops, and put out various publications such as the theoretical journal Nouvelle École and the magazine Éléments. GRECE also succeeded in infiltrating the editorial board of the well-established weekly Figaro-Magazine and other journals.[24] The Club de l'Horloge, founded in the early 1970s by students of the Grandes Écoles, the élite schools for the higher civil service, tried to spread its ideas at workshops for civil servants, conservative politicians and business people and through several publications of its own.[25]

The ideological coherence of the French New Right was put

increasingly into question by a variety of adjustments which Alain de Bénoist offered during the 1970s and 1980s.[26] Among these were shifts towards a pronounced paganism and complete rejection of Judeo-Christianity, anti-capitalism and anti-Americanism, and the so-call *tiers-mondisme*, a strategic alliance between Europe and the Third World against the superpowers. These doctrines put GRECE increasingly at odds with the pro-capitalist and pro-American *Club de l'Horloge* and all the political parties, including the far-right *Front National*, and blurred the dividing lines between the French Left and the New Right to the point where observers argued that the term 'right-wing' ceased to make sense as concerned the New Right.[27] The most important, and politically fruitful, doctrinal shift took place with the redefinition of racism. The New Right's concept of 'ethnopluralism', in borrowing from the left's terminology of *différence* (Derrida), rejects all notions of biological racism and racial superiority and replaces it with the acceptance of the co-existence of different races. As Taguieff has argued so convincingly, at the heart of 'ethnopluralism' still lies racism, that is, the rejection of any mix of races through marriage and immigration, or *mixophobie*.[28] A reformulated, or 'differentialist' (Taguieff) racism, 'ethnopluralism' is the New Right's countermodel to the New Left's multiculturalism.[29]

Underlying these doctrinal shifts remain some ideological constants such as the diagnosis of a crisis of European civilization and its attribution to universalist and egalitarian principles to be found in all major political philosophies from Christianity to liberalism to socialism/Marxism.[30] Consequently, on a political plane, the New Right rejects the concept of liberal, participatory democracy and favours an élitist political order based on an organic view of society in which politics has the primacy over economy and society. Socioeconomically, the New Right proposes a 'third path' between capitalism and socialism, rejecting the 'Cola-Vodka imperialism' of the USA and the former USSR in favour of a neutral Europe, but ultimately, the USA and the 'colonization' of Europe by the USA is seen as the main challenge (especially after the collapse of the Soviet empire). The underlying concept of 'national-bolshevism' and a strong state above society and individual rights is clearly inspired by older versions of the extreme right such as the anti-semitic revolutionary right of Edouard Drumont in pre-First-World-War France and the 'conservative revolution' of Carl Schmitt, Ernst Niekisch, and Moeller von den Bruck in Weimar Germany.[31]

In the early 1980s, parts of the *Nouvelle Droite*, responding to the Socialists' electoral victories, became involved in party politics. Alain de Bénoist's cynical applause of the Left's success, which implied that the French got what they deserved, alienated many of his colleagues and drove some of them to the *Front National* (FN). Likewise, some members of the *Club de l'Horloge,* such as Jean-Yves Le Gallou, Yvan Blot and Bruno Mégret (a former RPR parliamentary candidate) joined the FN, while others such as Michel Leroy sided with the RPR–UDF alliance hoping to achieve a cooperation between the conservative camp and the FN.[32]

By the early 1990s, the *Nouvelle Droite* has become marginalized and the fierce battles and controversies of the late 1970s and early 1980s seem to have become history. A recent appeal by concerned intellectuals, artists and others (Pierre Bourdieu, Jacques Derrida, Umberto Eco and 500 more) in mid-1993, the *Appel à la vigilance,* against the ongoing threat from the New Right provoked strong reactions but it divided rather than united the intellectual community and was as much about some intellectuals (particularly Taguieff's) 'lenient' handling of Alain de Bénoist as it was about the latter himself.[33]

More so than in the French case, the 'conservative revolution' is a major intellectual inspiration for the German New Right. Almost simultaneously with the emergence of the *Nouvelle Droite,* West German right-wing groups and intellectuals reorganized after the electoral failure of the extreme-right NPD in 1969 and the rise of the Left to power under Willy Brandt's leadership. In response to 1968 and the democratization and reform politics of the early 1970s, including the controversial *Ostpolitik,* neo-conservative intellectuals revived the distinctly German conservative idea of a strong state which keeps itself above party and social struggles, and combined this position with the ideas of economic growth and technological progress – ideas traditionally alien to German conservatives.[34] They complained about the overload of government and the decay of bourgeois culture and values[35] and they tried to counter the challenge of the New Left, especially in the educational realm, by emphasizing values like discipline, hard work, obedience, the well-known German *Sekundärtugenden,* or secondary virtues.

Later in the 1970s, some of these intellectuals such as Robert Spaemann, Arnold Gehlen or Gerd-Klaus Kaltenbrunner joined ranks with more nationalist right-wing and revisionist intellectuals like Armin Mohler, Bernard Willms, and Helmut Diwald – the German equivalent to the *Nouvelle Droite.* Though intellectually less original than de Bénoist and colleagues and much more loosely organized than they, the German New Right pursued the same strategy of establishing 'cultural hegemony', which in the German case included also a large portion of rewriting history and undoing the post-war consensus and *raison d'être* of the Bonn Republic.

One of their major mouthpieces is *Criticon*, in which Mohler, Kaltenbrunner, Caspar Schrenck-Notzing, Henning Eichberg and 'guests' like Alain de Bénoist write, and in which Mohler announced it was time to break the taboo that only the CDU/CSU was the 'home' for conservatives in Germany.[36] Other important magazines of the German New Right include *Nation Europa*, *MUT*, and *Junge Freiheit* (an offspring of the *Republikaner* in 1986). Similar to the GRECE takeover of the *Figaro-Magazine* in the early 1980s, New Right ideologues in Germany try to infiltrate established newspapers. In 1993, Nolte disciple Rainer Zitelmann became the manager of the cultural section of the mass-circulated *Die Welt* in which he tries to overcome the conservatives' 'appeasement *vis-à-vis* the left' and the 'double-trauma' of 1933 and 1968, thus steering the newspaper towards positions found in New Right magazines like the *Junge Freiheit*.[37] Besides its mass media, the New Right also has outlets to a wide network of publishers in which established German scholars, French New Right intellectuals, and holocaust-revisionists publish side by side, and it organizes workshops like the *Thule Seminar* in Kassel which co-operates closely with GRECE.[38]

The New Right organizational network – characterized as 'organized confusion'[39] – proved to be an important link between established conservatives and the right-wing extremist scene. Neo-conservative and New Right intellectuals, especially those participating in the *Historikerstreit*, or historians's debate, attempted to re-evaluate the Nazi past and to develop a new German national consciousness derived from a collective historical identity outside the 'shadow of Auschwitz'.[40] This was an effort to define a German national identity in clear demarcation from the New Left's approach to a post-national identity and a 'constitutional patriotism' by emphasizing the traditions of a German *Kulturnation* and a *völkisch,* that is ethnically based, nationalism. As Michael Stürmer, historian, advisor to the chancellor and obviously a disciple of Gramsci, put it: '... in a land without history, the future is won by those who supply memory, shape concepts and interpret the past.'[41] In this context, the New Right also massively criticized the New Left's agenda of civil rights, emancipation and democratization.

At the same time, the New Right, inspired and helped by the *Nouvelle Droite* and its concepts, developed its ideological base, one that disguises its criticism of liberal democracy as anti-Americanism and German self-determination, and its racism and anti-semitism in the concepts of ethnopluralism incorporating a modern scientific outlook derived from the natural science research of Konrad Lorenz, Hans Eysenck, Irenäus Eibl-Eibesfeldt and others.[42] With this new outlook, the New Right established common ground with conservatives and neo-conservatives well into the environs of the Kohl government while helping to legitimize basic tenets of right-wing extremism. For a closer look reveals that behind the talk of German sovereignty and normalization lie historical revisionism on the one hand, which ultimately rejects any specific German responsibility for the Second World War and the Holocaust, and the anti-liberal philosophy of Carl Schmitt and colleagues on the other, which puts the collectivity of the German nation and its newly regained nation-state above civil liberties and human rights.

The links between the 'metapolitics' of the New Right and the realities of German (party) politics are numerous but less obvious than in France during the 1980s. Unlike in France, the German New Right is less intellectual and more academically rooted with a traditional distance from party politics. However, many neo-conservative and New Right intellectuals are close to the CDU/CSU, and some have established ties to the *Republikaner*. Armin Mohler considers the Republikaner-chief Schönhuber his friend, and Helmut Diwald, a revisionist historian, contributed the preamble to the *Republikaner*'s 1990 party platform.[43]

In sum, the intellectual New Right in both France and Germany can be characterized as the 'counter-revolution' to the 'revolution' of 1968. It rejects everything that the New Left stands for regarding democratization, egalitarianism and multiculturalism. In the end, it is the substitution of an open society with an individualist and universalist basis by the return of the collectivism of the 'conservative revolution' of the 1920s. This is the most obvious sign of a 'Weimarization' of European politics. In itself it is hardly new. What makes the New Right new, however, is its adoption of modern strategies and technologies in the context of a post-industrial society where traditional social milieus are weakening and modern mass communication provides for a new phase of atomization and individualization.

In the French context, with the traditional interplay of revolution and counter-revolution, of left and right, this shift to the right might be interpreted as just another turn in the cyclical patterns of French history. In the German context, however, the lack of any strong revolutionary traditions and symbols and the newness of the civil society in the Bonn Republic raises more serious questions about the dangers of the New Right. A historical revisionism, coupled with the newly acquired sovereignty in a unified Germany puts into question the entire foundation of the democratic project of modern Germany. The following part of the paper exlores to what extent this reconfiguration of the political spectrum is mirrored in party and electoral politics with its more tangible political repercussions.

The New Right Parties and their Electorates: Front National,
Republikaner *and others*

France

The *Front National* (FN) was created in 1972 by leaders of the *Ordre
Nouveau,* a nationalist movement that was itself founded three years
earlier to overcome the fragmentation on the far right. Under the
leadership of Jean-Marie Le Pen who combined the political experience
of poujadism, anti-gaullism and tixiérism – he was the campaign
manager of the far right Presidential candidate Tixiér-Vignancour in
1965 – with his military experience in Algeria, the FN tried to attract
anti-republicans, authoritarians, conservative Catholics, imperialists and
racists.[44] In none of the elections up to 1983 did the FN attract more than
one per cent of the national vote and the party reached its electoral low
point in 1981 when Le Pen was not able to find the necessary 500
'sponsors' for his Presidential candidacy. Clearly, before 1981 Le Pen
was unable to mobilize a significant portion of the electorate although
the themes and issues that he developed through the FN were generally
the same he used after 1981. The *Front National* rose from obscurity to
prominence after its breakthrough in the 1983 local elections in a Paris
suburb and the 1984 European elections. Since then, the FN has
consolidated its national vote share at 10–15 per cent.

Part of the reason for the FN's sudden success – aside from the
personal appeal of its leader – is an ambiguous platform and a flexible
strategy at a time of the growing disenchantment of segments of the
French public with the established parties and institutions and an
increasing sense of crisis (see above). Although the party has different
factions or *familles,* the authority of Le Pen as its leader is undisputed
and the party's image is streamlined into homogeneity.[45] Thus Le Pen's
and the party's platform are almost indistinguishable. Immigration is the
FN's major campaign theme but the party's ideology is more complex
than that and defies the notion of a single-issue movement.[46] Echoing the
diagnosis of the intellectual New Right, Le Pen interprets the signs of an
economic crisis as an indicator of a crisis of the French nation and
culture. The FN reasserts a notion of French national identity that
comprises both revolutionary-republican traditions and the entire '4000
years' of French history. It attacks all notions of egalitarianism
(including the idea of human equality as preached in the Bible *and* in the
literature of the Enlightenment),[47] the left and the immigrants as the
major reasons for social and economic problems in France. At the same
time, the FN promotes the values of individual freedom, private property
and law and order. Le Pen finally rejects internationalist policies, has

become the most ardent critic of the process and policies of European integration, and opposed, as the only major politician, the US-led war against Saddam Hussein in 1991.[48]

The leaders of the FN made it repeatedly clear that their main political enemy is the PS under François Mitterrand as the major exponent of cosmopolitanism, egalitarianism, and so on, although they generally lash out against the 'gang of four' (PS, PCF, RPR, UDF) and the Establishment as selling out French interests.[49] Le Pen continuously seeks to distinguish himself from the political establishment by a more radical political discourse. On the other hand, the condemnation of the 'gang of four' has not prevented Le Pen from seeking respectability for his party through partial collaboration with the parties on the right, mostly at the local level, and a more moderate appearance in parliament.[50]

The ideology and behaviour of the party raise the question of its quality regarding democracy and the French political system and invite historical comparisons.[51] Its origins in the *Ordre Nouveau*, Le Pen's statement about the Holocaust as a historical 'detail', his racism and disguised anti-Semitism, and some similarities between Hitler and Le Pen in style and appeal may justify one in seeing some fascist elements in the FN. However, these are outweighed by the differences not only in content but also in context. The FN is neither revisionist nor revanchist (regarding Algeria, or the entire European order), nor does it propose a centrally directed economy or sociobiological élitism (thus setting it apart even from the more radical views of GRECE). From Poujadism, the FN has inherited the populist style but not its opposition to economic modernization, and it is clearly more structured, hierarchically organized and has a broader platform. The *Front National* stands for authoritarian presidentialism but not for the elimination of parliament and the democratic rules of the game, and it does not question the legitimacy of the Fifth Republic. If by anti-system party we mean a party that 'abides by a belief system that does not share the values of the political order within which it operates'[52] then the FN is not anti-system so far as the *political* aspect of the values are concerned. Values such as equality and tolerance are not essentiel ingredients of the current political order in France but as (controversial) components of French political traditions they have been part of the French belief system and key elements of what it means to be on the left.

The electoral fortunes of the *Front National* reflect a trend towards consolidation of voter support. Between 1984 and 1993, the FN obtained an average of 11.5 per cent in six nation-wide elections (three parliamentary, one presidential and two European elections). The early successes from 1984 to 1986 depended to a large extent on protest voting, fuelled by anti-party and anti-immigration sentiments and characterized by a low level of inter-election voting consistency. But the more recent elections have produced higher levels of consistency and an increasingly even spread of FN support across regions, classes and partisan background.[53]

This distinguishes FN support from the Poujadist movement of the 1950s which drew its support mainly from disgruntled shopkeepers and farmers and the breakdown of the petty bourgeoisie. In fact, the FN attracts voters from middle-class and working-class backgrounds, from the political right and political left alike. In the most recent parliamentary elections of March 1993, workers along with employees showed a slightly disproportionate support for the FN (18 per cent each, with 13 per cent being the national vote; the other outstanding demographic factor was age: 18 per cent was made up of 18–24-year-olds).[54] FN voters in 1993 exceeded all other parties' voters in their concern for the country's general situation rather than the situation in the electoral district as a motivation for the vote (86 vs. 13 per cent) and in their pessimism regarding the way democracy worked in France.[55]

Overall, the most distinct characteristic of the typical FN voter is not his or her sociodemographic profile but rather a strong concern with 'Frenchness', nationalism and immigration along with materialist value orientations and high levels of insecurity, pessimism, and authoritarianism.[56] A recent analysis of electoral support for the *Front National* concludes that traditional cleavage structures in French society (class, religion, region) play no significant role in the vote for Le Pen but that value dimension and issue concerns in combination with constituency-level measures such as crime, immigration and unemployment are decisive.[57]

Ideology has become a driving force behind the vote for Le Pen. More than four-fifths of the 1986 FN voters voted for Le Pen in the 1988 Presidential elections (first round), thus exceeding the 'transmission score' for any other party.[58] In the 1993 parliamentary elections, FN voters showed again the highest level of vote transfer from the 1992 regional elections (91 per cent of the 1993 FN voters had voted for the same party in 1992 followed by RPR–UDF voters with 87 per cent and Communists with 86 per cent). In addition, 71 per cent of FN voters in 1993 had already decided to vote for their party several months before the election (RPR–UDF voters: 66 per cent, Communists: 65 per cent).[59] The analysts of the FN electorate conclude: 'The high recall levels, when compared with partisans of other stripes, suggest a very hard ideological core of FN partisans. For that group, extreme-right ideology would seem capable of achieving near-full external status, acting as a more or less permanent lens through which to view political events.'[60] These findings strongly suggest that the FN is anything but a protest movement.[61] Rather, it is well rooted in the minds of the French electorate as a New Right party and has survived even the return from proportional representation to the single-member constituency system of elections in 1988 and lack of parliamentary representation.

Germany

In comparison with the French case, Germany stands out because of the unique role of the national and democratic question and the recent process of reunification. Moreover, the New Right in Germany is electorally fragmented into various parties, such as the *Deutsche Volksunion* (DVU), the older *Nationaldemokratische Partei Deutschlands* (NPD) and the new party of the *Republikaner* (REP). Unlike its French counterpart, the New Right in Germany has undergone a development of ups and downs, with the REP's 10.5 per cent in the 1992 Baden-Württemberg state elections being the electoral peak to be followed by complete electoral insignificance throughout the *Superwahljahr*, or 'super election year' of 1994. But as in France, the electoral successes of the New Right are a structural phenomenon and different from previous waves of right-wing extremism in Germany.

Whereas in France the immigration issue was introduced by the Communists and largely ignored by the political establishment until the FN's electoral breakthrough, the German establishment itself, most notably politicians of the government parties CDU/CSU throughout the 1980s put the immigration issue on the agenda and merged it with a discourse on a traditional German national identity.[62] This discourse was fed by, and fed back into, the rearrangement of the West German party system in which the emergence of a post-materialist New Left was countered by the rise of a New Right. Already in the early 1980s, there were two quite distinct ideological dimensions in the German mass public reflecting the concerns of Old Politics and New Politics based on changing cleavage structures. At the right-wing end of the Old Politics dimension, old conservatism clearly reflects the concerns of traditional CDU/CSU voters, that is the old middle class and Catholics, whereas in the New Politics dimension a 'neo-conservatism' was mostly determined by low levels of education and materialist value orientations and cut across party lines.[63]

By 1989 the ties of these 'neo-conservatives' to the established parties had weakened to a degree that many were ready to vote for the

Republikaner. The demographic profile of the supporters of the *Republikaner*, but also of those voting for the NPD or DVU, stresses the notion that these parties had mobilized the right-wing pole of the New Politics conflict axis which includes working-class and middle-class voters, union and non-union voters alike. The cross-cutting nature of the New Right vote is demonstrated by the fact that already in the 1989 Berlin and European elections, about 40 per cent of the *Republikaner* voters had previously voted for the CDU/CSU, 20 per cent for the SPD.[64] This pattern of previous party affiliation among voters for the New Right continued after reunification.[65] Along with support from union members and Catholics, the disproportional attractiveness of the New Right to members of the younger generation is another structural feature that was absent from earlier waves of right-wing extremism in West Germany.

Rather than by traditional cleavage factors such as social class or religiosity and bread-and-butter issues, New Right voters can be characterized by a more general sense of insecurity, exacerbated by fears of social and economic marginalization and of the 'threat' of immigration, together with materialist value orientations and political alienation.[66] These voters represent the 'normal pathological condition' in Western democracies (see above) and are driven by subjective problems of adaptation to modernization processes and a fear of losing status and entitlements in a more dynamic and complex world. In their electoral choice, xenophobia and racism mix with this defence of social entitlements, or *Wohlstandschauvinismus*.

In sum, the mobilization of electoral support for the parties of the New Right in West Germany as well as in other Western democracies is a consequence of a structural change. The rise of the New Right differs from previous waves of right-wing extremism in Germany because of its different adherents and demographic support patterns which draw voters from the CDU/CSU *and* SPD. This characteristic has an important impact on its place in the structure of German party competition. Unlike in earlier waves when the exchange of voters happened primarily between the CDU/CSU and the radical right, *both* major parties are affected and under pressure to react. Moreover, the CDU/CSU is now in a position to play the New Right card strategically against the SPD by putting pressure on it to conform to right-wing policies.

Before 1989, the *Republikaner* tried to establish themselves as the party of German reunification and traditional German national identity and, thereby, find their place in the political spectrum.[67] With reunification, the *Republikaner* lost their original theme to the Bonn government and have since focused more on immigration issues. However, reunification both hurt *and* helped the New Right after 1990.

It hurt the New Right by undermining the momentum it had acquired in 1989 and resulted in the subsequent failures in the 1990 elections. Moreover, with reunification, the New Right was faced with a particular structural constraint by the addition of an East German electorate which, despite its high levels of xenophobia,[68] was less receptive to the New Right than the West German electorate. In both series of elections in 1990 and 1994, the Republikaner, contrary to their initial expectations, scored significantly lower in Eastern than in the Western state and county-wide elections throughout 1994. Moreover, the Republikaner failed to build up an effective party organization in the East, with only about 2,000 members as compared with more than 20,000 members in the West.[69]

The Republikaner's limited electoral appeal in the East stems from a variety of factors. In general, despite some signs of economic recovery in the new Länder, party politics four years after reunification is still more discredited in the East than in the West.[70] More specifically, the Republikaner, in terms of their West German voters' concerns and despite their activists' rhetoric, are the party of a West German defensive nationalism. Far from expressing national solidarity with the Easterners and a willingness to sacrifice, the Republikaner voters in the West see the newly-added East German co-citizens and their massive financial and other needs as a threat rather than an enrichment (or even fulfilment) of national dreams. Apart from Green party and PDS voters, and for very different reasons, it was and is above all Republikaner voters who look at reunification and its consequences with scepticism rather than joy.[71]

In the West, reunification reinforced those dynamics which brought about the rise of the New Right and reaffirmed a traditional sense of German nationhood. The solution of the German question and the restoration of the Staatsnation of Bismarckian heritage in 1990 coincided with a new wave of immigration to Germany. Rather than restoring the public's confidence in the established parties, the policy of reunification and its consequences have only added to the perceived lack of competence, as the discussion about the Steuerlüge (tax lie), the confusion in financing reunification and the hysterical debate on immigration and the asylum law demonstrate. The pressure on the established parties to react reached its high point at the end of 1992, after a series of anti-foreigner attacks (most notably the riots in Rostock and the arson murder in Mölln) and the New Right parties' electoral successes in the state elections of Schleswig-Holstein and Baden-Württemberg.

The handling of the asylum debate by the major parties in 1992/93 demonstrates most tellingly the political spectrum's shift to the right on the New Politics dimension, thereby diminishing the political space in which New Right parties in Germany can legitimately operate. After reunification it seemed that the established right and the New Right were in an antagonistic relationship, competing for the same potential vote. But the nature of the New Politics' cleavage suggests that they were in a dialectical relationship into which even the SPD was drawn since it also had an electorate susceptible to the parties of the New Right.[72] The New Right used more extremist rhetoric and politicized the asylum debate to a degree where the CDU's own hard-line position seemed a legitimate compromise which made it difficult for the SPD to reject it. The alternative discourse on German identity, articulated before 1989 by the New Left in the SPD and the Greens alike, which strove for a redefinition of (West) German nationhood towards the model of a 'political nation' à la France or the United States, was abandoned by the SPD. A de facto Grand Coalition of CDU/CSU, FDP, and SPD reached a compromise in late 1992 and amended the Basic Law's asylum paragraph in 1993. Thus, the SPD gave in to the right-wing interpretation of the asylum issue and gave up its insistence on linking a change in the Basic Law on asylum with a liberalization of citizenship and immigration policies.

As a result of the shrinking opportunity structures of the New Right, its resource problems in ideology and organization became more visible in 1994. A comparison of the Republikaner's five party platforms from 1983 to 1993 reveals that the party walks a fine line between pro-system and anti-system positions. Their official commitment to the Basic Law is seasoned with calls for the direct election of the Federal President and for national referenda.[73] This seemingly democratic orientation contrasts with the repeated stress on the priority of the German people, the ethnically defined Volk, its nation and the state over special group interests, individual rights and party loyalties. This essentially anti-liberal and anti-pluralist thrust is hardly reconcilable with various republican principles of the Basic Law. Moreover, the rejection of local and other voting rights for non-Germans (including EC-citizens) and the call for an immediate stop to immigration reflect underlying xenophobia that wants a German state for ethnically defined German citizens. Finally, the 1993 platform does not recognize the German–Polish border of 1990 but calls for a 'completion' of German reunification with the Eastern territories. The platform repeatedly refers to the five new Länder as 'Mitteldeutschland', or Central Germany, and to reunification as 'partial reunification'.[74]

Clearly, the New Right voters' right-wing views which consist of a large dose of political alienation, racism and xenophobia, extreme national pride and a rather apologetic view of Germany's Nazi past corresponded to many of these or other positions the New Right has to offer.[75] However, besides its irrelevance to East Germans, the New Right's ideology, without the immigration issue and with the established parties' tougher image on law and order, has lost most of its distinctiveness and legitimacy in the West as well. At the same time, its more controversial aspects such as its questionable commitments to democracy and a strategic drift to the right has become more visible. Thus, during the 1994 campaign, Schönhuber decided to sharpen his party's profile and moved further to the right by sharing his anti-semitic and revisionist views with the German public and by reaching out to the more extremist DVU and their chief, Gerhard Frey.[76] But the position of Schönhuber as the party's leader had never been very secure. This came fully into the open during the 1994 election campaigns. Schönhuber's desperate attempt to overcome the self-defeating fragmentation of the right-wing spectrum by reaching out to the DVU's chief backfired within his own party. Schönhuber was ousted by the *Republikaner* leadership three weeks before the Federal elections and a new leadership quarrel ensued.[77] This is in dramatic contrast to the French scenario where a more charismatic Le Pen keeps his party together and himself on top.[78]

The vote for the New Right parties was never a simple protest vote but mixed ideological convictions with a sense of alienation from the political system and particular issue concerns such as immigration and law and order.[79] For the time being, the issues are taken care of by the major parties. The opportunity structures of the New Right were diminished in 1994 by the dialectical relationship between the New Right and the established parties, that is, a radicalization process in which the latter moved to the right along the new conflict dimension. As a result, the internal problems of the New Right, such as organizational disarray, became highlighted and more consequential in 1994. For the time being, right-wing politics is executed from within the political establishment. But the structural reasons which brought about the rise of the New Right have not disappeared. There is still a considerable right-wing vote potential and it remains open for as long as the New Right is contained.

Overall, the New Right party scene in Germany is characterized by a larger degree of revisionism and revanchism than the French *Front National* at the ideological level. Despite their official commitment to the Basic Law, the REP and DVU are less reliably pro-system in Sartori's sense since their call for plebiscitarian democracy, their anti-plural, xenophobic and nationalist stances, and their revanchist orientation throw basic values of the political order of the Federal Republic into question. At the organizational level, the New Right is fragmented to the point of self-defeat and the *Republikaner* may be finished as a party after their 1994 débâcle.

Conclusions

This chapter has analyzed the emergence of the New Right in France and Germany. It could be demonstrated that the intellectual New Right in seeming rejection of, and opposition to, the principles and realities of Western democracies and particularly in its modernization in the wake of 1968 is contributing to a 'Weimarization' of European politics. At the ideological level of the New Right parties in France and Germany, New Right ideas have only limited appeal, especially in France. The party platforms and political rhetoric do not rekindle the spirit of the conservative revolution or the historical fascist and Nazi movements.

At the electoral level, the New Right cannot be interpreted as an anti-democratic, revisionist force. All the new right-wing parties in Germany, France and other continental European countries (and the American New Right movement) have in common national-populist appeals to the 'common man', running against all established parties in order to return power to the 'people', authoritarian leadership by charismatic demagogues, and issues of nationalism, xenophobia, traditional values, and free enterprise.

If one defines right-wing extremists as anti-democratic authoritarians, as do Scheuch and Klingemann and others, then none of these parties or movements clearly qualifies as such, since all base their political ideology and action on basic principles of democracy, that is, the rejection of force as a political means, the acceptance of the existing party systems, the emphasis on their 'Constitutionality', and so on. They are 'extreme' not in terms of being against or outside the existing constitutional order but in terms of being extreme within that order.

On the other hand, the dividing line between these parties and movements and hard-core anti-constitutional right-wing extremists and neo-fascists is blurred by their anti-pluralist, xenophobic and even openly racist appeals and their authoritarian internal organization. In fact, they provide a crucial link between established conservatism (and neo-conservatism) and the openly anti-democratic extremists on the right by radicalizing (neo)conservative positions on the one hand, and legitimizing extreme right positions on the other. That is, they operate ideologically along the same political axis as the extreme right but 'soften' their positions in order to introduce them to the political discourse, which, in turn, forces the established parties to take more radical positions in order to prevent a cross-over of voters to the new right-wing parties.

Finally, the role of modernization processes for the emergence of the New Right and its implications for its support patterns must be specified. It is insufficient to interpret the New Right as a reaction of so-called 'modernization losers'.[80] As has been widely demonstrated, actual loss of status, unemployment, and so on is less relevant than the subjective dimension, that is the *perception* of threat to one's status, life-styles and values. Thus, the New Right in Western democracies has been aptly characterized as a *Wohlstandschauvinismus,* or 'chauvinism of social entitlements' rather than a traditional nationalist extremism of declining classes or status groups.

Notes

Earlier versions of this essay have been presented at the Ninth International Conference of Europeanists in Chicago, 31 March–2 April 1994, and the XVIth World Congress of the International Political Science Association in Berlin, 21–25 Aug. 1994. I want to thank Pascal Perrineau and Nonna Mayer of the CEVIPOF for their generous assistance during my research visits in Paris. I am also indebted to the Institute for European Studies at Cornell University for its financial support of these visits.

1. The metaphor of a 'hinge' concerning the New Right was introduced by Wolfgang Gessenharter, 'Die "Neue Rechte" als Scharnier zwischen Neokonservatismus und Rechtsextremismus in der Bundesrepublik', in R. Eisfeld and I. Müller (eds) *Gegen Barbarei. Essays R.M.W. Kempner zu Ehren* (Frankfurt/M.: Athenäum, 1989), pp. 424–52.
2. K. Mannheim, 'Das konservative Denken', *Archiv für Sozialwissenschaft und Sozialpolitik* 57 (1927), pp 68–142, 470–95.
3. S.M. Lipset and S. Rokkan, 'Cleavage Structures, Party Systems, and Voter Alignments', in Lipset/Rokkan (eds), *Party Systems and Voter Alignments*, (New York: Free Press, 1967), pp. 1–64.
4. See K. von Beyme, 'Right-wing Extremism in Post-war Europe', *West European Politics*, 11/2 (Apr. 1988), p. 1.
5. G. Sartori, *Parties and Party Systems* (Cambridge: Cambridge University Press, 1976), p. 133.
6. E.K. Scheuch and H.-D. Klingemann, 'Theorie des Rechtsradikalismus in westlichen Industriegesellschaften', *Hamburger Jahrbuch für Wirtschafts- und Gesellschaftspolitik*, 12 (1967), pp. 11–29.
7. See the discussion of the role of the past and of 'golden ages' for the radical right in P.H. Merkl, 'Conclusion: A New Lease on Life for the Radical Right?', in P.H. Merkl and L. Weinberg (eds) *Encounters with the Contemporary Radical Right* (Boulder: Westview Press, 1993), pp. 214–19.

8. Definitions of right-wing extremism based on ideology alone seem problematic. They lend themselves to an essentialist answer, arbitrarily excluding variations of ideology, styles and behaviour as well as variations of the phenomenon over time (e.g. anti-communism as an 'essential' component of right-wing ideology makes little sense in a post-communist era). Thus, behavioural aspects including public support patterns should also be taken into consideration.
9. See R. Inglehart, *The Silent Revolution* (Princeton, NJ: Princeton University Press, 1977), *idem. Culture Shift* (Princeton, NJ: Princeton University Press, 1990).
10. The term 'New Left' has various meanings, from specific revolutionary or Marxist cadre groups in the wake of 1968 to the whole array of social movements and new parties on the left in the 1970s. In this essay, the term is applied to such new social movements, new parties or wings within (old) left parties, which are characterized by new middle-class instead of working-class support, post-materialist instead of materialist value priorities and an élite-challenging instead of an élite-directed political style. For an informative overview, see A.S. Markovits and P.S. Gorski, *The German Left. Red, Green and Beyond* (New York: Oxford University Press, 1993), Introduction.
11. See R. Dalton, *Citizen Politics in Western Democracies,* (Chatham, NJ: Chatham House, 1988).
12. See J.A. Laponce, *Left and Right. The Topography of Political Perceptions* (Toronto: U. of Toronto Press, 1981); for a differentiated view see R. Rémond, *Les Droites en France* (Paris: Aubier, 1982), ch. 1. See also R. Cayrol, 'La droite, la gauche et les références idéologiques des Français', in SOFRES, *L'état de l'opinion 1992* (Paris: Seuil, 1992), pp. 57–72.
13. See Markovits and Gorski, *op. cit.,* ch. 2. In this otherwise excellent study of the German Left, it is curious that the SPD is excluded from the concept of 'the left' in (West) Germany and that the role of the New Left within the SPD or the interaction between the SPD and the New Left, Greens, etc. is only elaborated marginally.
14. See S. Barnes, M. Kaase *et al., Political Action: Mass Participation in Five Western Democracies* (Beverly Hills, CA: Sage Publications, 1979); Dalton, *Citizen Politics,* chs. 3 and 4.
15. See H.-G. Betz, *Radical Right-wing Populism in Western Europe,* (New York: St. Martin's Press, 1993).
16. See D. Roth, 'Wandel der politischen Einstellungen seit der Bundestagswahl 1990', *German Studies Review,* 16,2 (May 1993), pp. 265–98.
17. See É. Dupoirier, 'Les Français à l'épreuve de la crise', in SOFRES, *L'état de l'opinion 1994* (Paris: Seuil, 1994), pp. 55–75.
18. See Le Gall, *op. cit.,* p. 125. For an insightful analysis of ethnocentrism in France see N. Mayer, 'Ethnocentrism, Racism and Intolerance', in D. Boy and N. Mayer (eds), *The French Voter Decides* (Ann Arbor, MI: The University of Michigan Press, 1993), pp. 21–44.
19. See E. Wiegand, 'Zunahme der Ausländerfeindlichkeit? Einstellungen zu Fremden in Deutschland und Europa', *ZUMA-Nachrichten,* 31 (1993), pp. 20–22; see also Statistisches Bundesamt, ed., *Datenreport 1992* (Bonn: Bundeszentrale für politische Bildung, 1992), pp. 612f. For an overview of German xenophobia see M. Küchler, 'The Germans and the "Others": Racism, Xenophobia, or Self-Defense?', in *German Politics* (1994, in print).
20. See *ibid.,* p. 25.
21. For a summary overview see M. Wegierski, 'The New Right in Europe', *Telos,* Special Double Issue 'The French New Right. New Right – New Left – New

Paradigm?' Nos. 98–9 (Winter 1993–Spring 1994), pp. 55–69.

22. See P.-A. Taguieff, 'Les Droites Radicales en France: Nationalisme révolutionnaire et National-libéralisme', in *Les Temps Modernes*, No. 465 (April 1985), p. 1789; W. Gessenharter, *Kippt die Republik? Die Neue Rechte und ihre Unterstützung durch Politik und Medien* (München: Knaur, 1994), pp. 14–15.

23. The interpretation of the relationship between May 1968 and the *Nouvelle Droite* is a matter of debate. Some authors point out the links between the events of 1968 and the formation of GRECE (see C. Adelung, as quoted in H.-G. Jaschke, 'Frankreich', in F. Gress *et al., Neue Rechte und Rechtsextremismus in Europa* (Opladen: Westdeutscher Verlag, 1990), p. 45, and A. Hirsh, *The French New Left: An Intellectual History from Sartre to Gorz* (Boston: South End Press, 1981), ch. 6. Taguieff denies vehemently that GRECE was formed in response to May 1968 (see P.-A. Taguieff, *Sur la Nouvelle Droite* (Paris: Descartes, 1994), p. 10. But he concedes that the events have accelerated the splintering of the far right out of which GRECE emerged as a new force shaped by Alain de Bénoist's fascination with the intellectuals of the New Left and his adoption of the New Left's concept of 'cultural war' (interview with the author, 23 Nov., 1994). See also A.-M. Duranton-Crabol who argues that May 1968 and the surrounding sense of upheaval has driven many anti-communist academics and students to the right and also to GRECE in the early 1970s; A.-M. Duranton-Crabol, *Visages de la Nouvelle Droite* (Paris: Presses de la Fondation Nationale des Sciences Politiques, 1988), pp. 29–41).

24. See Taguieff, *op. cit.*, pp. 1826ff. and Christadler, 'Die "Nouvelle Droite" in Frankreich', in I. Fetscher (ed.), *Neokonservative und 'Neue Rechte'. Der Angriff gegen Sozialstaat und liberale Demokratie in den Vereinigten Staaten, Westeuropa und der Bundesrepublik* (München: Beck, 1983), p. 165.

25. See Christadler, *op. cit.*, pp. 174ff.

26. For a summary overview of the doctrinal evolution of the *Nouvelle Droite,* see P.-A. Taguieff, 'From Race to Culture: The New Right on European Identity', in *Telos*, Special Double-Issue 'The French New Right', Nos. 98–9 (Winter 1993–Spring 1994), pp. 99–125.

27. See M. Wegierski, *op. cit.*, p. 56; see also P. Piccone, 'Confronting the French New Right: Old Prejudices or a New Political Paradigm?', in *Telos*, Special Issue 'The French New Right', Nos. 98–9 (Winter 1993–Spring 1994), pp. 3–22.

28. See P.-A. Taguieff, *La Force du Préjugé* (Paris: Editions La Découverte, 1987) and his numerous writings on the *Nouvelle Droite*.

29. According to its proponents among the New Left, this concept, often misunderstood or misrepresented, does *not* mean an 'anything goes' with unlimited immigration and the right to be different in *any* respect; see for example D. Cohn-Bendit and T. Schmid, *Heimat Babylon. Das Wagnis der multikulturellen Demokratie* (Hamburg: Hoffmann und Campe, 1992), especially ch. 8, and C. Leggewie, *Multi kulti. Spielregeln für die Vielvölkerrepublik* (Berlin: Rotbuch Verlag, 1993), ch. 7.

30. This synopsis is derived from Jaschke, 'Frankreich', *op. cit.*, p. 60; see also Taguieff, *op. cit.*, pp. 1781–93, and Patrick Moreau, 'Die neue Religion der Rasse. der Biologismus und die neue kollektive Ethik der Neuen Rechten in Frankreich und Deutschland', in Fetscher, *op. cit.*, pp. 122–62; Christadler, *op. cit.*, pp. 181–97.

31. See Taguieff, 'Les Droites Radicales en France', *Les Temps Modernes, op.cit.,* pp. 1780–93; Jaschke, 'Frankreich', *op. cit.* p. 63. Taguieff points out the major dividing line between GRECE and *Club de l'Horloge* in the mid-1980s: 'On

comprend ce qui sépare fondamentalement la doctrine du GRECE de celle du *Club de l'Horloge*: l'individualisme modéré de celui-ci interdit d'aller au-delà de la mise en équation classique de Washington et de Moscou, tandis que l'anti-individualisme absolu de celui-là l'amène à l'abandon de l'anti-communisme en usage dans les milieux libéreaux (de droite et de gauche), en même temps qu'à l'identification du modèle américain (condensant un type de régime politique: démocratie libérale pluraliste, et un type de fonctionnement socio-économique: capitalisme) comme ennemi principal.' (Taguieff, 'Les Droites Radicales en France', *op. cit.*, p. 1833.)

32. See P. Fysh and J. Wolfreys, 'Le Pen, the National Front and the Extreme Right in France', *Parliamentary Affairs*, 45,3 (July 1992), pp. 316f. See also G. Birenbaum, *Le Front nationale en politique* (Paris: Balland, 1992), pp. 195–219, who identifies four *équipes* in the FN upper-level management, one of them being the *horlogers*, former members or friends of the *Club de l'Horloge*.

33. See F. Adler, 'Left Vigilance in France', *Telos*, Special Issue 'The French New Right', Nos. 98–9 (Winter 1993–Spring 1994), pp. 23–33.

34. See M. Greiffenhagen, *Das Dilemma des Konservatismus in Deutschland* (München: Piper, 1971); R. Lederer, *Neokonservative Theorie und Gesellschaftsanalyse* (Frankfurt/Main: Lang, 1979).

35. This they shared with an influential group of American neo-conservatives who became prominent during the 1970s; see J. Habermas, 'Die Kulturkritik der Neokonservativen in den USA und in der Bundesrepublik. Über eine Bewegung von Intellektuellen in zwei politischen Kulturen', in *Merkur*, 36 (Nov. 1982), pp. 1047–61, and M. Minkenberg, *Neokonservatismus und Neue Rechte in den USA* (Baden-Baden-Nomos: 1990), ch.3.

36. See M. Feit, *Die 'Neue Rechte' in der Bundesrepublik. Organisation–Ideologie–Strategie* (Frankfurt/Main: Campus, 1987), pp. 62–7.

37. Quoted in *Der Spiegel*, 11 (14 Mar 1994), p. 224. See also M. Gerste, 'Wenn Zitelmann zuschlägt', in *Die Zeit*, 11 (11 Mar 1994), p. 5, and Gessenharter, *Kippt die Republik?*, ch. 6. Needless to say, the New Right gets frequent support from the well established and respected *Frankfurter Allgemeine Zeitung*.

38. See M. Feit, *op. cit.*, pp. 48-77; C. Leggewie, *Der Geist steht rechts. Ausflüge in die Denkfabriken der Wende* (Berlin: Rotbuch, 1987); T. Assheuer and H. Sarkowicz, *Rechtsradikale in Deutschland. Die alte und die neue Rechte* (München: Beck, 1992), ch. 5; S. Mantino, *Die 'Neue Rechte' in der 'Grauzone' zwischen Rechtsextremismus und Konservatismus* (Frankfurt/Main: Lang, 1992), ch. 3.

39. Gessenharter, *Kippt die Republik?*, p. 123.

40. See H.-G. Betz, '*Deutschlandpolitik* on the Margin: On the Evolution of Contemporary New Right Nationalism in the Federal Republic,' in *New German Critique* (Spring/Summer 1988), pp. 127–58.

41. M. Stürmer, 'Geschichte in geschichtslosem Land', in *Frankfurter Allgemeine Zeitung* (25 April 1995), reprinted in R. Augstein *et al.*, *'Historikerstreit'. Die Dokumentation der Kontroverse um die Einzigartigkeit der nationalsozialistischen Judenvernichtung* (München: Piper, 1987), pp. 36–8.

42. See Feit, *op. cit.*, pp. 83–149; K. Schönekäs, 'Bundesrepublik Deutschland' in Greß *et al. op. cit.*, pp. 291–300.

43. See Leggewie, *Der Geist steht rechts*, p. 201; Gessenharter, *Kippt die Republik?*, pp. 147–55.

44. See J.-Y. Camus, 'Origine et formation du Front national, 1972–81', in P. Perrineau and N. Mayer (eds) *Le Front national à découvert* (Paris: Presses de la

Fondation Nationale des Sciences Politiques, 1989), pp. 17–19; W. Safran, 'The National Front in France: From Lunatic Fringe to Limited Respectability', in P.H. Merkl and L. Weinberg (eds) *Encounters with the Contemporary Radical Right* (Boulder, CO: Westview Press, 1993), p. 20.

45. See G. Birenbaum, *op. cit.*, ch. 1.
46. See S. Mitra, 'The National Front in France – a single-issue movement?', in *West European Politics*, 11,2 (Apr. 1988), pp. 47–64.
47. See Safran, *op.cit.*, p. 21.
48. See P.-A. Taguieff, 'Un programme "révolutionnaire"?' in N. Mayer and P. Perrineau (eds), *Le Front National à Découvert* (Paris: Presses de la Fondation Nationale des Sciences Politiques, 1989), pp. 195–227; H. Lagrange and P. Perrineau, 'Le syndrome lepeniste', in Mayer and Perrineau (eds) *Le Front National à Découvert*, pp. 228–47; P. Hainsworth, 'The Extreme Right in Post-war France: The Emergence and Success of the *Front National*', in Hainsworth (ed.) *The Extreme Right in Europe and the USA*, pp. 48–53.
49. See G. Birenbaum, *Le Front national en politique* (Paris: Balland, 1992), p. 309.
50. See Birenbaum, *op. cit.*, pp. 79–96.
51. For the following, see the illuminating discussion in Safran, *op. cit.*, pp. 21f, 29–35.; also, Birenbaum, *op. cit.*, pp. 76–78.
52. G. Sartori, *Parties and Party Systems. A Framework for Analysis* (Cambridge: Cambridge University Press, 1976), p. 133.
53. See Hainsworth, 'The Extreme Right in Postwar France', in Hainsworth (ed.) *The Extreme Right in Europe and the USA*, pp. 44–8; P. Bréchon and S. Mitra, 'The National Front in France', in *Comparative Politics*, Vol. 25, No. 1 (Oct. 1992): 63–82, *Le Monde* (23 March 1993): 4.
54. See N. Mayer and H. Rey, 'Avancée électorale, isolement politique du Front national', in *Revue politique et parlementaire*, no. 964 (March-April 1993), p. 46.
55. See *Libération* (23 Mar 1993), pp. 4–6.
56. N. Mayer and P. Perrineau, 'Why do they vote for Le Pen?', in P. Ignazi and C. Ysmal (eds), *Extreme Right-wing Parties in Europe. European Journal of Political Research*. Special Issue Vol. 22, No. 1 (July 1992): 129, 131; Hainsworth, "The Extreme Right in Post-war France", in Hainsworth (ed.) *The Extreme Right in Europe and the USA*, p. 46f.
57. See M. Lewis-Beck and G.E. Mitchell II, 'French Electoral Theory: The National Front Test,' in *Electoral Studies*, Vol. 12, No. 2 (June 1993), pp. 112–27.
58. *Ibid.*
59. *Libération* (23 Mar 1993), pp. 4–6.
60. *Ibid*, p. 125f.
61. For this view see P. Bréchon and S.K. Mitra, 'The National Front in France. The Emergence of an Extreme Right Protest Movement', in *Comparative Politics*, 25,1 (Oct. 1992), pp. 63–82.
62. See M. Minkenberg, 'Cultural Change and the Far Right in East and West Germany', *German Politics*, Vol. 3, 2, (Aug. 1994), pp. 169–92.
63. See Minkenberg, 'The New Right in Germany', pp. 62–70.
64. See R. Stöss, *Die Republikaner* (Köln: Bund Verlag, 1990), p. 97.
65. See Falter, *Wer wählt rechts?*, pp. 44–60.
66. See ibid., ch. 6.
67. The very founding of the party in 1983, in response to the CDU/CSU's perceived selling out of the national interest, i.e. the billion DM loan to the GDR negotiated by CSU chief Franz Josef Strauß and the continuation of *Ostpolitik* by the Kohl government, illustrates the initial thrust of the party.

68. See Küchler, 'Germans and "Others"'; also Minkenberg, 'German Unification and the Continuity of Discontinuities', op.cit. pp. 183, 186f.
69. See A. Pfahl-Traughber, *Rechtsextremismus. Eine kritische Bestandsaufnahme nach der Wiedervereinigung* (Bonn: Bouvier, 1993), pp. 46ff. 235ff.
70. See O. Gabriel, 'Institutionenvertrauen im vereinigten Deutschland', *Aus Politik und Zeitgeschichte* 22 Oct. 1993 (B43/93), p. 9.
71. See Michael Minkenberg, 'The Far Right in Unified Germany', in F. Weil (ed.) *Research on Democracy and Extremism*, Vol. 3, Baton-Rouge: Louisiana State University Press, 1995 (forthcoming).
72. See Falter, *Wer wählt rechts?*, pp. 23–6. In the Hamburg elections of 1993, the New Right parties were particularly successful among the working class, a sixth of whom voted for the *Republikaner* or the DVU; see *Der Spiegel*, 27 Sep. 1993 (39), pp. 29–33.
73. Die Republikaner, *Parteiprogramm 1993* (Augsburg 1993), p. 5.
74. For an examination of *Republikaner* platforms, see Gessenharter, *Kippt die Republik? Die Neue Rechte und ihre Unterstützung durch Politik und Medien* (München: Knaur, 1994), pp. 157–69. See also H.-G. Jaschke, *Die Republikaner. Profile einer Rechtsaußenpartei* (Bonn: Dietz, 1990), pp. 90–106.
75. See Falter, *Wer wählt rechts?*, chs. 6 and 7.
76. See *Der Spiegel*, 11 Apr. 1994 (15), pp. 18ff.; *Berliner Morgenpost*, 25 Aug., 1994, p. 4.
77. See *Der Spiegel*, 20 June 1994 (25), pp. 32–5; *Der Spiegel*, 15 Aug. 1994 (33), p. 50. On the mediocrity of the *Republikaner*'s personnel in the 1994 campaign, see G. Dachs, 'Die Banalität des Radikalen', *Die Zeit*, 29 Oct 1993, (44), p. 5.
78. See Leggewie, *Druck von rechts*, pp. 100–103.
79. See Falter, *Wer wählt rechts?*, pp. 136–53.
80. This interpretation is widespread in the current German debate on the far right and borrows largely from the influential book by U. Beck, *Risikogesellschaft. Auf dem Weg in eine andere Moderne* (Frankfurt/M: Suhrkamp, 1986). See for example H. Funke, *'Republikaner'. Rassenhaß, Judenfeinschaft, nationaler Größenwahn* (Berlin: Aktion Sühnezeichen, 1989), p. 116; C. Leggewie, *Die Republikaner* (Berlin: Rotbuch Verlag, 1989), W. Heitmeyer, *Rechtsextreme Orientierungen bei Jugendlichen* (Weinheim: 1987). For a critical discussion of this interpretation see A. Pfahl-Traughber, *Rechtsextremismus. Eine kritische Bestandsaufnahme nach der Wiedervereinigung* (Bonn: Bouvier Verlag, 1993), pp. 207–14.

4

The New Extreme Right-Wingers in Western Europe: Attitudes, World Views and Social Characteristics[1]

Lauri Karvonen

During the last 10–15 years, neo-fascism and right-wing extremism have definitely left their position as political curiosa to occupy a part of the centre stage in European politics. Although comparatively few commentators still view movements of this kind as an immediate threat to the stability of democracy itself in Western Europe, it has become increasingly difficult to dismiss them as insignificant and isolated groups (cf. Hainsworth 1994, 1–24).

The reasons for the growing concern with right-wing extremism are obvious. Whatever the actual number of convinced neo-fascists and right-wing extremists may be, their activity is today on an entirely different level from that of any previous period after the Second World War. Right-wing extremists have become much more visible, and they are visible in more spectacular ways than earlier. Race-related violence has increased dramatically especially since the late 1980s. Both the number of such incidents, the methods used and the outcome of the attacks belie any notion of isolated outbursts of spontaneous anger. Those who commit these acts of violence pick their targets in strikingly similar ways; refugee quarters, small businesses operated by foreigners, and Jewish cemeteries are recurrent objects of such crimes. Bombs and all kinds of firearms seem to be readily available to those who commit these acts. Not just injuries and loss of property result from this violence; increasingly, loss of life is the outcome of race-related violence in Europe (Björgo and Witte, 1993, 12–16).

Parallel to these trends, a more 'respectable' kind of extreme nationalism has gained ground in West European politics. The German Republicans (Kolinsky 1994, 61–91), the *Front National* in France (Hainsworth 1994 B, 29–57) and the *Movimento Sociale Italiano* (Sidoti 1994, 151–72) have enjoyed considerable successes in recent elections. Although careful not to be associated with outright fascism or with violent methods, these parties display several similarities with the extreme right-wing parties of the inter-war years. Clearly, their relative success contributes to a general impression of a new rise to prominence of the extreme right in today's European politics.

Convincing as such evidence may seem, it is important not to automatically view these expressions of extreme nationalism or ethnocentrism as parts of the same wave of 'right-wing extremism'. As Roger Eatwell (1994, 5–6) has aptly pointed out

> it seems unlikely that a hard-line, activist, fire-bombing German neo-Nazi can be subsumed psychologically in the same category as the French old age pensioner who votes once, or a few times, for the FN. Indeed, the evidence from opinion polls is that a typical FN voter is neither fascist, nor even particularly radical...
> ...it is important to begin by asking what exactly has changed recently. This may seem a bizarre question, given the dramatic [Fascist and Racist] manifestations... However, there may be less change at an *attitudinal* level... The relationship between political belief and action is complex.

The present paper focuses on the occurrence of attitudes and beliefs typical of fascists and extreme right-wingers in Western Europe over a ten-year period. It has a double aim. On the one hand, it focuses on attitudinal change over time. Has there been a marked increase in such beliefs and attitudes since the early 1980s? If that is the case, is this a general trend throughout the continent, or have there been conspicuous differences between individual countries as to these tendencies? In a word, has the dramatic increase in acts associated with neo-fascism and right-wing radicalism been accompanied by a parallel shift in fundamental attitudes at the level of the general public?

Irrespective of whether such a general change has occurred, this study also wants to portray those individuals that display characteristics associated with right-wing extremism. What are the typical social and psychological attributes of modern-day extreme right-wingers?

Design

The structure of the study follows the two main questions presented above. First, a descriptive account of the degree of attitudinal change from 1981 to 1991 is presented. After that, individuals displaying high values on variables associated with right-wing extremism in 1991 are analyzed. The exact dimensions and operationalized questions in connection with these two tasks will be presented separately below.

Data

The empirical material consists of individual-level data originating from *The European Value Study* (EVS).[2] The EVS comprises two rounds of interviews conducted in the West European countries in 1981 and 1990/91.

The longitudinal analysis of attitudinal change includes 14 countries: France, Britain, West Germany, Italy, the Netherlands, Denmark, Belgium, Spain, Ireland, Northern Ireland, Norway, Sweden, Iceland and Finland. The total number of respondents is 16,594 in the 1981 sample, 20,471 in the 1991 sample.

The second analysis, which concerns the correlates of attitudes connected to right-wing extremism, is based on cross-sectional data: all data are from the 1991 sample. As the 1991 interviews also contain data on Austria, this country is included in this part of our study. Consequently, the total number of cases is somewhat higher here (N=21,931).

Empirical Analysis I: Attitudinal Change, 1981–91

Dimensions of Extreme Right-Wing Attitudes

Several attitudinal dimensions characteristic of the extreme right can readily be culled from the literature: racism, extreme nationalism, anti-marxism, authoritarianism, intolerance and anti-parliamentarism (Payne 1980, 20–21; Gardberg 1993, 8–33; von Beyme 1988, 1–16). There were several questions that represent aspects of these dimensions in both rounds of the EVS interviews. The following indicators stand for these dimensions in operational terms.

Racism: Share of respondents that mention 'other races' among 'groups that they would not like to have as neighbours'.

Extreme nationalism: Share of respondents that mention 'foreign workers' among 'groups that they would not like to have as neighbours'; share of respondents that say that they are 'very proud of their nationality'.

Anti-marxism: Share of respondents that mention 'left-wing extremists' among 'groups that they would not like to have as neighbors'.

Authoritarianism: Share of respondents that think that 'greater respect for authority' would be a change for the better.

Intolerance: Share of respondents that think that homosexuality can 'never be justified'.

Anti-parliamentarism: Share of respondents that say that they have 'no confidence at all in parliament'.

Evidence

The results clearly indicate that cultural circumstances and national conditions strongly influence the way in which the various questions are perceived by the respondents. This means that the share of respondents choosing alternatives typical of extreme right-wingers varies greatly from country to country depending on the question. For instance, fairly low shares of respondents throughout Europe say that they would resent representatives of other races as neighbours; by contrast, an overwhelming majority in most Catholic countries would welcome a greater respect for authority, while Protestant Northern Europe is more sceptical of this proposition. Similarly, condemning homosexuality is clearly more common in Catholic than Protestant countries. About half of the West German respondents reject 'left extremists' as neighbours, whereas this is uncommon in Denmark and Finland; in the latter countries, a 'left extremist' is probably simply someone voting for the radical left, whereas the term evokes an image of Red Brigade terrorism in Germany.

The present paper does not, of course, argue that anyone taking this or that position on a particular question belongs to the extreme right-wing. Rather, one would expect these positions to become more common if the general support of the extreme right-wing were to become stronger over time.

This bird's eye view of Western Europe does not convey an entirely clear-cut impression. On five of the indicators, the direction of the change would seem to corroborate the notion of increased extremist attitudes; on two of them, the development runs counter to such a hypothesis. Moreover, on three of them the change is less than three percentage points and cannot therefore be regarded as particularly clear. No dramatic overall change can be said to have taken place as regards attitudes towards other races and foreign workers or concerning confidence in parliament.

On the other hand, it is somewhat more obvious that the attitudes towards 'left extremists' have become more negative over time. Apparently, the collapse of communism has made for a more hostile environment for the extreme left in Western Europe as well. Somewhat more people now say that they are 'very proud of their nationality' than ten years earlier. By contrast, clearly condemnatory attitudes towards homosexuality display an overall decrease over time. Interestingly enough, the 'age of AIDS' seems to have brought about a more tolerant rather than more restrictive mood. Moreover, there is some decrease as concerns the share of respondents that call for a greater respect for authority. Here, however, the relation to right-wing extremism may be very complex. It is quite conceivable that, for instance, neo-fascist activists may view socialist-led governments, police interfering with their demonstrations, or courts sending their colleagues to prison as 'authorities' – they should therefore perhaps not be expected to call for 'greater respect for authority'.

TABLE 4.1.
QUESTIONS REPRESENTING DIMENSIONS OF RIGHT WING-EXTREMISM: CHANGE 1981–91. MEAN VALUES FOR 14 COUNTRIES (PER CENT OF ALL RESPONDENTS).

	1981		1991		
Question	Max/min	Mean	Max/min	Mean	Change
'Other races'	11.4/3.3	7.9	24.8/5.9	10.8	2.8
'Left extremists'	48.2/0.2	22.5	50.8/5.8	28.4	5.9
'Foreign workers'	19.8/0.2	8.1	20.3/4.6	10.9	2.9
'Respect authority'	86.2/25.5	53.6	82.5/21.6	50.0	-3.6
'Homosexuality'	60.8/19.8	44.4	64.8/12.0	38.7	-5.7
'Nationality'	65.4/16.8	37.7	76.8/19.8	42.6	4.9
'Parliament'	26.9/2.2	10.5	22.6/5.1	12.0	1.5

Legend: For the definitions of the questions, see above section on 'Dimensions of extreme right-wing attitudes'. The figures are based on the percentage of respondents in each country who answered these questions as indicated in that section.

As the figures in Table 4.1 are mean values, it is of course necessary to examine the change for individual countries in order to determine how far the overall figures portray pervasive tendencies and to what extent they have been decisively affected by extreme levels of change in individual countries.

The EXACT figures for the 14 countries are presented in Appendix 1 at the end of this chapter. Table 4.2 shows the general direction of change on the various indicators for each country. If the share of respondents choosing a particular alternative on a question has not increased or decreased more than three percentage points from 1981 to 1991, the result is coded as 'no change' and marked '0'. If the increase has been more than three percentage points this is indicated by '+'. Correspondingly, a decrease of more than three percentage points is indicated by '-'.

TABLE 4.2
THE OCCURRENCE OF ATTITUDES ASSOCIATED WITH RIGHT-WING
EXTREMISM IN 14 COUNTRIES: CHANGE 1981–1991

Question

Country	'Other races'	'Left extrem.'	'Foreign workers'	'Authority'	'Homosexuals'	'Nationality'	'Parliament'	Tot.*
France	+	+	+	+	-	+	+	6
Britain	0	+	0	+	0	0	0	2
W. Germany	0	0	-	-	0	0	0	0
Italy	+	-	+	-	-	0	-	2
Netherlands	0	+	-	0	-	+	0	2
Denmark	+	0	0	0	0	+	-	2
Belgium	+	+	+	-	-	+	0	4
Spain	0	0	+	-	-	0	+	2
Ireland	0	+	0	0	0	+	0	2
N. Ireland	0	+	0	-	+	+	0	3
Norway	+	0	+	-	0	+	0	3
Sweden	0	+	+	-	0	+	0	3
Iceland	+	+	+	0	-	-	0	3
Finland	+	+	+	0	-	0	+	4
Tot.'	7	9	8	2	1	8	3	

Legend: For definition of questions see above Table 4.1 and section on 'Dimensions of extreme right-wing attitudes'
*) Includes only cases that display increase in the direction of more right-wing extremism.

The variation among the 14 countries would seem to belie any notion of a uniform increase of extreme right-wing attitudes in Western Europe. France and West Germany are the extremes. In France, the share of respondents choosing 'extreme right alternatives' has increased on all questions except the one concerning homosexuality; clearly fewer French respondents unequivocally condemned homosexuality in 1991 than ten years earlier. In Germany, by contrast, there was no clear increase of this kind at all. To the extent that there is any clear change at all, it reflects a more critical attitude towards authority and a more tolerant mood *vis-à-vis* foreign workers. Clearly, the Fall of the Wall did not immediately lead to increased extreme right-wing attitudes among West Germans.

As to the other countries, Belgium and Finland display an increase on four of the seven indicators, the remaining ten countries on two or three.

For many of these countries, decreased values were almost as common as increased ones.

Nevertheless, examining the table across variables rather than cases one may note that more than half of the cases displayed increased levels of intolerance towards left-wing extremists and foreign workers as well as of national pride. In half of the countries, intolerance against other races had increased. Only three instances of increased anti-parliamentarism and two of increased authority-orientation could be noted. Intolerance against homosexuality had generally decreased or remained unchanged.

The interpretation of the overall results therefore depends on how one wishes to weight the various questions as indicators of extreme right-wing attitudes. If ethnocentrism (national pride, intolerance against foreigners and other races) and anti-marxism are stressed, then there are clearly increased extreme right-wing attitudes in large parts of Western Europe. If the rest of the indicators are given equal weight, the picture becomes much more ambiguous.

Some highlights of the exact figures for each country on the various indicators are worth mentioning here (see Appendix 1). France, Belgium and Finland display an increase of more than ten percentage points in intolerance *vis-à-vis* left-wing extremists. The Finns have, moreover, become significantly more restrictive towards other races;[3] their distrust of parliament has also grown markedly.

Considerably fewer Italians view an increased respect for authority as something clearly desirable. Attitudes towards homosexuality have become clearly less condemnatory over time in Iceland, Italy, Finland and Spain. National pride has increased more than ten percentage points from 1981 to 1991 in Denmark, Sweden and Ireland.

In sum, the following may be noted as concerns attitudinal change 1981–91:

1) Most West European countries display clearly increased intolerance *vis-à-vis* left-wing extremism. There is also some increase in intolerance against other races and foreign workers.
2) National pride has increased significantly in large parts of Western Europe.
3) Calls for increased respect for authority have become less common.
4) Intolerance against homosexuality has decreased significantly in most European countries.
5) Of individual countries France displays most attitudinal change towards increased right-wing extremism; West Germany is the other extreme, displaying practically no increase at all.

Empirical Analysis II: Some Correlates of Extreme Right-Wing Attitudes in 1991

Focus

The aim of this section is to highlight some psychological and social characteristics of respondents who in 1991 displayed attitudes typical of right-wing extremists. The focus is on three groups of respondents:

Group 1 is selected on the basis of multi-dimensional criteria. It includes respondents who attain extreme right-wing values on three central dimensions simultaneously. These dimensions are: racism (respondents who reject representatives of other races as neighbours), authority-orientation (respondents who would welcome greater respect for authority) and anti-parliamentarism (respondents who have no confidence at all in parliament). This group could perhaps be called the 'hard core' of today's right-wing extremism.

Group 2 consists of those respondents who mention Jews among those groups that they would not like to see as neighbours. Unfortunately, the 1981 EVS data did not contain information on this dimension, which is why longitudinal analyses have not been possible. It is all the more important to provide a cross-sectional picture of the extent and correlates of anti-Semitism in Western Europe in the early 1990s.

Group 3 highlights the correlates of sexual intolerance. It consists of those respondents who would not accept homosexuals as neighbours.

The analysis of each of these groups starts out by a simple presentation of the relative frequencies of these attitudes by country. Apart from that the analysis does not differentiate between countries; all respondents irrespective of nationality will be treated together in each of the three groups.

The three groups will be examined from two angles. On the one hand, some basic elements of the respondent's world views will be at the centre of attention. The objective is to find out to what extent indicators used in the socio-psychological study of the *'Authoritarian Personality'* are valid for these groups as well. In this classical research initiated by Adorno and others in the 1940s nine different dimensions of personality were studied with the aid of a large number of questions with which respondents with authoritarian leanings were expected to agree.

The present study examines five of these dimensions. The list below defines these (the quotations are from Eysenck 1954, 149–51) and presents the questions used as measures in this study.

Projectivity. 'The disposition to believe that wild and dangerous things go on in the world; the projection outwards of unconscious emotional impulses'. In the present study, the question 'Generally speaking, would you say that most people can be trusted or that you can't be too careful in dealing with people?' is used to measure this dimension. Respondents displaying extreme right-wing attitudes are expected to choose the alternative 'can't be too careful'.

Superstition and stereotypy. 'The belief in mystical determinants of the individual's fate; the disposition to think in rigid categories'. Two questions are used to describe this dimension: 1) 'Some people feel they have a completely free choice and control over their lives, and other people feel that what they do has no real effect on what happens to them. How much freedom of choice and control do you feel you have over the way your life turns out?' 2) 'In the long run, do you think the scientific advances we are making will help or harm mankind?' To the former question, 'extreme right-wingers' are expected to answer 'little or no freedom and control'; as to the latter question, they are expected to choose the alternative 'scientific advances will harm mankind'.

Authoritarian aggression. 'Tendency to be on the lookout for, and to condemn, reject and punish people who violate conventional values'. 'Extreme right-wingers' are expected to agree with the following two propositions: a) 'There are absolutely clear guidelines about what is good and evil. These always apply to everyone, whatever the circumstances.' b) 'Regardless of what the qualities and faults of one's parents are, one must always love and respect them.'

Conventionalism. 'Rigid adherence to conventional, middle-class values'. Respondents are expected to mention 'good manners' among 'especially important qualities which children should be encouraged to learn at home'.

Authoritarian submission. 'Submissive, uncritical attitude towards idealized moral authorities of the in-group'. Respondents are expected to mention 'obedience' among 'especially important qualities which children should be encouraged to learn at home'.

As to the social characteristics of the respondents, the following three factors stand out as potentially important in the light of previous research. Right-wing extremists usually profess to be *anti-political*; thus, one would expect them to display a low degree of interest in politics. A low level of social sophistication has been found to be typical of them. Consequently, they can be expected to have a low *socio-economic status;* unskilled workers can be expected to be overrepresented among them. As to *age,* respondents displaying extreme right-wing attitudes are expected to be found at the extremes. On the one hand, previous studies of right-wing extremism indicate that movements of this kind attract young people in particular; on the other hand, rigid authoritarian attitudes are normally most common among the oldest age cohorts (Falter and Schumann, 1988, 104–7; Merkl, 1980, 764–81).

The analysis of the three groups – the 'hard core' of extreme right-wingers, the anti-Semites and the sexually intolerant – will be structured according to these psychological and social characteristics. The groups will be compared to the other respondents on the various dimensions; percentwise distributions will be presented and tested for statistical significance. Significance is determined on the basis of values of chi square.

Racism, anti-parliamentarism and authority-orientation: the 'hard core' of extreme right-wing attitudes

As expected, those who both rejected other races as neighbours, said they had no confidence in parliament whatsoever, and welcomed increased respect for authority turned out to be a very small minority of all respondents. Of a total of 21,931 respondents in 15 West European countries, only 183, or 0.8 per cent belonged to this group. Table 4.3 shows the distribution of this group by country.

TABLE 4.3
THE 'HARD CORE' OF RIGHT-WING EXTREMISM IN WESTERN EUROPE
BY COUNTRY

Country	N	% country	% sample
France	18	1.8	9.8
Britain	12	0.8	6.6
W. Germany	7	0.3	3.8
Italy	26	1.3	14.2
Netherlands	2	0.2	1.1
Denmark	4	0.4	2.2
Belgium	39	1.4	21.3
Spain	46	1.1	25.1
Ireland	6	0.6	3.3
N. Ireland	1	0.3	0.6
Norway	3	0.2	1.6
Sweden	5	0.5	2.7
Iceland	2	0.3	1.1
Finland	5	1.0	2.7
Austria	7	0.5	3.8
	183	x = 0.7	100.0

Due to large sample size combined with a high relative occurrence of the three attitudes, Belgium, Spain and Italy especially dominate the sample as a whole. As for France, the fairly large share of the sample is solely an effect of the relatively high occurrence of the attitudes; the French sample is medium-sized in the data as a whole. The fact that the southern and central areas of Western Europe dominate the sample is naturally a factor which should be kept in mind; the special conditions present in these regions but less important in Northern Europe may affect the analysis as a whole.

Table 4.4 depicts the correlates of this group in Western Europe as a whole. The small 'hard core' of extreme right-wingers is compared with the total population of West European respondents in the 1991 ESV data. The table shows the percent-wise distributions of respondents according to the crucial alternatives on each question. The levels of significance denote values of chi square calculated in most cases on the basis of 2 x 2 cross-tables.

TABLE 4.4.
THE CORRELATES OF THE 'HARD CORE' OF WEST EUROPEAN RIGHT-
WINGERS IN 1991

Question	Alternative	'Hard core' (%)	All (%)	Sign.
People trusted?	'Can't be too careful'	80.3	54.2	0.000
Freedom and control?	'Little or none'	36.0	26.9	0.01
Scientific advances?	'Will harm'	26.8	18.3	0.001
Good and evil?	'Absolute guidelines'	31.7	28.1	ns
Respect parents?	'Always'	68.9	63.6	ns
Mention 'good manners'?	Yes	89.6	76.4	0.001
Mention 'obedience'?	Yes	54.1	35.2	0.000
Interest in politics?	Little or none	80.4	56.7	0.000
Socioeconomic status?	Unskilled	24.0	16.5	0.01
Age?	Over 47	61.2	39.2	0.000
		N = 183	N = 21,931	

Legend: for comprehensive information on questions and alternatives, see text above in the section entitled 'Focus'. Significances are based on values of chi square

In most respects, the little group of 'hard core' right-wingers confirm the expectations presented above. Their level of trust in people is significantly lower than that among the respondents at large. They are less inclined than others to believe that they have freedom of choice and can exert control over their own lives; the level of significance here is, however, not particularly high. More than others they tend to believe that scientific advances are potentially harmful. Furthermore, they value good manners and obedience clearly more. There is also a clear difference in the level of interest in politics, extreme right-wingers being significantly less interested. Unskilled workers are somewhat over-represented among them.

As to questions about good and evil and respect for parents, there is no clear difference to be discerned. It is possible that these questions are not particularly accurate measures of the theoretical dimensions they are to portray. For instance, it is imaginable that a liberal person and a fascist might view human rights so that the former would see them as 'inalienable rights' whereas the latter could consider violating them should the 'good of the Fatherland' so require.

As for age, no overrepresentation of younger people could be discerned in the 'hard core' group. By contrast, the older age cohorts were clearly overrepresented in this group just as had been expected.

In sum, this small group of extreme right-wingers would seem to comply largely with the expectations concerning world views and socioeconomic characteristics based on previous research. The central traits of the 'authoritarian personality' seem to be well-represented among them. As expected, they also proved to be highly anti-political and more often than respondents in general belong to the group of unskilled workers.

The Correlates of Anti-Semitism

From a 'post-Auschwitz' perspective, one might have expected neo-fascist and ultranationalist movements in today's Europe to play down the anti-Semitic element in their propaganda. Quite the contrary, the more militant groups seem to have bought Hitler's anti-Semitism wholesale (Griffin, 1993, 161–74). Even the more 'respectable' ultra-nationalists such as le Pen and Schönhuber, while denying that they or their parties are anti-Semitic, have made statements about Holocaust and related questions that can clearly be interpreted as invitations to anti-Semites to join these movements.

Table 4.5 indicates that there is indeed some political potential in anti-Semitism. Out of 100 West European respondents, on the average eight mentioned Jews among those groups that they would not like to have as neighbours. Again, relatively clear differences could be noted between countries.

If percentages below five are classified as a low level of anti-Semitism, five to ten per cent as intermediate, and over ten per cent as a high level, then Denmark, the Netherlands and Finland have a low level of anti-Semitism, while Belgium, Italy and Austria have high levels. The remaining nine countries display intermediate levels of anti-Semitism. Looking at the two extreme groups, one might be tempted to stress that the three countries with high levels are all Catholic, whereas Denmark and Finland are Protestant countries and the Netherlands has as many Protestants as Catholics. Looking at countries like Ireland and Norway clearly indicates, however, that the religious factor in itself is not a sufficient determinant of the level of anti-Semitism, although it seems to have a certain impact.

TABLE 4.5.
ANTI-SEMITIC RESPONDENTS IN WESTERN EUROPE BY COUNTRY

Country	N	% country	% sample
France	67	6.7	3.5
Britain	100	6.7	5.3
W. Germany	152	7.2	8.0
Italy	249	12.3	13.1
Netherlands	34	3.3	1.8
Denmark	32	3.1	1.7
Belgium	364	13.0	19.1
Spain	410	9.9	21.5
Ireland	64	6.4	3.4
N. Ireland	19	6.3	1.0
Norway	110	8.9	5.8
Sweden	59	5.6	3.1
Iceland	51	7.3	2.7
Finland	28	4.8	1.5
Austria	166	11.4	8.7
	1905	$x = 7.5$	100.0

In the following, the group of anti-Semitic respondents will be analyzed *in toto* without national distinctions. Again, the large Spanish, Italian and Belgian samples may distort the analysis to some extent.

As for the structure of the analysis and the dimensions highlighted, the analysis is basically identical with the preceding section.

The 'Authoritarianism scale' of Adorno and others from which the attitudinal dimensions included in Table 4.6 have been selected is a product of a research project which originally focused on the emergence of anti-Semitism. Viewing the results of the present analysis one might be tempted to say that nothing indeed is new under the sun.

Today's anti-Semites in Western Europe – just as those in the US and Western Europe in the 1940s – are more distrustful and superstitious than other people in relation to the outside world. They more often have rigid standards for good and evil, and they adhere to conventional norms more frequently. They are also clearly more oriented towards authority than are other people.

In terms of social characteristics the anti-Semitic group similarly distinguishes itself from the rest. They are clearly less interested in politics than people in general. Their socio-economic status is on the average lower. Their average age is significantly higher than that of respondents at large. Again, there was no young group of right-wingers to be discerned.

TABLE 4.6.
THE CORRELATES OF ANTI-SEMITISM IN WESTERN EUROPE IN 1991.

Question	Alternative	'Anti-Semites' (%)	Others (%)	Sign.
People trusted?	'Can't be too careful'	71.6	57.0	0.000
Scientific advances?	'Will harm'	23.9	19.4	0.000
Good and evil?	'Absolute guidelines'	36.4	29.0	0.000
Respect parents?	'Always'	78.7	67.7	0.000
Mention 'good manners'?	Yes	84.3	75.6	0.000
Mention 'obedience'?	Yes	45.6	34.2	0.000
Interest in politics?	Little or none	67.1	55.8	0.000
Occupational status?	Low	50.9	37.1	0.000
Age?	Over 47	53.9	39.2	0.000

N = 1,905   N = 20,026

Legend: For comprehensive information on questions and alternatives, see above section on 'Focus'. Significances are based on values of chi square.

The present group of West-European anti-Semites clearly confirms the generalizations offered by earlier research. It is hard to escape the impression that there is something which could best be labelled *der ewige Antisemit.*

The correlates of sexual intolerance

Our third and final group consists of those respondents who in 1991 mentioned homosexuals among groups that they would not like to have as neighbours. We noted earlier that the condemnatory attitudes against homosexuality had decreased over time. This final analysis depicts the group that still clings to a negative attitude *vis-à-vis* homosexuality.
Again, the Netherlands and Denmark display conspicuously low levels of intolerance. The rest of Scandinavia and also Belgium and France this time have low to intermediate levels of intolerance. Austria and Northern Ireland display the highest levels of intolerance *vis-à-vis* homosexuality.

TABLE 4.7.
RESPONDENTS WHO REJECT HOMOSEXUALS AS NEIGHBOURS IN 1991

Country	N	% country	% sample
France	244	24.4	4.0
Britain	493	33.2	8.1
W. Germany	703	33.5	11.5
Italy	742	36.8	12.1
Netherlands	111	10.9	1.8
Denmark	121	11.7	2.0
Belgium	672	24.1	11.0
Spain	1206	29.1	19.7
Ireland	332	33.2	5.4
N. Ireland	146	48.0	2.4
Norway	242	19.5	3.9
Sweden	185	17.7	3.0
Iceland	141	20.1	2.3
Finland	148	25.2	2.4
Austria	634	43.4	10.4
	6,120	x = 27.4	100.0

Once again, the group as a whole is characterized by an overrepresentation from Spain, Italy, West Germany and Belgium. With the exception of the last country, there is thus an overrepresentation of respondents originating from countries where the level of sexual intolerance is rather high.

This analysis largely repeats the pattern observed earlier. Those respondents who resent homosexuals are similar to the anti-Semitic group of respondents and also to a large extent resemble the tiny 'hard core' of extreme right-wingers. This goes for attitudinal profiles as well as socioeconomic characteristics. One form of intolerance largely feeds the other.

TABLE 4.8.
THE CORRELATES OF SEXUAL INTOLERANCE IN WESTERN EUROPE IN 1991

Question	Alternative	Intolerant (%)	Others (%)	Sign.
People trusted?	'Can't be too careful'	68.4	54.4	0.000
Scientific advances?	'Will harm'	21.7	19.0	0.000
Good and evil?	'Absolute guidelines'	37.5	26.6	0.000
Respect parents?	'Always'	78.5	64.8	0.000
Mention 'good manners'?	Yes	83.6	73.6	0.000
Mention 'obedience'?	Yes	42.2	32.4	0.000
Interest in politics?	Little or none	62.2	54.6	0.000
Occupational status?	Low	44.1	36.1	0.000
		N = 6,120	N = 15,811	

Summary and Conclusions

This study represents a first preliminary analysis of a large body of survey data, which allow a detailed examination of attitudes and views usually associated with right-wing extremism. It aimed at providing an overview of the main changes in such attitudes over time as well as of some basic characteristics of those respondents who in 1991 displayed attitudes typical of right-wing extremism.

The results can be summarized in the following way:

1. Most West European countries display clearly increased intolerance *vis-à-vis* left-wing extremism. There is also some increase in intolerance against other races and foreign workers.
2. National pride has increased significantly in large parts of Western Europe.

3. Calls for increased respect for authority have become less common.
4. Intolerance against homosexuality has decreased significantly in most European countries.
5. Of individual countries France displays most attitudinal change towards increased right-wing extremism; West Germany is the other extreme, displaying practically no increase at all.
6. Right-wing extremists – whether they be defined by multi-dimensional criteria, in terms of anti-Semitism or in terms of sexual intolerance – comply with most of the character dimensions found in the work on 'the Authoritarian Personality' by Adorno and others. They display authoritarian aggression, superstition, authoritarian submission and conventionalism to significantly higher degrees than other respondents.
7. In terms of social characteristics, extreme right-wingers are distinguished by lack of interest in politics, low occupational status and higher average age than other respondents.

All in all, there seems to be an increase in attitudes normally associated with the extreme right-wing in Western Europe since the early 1980s. It should be noted, however, that there is no uniform pattern of increase either across countries or across variables. Many countries, notably Germany, display no significant increase at all. Moreover, such factors as authority-orientation and a clear aversion to homosexuality have become less common over time. Ultranationalism – national pride and aversion to other races and foreign workers – has, however, increased notably. These are factors at the very core of extreme right-wing propaganda today. It should be an urgent task for research to assess to what extent mainstream politics throughout Western Europe has tuned in on such changes in the attitudes of the general public.

Notes

1. Prepared for presentation at the XVI World Congress of the International Political Science Association, Berlin, 21–25 Aug. 1994 RC6.2: 'The Revival of Right-Wing Extremism in the 1990s', L. Weinberg and P. Merkl, convenors. Copyright IPSA, 1994
2. The data were made available by The Norwegian Social Science Data Services (NSD), Bergen, Norway. Special thanks are due to Jostein Ryssevik, Ewelyn Jordal, Anne Dueland and Lars Holm. The NSD or its staff are in no way responsible for interpretations of the data made in this article.
3. Incidentally, this seems to coincide with the first major experience the Finns have had with refugees (Somalis) coming into the country. Up until the late 1980s, Finland was a conspicuous exception among the West European countries due to her extremely restrictive refugee policies.

BIBLIOGRAPHY

von Beyme, K. (1988), 'Right-wing extremism in Post-war Europe', in K. von Beyme (ed.), *Right-Wing Extremism in Western Europe* (London: Frank Cass), 1–18.
Björgo, T. and Witte, R. (1933), 'Introduksjon', in T. Björgo and R. Witte (eds.) *Rasistisk vold i Europa*, Oslo: Tiden Norsk Forlag, 9–28.
Eatwell, R. (1994), *The Revival of Fascism and Racism in Europe: New Insights into Old Problems?*, (University of Bath, (mimeographed)).
Eysenck, H.J. (1954), The Psychology of Politics (London: Routledge & Kegan Paul).
Falter, J.W. and Schumann, S. (1988), 'Affinity towards Right-wing Extremism in Western Europe', in K. von Beyme (ed.), *Right-Wing Extremism in Western Europe,* (London: Frank Cass), 96–110.
Gardberg, A. (1993), *Against the Stranger, the Gangster and the Establishment. A Comparative study of the ideologies of the Swedish Ny Demokrati, the German Republikaner, the French Front National and the Belgian Vlaams Blok,* (Helsingfors: SSKH Meddelanden).
Griffin, R. (1993), *The Nature of Fascism* London: Routledge.
Hainsworth, P. (1994), 'Introduction. The Cutting Edge: The Extreme Right in Post-War Western Europe and the USA', in P. Hainsworth (ed.), *The Extreme Right in Europe and the USA* (London: Pinter Publishers), 1–28.
Hainsworth, P. (1994B), 'The Extreme Right in Post-War France: The Emergence and Success of the Front National', in P. Hainsworth (ed.), *The Extreme Right in Europe and the USA,* (London: Pinter Publishers), 29–60.
Kolinsky, E. (1994), 'A Future for Right Extremism in Germany?', in P. Hainsworth (ed.), *The Extreme Right in Europe and the USA,* (London: Pinter Publishers), 61–94.
Merkl, P.H. (1980), 'Comparing Fascist Movements', in S.U. Larsen, B. Hagtvet and J.P. Myklebust (eds.) *Who Were the Fascists. Social Roots of European Fascism,* (Oslo-Bergen-Tromsö: Universitetsforlaget), 752–83.
Payne, S.G. (1980), 'The Concept of Fascism', in S.U. Larsen, B. Hagtvet and J.P. Myklebust (eds), *Who Were the Fascists. Social Roots of European Fascism,* (Oslo–Bergen–Tromsö: Universitetsforlaget), 14–25.
Sidoti, F. (1994), 'The Extreme Right in Italy: Ideological Orphans and Countermobilization', in P. Hainsworth (ed.), *The Extreme Right in Europe and the USA,* (London: Pinter Publishers), 151–174.

APPENDIX 1

Share of respondents choosing 'extreme right alternatives' on seven questions in fourteen countries, 1981 and 1991. Per cent.

a) Share of respondents mentioning 'other races' among 'groups that they would not like to have as neighbors'

Country	1981	1991	Change 1981-1991
France	4.8	9.4	4.6
Britain	9.4	8.2	-1.2
W. Germany	9.7	9.9	0.2
Italy	6.2	12.1	5.9
Netherlands	8.4	7.4	-1.0
Denmark	3.4	7.0	3.6
Belgium	11.4	16.9	5.5
Spain	8.4	9.9	1.5
Ireland	6.7	5.9	-0.8
N. Ireland	9.0	6.9	-2.1
Norway	8.0	12.4	4.4
Sweden	6.1	6.5	0.4
Iceland	3.3	7.5	4.2
Finland	5.8	24.0	19.0

Mean change: 2.8

b) Share of respondents mentioning 'left extremists' among 'groups they would not like to have as neighbors'

France	9.6	23.5	14.2
Britain	25.7	33.3	7.6
W. Germany	48.2	50.8	2.6
Italy	35.3	29.2	-6.1
Netherlands	36.7	46.7	10.0
Denmark	5.9	5.8	-0.1
Belgium	19.7	35.4	15.7
Spain	24.8	24.8	0.0
Ireland	20.9	28.9	8.0
N. Ireland	28.2	34.5	6.3
Norway	17.7	18.6	0.9
Sweden	21.0	24.1	3.1
Iceland	21.0	30.1	9.1
Finland	0.2	12.1	11.9

Mean change: 5.9

c) Share of respondents mentioning 'foreign workers' among 'groups that they would not like to have as neighbors'

France	5.5	12.8	7.3
Britain	11.9	10.8	-1.1
W. Germany	19.8	16.2	-3.6
Italy	3.1	13.4	10.3
Netherlands	16.0	8.9	-7.1
Denmark	9.6	11.6	2.0
Belgium	15.2	20.3	5.3
Spain	1.9	8.8	6.9
Ireland	5.4	5.1	-0.3
N. Ireland	9.3	7.2	-2.1
Norway	9.4	15.8	6.4
Sweden	4.1	8.9	4.8
Iceland	1.9	7.7	5.8
Finland	0.2	4.6	4.4

Mean change: 2.8

d) Share of respondents who think that 'increased respect for authority' would be a change for the better

France	52.5	59.2	6.7
Britain	69.7	73.2	3.5
W. Germany	38.8	29.5	-9.3
Italy	61.8	47.2	-14.5
Netherlands	53.9	52.4	-1.5
Denmark	35.1	34.9	-0.2
Belgium	57.2	49.3	-7.9
Spain	75.0	67.6	-7.4
Ireland	84.1	82.5	-1.6
N. Ireland	86.2	81.6	-4.6
Norway	35.6	32.1	-3.5
Sweden	31.1	21.6	-9.5
Iceland	44.0	42.3	-1.7
Finland	25.4	26.2	0.8

Mean change: -3.6

e) Share of respondents who think that 'homosexuality can never be justified'

France	44.8	39.5	-5.3
Britain	40.8	42.3	1.5
W. Germany	41.2	32.3	-8.9
Italy	60.8	42.3	-18.5
Netherlands	19.7	12.0	-7.7
Denmark	33.5	36.4	2.9
Belgium	45.9	41.5	-4.4
Spain	52.6	41.7	-10.9
Ireland	51.8	51.0	-0.8
N. Ireland	59.9	64.8	4.9
Norway	45.2	45.0	-0.2
Sweden	34.5	37.0	2.5
Iceland	43.7	24.1	-19.5
Finland	46.9	31.6	-15.3

Mean change: -5.7

f) Share of respondents who say that they are 'very proud' of their nationality

France	28.5	34.9	6.4
Britain	51.0	52.5	1.5
W. Germany	18.4	19.8	1.3
Italy	38.4	40.1	1.7
Netherlands	16.8	22.8	6.0
Denmark	27.9	42.2	14.6
Belgium	24.9	30.6	5.7
Spain	47.9	45.4	-2.5
Ireland	65.4	76.8	11.4
N. Ireland	45.5	53.5	8.0
Norway	40.0	44.8	4.0
Sweden	28.4	40.6	12.2
Iceland	57.0	54.0	-3.0
Finland	38.2	38.1	-0.1

Mean change: 4.9

g) Share of respondents who say that they have 'no confidence at all in parliament'

France	11.3	17.3	6.0
Britain	11.5	11.5	0.0
W. Germany	5.0	7.0	2.0
Italy	26.9	22.6	-4.9
Netherlands	8.7	7.6	1.1
Denmark	15.1	9.6	-5.5
Belgium	15.8	14.3	-1.5
Spain	13.0	18.7	5.7
Ireland	9.2	10.4	1.2
N. Ireland	10.9	9.9	-1.0
Norway	2.2	5.1	2.9
Sweden	8.4	11.1	2.7
Iceland	5.8	8.2	2.4
Finland	2.8	15.1	12.3

Mean change: 1.5

5

The Extreme-Right Political Movements in Post-Communist Central Europe

Thomas S. Szayna

Five years after the ouster of the communists from power in the former Soviet satellite states in Europe and the initiation of a process of setting up liberal democratic regimes in their place, the political party systems in these countries remain in a highly fluid state. The number of significant political parties and movements reaches well into double figures in each country, the parties constantly splinter and amalgamate, 'charismatic' politics (centring on personalities rather than ideologies) play a large role in each country, and the electoral laws in these countries have undergone many modifications, with the effect of changing the 'rules of the game.' And yet, the consolidation of the democratic regimes will depend, in part, on the development of a functioning party system composed of strong institutionalized parties and having a dominant ideological middle and weak fringes. There seems little disagreement on this point. Political parties, elections, and legislatures comprise the three main institutions of public choice and they are commonly accepted as necessary components of any democratic political system. Whatever one's theoretical perspective may be, the institutionalization of political parties, whereby the electorate has several sets of office-seekers and policies to choose from, remains a cornerstone of the successful transformation of the monopolistic political systems of the former communist countries into multi-party democracies.[1]

One trend in the realm of political party system formation in the former communist states has been the emergence (and partial success) of figures and parties espousing ultra-nationalist positions and using populist and demagogic appeals. The allegiance to pluralism of such political actors is suspect and their actions have had the effect of disrupting the democratic political process. Political movements fitting such a mould have become vocal and sometimes serious political players in all former communist countries in Europe during the last five years. Even if they do not come to power, such political parties will play (or have played already) a role in the evolution of the political systems in the newly emerging democracies by shifting the political spectrum, influencing the makeup of ruling coalitions, or by preventing the smooth functioning of legislatures. Put in a different way, if fringe political parties aiming to subvert the democratic process become strong enough, they may paralyze the functioning of the legislature, bring about a political crisis and, eventually, perhaps put an end to the current democratic experiment in the region.

This chapter explores the origins, sources of support, and the potential for further political gains of the disruptive extreme right-wing political movements in four former communist countries of central Europe: Poland, the Czech Republic, Slovakia, and Hungary. Disruptive extremist political movements that have emerged in these states have met with varying degrees of success. Although populist figures have had some successes in all the countries under consideration (presenting some important lessons about the susceptibility of the electorates to populist appeals), the extreme right has met with very little positive response from the electorates. Indeed, after the success of conservative parties in the elections in 1990–91 (with a few extreme-right elements also garnering some support) in a seeming reaction to the many decades of communists in power, the Polish and Hungarian elections in 1993–94 brought the 'reformed' communist parties back to power. In Slovakia, populist-nationalist elements have governed with only a brief interruption since the watershed elections in June 1992 that led to the division of Czechoslovakia. In the Czech Republic, a coalition of conservative free-market forces has steered uninterruptedly the country's transition. The extreme right, as the label implies, has been consigned to a vocal but marginal fringe in all four countries. Nevertheless, while the extremist movements may be on the fringe currently, the volatility of the electorates and the enormous social and economic upheavals going on in these countries mean that a potential threat to the democratization process from the extreme right remains.

What is the Extreme Right?

The use of Western terminology comprises probably the most analytically treacherous and potentially misleading area in any discussion of political currents in the emerging party systems in post-communist central Europe. The left–right political distinctions used commonly in discussions of party systems in the developed Western democracies have only partial applicability to contemporary central Europe because of some important economic differences between the two regions and the resulting different political cleavages.[2] For that reason, an operational definition of the term 'extreme right' is in order.[3]

The term 'extreme right', as used here in the context of post-communist central Europe, refers to political movements characterized by suspect allegiance or downright rejection of pluralism and democratic institutions, combined with a proclivity towards authoritarian modes of rule. The extreme right has a fundamental chauvinistic nationalist orientation (an ultra-nationalist outlook) that underlies many of the other beliefs. The 'nation' (with a strong leader as the embodiment of that nation) is seen as the mythical ideal to which the society must be subordinated, through corporatist political structures if necessary. The extreme-right movements tend to have an ascriptive (even bordering irrationally on the biological) understanding of ethnicity. In an ethnically exclusivist manner, they see ethnicity so defined as the only justifiable criterion for citizenship. They also have xenophobic fears about keeping the nation 'pure'. Outright racism, anti-Semitism, and fears of other polluting groups, such as the Roma (Gypsies), tend to pervade such views. Anti-alien sentiments, hostility to anyone labelled as 'different,' and general social intolerance fall into the same category. Acceptance of violence or at least non-rejection of violence as a means of accomplishing these goals forms a component of the extreme-right beliefs.

Because of the ascriptive understanding of ethnicity, the extreme right tends not to distinguish greatly between the specific main national group and its co-ethnics who may live across the border in neighbouring countries. Such views lead to irredentist leanings and tendencies towards 'recovering' lost territories, which the extreme right sees as 'inalienable' lands somehow necessary for national survival.

Because of its underlying ethnic nationalism, extreme-right movements are suspicious of supra-national movements, and they reject both communism and liberalism. Stemming from the view of modern Western democratic societies as alien and morally corrupt and embracing corporatism as the preferred model of organization of the society, the extreme right places an emphasis on discipline, hierarchy, and 'law and order'. The extreme right in post-communist central Europe has an essentially statist outlook; it favours a considerable state role in the economy as well as in the distribution of resources. It favours a 'gradual' reform of the economy, prefers state control over some of the industry and a mixed system as the final goal (for the extreme-right forces do not trust that profit-seeking by individuals will benefit the 'nation' sufficiently). It also tends to look with suspicion on foreign participation in the economy because of a xenophobic assumption that foreigners invariably aim to harm the security of the state.

The views on the economy carry implications for the role of the individual in society, with the extreme-right movements favouring an extensive paternalistic involvement of the government in guaranteeing the welfare of the citizens. In terms of its appeals to the electorate, the extreme right exhibits far-reaching populism, with demagogic slogans dominant.

There is a fundamental divide between the extreme right and conservative parties that embrace economic liberalism with touches of traditionalism in social outlooks. In fact, the extreme right in post-communist central Europe has much in common with some of the unrepentant communists, whereas the traditionalist-minded liberals represent the ideological centre. That is not a surprise, since both communism and nationalism are essentially anti-individualistic movements emphasizing the collective. The proper contrast of both extremist groups is with the liberal parties that prefer to limit the role of the government to that of creating an environment for individual initiative to bear fruit.

Because extreme-right movements have a nationalistic core, their content is country-specific, for they use the symbols and relate to the experiences of the given nation.[4] In other words, the extreme-right movements in Poland, Slovakia, the Czech Republic, and Hungary place different degrees of emphasis on the issues mentioned above due to different national symbols and concerns. Each country is discussed in more detail below.

Poland

The process of formal ouster of communists from power in Poland occurred with the semi-competitive parliamentary elections in June 1989. Fully competitive parliamentary elections took place in October 1991 and in September 1993. Presidential elections were held in November and December 1990 (two-round process). Local-level elections took place in May 1990, and in June 1994.

From the perspective of tracing the overall political preferences of the Polish electorate, the parliamentary elections in 1991 and 1993 provide the only completely accurate 'poll', for only then did the Polish voters have a clear choice between a variety of parties putting forward different solutions for the country's problems. The initial parliamentary elections in June 1989 were not fully competitive, took the form of a plebiscite on communist rule, and constituted a pathbreaking step on the road to transition away from communist rule. The presidential elections played the role of the first fully free national level elections, but the contest ultimately came down to personalities and a measure of Lech Walesa's prestige in Poland. The first local elections represented transitional elections from the old regime; the second local elections took place in conditions of more established parties but in a myriad of local coalitions.

The Polish political party system has gone through substantial consolidation over the past five years. The initial elections in 1991, held under a generous proportional representation law, produced an extremely fractionated parliament (18 parties or movements with more than a single MP and 11 additional organizations with one MP in the lower house, and 12 parties with more than a single MP and 16 additional movements with one MP in the upper house).[5] A changed election law for the 1993 elections put in place threshold limits on party support for representation (five per cent for parties, eight per cent for coalitions). The result was that only seven political movements gained representation in the lower house (including one ethnic minority organization exempt from the limits); the upper house was more differentiated internally, with six movements having more than one MP represented and ten additional movements with a single MP (however, two parties controlled 73 per cent of the upper house MPs).[6]

The Polish party system that has emerged is fairly differentiated, from a strong socialist and social-democratic left, to a liberal-centrist middle, and a conservative-clerical-nationalist right.[7] The rightist groupings made a dismal showing in the 1993 elections (failing to place any MPs in the lower house) because of disunity, but they are likely to obtain a better result in the next elections. Indeed, the local elections in 1994 already point to greater success on their part.[8] Social- and economic-based political cleavages predominate, though there are also others, religious-secular, regionalist- (most importantly in Silesia) and ethnic-based.

The Clerical-Nationalist Right

The conservative-clerical-nationalist right in Poland includes a couple of dozen significant parties. Some of the parties stressing their Christian or national credentials fall outside the usual Western norms in terms of their platforms, the manner of their appeals, and the principle of separation of church and state. The most important party that falls into this category is the Christian-National Union (*Zjednoczenie Chrzescijansko-Narodowe*, or ZChN). The ZChN has been dedicated to putting in place what amounts to a confessional state, with the party seeing its role as little more than an agent to administer Catholic dogma in the political sphere. In ZChN's outlook, Catholic teachings should underlie all social policy. ZChN's social platform is combined with an interventionist and protectionist economic policy; indeed, studies by Polish political scientists portray the party as more statist-oriented than the main successor party to the communists. ZChN has made appeals to the electorate on the basis of clearly Polish nationalist themes, including thinly-disguised anti-Semitism,[9] great concern for the fate of the ethnic Poles in the post-Soviet countries to Poland's east, and paranoia about Poland's integration into Europe and close ties with Germany.

In the elections in 1991, the party, running as the main member of a Catholic political coalition, received 8.73 per cent of the popular vote for the lower house of parliament (giving it 53 seats, or 12 per cent of the lower house). Adding the votes for the Party of Christian-Democrats (PChD), which ran separately, but whose views were similar to those of ZChN and which joined ZChN in a coalition in 1993, the total vote for the clerical-nationalist forces came to 9.84 per cent. In the 1993 elections, the party (again running as the main member of a Catholic-nationalist coalition) received 6.37 per cent of the popular vote for the lower house of parliament[10] (failing to put any deputies into the lower house). The largest sources of support for ZChN comes from the elderly and from the south-eastern (least developed and predominantly rural) part of Poland.

The Radical-Populists

Several significant parties with a radical-populist orientation share the mode of operation and system of beliefs of the extreme right, though they cannot be described properly as belonging to it.[11] Three parties with widely divergent backgrounds fall into this category: the Confederation for Independent Poland (*Konfederacja Polski Niepodleglej*, or KPN), Party X (*Partia 'X'*), and Self-defence (Samoobrona).

The populist, opportunistic, and maverick nature of the KPN defies easy labels.[12] The KPN combines nostalgic dreams of Poland as a great power with a paternalistic, corporatist vision of the state and with strong leadership. Founded in 1979, the KPN's genesis dates back to the nationalist anti-communist opposition circles in Poland in the 1970s. Portraying itself as an alternative to the communists and to Solidarity, KPN managed to attract a limited following during the 1980s. Since

1989, the KPN has used populist slogans, focusing on 'complete decommunization' (insisting that, throughout the post-1989 era, Poland has remained under the 'hidden hand' of the communists), a foreign policy aimed at establishing a counterweight to the EC by putting together a Polish-led bloc of central and east European states, and protectionism and opposition to a rapid transformation to a market economy but offering little more than sloganeering as an alternative. The KPN has evolved from a pro-church to an outright anti-clerical stance, and then back to a pro-church view. It has portrayed itself as a party 'above ideology,' claims that 'service to the nation' is its only motive, and proudly traces its roots to the pre-Second World War Pilsudskiite tradition (popular Polish leader who staged a coup in 1926 and imposed a conservative-authoritarian regime with a strong Presidency). The leader of the KPN, Leszek Moczulski, a journalist with a keen interest in military history, has maintained unchallenged control over the party since its founding. Although Moczulski's distant past includes anti-Semitic vitriolics, the party has largely abstained from such appeals during the past few years. In disruptive outbursts in the parliament, KPN MPs have variously labelled the post-Solidarity governments lackeys of Western bankers, German irredentists, or Russian imperialists, depending on the occasion. On many occasions Moczulski has threatened 'unconventional' or 'revolutionary' actions.

The KPN has a strong party organization and it has achieved considerable success in both of the fully competitive parliamentary elections. In 1991, the KPN garnered 7.50 per cent of the popular vote for the lower house of parliament (and, with the clever use of obscure election regulations, managed to raise the KPN bloc of MPs to 51, the third largest grouping in the lower house). In the 1993 elections, the KPN received 5.77 per cent of the vote to the lower house (giving it 22 seats in the lower house).

In contrast to the anti-communist roots of the KPN, Party X and Self-defence have strong nationalist-communist backgrounds in their leaderships. They employ purely demagogic activist appeals, usually centring on conspiracy theories with supposed attempts by outsiders (international Jewish conspiracy, IMF, the World Bank, Germans, communists, liberals, or any combination of the above), and they are prone to outright bizarre pronouncements that stray well beyond the rational. Their appeal is to the most disaffected in society.

Party X came onto the Polish political scene as a consequence of Stanislaw Tyminski's run for president during the 1990 elections. An emigré, with a shadowy past that included ties to the communist-era Polish secret police, Tyminski appeared in mid-1990 and finished second (with 23 per cent of the vote) in the first round of the presidential elections, beating the prime minister, Tadeusz Mazowiecki, and forcing a runoff with Lech Walesa. Building on his success in the elections, Tyminski founded his own party, Party X, in March 1991. He owed his success in the presidential elections to the exploitation of the dissatisfaction with the Balcerowicz programme of economic reforms, initiated at the beginning of 1990, designed to bring a market economy to Poland at a fast pace. It was this theme that he planned to exploit further. In fact, the party was initially going to be called the 'Party of Pain', so as to underline its opposition to the painful disruptions that came about as a result of the economic reforms. The party quickly built a national structure but it has fizzled since that time.

It is difficult to speak of a coherent set of views that the party represents; in fact, the party has served as little more than a vehicle for Tyminski's bizarre pronouncements. These include claims of having achieved a 'fourth dimension' of spirituality, boasts of experimenting with hallucinogenic drugs, and his supposed discovery of a 'cybernetic algorithm' that holds the secret to a Polish economic success. The membership of Party X includes a variety of figures associated with the communist regime, including members of the rabidly anti-Semitic Grunwald association. The Party has spoken out against the economic reform and privatization programme, vilifying it as a supposed Jewish conspiracy that aims to partition Poland again. In fact, conspiracy theories, usually centring on foreign attempts to rob Poland of its supposed riches, underlie most of Party X's statements. Although the party has staged loud protests and has been most of all a disruptive force, Tyminski and his party deserve the label of political cranks.

Party X received 0.47 per cent of the vote to the lower house in the 1991 parliamentary elections, which was enough to give it three deputies. The party has lacked cohesion, and has been prone to factionalism; the deputies elected in 1991 promptly joined other parties. In the 1993 parliamentary elections, the party received 377,408 votes, or 2.74 per cent of the vote to the lower house. Due to more stringent election rules, it failed to gain representation.

Self-defence appears to be a rural counterpart of Party X, combining its conspiracy theories and anti-Semitism with more violence and an emphasis on publicity-seeking disruptive behaviour. Self-defence was founded in 1992, by a former communist party member, Andrzej Lepper, as a movement to give political expression to indebted farmers who faced bankruptcy and foreclosure. The party quickly gained national prominence because of its methods. It organized roadblocks, occupied government buildings and, in its best known action that took place a few months before the 1993 elections, a group of Self-defence activists stormed a city hall in a small town in central Poland and manhandled the mayor. The most common activity of Self-defence has been its use of paramilitary activists to prevent banks from foreclosing on indebted farmers' property.

Self-defence is little more than a vigilante-style organization that has tried to channel the anger of farmers hurt by the economic reforms into political ends. It explains the initiation of the economic reforms in Poland in 1990 as an international conspiracy. Because it focuses on farmers' grievances, the party's greatest ire is directed at the EU, so as to exploit the resentment among hard-hit Polish farmers towards the EU restrictions on Polish agricultural imports. Just as with Party X, the membership of Self-defence includes nationalist figures associated with the communist regime, including Bohdan Poreba, the leader of the anti-Semitic Grunwald association, and Edward Kowalczyk, a former deputy prime minister in General Jaruzelski's martial law government in Poland in the early 1980s. The party openly advocates the breaking of the law and its appeals are meant to incite the people hurt by the economic reforms to violent activism. It justifies such advocacy because of the treason it accuses the political leadership of Poland since 1989. Its appeals clearly allude to Polish ultra-nationalism, including a heavy dose of anti-Semitism, and the sense of being wronged by ill-intentioned outsiders.

Self-defence received 383,967 votes, or 2.78 per cent of the vote to the lower house in the 1993 parliamentary elections. Running personally in Koszalin region (north-western Poland), Lepper was the single highest vote-getter in the district (13 per cent); at the time, the heavily rural region had the highest unemployment rate in all of Poland. The party failed to gain representation in the parliament but it has not faded completely from the scene. It continues to engage in violent demonstrations and intimidates local-level officials.

The Polish Extreme Right

Although the ideological underpinnings of the contemporary Polish extreme right fall squarely into the general outline of the central European extreme right presented earlier, the peculiarities of the extreme-right fringe in Poland revolve around the strong elements of insecurity in contemporary Polish ultra-nationalism about the survival of an independent Polish state. Anti-German feelings form the core of the xenophobic and paranoid beliefs. The anti-Russian and anti-Ukrainian feelings are moderated by pan-Slavic tendencies and they differ from the anti-German feelings because of perceptions of Polish superiority over the East Slavs. The 'recovery' of former Polish territory, currently part of Ukraine, Belarus, and Lithuania, complements such views, sometimes in the context of a 'Greater Poland' and emphasis on supposed Polish martial qualities. Ethnically based virulent anti-Semitism, with Jews portrayed as exploiters and tools of foreign oppression of ethnic Poles, forms a main component of Polish ultra-nationalism. Racist attitudes towards foreign students (Africans and Arabs) and anti-Roma perceptions stem from the general xenophobia and the struggle for 'purity' of the Polish 'nation'. The mythical vision of a harmonious, hierarchical Polish nation and the close relationship between a nativist version of Catholicism and Polish nationalism reinforce the distrust of the profit motive and the rejection of 'vulgar' capitalism. In a connection of several aspects of Polish ultra-nationalism, the extreme right sees the sale of land or industry to foreigners as tantamount to treason, and it identifies a Jewish or German conspiracy behind the influx of foreign capital into Poland. In the same way, Polish ultra-nationalists see Polish integration into West European supra-national institutions as a fundamental evil that aims to destroy the Polish state. An idealized image of Poland for the ultra-nationalists is a highly centralized, corporatist state.

A number of extreme right parties and organizations, almost all with a miniscule or non-existent membership, operate in Poland. Several organizations claim continuity with the National Democracy (*Endecja*) movement of Roman Dmowski (a nationalist, anti-Semitic, anti-German, clerical political organization that was a significant political force in Poland prior to the Second World War): the National Democratic Party (*Stronnictwo Narodowo-Demokratyczne*),[13] the National Party (*Stronnictwo Narodowe*), and the National Rebirth of Poland (*Narodowe Odrodzenie Polski*).[14] However, the two most successful movements that are likely to be heard from in the future and that exemplify the violent, ultra-nationalist extreme fringe in Poland are: the Polish National Commonwealth–Polish National Party (*Polska Wspolnota Narodowa–Polskie Stronnictwo Narodowe*, or PWN–PSN), and the Polish National Front (*Narodowy Front Polski*, or NFP).[15] Both movements appeal to neo-fascist sentiments and have relied on skinheads for a portion of their support.

In its current version, PWN–PSN resurfaced in December 1990.[16] In the parliamentary election in 1993, the party had trouble putting together enough signatures necessary for registration. It managed to run only in a handful of districts, winning 14,989 votes, or 0.11 per cent of the total vote. Under the leadership of Boleslaw Tejkowski, the party proclaimed itself as a nationalist movement unifying all Polish 'national' forces, and claiming common heritage with Roman Dmowski's National Democracy movement. The party claims to be for a 'national' Poland, where only 'Poles' would have political and economic rights, and where 'pure Polish' culture would flourish. It is difficult to speak of a coherent party platform since the PWN–PSN's ideas stray well into the irrational, but its views generally follow closely the outline given above. The party has insisted that a Jewish conspiracy, aiming to seize the alleged tremendous Polish wealth (in response to the privatization of Polish industry, Tejkowski has advocated nationalization with no compensation for all enterprises bought by foreign capital), has taken over Solidarity, the former communists (which it always supposedly controlled), and the Catholic Church. In a classic version of anti-Semitism without the Jews, the party claims that three million Jews remain in Poland, though they are 'hidden' Jews. The party has some pan-Slavic tendencies, in that it is most open to co-operation with other Slavic countries while fearing closer ties and integration with the West European countries (including a rejection of NATO membership). Skinheads and their sympathizers form the core of support for the party, a fact that adds a violent element to the party's demonstrations.

The party's poor showing is not due to a lack of awareness of it by the electorate. Extensive opinion polls in May 1992 showed that 24 per cent of the respondents had heard of the party. What comes across is a clear rejection of the party, with 60 per cent of those who have heard of it agreeing with the decision to prosecute Tejkowski.[17] Although it is the most important of the extreme-right Polish political movements, the PWN–PSN seems consigned to the lunatic fringe (literally, in view of Tejkowski's legal troubles and his court-ordered psychiatric examination). Tejkowski announced his intention to run in the 1995 presidential elections but the result probably will reconfirm the negligible support for Tejkowski's views among the Polish electorate.

The NFP had existed since March 1991 as a fringe organization relying on skinheads and devoted to the cause of a 'Greater Poland', militarism, statism, corporatist political structure, and deep hostility to all ethnic minorities. The party openly stood for the eradication of everything that is not 'national' in Poland, including the setting up of labour camps where politically suspect elements would be 're-educated' and the expulsion of the Roma. In the parliamentary election in 1993, the party had problems gaining enough support for registration; it ended up winning 565 votes, or 0.004 per cent of the total vote. However, the party gained a new lease on life with the defection of Janusz Bryczkowski in March 1994 from Self-defence (where he was one of the leaders of the organization) and his accession to the NFP's leadership position. Under Bryczkowski, the party has continued its xenophobic ways, putting greater focus on anti-Semitism (probably an indication of the membership of Bryczkowski during the communist era in the official 'patriotic', anti-Semitic Grunwald association). The NFP's pan-Slavic feelings were evident during the party's congress in March 1994, attended by Vladimir Zhirinovsky. With a shadowy past, links to the secret police during the communist era, favourable comments about the Nazi party, and a 'legion' of baseball bat-wielding skinheads for protection, Bryczkowski represents a strain of native fascism. The NFP seems to be competing for the same support base as the PWN–PSN. It also seems consigned to the same realm of insignificance as the PWN–PSN.

Conclusions

In both of the fully competitive Polish parliamentary elections, the extreme right made only a miniscule showing. Based on their dismal failure in the elections and consistently negligible standings in opinion polls, there is very little support for extreme-right movements in Poland, even though they do exist and they are vocal and noticeable well beyond their extremely limited base of support. The more important political phenomenon in post-communist Poland has been the appearance of several populist political movements that have some characteristics of the extreme right and which appeal to Polish nationalist themes shared more widely among the population, though their incoherent or absent party platforms make it impossible to include them in any easily definable political category.

The almost six per cent of the Polish electorate that voted for the Polish extreme-right and the radical populist political movements that share many ideas of the extreme right (Party X and Self-defence) in the 1993 parliamentary elections represents a fringe that seems impossible to integrate into the mainstream of the political life in Poland. The political movements of the extreme right and elements supportive of it have attempted to play on feelings of insecurity and to exploit the disruptions that came with the economic reform in Poland so as to mobilize support. And yet, despite unemployment levels of about 15 per cent nation-wide (and over 20 per cent in some especially hard-hit districts), the extreme right failed to convert the disenchantment and dissatisfaction into political gains in the 1993 elections. Since unemployment levels may have peaked and, in view of Poland's high economic growth rates, may soon start to come down, the appeals of the extreme right seem likely to meet with less success in the future.

Other populist forces (most of all, the KPN) and traditionalist-national-clerical elements (exemplified by the ZChN) use milder appeals that aim to exploit dissatisfaction or to allude to national-chauvinistic themes, respectively.[18] Support for those two forces came out to a little over 12 per cent in the 1993 elections. But support for them has varied substantially over the past 3–4 years. Opinion polls showed KPN receiving as much as 12 per cent support in 1992, though the party has hovered in the 4–6 per cent range since the 1993 elections. ZChN support also has varied considerably, from a high in the low teens to a low of 5–6 per cent. Some of the voters for both parties might be susceptible to voting for a charismatic extreme-right candidate who might emerge on to the Polish political scene in the near future.

The Czech Republic

A bloodless and rapid 'velvet revolution' drove the communist regime out of power in Czechoslovakia in a matter of days in November and December 1989. Elections in June 1990 brought about freely elected central and republican (Czech and Slovak) parliaments in Czechoslovakia. Czechoslovak local elections took place in November 1990. The June 1992 elections to the federal and republican parliaments demonstrated vividly the deep split between the Czech lands and Slovakia. In effect, the elections sealed the fate of the federation, since the diametrically opposed results in the Czech Republic and Slovakia caused a hopeless deadlock at the federal level and a clear mandate to pursue different policies at the republican level. The Czech Republic became an independent state at the beginning of 1993. With the federal parliament dissolved, the Czech republican parliament gained the status of a state-level legislature. Local-level elections in November 1994 have been the only elections held in the Czech Republic since the breakup of Czechoslovakia.

From the perspective of tracing the overall political preferences of the Czech electorate, the elections in 1992 provide the only completely accurate 'poll' of voters' preferences. The initial federal- and republican-level elections in 1990 had a fully competitive character but they had the form of a plebiscite on communist rule. As such, the initial elections played the role of a mechanism of regime transition. The parliamentary elections in 1992 amount to the first truly representative elections in Czechoslovakia in the post-communist period, because the electorate faced a wide range of options, rather than a simple pro- or anti-communist choice.

The Czech political party system has changed little since 1992. The electoral law governing the 1992 elections established proportional representation with a five per cent threshold level and limits on coalitions so as to block the fragmentation of the parliament. Eight parties entered the newly-constituted Czech Republic National Council (the Czech republican legislature).

The Czech party system that has emerged has a strong liberal-centrist and Christian-democrat middle, with a substantial socialist/communist and social-democratic left wing, and a weak but unified nationalist right. Social- and economic-based political cleavages predominate, though there are also strong regionalist- (Moravian-Silesian) and some religious-secular cleavages. A coalition of the civic- and Christian-oriented liberal (free market) parties has been in power since the 1992 elections. The Christian-democratic parties place greater emphasis on Christian teachings in their views on social issues than the purely civic liberal parties, but they recognize the division between church and state and they are similar in outlooks to Christian-democratic parties in Western Europe. The governing liberal-oriented coalition parties and independents were the main winners in the local elections, held in November 1994.

The Czech Extreme Right

The peculiarities of the contemporary Czech extreme right centre on anti-German sentiments and a xenophobia that scapegoats especially the Roma. There is some affinity with the Russians, stemming from a strong dose of pan-Slavic feeling. The extreme right sees the breakup of Czechoslovakia as deeply troublesome because it viewed Slovakia as a component of a Czech-dominated Czechoslovakia. The breakup has reduced the Czech Republic to a minor country, and exposed it to a supposed greater threat from Germany. Anti-Semitism exists but it is the Roma who are seen in a racist perspective as the main 'pollutant' of the Czech 'nation'. The vision of a homogeneous Czech nation also shows distrust of capitalism and it borrows elements of religious mysticism. The Czech extreme right has an understanding of sovereignty that is synonymous with self-sufficiency and autarky. It views the integration of the Czech Republic into West European supranational institutions as tantamount to a German takeover. A corporatist vision of the state underlies the idealized view of the Czech Republic.

While a number of openly racist organizations (including a Ku Klux Klan organization) and at least a dozen skinhead associations have emerged in the Czech Republic, there is only one significant political party that fits the extreme right label, namely, the Republican Party Association for the Republic (*Republikanska Strana – Sdruzeni pro Republiku*, or RS–SR), also known as the Republicans. After receiving 0.94–1.00 per cent of the vote in the transitional elections in June 1990, the party fared surprisingly well in the elections in 1992.[19] The RS–SR received 5.98 per cent of the vote in the republican elections. The vote for RS–SR was even greater to the federal-level bicameral parliament, ranging from 6.37 per cent for the lower house to 6.48 per cent for the upper house. The strong vote raised it above the required five per cent threshold for representation and placed 14 RS-SR deputies in the 200-member Czech National Council (currently a unicameral parliament). The party has been prone to factionalism. Despite the lack of new parliamentary elections, intra-party splits resulted in only six deputies remaining in the RS–SR by late 1994.

The leader of the RS–SR, Miroslav Sladek, a low-level functionary in the censorship office under the communist regime, has retained a tight grip on the party since its formation in December 1989. Sladek remains the unchallenged charismatic leader of the party with little apparent threat to his position. Periodic intra-party rumblings usually lead to some other higher party officials leaving the party or being expelled.

The RS–SR evokes strong parallels with the German *Republikaners*, although its anti-German perceptions constrain it from showing its sympathies openly. The RS–SR combines dreams of a greater Czechoslovakia with an 'ethnically pure' (limiting it to the various Slavic groups) paternalistic and corporatist state. Sladek has claimed that the party represents a continuation of the pre-Second World War Agrarian Party,[20] a mainstream political organization that glorified the peasantry and the 'simple life', and which turned towards authoritarianism in the late 1930s. The party has a secular orientation though it claims to sympathize with religious organizations.

The RS–SR has used populist and outright racist slogans to mobilize support, accompanied by publicity-seeking demonstrations and meetings, some of which have dissolved into anti-Roma violence.[21] Sladek's speeches clearly aim to whip up racist and chauvinistic feelings and he has, on occasion, called for his supporters to arm themselves for their demonstrations. The party's spokesmen openly call for the 'resettlement' of the Roma, identifying them as criminals and as lazy people living off welfare.[22] Anti-Semitic comments and, in the initial post-1989 period, calls for the expulsion of the Vietnamese and Cuban guest workers, have also surfaced in the party's declarations. As the Czech skinheads' violent attacks on the Roma became a widespread phenomenon in 1990, Sladek attempted to co-opt them into the party, publicly defending the skinheads on a number of occasions. However, by 1991, Sladek distanced himself from the skinheads having found it impossible to organize them.

The party had opposed vehemently the division of Czechoslovakia, even initiating criminal proceedings against the Czech prime minister, Vaclav Klaus, on the charges of treason for engineering the split of the country. The RS–SR remains unreconciled to the breakup, calling for the 'reunification' of the country even though opinion polls show widespread acceptance of the split in both the Czech lands and Slovakia. In order to underline its commitment towards that end, the RS–SR set up a Republican party in Slovakia in 1994.[23] On a downright bizarre Czechoslovak nationalistic note, the RS–SR emerged as the only group publicly calling for the 'return' of the Transcarpathian *oblast* (county-level region) in Ukraine to Czechoslovakia. Annexed by the USSR in 1945, the Ruthenian-inhabited region had belonged to Czechoslovakia in the period between the two world wars.

The RS–SR is openly anti-German and it has tried to exploit popular-level fears of German investment in the Czech Republic as supposedly leading to renewed domination by Germany. Associated issues, such as the Czech–German controversy over apologies and compensation to the Sudeten Germans expelled from Czechoslovakia after the Second World War,[24] have provided another populist issue for the party, with Sladek accusing the Czechoslovak and then the Czech government of betrayal and of selling off Czech lands to the Germans. The party's stance has evolved to embrace pan-Slavic themes. In March 1994, one of the highest-ranking RS–SR officials met the Russian extremist, Vladimir Zhirinovsky, at the congress of the Polish National Front in Warsaw.

The RS–SR's economic programme has been driven by populism. Initially, the party advocated a rapid path towards capitalism, with little state intervention in the economy. As unemployment and fears of economic changes grew in the Czech lands, the RS–SR modified its stance, eventually calling for a gradual programme of change, with a mixed economic system as the final result, and a massive spending programme to create jobs and improve the standard of living. The RS–SR has persisted with its view that the transition process is actually a plot to destroy the country and that, in any event, the country remains under the control of communists and their collaborators. In Sladek's view, every other party remains a tool of the communists, the Czechoslovak 'velvet revolution' was in fact engineered by the communists, and leaders such as Havel are 'crypto-communists'.

Sladek relishes controversy and attention. In fact, in a seemingly deliberate political strategy, he has tried to stage occasions that would lead to media coverage and increase his notoriety. His planting of a Czechoslovak flag in Mukachevo in Ukraine's Transcarpathian region, his venomous and racist speeches at public meetings, combined with his denunciations of every other politician and political party in Czechoslovakia as traitors all add up to actions of a political crank. However, Sladek's tactics have some appeal to the disaffected and cynically-disposed and they serve to undermine the legitimacy of the system as a whole. The party's support comes predominantly from young urban males in Bohemia's smaller cities (which have been the economically hardest-hit areas during the transition process from communism). The regionalist Moravian–Silesian movements siphoned off some of the protest vote in Moravia. Widening the base of support will probably be difficult for Sladek to accomplish.

The only other significant political force in the Czech Republic with some affinity for the extreme right is one strand of the regionalist Moravian–Silesian movement. Several Moravian–Silesian political movements exist and they are represented in the Czech parliament, though their importance has decreased over the past three years. Their demands also have changed, from a strong initial drive for autonomy to pressing for a greater regionalist voice. One political movement exceeded those bounds and adopted an uncompromising autonomist-nationalist agenda: the Moravian National Party (*Moravska Narodni Strana*, or MNS).[25] Initially, the party was represented in the parliament (as part of a larger coalition of Moravian–Silesian regionalists) but the deputies left the party in April 1994. The party's future is uncertain, especially in view of the decline in support for Moravian–Silesian radicalism. The presence of the MNS and other minor radical Moravian–Silesian movements notwithstanding, the primary extreme-right movement throughout the Czech Republic is RS–SR.

Conclusions

The populist-extreme right clearly has struck a responsive chord with a small but noticeable portion of the Czech electorate. Its support has remained relatively steady, hovering between 4–5 per cent in opinion polls since the 1992 elections. More than any other party, the RS–SR occupies the position of an ultimate protest group. However, the party's clear anti-Roma views, xenophobia, and its paranoid anti-German positions appeal to more widely-shared sentiments and broaden its appeal beyond just the unemployed and the disaffected.[26] The party's tactics also have brought it high negative ratings, seemingly establishing a low ceiling for the level of its support. In addition, the RS–SR's antics are a source of embarrassment to most Czech politicians, and other parties have refused to have anything to do with the RS–SR, thus marginalizing it within the parliament.

Slovakia

Slovak politics took a different turn from Czech politics almost immediately after the 'velvet revolution' in 1989. While the issue of the most rapid progress toward a Western-style liberal state emerged foremost in the Czech lands, the issue of Slovakia's status within Czechoslovakia soon became dominant in the eastern part of the country, and it subsumed discussions over economic policies. In contrast to the more fragmented Czech parliament, the Slovak National Council emerged from the June 1992 elections with only five parties represented and with the former Premier Vladimir Meciar's Movement for a Democratic Slovakia (*Hnutie za Demokraticke Slovensko*, or HZDS) commanding almost a half of the votes in the Slovak parliament.[27] Reflecting the dominant issue in Slovakia, during the campaign prior to the 1992 elections, almost all Slovak political groupings of any importance advocated a greater degree of independence for Slovakia, with differences between them centring on the level of autonomy sought. A few parties, the most important of which was the Slovak National Party (*Slovenska Narodna Strana*, or SNS) embraced a clearly secessionist platform, tying all of Slovakia's problems to the republic's supposed inferior and discriminate status in the federation.

The single issue that dominated Slovak politics in 1990–92 disappeared as Slovakia became independent at the beginning of 1993. With the federal parliament dissolved, the Slovak republican parliament gained the status of a state-level legislature. Meciar's movement began to lose its cohesiveness soon after the achievement of Slovakia's independence. The splintering of the HZDS led to the ouster of the Meciar government in March 1994 and a short-lived liberal–socialist coalition coming to power. However, elections at the end of September 1994 gave the HZDS a plurality of the votes, leading to the formation of a coalition government again led by Meciar and with the participation of SNS and a communist-style, populist, 'workers' party, the Association of Slovak Workers (*Zdruzenie Robotnikov Slovenska*, or ZRS). The parliamentary elections in September 1994 represented the first Slovak elections where preferences were no longer skewed by the sovereignty issue.[28] Local-level elections in November 1994 for the most part reflected the results of the parliamentary elections.

Seven parties or movements entered the Slovak National Council as a result of the 1994 elections, up from a total of five following the 1992 elections. The Slovak party system is still in a formative stage: it has an amorphous quality, is complicated by multidimensional cleavages, and 'charismatic' politics dominate. The overriding link between the three parties in the governing coalition is populism, statism, and nationalism. An ideologically-undefined populist-nationalist movement (HZDS) is the dominant political force, controlling two-fifths of the parliament and having received about a third of the popular vote. About one-fifth of the deputies belong to the left wing, consisting of a socialist/social-democratic coalition. Liberal and Christian-democratic parties combine for another one-fifth of the parliament. An ethnically oriented Hungarian political coalition amounts to about a tenth of the MPs. A nationalist party with extremist tendencies, the SNS, rounds out the Slovak political parties represented in the parliament.

Meciar's HZDS clearly exploited Slovak nationalist themes in its quest for political power. At times, especially on questions concerning Hungary or ethnic Hungarians, the HZDS embraced what amounted to ethnic exclusivist positions. However, the HZDS is too much of an amorphous grouping to be considered as anything but a populist mass movement subject to further splintering. The 'mainstream' Slovak parties (the socialist coalition and the Christian-democrats) also engaged in appeals to Slovak nationalism, but at a much less limited level. Though none of these parties fits the chauvinistic extreme right category, their appeals may end up strengthening the extreme right.

The Slovak Extreme Right

While the ideological outlines of the contemporary Slovak extreme right fit well within the bounds of the general central European extreme right, the peculiarities of the Slovak extreme-right fringe centre on the paranoia about safeguarding the newly-won independence of the Slovak state. The paranoia is focused primarily on Hungary, which is perceived as an 'ancient enemy' bent on subjugating the Slovaks. The Slovak extreme right has a strong dose of pan-Slavic views, which also has a flip-side in its suspicion of supposed German designs on Slovakia. There is also distrust and resentment of the Czechs, based on feelings that the Czechs exploited Slovakia for decades. The large ethnic Hungarian minority in southern Slovakia is viewed by the Slovak extreme right as a 'fifth column', bent on destroying the Slovak state from within, as part of a larger Hungarian plot. Deep anti-Semitism, both religious- and ethnic-based, pervades the views of the Slovak extreme right, while the

Roma are seen in a racist perspective as a 'pollutant' and a threat to the Slovak 'nation'. The Slovak extreme right distrusts capitalism, is heavily paternalistic, and has a thoroughly corporatist ideal of the Slovak state and nation. The usual suspicion of supranational institutions common to the extreme right is strengthened in Slovakia because of the relatively new phenomenon of the establishment of a Slovak state and the continuing deep insecurity over its survival.

A large number of extreme-right movements and organizations emerged in Slovakia after 1990. Their strength peaked at about the time of the watershed elections in 1992 and it has decreased markedly since that time, though the overall level of political discourse has moved towards a greater acceptance of Slovak nationalist themes. The changing fortunes of the Slovak extreme right are illustrated by the vote it received in the 1992 and the 1994 elections. In the 1992 elections, the six extreme-right parties[29] together gathered 11.88 per cent of the total vote to the Slovak National Council, with only the SNS crossing the five per cent threshold necessary to win representation. In the 1994 elections, the two extreme right coalitions together won 7.45 per cent of the vote,[30] again with only the SNS gaining representation.

The most obvious explanation for the reduced support for the extreme-right parties is that these were single issue movements (Slovak independence) and when that issue went away they were left without their main basis for appeal. The two extreme-right groupings that took part in the 1994 elections were: the SNS, and the Christian Social Union (*Krestanska Socialna Unia*, or KSU). The Slovak People's Party put up candidates on the KSU list. A variety of extreme-right political movements that had run independently in the 1992 elections had disappeared from the political scene by 1994, having either merged with other parties, fallen apart, or failed to retain an active status.[31]

In addition to the extreme-right political parties, there are also a number of prominent outwardly non-political organizations that promote the views associated with the extreme right, the most important of which is the Slovak Motherland association (*Matica Slovenska*). The Slovak Motherland association has focused its activities in the cultural realm and the promotion of Slovak language and culture. It has strong anti-Hungarian sentiments and its public statements are generally in line with the views of the Slovak political parties of the extreme right. Another group, the Jozef Tiso Association, is a historical group dedicated to the rehabilitation of the Slovak state that was established under the auspices of the German Nazi regime in 1939 and that state's leader, Jozef Tiso (executed as a war criminal after the Second World War). Members of the Jozef Tiso Association generally sympathize with the Slovak People's Party (the party in contemporary Slovakia claiming continuity with Jozef Tiso's party). Its membership has neo-fascist sympathies.

The SNS has gone through substantial changes since its founding in 1989, starting off on a secessionist and nationalist stance, moderating its policies and tactics in 1991–92, and veering off into almost a respectable status as a conservative-oriented political movement in 1993, before splintering and embracing an extreme-right orientation in 1994. Because of its adaptability and populism, the SNS defies easy labels. However, the split within the party in late 1993 ended the attempt to transform the SNS into a conservative Western-style liberal party and elevated to power the ultra-nationalist elements within the movement. Despite the internal shift, SNS spokesmen have resisted the extremist label. In addition, since the SNS entered into the three-party coalition government in December 1994, SNS spokesmen have had to moderate their public comments lest they cause a crisis for the government. Nevertheless, the views of the SNS, especially in its post-February 1994 stage, match closely the central European extreme right checklist.

The SNS emerged in December 1989 (though the party officially registered in March 1990), claiming continuation with the pre-Second World War movement by the same name that had pressed for Slovak autonomy and independence and some of whose members had played an important role in the German Nazi wartime puppet state of Slovakia. The quick seizure of the 'national question' by the SNS in 1990 gave it some prominence and elevated it to electoral success in the June 1990 federal and republican elections (garnering 10.96–13.94 per cent of the vote in Slovakia) and entering the central and republican legislatures.

The first SNS chairman, Vitazoslav Moric, promoted confrontational tactics. Blaming all of Slovakia's ills exclusively on the Czechs, he appealed to Slovaks not to follow the laws of the Slovak parliament (he viewed the parliament as illegitimate – a tool of Czech domination of Slovakia), pressed for a discriminatory Slovak language law, and openly defended Jozef Tiso (leader of the Slovak Nazi puppet state during the Second World War). Moric's occasional xenophobic outbursts against the Hungarians, Czechs, and Jews, brought charges of fascism against the party and censure by the Slovak parliament. The SNS also organized some of the first anti-Hungarian demonstrations and rallies in post-1989 Slovakia. The involvement of SNS activists in violent incidents gave the party some notoriety.

The SNS fared poorly in the local-level elections in November 1990, receiving only 3.2 per cent of the vote. The electoral débâcle brought into the open a rift between the moderate and extremist strains within the party and led to the election of Jozef Prokes as chairman of the SNS in March 1991. The leadership change marked a shift in the tactics of the SNS towards less confrontation. Prokes affirmed the SNS's resolve to honour the democratic process, abandoned the idea of achieving Slovakia's independence at any cost, and called for an end to the violence that sometimes accompanied the SNS rallies. The SNS assumed the role of a non-constructive opposition, probably assisting in shifting public opinion towards secessionist sentiments by obstructing any progress in the Czech-Slovak talks over the set-up of the state and by continuously blaming the mounting Slovak economic problems on the Czechs. The shift in tactics did not mean the abandonment of basic goals. The SNS fully supported the Declaration of Slovak Sovereignty in March 1991, put together by several Slovak nationalist groupings.

The SNS's less combative tactics appear to have regained it some popularity in the June 1992 parliamentary and republican elections, though the gains were overshadowed by Meciar's clear victory. The complementary nature of the views of Meciar's movement and the SNS led to collaboration between the two political forces. However, the SNS was always deeply split about the wisdom of co-operating with Meciar. When the SNS agreed to participate formally in a coalition government with the HZDS in October 1993, the party splintered. Ludovit Cernak, the chairman of the SNS since 1992, and six SNS deputies left the party and formed the National Democratic Party in February 1994. Cernak's departure represented a victory for the ultra-nationalist elements within the SNS and spelled the end of the effort to transform the SNS into a liberal conservative-oriented party.

The SNS chairman since February 1994, Jan Slota, has taken the party fully into the extreme-right category. Under Slota, the SNS has stressed the 'national principle' for Slovakia, which in practice translates into ethnic exclusivism and policies aimed at a rapid assimilation of the ethnic Hungarian minority. Claiming that ethnic Slovaks face discrimination in their own state, the SNS has advocated far-reaching anti-Hungarian policies. SNS spokesmen have accused the ethnic Hungarians of attempting to destroy Slovakia and called for the outlawing of ethnic Hungarian political parties in Slovakia as well as the banning of any displays of Hungarian symbols. The SNS has clear anti-Semitic tendencies, with allusions to an international Jewish conspiracy against Slovakia sometimes creeping into public statements by party spokesmen. In mid-1994, in a well-publicized incident, the SNS newspaper published Nazi symbols (swastikas) and the party has consistently portrayed the Second World War-era Slovak Nazi puppet state in a positive light. Stemming from a basic xenophobia, there is a conspiratorial aspect to SNS explanations for Slovakia's problems, with communists, a supposed international Jewish conspiracy, Czech 'exploiters', Roma criminals, or Hungarian irredentists as the culprits.

The SNS has strong pan-Slavic views, which come across mainly in the form of Russophile tendencies. Deputy chairman of the SNS, Juraj Molnar, attended Zhirinovsky's party congress in Moscow in April 1994. Other SNS leaders, including the chairman, Jan Slota, also have evaluated Zhirinovsky in a positive light, and SNS publications promote the idea of pan-Slavism (with an East Slav orientation). For his part, Zhirinovsky has spoken fondly of Slovakia, once even promising to make Bratislava the capital of his planned Slavic East European Union.

Showing a preoccupation with the security of Slovakia's borders and often referring to a Hungarian 'threat', the SNS has consistently been interested in military matters, and, since independence, has called for the strengthening of the Slovak armed forces. The interest in military issues warrants a more detailed discussion since SNS representatives received the posts of defence and education ministers in the Meciar-led government formed in December 1994. Putting a SNS member in charge of the Ministry of Education means a difficult time for Hungarian language instruction in schools in Slovakia and it represents the beginning of an attempt to 'educate' Slovak youth with far-reaching Slovak nationalist ideas. But the SNS control of the Ministry of Defence entails an even greater danger of Slovak ultra-nationalist ideas becoming dominant in the military.

The SNS was always distrustful of Czechoslovak institutions, considering them tools of Czech domination, and the Czechoslovak military was no exception. The SNS initiated the spread of direct ethnic tensions to the Czechoslovak military in October 1990, when it called for the formation of two armies in Czechoslovakia (one Czech, one Slovak) and appealed to Slovaks in the military to form their own organization. Heeding the call, the Association of Slovak Soldiers (*Associace Slovenskych Vojakov*, or ASV), a chauvinistic nationalist organization, emerged. The ASV issued a steady stream of venomous complaints about the alleged ethnic discrimination in the Czechoslovak military and it subverted the normal functioning of the Czechoslovak armed forces.[32] One of the most notorious spokesmen of the ASV was elected to the federal parliament on the SNS list in the June 1992 elections. The ASV has continued in existence in independent Slovakia. At first it attempted to intimidate ethnic Slovak soldiers who had been stationed in the Czech lands so as to prevent them from returning to

Slovakia (because they saw such personnel as 'polluted' by federalist ideas). In the 1994 elections, the SNS electoral list also included a representative of the ASV.

The entry of the SNS into a coalition government with the HZDS in December 1994 entailed the granting of the long-sought post of the defence minister to the SNS. Exemplifying anti-Hungarian feelings and pro-Russian sympathies, the new defence minister, Jan Sitek, has attempted to put the SNS agenda into practice. Sitek has freely acknowledged his close ties with the ASV and has stressed the improvement of 'patriotic education' for conscripts in the armed forces. In practice, the stress on education amounts to the strengthening of chauvinistic Slovak nationalism permeating the Slovak military. The institutionalization of such outlooks in the military may become a long-term problem. In addition, a Slovak military permeated by ASV/SNS influence seems unlikely to shirk from a loosely-interpreted internal security role in case of any outbreak of disturbances in the heavily Hungarian-inhabited southern Slovakia.

The greater SNS voice also has implications for Slovakia's defence industry. The chairman of Armex, the government-owned Slovak arms trading company, is Vitazoslav Moric, the first chairman of the SNS. In late 1994, Moric announced plans for increased Slovak arms sales to several developing countries. The more nationalistically inclined Slovak political figures always saw the Slovak defence industry as a source of prestige and strength for Slovakia and they have been chagrined at the industry's decline. The industry has shrunk to only a fraction of its 1987 size, but the SNS preoccupation with defence issues may lead to an attempt to revive it. It is in the sense of sales of Slovak arms to rogue regimes that the SNS influence in defence matters may become felt abroad.

The SNS did not have an economic programme to speak of for the first two years of its existence. Its economic pronouncements consisted of populism and laying blame for everything imaginable on Slovakia's supposedly subservient status in the federation and insisting that the Czechs engaged in a continuous robbery of Slovakia's resources. When finally drafted in 1992, the SNS economic policy programme called for increasing employment, protectionism, and a mixed system. Slota's SNS returned to these themes in the 1994 elections, modified with the populist call of cutting taxes by a quarter. The SNS vehemently opposes the sale of land to foreigners and it is deeply distrustful of foreign investment. It accepts a paternalistic state role in the provision of welfare to the citizens. Although the SNS pays lip-service to the goals of entry into the EU and NATO because of its participation in the Meciar-led government, the SNS clearly distrusts any supranational organizations. Not only does it see the EU as an agent of destruction of Slovak sovereignty but it opposes vehemently even the creation of 'Euroregions' (cross-border local-level co-operation schemes) as back-door attempts to carve up Slovakia.

The success of the SNS in winning representation in three parliamentary elections suggests that it is not a temporary phenomenon. Indeed, the SNS has a wide base of support, with skilled workers, the intelligentsia, and youth all forming important sources of its strength. The SNS has attracted some of the protest vote of the unemployed in central Slovakia but, somewhat surprisingly, in all of the elections the SNS received its greatest number of votes in the Bratislava region, the intellectual centre of Slovakia and an important bellwether of political currents. The SNS has been successful despite four party chairmen, indicating enough institutional coherence to survive some serious internal bickering. Following the intra-party split in early 1994, its appeal decreased and polls indicate that the party hovers at about 4-5 per cent in the level of support. However, the party seems likely to become a long-term actor on the Slovak political scene.

In addition to the SNS, the KSU is the only other extreme right political party in Slovakia that has received more than just a miniscule measure of support in post-1989 elections. The party, led by Jan Klepac, emerged in March 1992 as a splinter group from the Christian Democratic Movement (KDH). The party came about because of the openly secessionist stance of some of the KDH members and their dissatisfaction with the dominant KDH line of a loose association with the Czech lands.[33] The KSU exemplifies a statist and collectivist orientation (perceived as 'leftist' by many KDH members) regarding the economy and the role of the individual in the society. Its views regarding the danger from Hungary border on the paranoid; party spokesmen have spoken out repeatedly against supposed smuggling of weapons to the ethnic Hungarians in Slovakia from Hungary by irredentists. In the 1994 elections, the neo-fascist Slovak People's Party (the party claiming continuity with the main political movement that ruled in the Second World War-era Slovak Nazi puppet state) placed candidates on the ballot together with the KSU. The KSU failed to win representation in both the 1992 and 1994 elections; in 1994, the KSU-led coalition won 2.05 per cent of the vote, with its greatest source of support coming from the economically-depressed central and eastern Slovakia. Its ability to remain a significant actor on the Slovak political scene is in doubt.

Conclusions

The Slovak extreme right has been successful in gaining representation in the state legislature and it currently has a voice in the government. The extreme right seized on the populist issue of sovereignty and it reached a high point in 1992, but its strength has decreased since that time. In independent Slovakia, the extreme right has taken up the issue of defending the state from supposed foreign (mainly Hungarian) threats against it, but it is uncertain whether that cause will allow it to win greater popularity in future elections. Nationalist-populist political movements, having some commonalities with the extreme right (in the sense of uniting interventionist economic views and nationalistic scapegoating but without the far-reaching chauvinism and the paranoid and sometimes violent edge associated with the extreme right), have been dominant in Slovakia for the last 3–4 years.

The success of the nationalist-populists and the respectable showing of the extreme right in Slovakia during the last two elections make it clear that a coherent political party system is still far off and that open appeals to chauvinism still carry a good deal of weight in Slovakia. As exemplified best by Meciar, Slovak politics are charismatic. The high unemployment rate (close to 15 per cent overall, and over 20 per cent in several localities), its structural nature, and dim prospects for improvement in the near-term mean that a large pool of voters will remain susceptible to populist and nationalistic appeals.

Hungary

The gradual transition from communist rule in Hungary led to the holding of competitive parliamentary elections in March and April 1990, the first fully competitive elections in the region since the 1940s. The elections had the hybrid role of a plebiscite on communist rule and the establishment of a new legislature under conditions of weak party formation. Local-level elections followed in October 1990. A few by-elections took place in 1992–93, but the next full parliamentary elections took place in May 1994, while other local-level elections followed in December 1994.

The Hungarian political party system has remained largely intact since 1990, with the same six parties gaining representation (five per cent threshold) in both elections. The mixed electoral system produced a clear victory in 1990 for the Hungarian Democratic Forum (*Magyar Demokrata Forum*, or MDF), a conservative nationalist-leaning coalition of anti-communist forces. Although the MDF received just under 25 per cent of the popular vote in the first round of voting, it ended up with a total of 165 seats (out of 386) in the parliament after the second round.[34] The MDF entered into a coalition with two other parties, the Independent Smallholders Party (Fuggetlen Kisgazda Part, or FKgP) and the Christian Democrats (KDNP) and, despite some fractionating within the parties, the ruling coalition held together until the 1994 elections. The socialists won a resounding victory in the 1994 elections, receiving 33 per cent of the vote and ending up with an outright majority in the parliament after the second round (54 per cent of the seats).[35] The socialists entered into a coalition government with one of the liberal parties.

The Hungarian party system that has emerged has a strong socialist left, a liberal-centrist middle, a conservative-clerical right, and a populist-nationalist right. The rightist groupings performed poorly in the 1994 elections but the results led to an effort to overcome the disunity on the right and the right seems likely to obtain a better result in the next elections. Social- and economic-based political cleavages dominate, though religious-secular and urban-rural splits, as well as generational issues also play a part.

The Radical-Populists

The FKgP has emerged as an important conservative-populist party. The FKgP takes its name from a pre-Second World War party that appealed to the economic interests of farmers and small businessmen but which also focused on the themes of social justice and national pride and had some extreme-right leanings. The FKgP won the 1945 elections but was then subverted by the communists. The party resurfaced in 1988. Initially, the reborn FKgP was a conservative party with traditionalist inclinations and pervasive anti-communist proclivities. The party appealed mainly to the farmers and made land restitution its central concern. It won 11.73 per cent of the vote in the 1990 elections, giving it 44 deputies in the parliament. Considerable intra-party conflicts were kept in check until February 1992, when Jozsef Torgyan took *de facto* control of the party and left the governmental coalition. Although only nine deputies followed Torgyan, the leadership of the party and most of the rank and file supported him. Torgyan's party (renamed the Independent Smallholders and Civic Party) won nine per cent of the vote and gained 26 seats in the parliament in the 1994 elections. The non-Torgyan deputies never managed to organize a viable party.[36] The FKgP has a solid base of support in the Hungarian countryside.

The ideology underlying Torgyan's party is a deep distrust of communists and socialists and the belief that a change of regimes had never taken place. The FKgP also has focused on the issue of land ownership, exploiting the disappointment and disenchantment of Hungarian farmers with the manner of post-communist land restitution. Although references to 'real Hungarians' often creep into the party's statements, the FKgP has taken pains not to appear outwardly chauvinistic, and anti-Semitic statements have been absent from comments by FKgP spokesmen. The party has made the issue of the treatment of ethnic Hungarian minorities in the neighbouring countries a major theme in its platform, though party spokesmen have eschewed outright irredentist views. These seemingly conservative but respectable outlooks have been accompanied by the unofficial co-operation and sympathy of some members of the FKgP with the skinheads, their participation in other extreme-right organizations, and nationalist rhetoric and demagoguery. While not an extreme-right movement *per se*, the FKgP has used the symbols and discourse common to that of the extreme right. In the current parliament, Torgyan's party is the most nationalist-oriented grouping and it may gain strength as a result of its vitriolic opposition to the socialist-led government.

The Hungarian Extreme Right

The peculiarities of the contemporary Hungarian extreme right revolve around the strong sense of injustice regarding the fact that several million ethnic Hungarians live beyond Hungary's borders (a result of the 1920 Treaty of Trianon), mainly in Slovakia, Ukraine, Romania, and Serbia. The physical separation of so many ethnic Hungarians from the Hungarian state is seen by the extreme right as part of a plot to thwart the supposed natural genius of the Hungarian 'nation' from flourishing. In this sense, the 'recovery' of the historic (pre-First World War) Hungarian lands and the unification of the ethnic Hungarians with Hungary is seen as crucial. There is a deep sense of Hungarian ethnic distinctiveness (seen in racial-biological terms), complemented by strong xenophobic feelings towards all other ethnic groups, with an especially strong fear of being swallowed up in a 'sea of Slavs'. There are also strong perceptions of cultural superiority towards the neighbouring peoples, with the Romanians seen as the most inferior. The sense of superiority also translates into a Hungarian civilizing mission to the neighbouring nationalities and complements the view on 'unification' of all Hungarians in the Danube basin. Ethnically based virulent anti-Semitism, with Jews portrayed as tools of foreign interests and oppression, forms a central part of Hungarian ultra-nationalism. Racist attitudes towards non-Europeans and anti-Roma perceptions (with the Roma seen as a dangerous and genetically defective element within the Hungarian 'nation') form the other component of Hungarian xenophobia. Underlying the ideal of the extreme right is a vision of a harmonious Hungarian nation, perceived as some kind of a living entity of its own. A sense of social justice for all Hungarians permeates such views, resulting in distrust of capitalism. Often, there is also an idealized view of Hungarian peasant life, sometimes with a good dose of fundamentalist clerical sentiments. Hungarian ultra-nationalists see Hungarian integration into supranational institutions as another attempt to destroy the Hungarian 'nation'.

A considerable number of extreme-right parties and organizations has emerged in Hungary since 1988–89, most with a miniscule or small membership base. These organizations have an outright neo-Nazi orientation and a strong skinhead component, and they claim ideological continuity with Ferenc Szalasi's 1930s- and 1940s-era Arrow Cross movement. Three such movements (Istvan Gyorkos' Hungarian National Front, Albert Szabo's World National Popular Rule Party, and Kemal Ekrem's Alliance of the Victims of Communism) re-established the neo-fascist Hungarist Movement in April 1994. Other major neo-fascist movements that act as umbrella organizations for skinheads include the Independent National Youth Front (*Fuggetlen Nemzeti Ifjusagi Front*), the Holy Crown Society (*Szentkorona Tarsulat*), and the 1956 Anti-Fascist and Anti-Bolshevik Association (*1956-os Antifasiszta es Antibolseviszta Szovetseg*).[37] A previous MDF member, Izabella Kiraly, has been among the most outspoken defenders of the skinheads. She founded the Hungarian Interest Party in 1993 specifically to defend the 'national-spirited youngsters', as she refers to the skinheads. None of these organizations or parties has managed to attract more than a handful of supporters, though they have attracted a good deal of publicity through their violent demonstrations.

The above groupings notwithstanding, the most important figure on the Hungarian extreme right is a former deputy chairman of the MDF, Istvan Csurka. The MDF was founded in 1987 as an anti-communist coalition of three diverse political currents: the Christian-Democrats, the Populists, and the Liberals. Since even the three groupings were far from homogeneous, the MDF was always difficult to place ideologically. Some of the figures within the Populist faction, such as its leader, Csurka, professed clearly extreme nationalist views that bordered on the neo-fascist. Other prominent figures within the Populist faction had a staunch nationalist orientation without Csurka's extremist inclinations. The conflict between the factions came to a head in 1992–93 and led to the expulsion of Csurka and his closest associates from the MDF in May 1993.

In anticipation of an intra-party showdown, and trying to push the MDF towards his own extremist beliefs, Csurka established the Hungarian Path (*Magyar Ut*) discussion circles in February 1993. These circles had the function of bringing together a variety of extreme rightists and ultra-nationalists (from within and without the MDF). Some of Torgyan's supporters have joined the Hungarian Path circles. After being expelled from the MDF, Csurka set up his own party in June 1993, the Hungarian Justice and Life Party (MIEP).[38] Although not formally affiliated with the MIEP, the Hungarian Path circles bring forth the message of the MIEP to a wider audience. A total of 13 deputies joined the MIEP faction in the parliament. The MIEP was the most significant extreme right party on the ballot in the May 1994 elections, but it performed poorly, gaining only 1.59 per cent of the total vote and failing to win representation in the parliament. The failure stands in contrast to the success of Torgyan's FKgP.[39]

Csurka's leadership position in the MDF prior to 1993 stemmed from his dominant position within MDF's Populist faction. The name of the Populist faction derives from the affinity of its members with the populist writers of the 1930s and 1940s in Hungary, whose anti-modernization views tended towards the glorification of the Hungarian traditions, the rejection of outside influences (which included a dose of anti-Semitism), and the promotion of a paternalistic state that would serve the whole Hungarian 'nation'. Csurka, a playwright by profession, turned the populist views into one coherent xenophobic whole in his political treatise that was published in August 1992.[40] The manifesto did not mean a new stage of Csurka's political thinking; prior to its publication, Csurka did not conceal his views and, as a result, had already achieved notoriety and some popularity.

Csurka's beliefs correspond closely to the usual extreme-right views, though they are a peculiar mix of nativism and pre-rationalism. At the core of his beliefs lies an almost biological understanding of the Hungarian 'nation' as a living entity whose survival faces a number of threats. An international Jewish conspiracy generally underlies these threats, whether it comes in the form of communists or Western bankers. Csurka and his group believe that only they truly speak for the nation, asserting that the communists had infiltrated all other political forces in Hungary, including the Western-style liberal parties.

There is a strong dose of irredentism in Csurka's thinking. Without openly advocating a change of borders by force, Csurka has claimed that the Yalta agreement expires in 1995 and suggested that an opportunity existed to rectify the supposed historical injustices inflicted upon Hungary by the Treaty of Trianon, to regain the 'lost territories', and to unite all Hungarians with their nation. Csurka's use of the phrase 'living space' for Hungarians in his treatise translates uncomfortably into German as 'lebensraum' and it won him international notoriety. The irredentism of Csurka and his followers within the MDF became evident in May 1993 during the parliamentary debate on the ratification of the Ukrainian–Hungarian state treaty. Csurka objected to the treaty's clause on the mutual renunciation of territorial claims, since it dashed the hopes for 'reuniting' the ethnic Hungarian-inhabited Transcarpathian portion of Ukraine with Hungary.[41]

There is a profound collectivist vision of the nation in Csurka's views, evident in his acceptance of a paternalistic state that would care for the 'lower strata' of the population and which would pursue a 'third way' between capitalism and communism. The latter amounts to private ownership in a mixed economy that would serve the nation. Csurka's ideal government would have little tolerance for such pollutants of the Hungarian nation as consumerism. In addition, the government would reimpose law and order. Accusations of Jewish-organized conspiracies underlie the entire discourse. In addition to the strong anti-Semitic sentiments, Csurka alludes to the deterioration of the genetic pool by the Roma and implies that the time has come to be rid of them. Such comments have made Csurka the ideological leader for many of Hungary's skinheads.

Although Csurka clearly overstepped the bounds of permissible discourse and took intra-MDF squabbles to a new level through his use of nationalist appeals in a demagogic fashion, the MDF initially reacted mildly to the manifesto. The subdued response stemmed from the need to keep the party together, an exaggerated opinion about the level of support Csurka had within the MDF, and because some of the themes that Csurka touched on had resonance in the MDF as a whole (for example, the 'third way' option and the issue of ethnic Hungarians in the neighbouring countries). This is not to say that the MDF identified with Csurka's views but that the conservative-nationalist elements within the MDF agreed on the importance of the issues touched on by Csurka.[42]

Csurka's line of blaming the ills that have come with the transformation away from communism on incomplete 'decommunization' or on conspiracies by outside groups (Jews in Csurka's case) would seem to appeal to the disenchanted. And yet, in the May 1994 elections, the electorate spurned the extreme right and voted for the socialists. Rather surprisingly, Csurka's support was proportionately greater among the wealthier classes than among the workers. The expected support base for a party with neo-fascist views represented by Csurka failed to materialize. The drop of the unemployment rate in Hungary to just above ten per cent by late 1994, if sustained, probably will undercut further the ability of a party such as the MIEP to appeal to a wider electorate. However, the danger of a major devaluation of the Hungarian currency in 1995 and the consequent political problems could provide a lively injection of support for the extreme right.

Conclusions

The Hungarian extreme right had managed to gain some prominence as a result of having had a voice in the ruling MDF coalition between 1990–93. Its actions gained it a good deal of notoriety domestically and internationally but ultimately its appeal proved to be almost insignificant. A nativist radical-populist political movement, sharing some aspects with the extreme right was the only force on the right political fringe to have some success in the 1994 elections. The extreme right's popularity is likely to grow if the socialist-led government falters on economic issues.

Final Observations

Political pluralism in the aftermath of the collapse of the communist systems in central Europe has brought with it the emergence of political movements of the extreme right. These movements usually combine a mix of a pre-rational anti-modernist core and claims of continuity with native pre-Second World War authoritarian or neo-fascist movements,[43] while exploiting the far-reaching social and economic disruptions that have come as a result of economic reforms designed to put in place free market systems. The themes of a conspiracy or a plot by outside ill-intentioned forces are common to all of these movements. Most of them claim that the liberal political forces that came to power in the aftermath of the communists represent a sell-out of the true revolution, for, in their view, the ultra-nationalist extreme-right elements are the only true representatives of the 'nation' (only they know the true national path and key to national salvation) and any viewpoint contrary to theirs has no legitimate basis on which to govern. They see the return of former communists to power (in Hungary, Poland, and temporarily in Slovakia) as the final proof that nothing of political significance has changed in these countries over the past few years. The virulent anti-communism of these movements, inflated with paranoia, is paradoxical, since they share the statist views of the unreformed communists. None of the extreme-right movements have any great love for the developed Western democracies, distrusting supranational liberalism and fearful of consumerism.

All of these movements have a preoccupation with defence of the state from the supposed myriad threats to it, both internal and external. Ethnic minorities bear the brunt of their xenophobia, with Jews and especially the Roma[44] as the most common targets of exclusivist tendencies. Conversely, the extreme right mourns its ethnic brethren across the border as people deprived of the supposedly great privilege of living with their co-nationals. Since they are preoccupied with the defence of the state, most of the extreme-right forces have a deep interest in the military. All of the movements, almost by definition, have had some involvement in inciting violence, usually based on ethnic animosities. Skinheads often form a source of support for these groups.

The extreme right generally uses negative and populist appeals almost to the exclusion of having any real programmes for development and economic reform. However, the appeals so far have found little resonance, despite double-digit unemployment figures (except in the Czech Republic, where the low figures hide substantial underemployment). Progress in the economic transformation of these countries and the elimination of fears about the security of these states holds the keys to containing the evolution of the extreme right in the region, because only economic success can undercut the potentially wider sources of electoral support for the extreme right. Also, only then will a centrist-oriented stable political party system become fully established. Because of its new sovereign status and its relatively greater economic problems, Slovakia warrants the greatest attention regarding the growth of the extreme right.

The emergence of the extreme right in post-communist central Europe must be placed in a larger context. In conditions of no constraint on the right of assembly, political movements spanning the political spectrum are bound to appear. The discrediting of the communists in central Europe strengthened the rise of movements diametrically opposed to them and it should be no surprise that some national-oriented political movements initially gained a measure of support. Because of the structural nature of the economic disruptions and the likelihood that it will take many years to bring to the region a level of prosperity similar to that in the countries west of them (which are the benchmark for comparison), it is likely that the electorate will be highly volatile and political elections will result in constant seesawing between the socialists and the liberals. In such conditions, the extreme right might gain on the coat-tails of an anti-left swing.

The actual strength of the extreme right ranges from insignificant to minor in all four of the countries discussed here. However, in conditions of a party system still forming, fractionated parliaments, and weak coalition governments, these even minor movements can sometimes gain a voice in governing the country that is out of all proportion to their standing among the electorate (the success of the SNS in Slovakia is a case in point). In addition, a variety of populist parties impossible to place ideologically has sprung up and they have been more successful. These movements use some of the themes of the extreme right but they have a much broader appeal. They are dangerous to the democratization process, since they are disruptive, add little to a constructive political discourse, and only give credibility to the themes of the extreme right. The elections held so far show that the extreme-right movements in post-communist central Europe usually cannot breach the five per cent threshold necessary for representation. When they do, as in the case of the RS–SR or SNS, it is due to special circumstances. However, the radical-populist movements have scored much greater electoral successes, gaining representation in several legislatures.

Finally, the experience of a developing political party system and the emergence of fringe movements on the right in post-communist central Europe is worth comparing to the initial post-Second World War West European experience. In such a comparison, post-communist central Europe comes off quite well. The growing pains of democracy in West Germany (which had 12 parties in its first parliament and the real spectre of a powerful neo-Nazi party certainly existed) or the presence throughout the post-Second World War period of an outright fascist party (tracing its roots to Mussolini) in the Italian parliament are just two examples that come to mind.

Notes

1. Scholars of transitions to democracy in Latin America and southern Europe have noted the importance of this point. For some recent literature, see R.H. Dix, 'Democratization and the Institutionalization of Latin American Political Parties,' *Comparative Political Studies*, Jan. 1992, pp. 488–511; S. Mainwaring, 'Political Parties and Democratization in Brazil and the Southern Cone', *Comparative Politics*, Oct. 1988, pp. 91–120; G. Pridham, 'Political Actors, Linkages and Interactions: Democratic Consolidation in Southern Europe,' *West European Politics*, Oct. 1990, pp. 103–17.
2. Kitschelt's central argument is that the different political cleavages add up to an entirely different axis of political competition in the former communist states. The argument is insightful but not yet proven. H. Kitschelt, 'The Formation of Party Systems in East Central Europe', *Politics and Society*, March 1992, pp. 7–50.
3. The definition is my modification of the nine traits of extreme-right movements proposed by B. Hagtvet in 'Right-Wing Extremism in Europe', *Journal of Peace*

Research, Vol. 31, No. 3, 199, pp. 241–6.

4. For longer treatment of the specific countries' nationalism, see the classic but still useful work by P.F. Sugar and I.J. Lederer (eds), *Nationalism in Eastern Europe* (Seattle, University of Washington Press, 1969).

5. For analyses of the 1991 elections, see F. Millard, 'The Polish Parliamentary Elections of Oct. 1991,' *Soviet Studies*, Vol. 44, No. 5, 1992, pp. 837–55; L.L. Wade, A.J. Groth and P. Lavelle, 'Estimating Participation and Party Voting in Poland: The 1991 Parliamentary Elections in Poland,' *East European Politics and Societies*, Vol. 8, No. 1, Winter 1994, pp. 94-121; W. L. Webb, 'The Polish General Election of 1991', *Electoral Studies*, Vol. 11, No. 2, 1992, pp. 166–70. A group of Polish social scientists have put together a fine analysis of the elections, S. Gebethner and J. Raciborski (eds), *Wybory 91 a Polska Scena Polityczna* (Elections 91 and the Polish Political Scene) (Warsaw, University of Warsaw, 1992).

6. For an analysis of the 1993 elections, see F. Millard, 'The Polish Parliamentary Election of September, 1993', *Communist and Post-Communist Studies*, Vol. 27, No. 3, 1994, pp. 295–313; H. Tworzecki, 'The Polish Parliamentary Elections of 1993', *Electoral Studies*, Vol. 13, No. 2, 1994, pp. 180–5; L. Vinton, 'Poland's Political Spectrum on the Eve of the Elections,' RFE/RL Research Report, Vol. 2, No. 36, 10 Sept. 1993, pp. 1–16.

7. F. Millard, 'The Shaping of the Polish Party System, 1989–93,' *East European Politics and Societies*, Vol. 8, No. 3, Fall 1994, pp. 467–94; P.G. Lewis, 'Political Institutionalization and Party Development in Post-Communist Poland,' *Europe-Asia Studies*, Vol. 46, No. 5, 1994, pp. 779–99.

8. A. Sabbat-Swidlicka, 'Local Elections Redress Political Imbalance in Poland', *RFE/RL Research Report*, Vol. 3, No. 27, 8 July 1994, pp. 1–8.

9. Polish anti-Semitism is a controversial topic. For some recent, methodologically sound analyses of its extent, see H. Datner-Spiewak, 'A First Glance at the Results of the Survey 'Poles, Jews, and Other Ethnic Groups', *East European Jewish Affairs*, Vol. 23, No. 1, 1993, pp. 33–48; R. Cohen and J.L. Golub, *Attitudes toward Jews in Poland, Hungary, and Czechoslovakia: A Comparative Survey* (New York, 1991).

10. It should be noted, though, that the three smaller parties forming a coalition with ZChN were not nearly as conservative and traditional-minded as the ZChN. The Conservative Party (*Konserwatywna Partia*) especially was a liberal (free market-oriented) party with conservative social tendencies. The party joined in a coalition with ZChN out of tactical considerations. A. Sabbat-Swidlicka, 'The Polish Elections: the Church, the Right, and the Left', *RFE/RL Research Report*, Vol. 2, No. 40, 8 Oct. 1993, pp. 24–30.

11. For more detailed information about the movements described in this section, see L. Vinton, 'Outsider Parties and the Political Process in Poland', *RFE/RL Research Report*, Vol. 3, No. 3, 21 Jan. 1994, pp. 13–22; L. Vinton, 'Poland', *RFE/RL Research Report* (Special Issue, 'The Politics of Intolerance'), Vol. 3, No. 16, 22 April 1994, pp. 62–7.

12. For more information about the KPN, see L. Vinton, 'From the Margins to the Mainstream: The Confederation for an Independent Poland', *Report on Eastern Europe*, 15 Nov. 1991, pp. 20–4; T.S. Szayna, 'Ultra-Nationalism in Central Europe', *Orbis*, Vol. 37, No. 4, Fall 1993, pp. 527–50.

13. This party, founded with support from the emigré-based National Party (in London), managed to have a representative (Jan Zamoyski) elected to the upper house of the parliament in the 1991 elections. The success came more because of name recognition (old noble name) than support for the party platform. This party

claims to be in the same category as the Gaullist movement in France but, in fact, it is much more nationalist and statist.

14. For more information about these movements, see J. Bugajski, *Ethnic Politics in Eastern Europe: A Guide to Nationality Policies, Organizations, and Parties,* (Armonk, New York, 1994), pp. 376–9, A. Rok, 'Antisemitic Propaganda in Poland – Centres, Proponents, Publications', *East European Jewish Affairs,* Vol. 22, No. 1, pp. 23–37; Paul Hockenos, *Free to Hate: The Rise of the Right in Post-Communist Eastern Europe* (New York, Routledge, 1993) (the chapter on Poland, pp. 237–69).

15. For more information about the movements described in this section, see L. Vinton, 'Outsider Parties and the Political Process in Poland', *RFE/RL Research Report,* Vol. 3, No. 3, 21 Jan. 1994, pp. 13–22; L. Vinton, 'Poland', *RFE/RL Research Report* (Special Issue, 'The Politics of Intolerance'), Vol. 3, No. 16, 22 April 1994, pp. 62–7; W. Oschlies, 'Rechtsradikalismus im postkommunistischen Osteuropa; Teil 1: Fallstudien' (Right-Wing Radicalism in Post-communist Eastern Europe; Part 1: Case Studies), *Bundesinstitut für ostwissenschaftliche und internationale Studien,* No. 29, 1992.

16. The party was founded in 1955 but was dormant for several decades.

17. H. Datner-Spiewak, 'A First Glance at the Results of the Survey 'Poles, Jews, and Other Ethnic Groups,'' *East European Jewish Affairs,* Vol. 23, No. 1, 1993, p. 47.

18. The two parties appeal to very different voters. M. Cline, 'The Demographics of Party Support in Poland,' *RFE/RL Research Report,* Vol. 2, No. 36, 10 Sept. 1993, pp. 17–21.

19. For an analysis of the elections, see J. Obrman, 'The Czechoslovak Elections', *RFE/RL Research Report,* 26 June 1992, pp. 12–19; G. Wightman, 'The Czechoslovak Parliamentary Elections of 1992', *Electoral Studies,* Vol. 12, No. 1, 1993, pp. 83–6.

20. Indeed, the very name of RS–SR alludes to the full name of the Agrarian Party: the Republican Party of Agriculturists and Small Peasants.

21. For more information, see J. Pehe, 'The Emergence of Right-Wing Extremism', *Report on Eastern Europe,* 28 June 1991, pp. 1– 6; J. Pehe, 'The Czech Republic', *RFE/RL Research Report* (Special Issue, 'The Politics of Intolerance'), Vol. 3, No. 16, 22 April 1994, pp. 50–4; W. Oschlies, 'Rechtsradikalismus im postkommunistischen Osteuropa; Teil 1: Fallstudien' (Right-Wing Radicalism in Post-communist Eastern Europe; Part 1: Case Studies), *Bundesinstitut für ostwissenschaftliche und internationale Studien,* No. 29, 1992; P. Hockenos, *Free to Hate: The Rise of the Right in Post-Communist Eastern Europe,* (New York, Routledge, 1993) (the chapter on the Czech Republic, pp. 209–31).

22. In this sense, the antics of the RS–SR strike a popular chord. The Czech citizenship law, passed in 1994, deprived some 75,000 Roma of their claim to be citizens of the Czech Republic on the justification that they had no fixed address. The law exploited the nomadic style of some of the Roma and it showed the prevalence of anti-Roma feelings in the country (including among the mainstream parties).

23. To stress its commitment to Czechoslovakia, the RS–SR made it a special point to campaign in both republics of the federation prior to the June 1992 elections. However, the party had virtually no appeal to Slovaks and it garnered only 0.32–0.36 per cent of the vote in Slovakia, showing the Czech rather than the federal nature of the party. The success of the Republican party in Slovakia is unlikely, since opinion polls and surveys point to an overwhelming acceptance of the division of Czechoslovakia as final in both successor states. S. Fisher, 'Czech–Slovak Relations Two Years after the Elections', *RFE/RL Research*

Report, Vol. 3, No. 27, 8 July 1994, pp. 9–17.

24. J. Obrman, 'Sudeten Germans Controversy in the Czech Republic', *RFE/RL Research Report*, Vol. 3, No. 2, 14 Jan. 1994, pp. 9–16; P. Bren, 'Czech Restitutional Laws Rekindles Sudeten Germans' Grievances,' *RFE/RL Research Report*, Vol. 3, No. 2, 14 Jan. 1994, pp. 17–22.

25. For more information about the Moravian–Silesian movements, see J. Bugajski, *Ethnic Politics in Eastern Europe: A Guide to Nationality Policies, Organizations, and Parties* (Armonk, New York, 1994), pp. 306–10.

26. The relative prosperity of the Czech Republic, as compared to the post-communist Balkan states or the successor states of the USSR have led to a considerable influx of immigrants from those states into the Czech Republic. The growing number of crimes committed by such immigrants has emerged as a political issue in the Czech Republic and it may translate into greater support for the xenophobic forces, such as the RS–SR. Czech figures have shown a steadily increasing number of attacks against the Roma and foreigners in the Czech Republic.

27. For an analysis of the elections, see J. Obrman, 'The Czechoslovak Elections', *RFE/RL Research Report*, 26 June 1992, pp. 12–19; G. Wightman, 'The Czechoslovak Parliamentary Elections of 1992', *Electoral Studies*, Vol. 12, No. 1, 1993, pp. 83–6.

28. For an analysis of the elections, see S. Fisher, 'Uncertainty in Slovakia after the Elections', *Societies in Transition*, 15 Nov. 1994, pp. 11–17.

29. These parties and the per cent of the vote they received for the Slovak National Council were: the SNS (7.93 per cent), the Slovak Christian Democratic Movement (3.05 per cent), the Party of Freedom and Party of National Unity (0.30 per cent), the Slovak People's Party (0.29 per cent), the Slovak Liberation Movement (0.23 per cent), and the National Liberal Party (0.08 per cent).

30. The Slovak sister party of the Czech SR–RC, the Assembly for the Republicans (*Zdruzenie pre Republiku–Republikani*, or ZpRR) was also listed on the ballot and it won 0.04 per cent of the vote, lifting the total extreme right vote to 7.49 per cent. The ZpRR has no appeal in Slovakia; it was founded by Sladek to emphasize his commitment to a Czechoslovakia rather than to participate seriously in the Slovak electoral process. The leader of the ZpRR, Jozef Horvath, has pursued a very different line from Sladek, eschewing radical statements.

31. For more information about the movements described in this section, see J. Bugajski, *Ethnic Politics in Eastern Europe: A Guide to Nationality Policies, Organizations, and Parties*, (Armonk, New York, 1994), pp. 336–40; S. Fisher, 'Slovakia', *RFE/RL Research Report* (Special Issue, 'The Politics of Intolerance'), Vol. 3, No. 16, 22 April 1994, pp. 68–71.

32. For a lengthier elaboration on the ASV, see T.S. Szayna, *The Military in a Postcommunist Czechoslovakia*, (N-3412-USDP, RAND, 1992), especially pp. 72–9.

33. Klepac's militant stance on the issue of Slovak sovereignty was clear long before the formal fractionating of the KDH. In July 1991 Klepac called for the formation of a Slovak Home Guard, in effect trying to set up a Slovak-controlled military.

34. There have been a number of English-language analyses of the elections; B. Racz, 'Political Pluralisation in Hungary: the 1990 Elections', *Soviet Studies*, Vol. 43, No. 1, 1991, pp. 107–36; K.C. Martis, 'The Geography of the 1990 Hungarian Parliamentary Elections', *Political Geography*, May 1992, pp. 283–305; J.R. Hibbing and S.C. Patterson, 'A Democratic Legislature in the Making: the Historic Hungarian Elections of 1990', *Comparative Political Studies*, Jan. 1992, pp. 430–54.

35. E. Oltay, 'The Former Communists' Election Victory in Hungary', *RFE/RL*

Research Report, Vol. 3, No. 25, 24 June 1994, pp. 1–6.

36. For a short history of the intra-FKgP troubles from 1989–94, see J. Pataki, 'Hungary's Smallholders Fail to Unite before National Elections', *RFE/RL Research Report*, Vol. 3, No. 10, 11 March 1994, pp. 15–19.

37. For more information about the movements described in this section, see J. Bugajski, *Ethnic Politics in Eastern Europe: A Guide to Nationality Policies, Organizations, and Parties*, (Armonk, New York, 1994), pp. 413–15; P. Hockenos, *Free to Hate: The Rise of the Right in Post-Communist Eastern Europe*, (New York, Routledge, 1993) (the two chapters on Hungary, pp. 105–65); E. Oltay, 'Hungary,' *RFE/RL Research Report* (Special Issue, 'The Politics of Intolerance'), Vol. 3, No. 16, 22 April 1994, pp. 55–61.

38. E. Oltay, 'Hungarian Democratic Forum Expels Radical Leader,' *RFE/RL Research Report*, Vol. 2, No. 31, July 1993, pp. 24–9.

39. A personal rivalry between Torgyan and Csurka has prevented a closer co-operation between them, despite the fact that supporters of the two politicians often interact. While both figures employ populist appeals, Torgyan has found Csurka's chauvinism, anti-Semitism, and irredentism unpalatable. Csurka and Torgyan held a joint rally in February 1994 (also attended by skinheads and openly neo-fascist groups) but more formal co-operation between them failed to materialize. The same problem hampered more extensive co-operation between Csurka and Torgyan in the local elections in 1994.

40. For the text of Csurka's treatise, see *Magyar Forum*, 20 August 1992, translated fully in FBIS-EEU, 17 Sept. 1992 (Supplement), pp. 1–20. For several analyses of the treatise, see J. Pataki, 'Istvan Csurka's Tract: Summary and Reactions', J.F. Brown, 'A Challenge to Political Values', E. Oltay, 'A Profile of Istvan Csurka', all in *RFE/RL Research Report*, 9 Oct. 1992, pp. 15–22, 23–5, 26–9.

41. The Transcarpathian *oblast* was a part of Czechoslovakia in the period between the two world wars but it had formed a part of Hungary prior to 1919. Hungary seized southern portions of the area in 1938 and then annexed it fully in 1939. The area was annexed to the USSR as part of Ukraine in 1945. Although most of the population of the *oblast* is ethnically Ruthenian and Ukrainian, about 180,000 ethnic Hungarians also inhabit the *oblast's* south-western portion.

42. The mainstream MDF came under criticism domestically and internationally for actions that seemed to stretch the bounds of conservatism, such as its supposed lax reaction to the violence perpetrated by the skinheads, the defence minister's statements that implied irredentist views, the ceremonial burial of Hungary's Second World War-era leader, Admiral Horthy, and the ideologically motivated personnel purge in the Hungarian media in early 1994. For more information on the last two issues, see E. Oltay, 'Horthy's Reburial Sparks Controversy in Hungary', *RFE/RL Research Report*, Vol. 2, No. 43, 29 Oct. 1993, pp. 33–7; J. Pataki, 'Hungarian Radio Staff Cuts Cause Uproar', *RFE/RL Research Report*, Vol. 3, No. 19, 13 May 1994, pp. 38–44.

43. For a good overview of the political movements in the four countries discussed here in the period between the two world wars, see J. Rothschild, *East Central Europe between the Two World Wars* (Seattle, University of Washington Press, 1974).

44. It is the Roma, rather than the Jews, who are the most disliked and persecuted ethnic group in the four countries examined here.

6

Post-Communist Right Radicalism in Romania[1]

Henry F. Carey

The Romanian right consists primarily of the former nationalist-communist faction in or reporting to the repressive, disinforming, and personalistic sections of the Interior Ministry's State Security department (*Securitate*). This was the strongest and most hated institution in the Ceauşescu regime. Its propaganda campaigns were, according to expatriate novelist Norman Manea,

> 'a consequence of Ceauşescu mixing nationalism and Stalinism. But it was not out in the open. It was done in a sly, hyper-critical way, playing the game of the West, playing the game of the nation. After the change, many of the terrible, nasty slogans came back. That for me was a big shock, to see the right-wing ideology. It is sometimes hard to take.'[2]

Securitate's *Stasi*-type surveillance and informer networks and its mystique and power resulted from managing Ceauşescu's personalistic and nationalist propaganda. They were comparable in their inspiration only with Kim Il-Sung's North Korea and Mao Ze-dong's China. There may be some truth to Paul Johnson's explanation that the *Securitate*'s loyalty to Ceauşescu occurred because 'Its members were recruited largely from state orphanages' who regarded the Ceauşescus 'as parents'.[3] Other ultra-nationalists came from the pre-War fascist Iron Guard.[4] Most important was Ceauşescu's decision to appoint nationalist ideologues to manage the *Securitate*, which would dominate the regime. Nationalist ideology had legitimated Ceauşescu, while giving the *Securitate* élites a privileged position that they initially lost under his successor, Ion Iliescu. Unlike Eastern Europe's anti-communist revolutions, Romania's had combat force, though less than reported, from a military trained to kill without a Soviet presence. A split in the élite *Securitate* counter-insurgency was the tactical turning point on the night of 21 December 1989, though fighting mostly between the two factions occurred for three more days. Had they not split, Romania could have been ruled by ultra-nationalists from the *Securitate* on 21 December rather than by the *perestroika* cabal of Iliescu linked to the Communist Party.

Many ex-*Securitate* élites still consider Iliescu a traitor, who assassinated their leader and hero, Ceauşescu, and became the KGB's new 'man in Bucharest'.[5] These rightists had been thrilled that Israel and Germany paid Romania for exit visas for dominant ethnic Jews and Germans, which also raised funds, qualified Romania for US trade access under the Jackson–Vanick law, and exported these minorities. From their standpoint it was unfortunate that Hungary would not take back its ethnic minorities because its own economy could not easily absorb them, and because, they felt, Hungary needed them to reconquer Transylvania. The rightists also lauded Ceauşescu's plans to rid Romania of nearly all its villages, especially the ethnic minority ones, as well as destroying urban, ethnic minority neighbourhoods. Ceauşescu had nearly paid off Romania's foreign debts and no longer had to kow-tow to foreign imperialists. Their *conducător* reversed Alexander Dubček's policy by criticizing the Warsaw Pact's 1968 invasion of Czechoslovakia but controlling the populace at home, thereby avoiding Soviet intervention, while producing a 'kind of national reconciliation', according to Pavel Câmpeanu.[6] By 1989 only *Securitate* loyalists supported Ceauşescu, but their ideology and networks outlived him.

The epitome of *Securitate* propaganda and rightist ideology has been the rehabilitation of Marshal Ion Antonescu, rightist dictator, at times a mass murderer and at others, protector of Jews and Roma. From 1947 to about 1980 the communists deemed Antonescu a 'fascist' enemy of the people. Since his 1980s' rehabilitation by *Securitate* propagandists, Antonescu has became a national hero and, by 1990, a martyr, rather than the popular, but ambiguous figure that he was. A statue of Antonescu, for example, was built in 1994 in Târgu Mureş, the former Hungarian capital of Transylvania, which the dictator never visited, just to spite the ethnic Hungarian community and its political party. The effort has been condoned by the Iliescu regime in order to delegitimate the exiled King Michael I, whom the regime perceives as a democratic threat.[7]

Some of these anti-Iliescu rightists, as well as pro-Iliescu agents, initially joined the two main opposition parties that competed in the 1990 elections and opposition newspapers.[8] Silviu Brucan, originally part of the Iliescu cabal, claimed that 80 per cent of editors of the opposition newspapers had earlier worked for the former *Securitate*.[9] This infiltration has distorted the development of a democratic opposition.

Other more radical rightists engaged in anti-Iliescu activities in 1990 under the torch of anti-neo-communism or pro-democracy. The full details of various protests have never been fully reported because of their semi-covert tactics and the infiltrated Romanian press, whose history also compromises it.

Manifestations of rightist, informal networks derived from the *Securitate* became evident on 12 January 1990, three weeks after the revolution-*cum*-coup of 22 December 1989. The ruling National Salvation Front planned a mass rally to commemorate the victims of the Revolution. However, the occasion, which turned out to be Iliescu's last time close to the public, was disrupted by *Securitate* loyalists and disgruntled Army officers who yelled, 'Don't sell out the country' and 'Let's end communism'. Dumitru Mazilu, number two in the National Salvation Front, joined the protests, probably not as a result of a sudden conversion but rather in the nature of nationalist power play.[10]

A second anti-Iliescu manifestation occurred a month later on the night of 12 February 1990, when eight young officers went on television with 13 demands including the removal of the Defence Minister, Nicolae Militaru, who had appeared with Iliescu on television on the night of 22 December 1989 to claim the new government. They objected that Militaru and other of Iliescu's senior military officers were KGB agents, who had trained at the Soviet Voroshilov Military Academy and tolerated Hungarians.[11] The next day over one thousand soldiers and officers demonstrated at Victory Square in Bucharest. Militaru and other officers were eventually removed. A young officer corps, that was actually allied to the chauvinists, was officially recognized to lobby for reforms. This Action Committee for Democratization of the Army called itself democratic, its main plank being to demand military autonomy from any civilian control or authoritarian measure.

In communal rioting in Târgu Mureş during 19–20 March 1990, between six and 30 people died and over 240 were wounded because the police and army intervened more than a day late, and only after a request from the local leader of the group generally believed to be responsible, *Vatră Românească* (Romanian Hearth or Cradle).[12] Many believe that the *Securitate* had formed *Vatră*, or its precursor, because the attacks, first on the ethnic Hungarian Party (UDMR in Romanian) and then against ethnic Hungarians and Roma, were so well-organized.

Several weeks after these riots, President Iliescu publicly announced the existence of his own intelligence agency, the Romanian Information Service (SRI), which had already been operative. SRI has been headed by Virgil Măgureanu, whom the right despises.[13] Iliescu had dissolved the *Securitate,* but retained about five thousand in the SRI out of an estimated 20,000 to 25,000 *Securitate* agents.[14] The *expulsions* of Securitate agents from the SRI helped to minimize citizen fear and somewhat reduced threats to the new regime. Most of the younger ones became rich businessmen, while others eventually joined what grew into up to eight intelligence agencies.

Beginning on 22 April the four-month 'anniversary' since the 'coup', as the right had been calling it, anti-neo-communist protests at University Square began in earnest, possibly modelled on those that had taken place on Tiananmen Square in Beijing the year before. A core of student leaders attracted evening crowds of tens of thousands after work over the next month.[15] Despite several orders during April and May, the police did not clear the 'neo-communist' free-zone of anti-Iliescu protesters. A major unanswered question is whether the police refused out of solidarity with, or fear of, the rightists who had organized the key protests, or because they could not control the crowds without resorting to lethal force. Similarly it is not known whether Iliescu used miners because they were his only loyal agent, of coercion or because only they would not use lethal force.

After the 20 May 1990 landslide for Iliescu and the Front, the democratic students and civilians stopped going to University Square in the evenings. A hard core of anti-Iliescu, nationalist 'students', continued to protest, mostly without the large democratic cover of the preceding four weeks. On 13 June, without many civilians present, the police really tried to clear the Square, but apparently were only half successful. Some 'students' then attacked the television station, and according to Iliescu, tried to set fire to the Police and Interior Ministry headquarters on 13 June 1990.[16] The head of Romanian Television, Răzvan Theodorescu, accused the students of being *Securitate* agents. Martyn Rady notes that 'former *Securitate* agents attacked the television station after the crowds were dispersed at University Square'.[17] Two ex-*Securitate* broadcasters, T. Brateş and Alexandru Stark, who had switched to and promoted the new Iliescu regime during the coup, claimed that they were beaten up at the television station.

Iliescu mobilized thousands of miners, whom he had sent to Bucharest twice before that year.[18] They travelled from the Jiu Valley and elsewhere in trucks and trains to Bucharest. On 14–15 June, they bludgeoned an unknown mix of democratic opponents, students, pseudo-student impostors, and ex-*Securitate* agents, who had been protesting against 'neo-communism'. Victims included six reported deaths, four of whom had been shot, and 500 wounded. One thousand were arrested, 250 punished, and only 34 tried.[19] Among those beaten up was the most famous protester, Student League President Marian

Munteanu, and former Iron Guard Treasurer, turned *Securitate* agent based in Italy, Iosif Constantin Drăgan. The offices of the opposition Peasant and Liberal Parties' headquarters, the architecture and geology faculty buildings, and the home of Dumitru Mazilu were all sacked and searched.

Iliescu praised the paramilitary violence against the 'Legionnaires', his term to denigrate the larger group of Ceauşescu loyalists in the former *Securitate*.[20] Iliescu survived what Drăgan called a 'coup attempt'.[21] The 'student' attacks did succeed as a 'white coup'. Iliescu bargained with the right, lest he might have to repress protesters again and lose indispensable Western aid. In due course, he permitted the right to start up newspapers, buy private television stations, and form political parties. The balance of this chapter considers the three most significant parties, Romanian National Unity, Socialist Party of Labour, and Greater Romania.

By 1992, out of a mutual desire for power, President Iliescu and the radical right formed an electoral alliance that lasted at least through the ensuing four-year elected term. In January 1995 they formalized the relationship with a publicly signed protocol. The right has used democratic freedom and forms to advocate ethnic based nationalism with ambiguous commitments to the parliamentary institutions in which they participate. Two different views about the relationship between the post-communist right and President Iliescu exist: mutual symbiosis versus strange bedfellows.

The first, a suspect one, holds that the two groups have more in common than otherwise. Their apparently different but less important ideologies are submerged in their common desire to keep power by utilizing appeals to nationalism. Those holding this perception feel that the President, like Brutus, 'protests too much' about how difficult his relations with the ultra-nationalists are. The latter's scare tactics may or may not be distasteful to the President, but they are the best way to scare the risk-averse, mass underclass from supporting the nascent, democratic opposition, as well as the West, which fears another Milosevic. If the right's ethnically intolerant discourse really bothered President Iliescu, he would find a new governing coalition partner from the democratic opposition. The right's rhetoric makes President Iliescu seem like a moderate. Furthermore, hate speech is illegal in Romania and unlawful under the terms of Romania's membership in the Council of Europe since September 1993. Yet no prosecutions have occurred. Furthermore, the President periodically lapses into jingoistic rhetoric, showing his true, anti-minority colours. His government has failed either to enact any laws protecting minorities or to conclude a peace treaty with

Hungary, both required under its Council of Europe membership. Both actions should be routine for a democratic country. While all the Romanian political parties made a pledge to integrate with the West in the 21 June 1995 'Snagov declaration', Romania has not renounced the 1991 mutual defence treaty with the Soviet Union. Most importantly the party system itself is weak. No matter how autonomous the rightist parties may be, they are subordinate to the presidency and its intelligence agencies.

The other, sympathetic interpretation of Iliescu's difficult relationship with the rightists holds that the rightists are unavoidably difficult allies, with whom the President must negotiate because realistically, he could not form a stable government with the perhaps democratic, but inexperienced and probably just-as-corrupt opposition. Romania would be ungovernable if a liberal group tried to govern against the will of the *nomenklatura*. This view argues that it is more realistic to try to reform the authoritarians than to empower the naive, who would face riots from manipulated or provoked unemployed workers from privatized state industries. Iliescu must deal with the autonomous right, which threatens him and the West with demands against normalizing relations with Hungary and integrating into NATO unconditionally. Any jingoist rhetoric by the President is the same as US politicians speaking about US national interests. This realist view, held by the US Embassy under John R. Davis, Jr. from 1992–94 and Alfred Moses from 1995 to the present, holds that Iliescu can be trusted, or at least be given a chance, and that the radical right cannot. The uneasy but stable coalition existing from at least 1992–96 has been a triumph of Iliescu's leadership, mutual political necessity, and constant negotiation. The right is authentically nationalist. Freedom has liberated their hateful statements, which should be taken seriously. Even though the presidency and intelligence agencies are powerful, the parliament has grown in importance, and with it, the rightist parties.

Both of these two versions are partly true, part of the time. Collaboration between both sides has been the bottom line since 1992 though a *putsch* from the right remains a small threat. Distinctions between the two sides are not only blurred, but in flux. Furthermore, the right is divided ideologically between nationalist-collectivists and nationalist-oligarchs. This internecine conflict, nevertheless, has become more significant since the fall of communism, given Romania's inactive but divided political culture between the Eastern civilization of the 'Old Kingdom' embraced by the rightists and the threatening Western civilization in Transylvania embraced by liberal intellectuals. The Iliescu–rightist electoral pact has suddenly engendered stability and consolidated a soft authoritarian rule. The skinheads of other East European transitions are absent, partly because of lower unemployment resulting from less privatization, and because its political culture may be more tolerant than others, while lacking superiority complexes. With the exception of the March 1990 Târgu Mureş riots, any xenophobic or racist attacks have been decentralized pogroms by irate villagers, without state provocation. Political violence has consisted of several dozen, mostly unreported, suspicious deaths, especially of Iliescu partisans and opponents that used to work for the *Securitate*.

Iliescu's relations with the Romanian right can be compared with similar splits in Serbia and Russia. The ultra-nationalist Radical Party of Serbia also makes the President, Slobodan Milosevic and his Socialist Party look like moderates. Both Iliescu and Milosevic have used nationalism to inhibit democratization, which might have elected moderates in fairer and more credible elections. Unlike Milosevic, however, Iliescu has faced fewer if any ethnic armies against whom the regime could then wage war to remain in power. This could occur in a Romania with its pre-Second World War population and boundaries, then one of Europe's most heterogeneous countries.

Parallels with Gorbachev suggest that Iliescu has come closest to implementing *perestroika* and *glasnost* policies. Yeltsin has since gone beyond them, more directly attacking the interests of Russian nationalists embedded in its *nomenklatura*. They threaten consequently the Russian regime more regularly and greatly. As in Romania's 1992 elections, the dubious 1991 and 1993 Russian parliamentary elections produced more ultra-nationalist legislators than were really elected. The Russian opposition has had constant battles with Yeltsin under the same dual executive constitution as Romania. Unlike in Gorbachev's fall from power and Yeltsin's insecurity, Iliescu's durability has been bolstered, possibly with KGB advice, by coalescing instead with the right.

The most important role of the radical parties is to antagonize the ethnic Hungarian party, UDMR. It is indicative President Iliescu does not make it clear whether he directs, condones, or opposes the ethnic intolerance of the right. In the 1990 election, the ethnic Hungarian party received seven per cent of the total vote, which it protected against any rigging attempts by the establishment. This was the second highest vote of any party. The rightist parties have exploited memories of underclass Romanians being maltreated by nineteenth century Magyarization campaigns and the Horthy dictatorship's occupation of northern Transylvania.

Rightist tactics for Iliescu's strategy of divide and rule are epitomized by the conflict over the Council of Europe law no. 1201 requiring 'ethnic autonomy'. The Romanian government has simultaneously preached the virtues of Council membership and complained that its rules could stimulate an ethnic Hungarian secession and/or war with Hungary. On this matter of ethnic autonomy, even the democratic opposition has agreed. Corneliu Coposu, leader of the National Peasant Christian Democrat Party, as well as other smaller parties in the Democratic Convention, also opposed ethnic autonomy in 1995. They advocated implementing federalism mandated by one interpretation of the Romanian Constitution. However, its Article One says that Romania is a 'unitary national state', which undermines decentralization. The rightist parties claim the latter provision violates the Romanian constitution, and during 1995, constantly demanded UDMR's legal abolition.

In the UDMR's 1993 Congress in Braşov, of the three main factions only the radical one insisted upon ethnic autonomy in Covaşna and Harghita counties and other majority, ethnic Hungarian areas. This faction is mostly led by former nomenklatura persons.[22] During 1993–94, Iliescu appointed loyal, ethnic Romanian prefects to the two ethnic Hungarian majority counties, Hargoviţa and Covaşna, and given the country's 42 prefects more budgetary power than the elected mayors, based on laws inherited from communism. By 1995, at the UDMR Congress at Cluj, there were no longer any factional disputes. The ethnic Hungarian Party supported territorial autonomy, under the European Parliament law no. 1201. The move divided the democratic opposition, without any responsible party advocating even limited, local autonomy as a compromise. This failure, which led to the *de facto* dissolution of the Democratic Convention in March 1995, was a dismal example of an irresponsible democratic opposition. This rightist triumph also polarized Hungarian–Romanian foreign relations and thereby preserves the salience of the rightist agenda.

Romanian resentments against Hungarians fit not only East European patterns, but earlier periods in Western Europe.[23] Psychoanalysts might use terms like victimization or inferiority complex to describe rightist xenophobia, whose focus on ethnic Hungarians far exceeds either mass or élite modal views. Perhaps, outsiders can never understand their mentality, but the perceived threat from the minority seems quite contrived, even granting some Hungarians have superiority complexes towards Romanians. An outbreak of war between Hungary and Romania seems unlikely, but possible, resulting from the stupidity of self-fulfilling prophecies of rightists on both sides of the border. While Romanian rightists are not monolithic, some are close to being fascist, with expansionist goals and a collectivist state.

The Radical Parties and Political Society

As of late 1995 two general elections have been held, including one second presidential round vote in the second, as well as a constitutional plebiscite and one set of local elections. The 20 May 1990 general elections produced a hegemonic party system that has been dominated by President Iliescu. Most rightists were too busy trying to oppose Iliescu outside parliamentary politics to take the election seriously.[24] The ruling National Salvation Front appointed loyal prefects and mayors throughout the country to boost the presidential and electoral results in its favour, both legitimately and fraudulently. Romania had a one-party mentality until the February 1992 local elections, during which the new Democratic Convention opposition was able to guard its vote and win in most major cities except Cluj, a result which was as shocking to the regime as to the victors. Iliescu's intelligence agents started to do their arithmetic and decided that they needed to join the radical parties to maintain control of a government they felt that they could not afford to lose in the upcoming general election. In the 27 September 1992 parliamentary votes only Romanian National Unity (PUNR) probably really received more than the three per cent minimum of votes legitimately cast.[25]

TABLE 6.1
OFFICIAL RESULTS OF THE 1992 PARLIAMENTARY ELECTIONS

		Chamber of Deputies			*Senate*	
Ruling Party	FDSN	3,015,708	27.71%	FDSN	3,102,201,	28.29%
Dem. Convention	CDR	2,177,144	20.01%	CDR	2,210,722,	20.16%
P Roman faction	FSN	1,108,500	10.88%	FSN	1,139,033,	10.38%
Romanian Unity	PUNR	839,586	7.71%	PUNR	890,410,	8.12%
Hungarian Party	UDMR	811,290	7.45%	UDMR	831,469,	7.58%
Greater Romania	PRM	424,061	3.89%	PRM	422,545	3.85%
Socialist Work.	PSM	330,378	3.03%	PSM	349,470	3.18%
Dem. Agrarians				PDAR	362,427	3.30%

Officially the four radical parties received about 18 per cent of the national parliamentary vote, but only 11 per cent of the presidential vote. (Their real parliamentary figure was about 14 per cent.) This exceeds the 1993 and 1995 percentages of votes of the French *Front National*, though the latter won some local elections in 1995 and most radical parties in the six former East European Soviet satellites. Iliescu casually proposed majoritarian elections in May 1994, but opposition from the radical parties would probably explain why it has gone nowhere. Yet, even with single member districts, most of Transylvania would probably be represented by the same two polarized, ethnic parties as now.

Romania's nascent party system is more a venue for polarizing polemics than interest aggregation and compromise. The radical nationalists have the function of eliminating the space for class-based politics and to increase the importance of ethnic debate. The radicals would have no *raison d'être* if they reconciled themselves to their political and ethnic opposites. Given their preference for power-sharing, the radicals from at least 1992 onwards have been tentatively reconciled to President Iliescu's dominance, rather than to that of the opposition or to the rule of law.

Parties of Radical Right Continuity

Michael Shafir has distinguished between ultra-nationalist parties.[26] Those with an intense Orthodox Christian ethos and with the 1930s Iron Guard as a model are 'parties of radical revival'. None of them, including the fastest growing party, Movement for Romania, qualified for parliament in 1992. The latter's leader, Marian Munteanu, was rumoured to have lost his life in a 1995 trainwreck but is still very much alive today.[27] Those which are atheist or agnostic and whose ideology and interests are derived from the nationalist communist state are 'parties of radical continuity'. President Iliescu's prominently and newly displayed religiosity, but contempt for the Iron Guard, distinguishes him from both types.

The most important party of radical continuity since the 1992 elections in votes, wealth, and in the youthfulness of its leaders has been that of Romanian National Unity. It claims to be a 'centrist party' interested in privatization. Indeed, its banking, export-import and retailing industries, many of which are organized by members of the former *Securitate,* produce enough resources for President Iliescu to fear that this radical nationalist formation could dominate the purchase of state firms, if privatization proceeds. Far more important than its ambiguous economic liberalism is PUNR's vulgar obsession with Hungarian issues. The Party President since 1992, Gheorghe Funar has chosen to attack and harass the UDMR and antagonize ethnic Hungarians.[28] Should his behaviour become too embarrassing, he could be dispensed with and a replacement found.

Romanian National Unity began as a regional Transylvanian party (PUNRT), but attempted in 1991 to become a national party and changed its name to PUNR. Radu Ceontea, then head of *Vatră,* became its first President, and called Iliescu a 'Bolshevik'.[29] In both the February 1992 local and September 1992 general elections, PUNR was particularly strong in the Transylvanian counties of Cluj, Bihor, Mara-Mureş, Bistrita-Năsăud, and Alba. After the local elections, in which Funar was elected Mayor of Cluj, the Cluj wing of PUNR began to dominate over the other, Târgu Mureş, faction of the party. The two reflect the two cities where the two ethnic groups live closest together. Funar then became the new Party President, through the machinations of Party Vice-President Ioan Gavra, a former communist youth newspaper editor. In the general election of September 1992, PUNR alone received about eight per cent of the 1992 parliamentary vote and 10.9 per cent of the presidential race, as Funar was the only presidential candidate from the four radical parties.

PUNR is known for constructing nationalistic, public monuments and sculptures, and other displays. In late 1992 Funar placed an anti-Hungarian quote from nationalist historian Nicolae Iorga on the Hungarian King Matthew (*Matthias Corvinus*) statue in the central square of Cluj facing the Hungarian cathedral. In 1994 Gheorghe Funar proposed removing the Latin name-plate on the King Matthew behemoth. Also a year later Funar built a statue of Avram Iancu nearby, close to the Opera House. Iancu was the martyred Romanian guerrilla of the 1848 uprising, who managed to defeat the Hungarian and Austrian armies before being betrayed and assassinated. Financed from the PUNR-sponsored Caritas game,[30] it was built in about two months in time for National Day, 1993.

Mayor Funar is notorious in Western circles for a Cluj City ordinance requiring his permission for all public rallies; banning Hungarian-language street signs and the Hungarian language in Hungarian schools; placing Romanian flags around the square containing King Michael's statue and broadcasting Romanian Orthodox services right outside the Catholic Church. These all violate the letter or the spirit of Romania's human rights commitments as a member of the Council of Europe and the two human rights Covenants. Funar constantly uses the term 'Gypsy' (ţigan) to disparage his adversaries, including President Iliescu. He helped enact the racist banning in 1995 of the proper nouns and adjectives 'Rom' (singular), 'Roma' (plural) or 'Romany' (adjective), the names chosen by this ethnic group, supposedly because they sound close to *Român,* ('Romanian'.)

Funar has faced challenges from various party factions, such as the parliamentary delegation in Bucharest. For example, he has accused party member Ioan Gavra of reaching an understanding with Iliescu and

Măgureanu, because Gavra withdrew his opposition to the nomination of Alfred Moses as US Ambassador to Romania in October 1994. In late November 1994, Gavra and Valer Suian accused party members Cornel Brahaş and Teodor Ardelean of being 'the men of *Cotroceni*' on issues of privatization.[31] This third faction split in 1995. Brahaş founded his own new party.

The PUNR has anti-Semitic elements, as indicated by its letter written to oppose the nomination of Alfred Moses as Ambassador to Romania. On 21 September 1994 PUNR Senator Adrian Moţiu, PUNR Vice-President of the Senate Foreign Affairs Committee, organized signatures of six other Romanian Senators in a letter addressed to the Senator Jesse Helms, then ranking minority member of the US Senate Foreign Relations Committee. It urged him to oppose the ratification of Moses through his acknowledged influence. This was several days before Iliescu was to meet Clinton for the first time in Washington. A lobbying effort was organized against Moses by the Romanian-born son-in-law of Congresswoman Barbara Kennerly, who allegedly wrote the letter. Originally, the PUNR executive board endorsed the letter. Later, Gavra, feeling intense pressure from the *Cotroceni* Presidential Palace, disavowed his ability to control the two PUNR members who signed the letter.[32] It accused Moses of being 'a close associate of the Ceauşescu's' for supporting Most Favoured Nation (MFN) trading status in the 1980s, an unfortunate but bipartisan US policy in retrospect. The letter omitted the various qualifications that Moses made in Congress, when condoning the policy. He criticized Romania's treatment of religious minorities other than Jews, especially Baptist and Uniate Christians (Greek Catholics). Ambassador Moses told me that the letter 'was motivated only by anti-Semitism'.[33]

The democratic opposition first brought a censure motion under Article 112 of the Constitution on 19 March 1993. Without the support of the rightists, the motion failed miserably, 192 to 26 with 32 abstentions. Once they threatened to support such motions, the danger of the Văcăroiu government falling became more real. PUNR first threatened a no-confidence motion and presidential suspension under Article 95 of the Constitution in late August 1993. The stimulus was a motion of the consultative Council of Minorities, whose majority of members are ethnic minorities. The non-binding motion condemned Cluj Mayor Funar's ordinance banning street signs in the Hungarian language. The ruling Party of Social Democracy's Senate President, Oliviu Gherman, favoured the use of some bilingual signs, while the Party's Senate group spokesman, Vasile Vacaru, added, 'The government is not bound by the Council's recommendation.' PUNR

Vice-President Ioan Gavra prevailed in a secret party vote over Funar's demand for a censure vote in parliament. Instead PUNR made an undefined 'ultimatum' to Iliescu to keep the Hungarian sign ban and to replace the young technocrats appointed by the first Prime Minister Petre Roman with PUNR's young cohorts.

Several days later the ethnic Hungarian Party withdrew its three representatives from the Council of Minorities because the government had 'no political will to permit Hungarian identity', according to UDMR Executive President, Takacs Csaba. As a result of PUNR's first threats, Prime Minister Nicolae Văcăroui began his first exploratory talks with PUNR to join the government, which occurred in Spring 1994. PUNR then dropped its threat of censure, and Iliescu refused to end the banning of Hungarian signs in Cluj. Several weeks later, the Roma representatives also withdrew from the Council on Minorities.

PUNR's influence was felt in foreign relations, as well. Funar protested against Foreign Minister Teodor Meleşcanu's invitation to Hungarian Foreign Minister Geza Jeszenszky to visit Bucharest. When the latter arrived in September 1993, the two diplomats reached a tentative accord on a treaty to normalize relations between the two countries. On 16 September 1993 President Iliescu publicly lambasted his own Foreign Minister for selling out Romania's sovereignty. Meleşcanu probably could not have negotiated the agreement without prior Presidential authorization. Either PUNR's ultimatum or Iliescu's planned change of position produced the public scolding. Bilateral relations apparently improved the following year as Iliescu met Hungarian President Arpad Goncz at the Conference on Security and Co-operation in Europe (CSCE) in Budapest on 6 December 1994 and invited him to Bucharest with a view to concluding a basic treaty. By mid-1995 the treaty seemed impossible, given Iliescu's explicit opposition to Council of Europe regulations.

In October 1993 Funar tried or pretended to try to show that his party could not be considered Iliescu's 'satellite' (the first interpretation described above.) He went so far as to meet with the opposition's National Peasant Party to form a new government after a theoretical no-confidence vote. During spring 1994 PUNR's censure threats and motions with the Democratic Convention, protesting the second Văcăroui budget, corruption, and economic mismanagement, led to planted rumours of 'anticipated elections'. There was never any chance of these being held. Another no-confidence vote came closer to passing than any of the more than half a dozen motions since the 1992 elections, but failed because not everyone in the PUNR supported it.

In early March 1994 four ministers with military rank were replaced with civilians with unacknowledged PUNR links and *Securitate* credentials: Defence Minister Gheorghe Tinca, Justice Minister Iosif Gavril Chiuzbaian, Interior Minister Ioan Dorut Taracila, and Transportation Minister Aurel Novac. Because the Council of Europe wanted civilians to replace generals, Tinca replaced Defence Minister Nicolae Spiroiu, who was reportedly too pro-NATO and anti-Russian for the President and allegedly to the KGB's liking. Chiuzbaian is allegedly linked to Drăgan.

Greater Romania Party

The most ultra-nationalist party, Greater Romania, was formed in May 1991, 11 months after a newspaper reached newsstands with the same name and by the same organization. It appropriates the name used for the 'Great Unification' of 1918. Greater Romania used to lack the extreme ethnic intolerance and hate that the name now connotes. Older members of Ceaușescu's regime like Mircea Mușcat, Maria Covaci and Radu Teodoru had obtained the services of the two most outrageous polemicists of that regime. Eugen Barbu and Corneliu Vadim Tudor were former editors of the extremist, communist 'cultural' weekly, *Săptămâna,* the exponent of proto-chronism, a polemic arguing that many Western discoveries were anticipated in Romania. In a 5 September 1980 editorial entitled 'Ideals', they attacked 'teachers of democratic tarantella clad in stinking tartans, Herods who are strangers to the interests of this nation...'[34] Tudor the 'poet' penned the phrase 'years of light' to depict the Ceaușescu regime.[35]

The newspaper, *România Mare,* may have the largest weekly circulation, ranging officially from 100,000 to 300,000 without any advertising. It was allegedly launched with the approval of then Prime Minister Roman,[36] though since 1992, it has been the most strident opponent of Iliescu of the rightist parties and newspapers. Moreover, it thrives on foreign pressure to keep out extremists, which confirms all its vast suspicions and prejudices. Greater Romania is widely believed to be financed by Drăgan and the *Securitate* network, which also finances the other worst-of-the-worst hate weeklies, *Europa.* Its *Securitate* contacts provide intelligence files used to attack opponents, as well as signals about whom and when to attack.

Greater Romania's President, Corneliu Vadim Tudor, is as notorious as Zhirinovsky, though less dangerous and popular for now. He drives a $100,000 Mercedes 7000-SL; has a dozen bodyguards; attacks curious journalists; picks fights with fellow Senators; and uses foul language publicly, even to the President. Tudor became more antagonistic to Iliescu after 1992–93, supposedly to protest the President's pro-Hungary and pro-Jewish policies. Iliescu had not only negotiated with Hungarians, but wore a yarmulke and went to the Holocaust Museum's 1993 opening. However, when so ordered by Iliescu, Tudor keeps quiet, such as during Iliescu's visits to NATO in 1993 and Israel in 1994.

For Vadim Tudor Jews is a code word for 'communists', including two in Iliescu's 1989 cabal, Roman and Silviu Brucan. During the 1992 elections, Tudor stated that Jews should not hold public office, just practise their religion in private. After the first round Tudor claimed that 'US policy is orchestrated by Jewish and Hungarian mafiosi'.[37] On the occasion of the 50th anniversary of the Iaşi pogrom, both *Romania Mare* and *Europa,* printed denials of the Holocaust.[38] In mid-June 1994 Tudor predicted that the treasonous opposition had planned to assassinate Iliescu so as to reinstate King Michael. Tudor included Jews and Roma as part of the opposition conspiracy to lend credibility to his ludicrous and unfulfilled prediction.

Socialist Party of Labour

The third rightist party, the Socialist Party of Labour (PSM), is leftist on class issues and rightist on nationalism. It is considered rightist because its chauvinism is not a valence issue, as the democratic opposition and voters prefer civic patriotism. Class issues are salient and the difference should be taken into account, especially since PSM claims the mantle of the Romanian Communist Party. Although communism is currently illegal, its return is no more unimaginable than it was in Lithuania, Poland and Hungary. Unlike in those latter countries, however, PSM did not return to power by winning elections honestly. It has not had to readapt its ideology significantly, and its role has been to make Iliescu appear moderate, whether or not it so intended. Like the Greater Romania Party, PSM plays on nostalgia for the communist period, especially subsidized housing and food, and guaranteed employment, as well as employing vulgar jokes and minority-baiting to gain attention.

The PSM president, Ilie Verdeţ, was Ceauşescu's Prime Minister from March 1979 to May 1982, as well as Ceauşescu's brother-in-law. He has helped the Iliescu government, on behalf of whom he visited Iraq in September 1993 to re-establish bilateral relations on behalf of President Iliescu. Romania is sometimes accused of selling arms to Iraq, despite the UN embargo.

PSM's most famous spokesman is Adrian Păunescu, who used to sport a crew cut while a communist editor, poet, and concert impresario.

Now his equally self-conscious look resembles a medieval monk and a Hell's Angel, without a pony-tail. Păunescu had been demoted by Ceauşescu apparently because he was too popular among youth. Many Romanians were scandalized when Păunescu was included in the first Romanian parliamentary delegation to the Council of Europe in the early months of 1993, when Romania was still under consideration for membership. In early September 1993, Păunescu took the lead in the Romanian Senate condemning the Hungarian Party (UDMR) leader Marko Bela for writing to the European Community's Romania representative Catherine Lalumière that more conditions should be placed on Romania's entry into the Council.[39] When the Council of Europe did admit Romania in September 1993, the West implicitly accepted the rightist role in what amounts to Romania's democratization. Păunescu also led the charges that the plebiscite and parliamentary elections in the Republic of Moldova in February and March 1994 were stolen. This was an ironic charge, since it takes a thief to know one. The Moldova votes effectively killed the dream of unification of the two Romanian nation-states. Curiously, Tudor said that the results did not surprise him. The bearded behemoth Păunescu, and the clean-cut, but also obese Tudor, receive extraordinary amounts of television coverage for their similar diatribes.

In December 1993 Socialist Labour brought a censure motion, which had Greater Romania Party's support. It argued that the government was 'neglecting the contributions of workers to the country's wealth' and 'developing an anti-inflation package at the expense of the workers'. Speculations and televised rumours that the Văcăroui government might fall were false since the Democratic Convention had a different incompatible censure motion, whereas the rightist resolution condemned privatization.

In 1994 the Socialist Labour Party Vice-Presidents for Propaganda, Tudor Mohora, as well as another Vice-President, Traian Dudaş, tried to moderate PSM's ideology, calling for greater Westernization and criticizing Păunescu and Verdeţ for supporting the inclusion of the Greater Romania Party into the government and their opposition to privatization. The split led to Mohora forming the Socialist Party, which held its first Congress on 17–18 June 1995.

Finally, the small Romanian Democratic Agrarian Party only just qualified for the Senate in 1992. PDAR tried to unite with the Romanian National Unity Party in 1993, but the negotiations between Funar and PDAR President Victor Surdu to create a National Unity Bloc failed in 1993. The party's electoral base is from presidents, vice-presidents and economists from the communist agricultural co-operatives, the new name for state farms given by Ceaușescu. PDAR was also one of three parties outside the National Salvation Front to join the Theodor Stolojan government after the September 1991 dismissal of Prime Minister Petre Roman. In late 1994, PDAR split, with a faction joining the opposition. It did not sign the January 1995 protocol between President Iliescu and the three main rightist parties examined, Greater Romania, Socialist Labour, and Romanian National Unity. This pact solidified the many appointments and patronage extended to the rightist parties in return for their recognizing both the legitimacy of the Iliescu regime and Magureanu as the intelligence authority to ensure its security.

Comparisons of Rightist Parties

Many describe the Romanian National Unity Party as 'nationalist' but the Greater Romania Party as 'fascist'. Nationalist is perhaps not strong enough to depict PUNR, whose Bucharest press conferences are virtually unidimensional harangues against Hungarians. Fascist is perhaps too strong for PRM, which has never enjoyed the high popularity that the term conventionally requires. I would use chauvinist for PUNR and ultra-chauvinist for PRM. Greater Romania, and its newspaper of the same name, are even more vulgar and ethnically intolerant than Romanian National Unity. Moreover, it not only attacks Roma and Hungarians, but also Jews and independent trade unions ('led by American chauffeurs').[40] The excesses of communism are attributed entirely to the Jewish Romanians, even though the worst Stalinist measures were mostly ordered and carried out by ethnic Romanians.[41] Unlike PUNR but like the third radical party, Socialist Labour, Greater Romania still praises Ceaușescu and regards capitalism as a threat to national unity because ethnic minorities exploit ethnic Romanians. This criss-crossing cleavage divides and inhibits the overt violence. However, conflict over ownership of state firms could eventually produce violence if privatization ever begins in earnest. Violence is also possible because both Greater Romania and Romanian National Unity advocate political-military action against Hungarian subversives in Transylvania and for the recovery of Bessarabia. All three parties prefer dictatorship and support democracy tactically.

Public Opinion and the Radicals

Western and Romanian journalists, who manage to attend the press conferences of the two chauvinist parties, the Greater Romania and Romanian National Unity Parties, hear diatribes by party spokesmen that seem surrealistic. If reporters inquire why Hungarian signs or meetings should be banned in Cluj or what is the evidence for Hungarian paramilitary organizations in Transylvania, they are shouted down by planted journalists. Romanian journalists that dare to so inquire are sometimes permanently expelled.[42] In spite of their highly undemocratic and contrived statements, the radical right receives little press criticism and substantial coverage on the *de facto* television monopoly.[43]

In a study commissioned by the Project on Ethnic Relations, three University of Bucharest sociologists found that the 'empirical pattern' of Romanian ethnic groups is peaceful coexistence, with a near 'universal' (positive) attitude towards ethnic Germans and one almost as friendly towards Jews, though the attitudes towards Roma were intolerant and 'ethnocentric'. Their conclusion is that friction and polarization are caused by intellectuals and political parties. The study found more intolerant attitudes towards Roma, but a general tolerance.[44]

By contrast, in their June and early July 1992 survey, funded by the US National Science Foundation, William Crowther and Georgeta Muntean found that ethnic hostility is far more pervasive throughout Romania, and may not require provocation to be elicited. Every group has approximately the same proportion of tolerant and intolerant communities. The survey shows that as a consequence of Romania's inter-war history and Ceauşescu's legitimation strategy, there remains an intense undercurrent of ethnic hostility within Romania.[45] Ethnic Hungarians were most dissatisfied with the lack of administrative autonomy, a view which polarizes Romanians the most, even in ethnically mixed areas which have a high consensus on other issues. Only in medium-sized cities is hostility towards Roma somewhat greater than in villages or in larger cities. Mureş is somewhat worse than most of Romania's 42 counties. Racial intolerance is Romania's most distinct social attitude. Sadly, on this latter point, there was less disagreement with the Bucharest sociologists.

Crowther and Muntean also found that Romanian attitudes were less tolerant than those in the Republic of Moldova. Romania's minorities come from Western and Eastern Christianity, while the Moldovans are all from the latter.[46] Furthermore, as a new country, Moldova's nation-state building has not been subjected to a century of frictions, motivated different goals, interests, differential economic experiences and aggregate development. The results are in the following two tables:

TABLE 6.2
ATTITUDE TOWARDS MINORITY RIGHTS SCALE

Favours Extensive Minority Rights

Scale	per centage Moldova	per centage Romania
1.00	20.2	8.3
1.25	26.9	12.0
1.50	28.0	20.5
1.75	14.9	33.9
2.00	4.8	19.2

Favours Limited Minority Rights

The scale is based on responses to nine questions with yes/no answers, with yes responses on all nine providing a score of 1.0 and no responses on all nine providing a score of 2.0.

TABLE 6.3
ATTITUDE TOWARDS MINORITIES SCALE

Scale	per centage Moldova	per centage Romania

Negative Attitude Towards Minorities

Scale	per centage Moldova	per centage Romania
1.00	31.7	43.0
1.50	31.0	28.0
2.00	19.6	14.9
2.50	5.9	2.7
3.00	3.2	0.9

Positive Attitude Towards Minorities

The second scale is based on responses to four questions that allowed respondents to say something positive or negative about minorities, based on the mean responses.

A UK-Gallup poll released on 23 August 1993, the 49th anniversary of King Michael's coup, indicates the complex relationship between ethnic attitudes and foreign policy views. Fifty-seven per cent said that Romania's national security was threatened by Hungary; next on the list of countries to be feared by the Romanians was the Ukraine, by which only 13 per cent felt threatened; only nine per cent felt threatened by Serbia, whose aggression has never been directed at Romania. Only 23 per cent of Romanian respondents said that the country's current boundaries were 'wholly acceptable'; 24 per cent said that they were unacceptable, but could not be changed; 32 per cent responded that they were unacceptable, but now was not the time to raise the issue. Sixty-one per cent said that at least one foreign country wanted to conquer at any rate part of Romania. Yet, only 17 per cent said that Romania should use force to conquer its lost territories; 89 per cent said that minorities should have equal rights.[47]

Data on the political parties should be taken with a grain of salt.[48] They are about as indicative as the official voting results. William Crowther and Georgeta Muntean found that Romanians perceive two clusters of political parties that can be deemed 'collectivist-nationalist' and 'liberal-universalist'. The two main variables distinguishing their perceptions are attitudes towards reform (privatization and income differentiation) and attitudes toward nationalism. The focal points of the collectivist-nationalist voters were the ruling party (then FDSN), the radical parties under study, plus, the Petre Roman faction that had not yet distanced itself in the opposition. Liberal universalist voters supported the four parties identified in the opposition Democratic Convention. The Beta scores show that those who were opposed to minority rights tend to favour the radical parties, with the highest negative relationship for supporters of Greater Romania. Conversely those who most strongly favour minority rights are supporters of the ethnic Hungarian Party, with supporters of the Civic Alliance Party also exhibiting a strong association with support for minority rights. All the scores are statistically significant.

TABLE 6.4
ATTITUDE TOWARD MINORITY RIGHTS SCALE BY CONFIDENCE IN
PARTY

	R-Square	Beta	Significance of F
Collectivist-Nationalist			
România Mare (Greater Romania)	0.018	-0.138	0.000
FDSN (Iliescu)	0.015	-0.129	0.000
PUNR (Romanian National Unity)	0.014	-0.122	0.000
FSN (Roman faction)	0.009	-0.100	0.0005
PDAR (Agrarians)	0.009	-0.100	0.0008
PSM (Socialists)	0.005	-0.080	0.0077
Liberal-Universalist			
UDMR (Hungarians)	0.143	0.379	0.000
CAP (Civic Alliance)	0.054	0.234	0.000
PNT-CD (Peasants)	0.036	0.192	0.000
PNL-AT (Liberal youth)	0.015	0.127	0.000

A poll of 1,100 Romanians in November 1993 by the sociologist Pavel Câmpeanu's Independent Centre of Social Studies and Polls, found that PUNR was the only party that showed some increase in support in the 13 months after the general elections.[49] That situation changed the following year however. The 'Social Barometers' public opinion poll series, financed by the Soros Foundation, produced three polls with identical questions. These included preferences for the parties in the parliament, with all the parties in the Democratic Convention listed separately.

Of those who expressed preferences, the four radical right parties received 22 per cent, 20 per cent, and 16 per cent, a steady decline over the nine month period. The decline of the Romanian National Unity Party, in the wake of the Caritas 'Ponzi' scam, to only two per cent, is still quite surprising. The other three radical parties gained more popularity than they received in the 1992 elections. Since then, the four qualified for parliament, three of them, PSM, PRM, and PUNR, have received regular television coverage. Their expected vote shares are now well above the three per cent entry threshold, making future cheating to reach the minimum unnecessary.

Future Influences

As transitions go Romania began turbulently and achieved comparative normalcy with Iliescu's 1992 electoral pact with the extremist parties. Most of these parties' leaders had been ideological national communists attached to the frightening *Securitate* bureaucracy. They do not have a track record of mass murder, which mostly occurred before 1953, just emotional belligerence, yearning for attention, absence of guilt and abject disregard for the truth. Combined with malintentioned intelligence agencies, they could be dangerous some day. Romanians are quick to assert that a post-Yugoslavia scenario could never apply to them. Political stability could be threatened if the Autumn 1996 general elections force the now consolidated Iliescu–rightist coalition to give up its power or wealth, like the 1990s Nicaragua scenario. Even that nightmare of ungovernability and provocation is still short of civil war. It seems improbable so long as President Iliescu remains in charge of the coalition, and the radical parties enjoy their separate 'pieces of the action.' Enjoying the privileges of the new class under oligarchic capitalism, their bark should continue to exceed their bite, shocking as it is.

Macro-economic performance and government policies with Hungary should affect the behaviour of the radical right. Though the law on privatization was belatedly enacted in 1995, it remains to be seen whether state firms are ever really privatized and whether it is done efficiently and honestly. President Iliescu has repeatedly pledged to normalize relations with Hungary, but a treaty as of mid-1995, has still not been signed and ratified by parliament. Four scenarios are possible:

TABLE 6.5
FACTIONS FORMED WITHIN THE ROMANIAN RIGHT
NORMALIZE RELATIONS WITH HUNGARY

		Peace-treaty with Hungary	No treaty with Hungary
ECONOMIC			
REFORM	Privatize	Greater Romania gets very angry	Greater Romania complains
	Do Not Privatize	Romanian Nat'l Unity reacts with *Vatră*	Romanian Nat'l Unity mildly complains

The two dimensions of domestic and foreign policy suggest which party will complain and which will mobilize more of the two most chauvinist and active parties during 1992–1996. Greater Romania, representing the most extreme older generation, insists on preserving the collectivist aspects of the new regime, while Romanian National Unity demands liberalization. Both, along with the other radical parties, oppose normalization of relations with Hungary, even though a more collectivist government was elected there in May 1994. The Romanian right cannot afford to lose a potential enemy in Hungary. The *status quo,* as of mid-1995, is found in the lower right-hand cell, with PUNR complaining the most.

Part of the Romanian right will be much more powerful if privatization proceeds. These are the younger Securitate agents that were purged or left the presidential intelligence agencies. On the other hand, the older agents, who did not have the motivation to go into business, stand to lose economically if privatization proceeds, and have generally supported the more extreme parties and newspapers opposing any departure from nationalism *and* collectivization.

Economic decline is usually associated with radical revival, especially if foreign powers or minorities can be scapegoated. Romania's inflation, however, was stabilized to a certain degree after the December 1993 IMF accord, which forced the government to stop monetizing the *leu* currency. Many are suffering from steady drops in standards of living because they are employed at very low wages by uneconomical state industries. Foreign-mandated or encouraged, shock therapy, which has not been tried in Romania, is presumably more likely to foster chauvinism. Economic impoverishment of a large poor majority remains the long-term forecast, and markets and banks do not yet operate under open competition. Popular discontent or anomie appear to be strong, leaving the theoretical openness vulnerable to demagoguery or worse – even if conditions are better than in Russia or the Ukraine. So far the radicals have not criticized democracy itself, but merely the economic policies of the government, though the line between the two would be thin if the coalition were to break down.

The January 1995 protocol between President Iliescu and the three rightist parties consolidated a three-year pact-making process that has stabilized the post-communist regime and by June 1995 produced open cabinet appointments from these satellite parties. The scheduled 1996 elections could force another crisis if the post-1992 coalition cannot be preserved on Iliescu's terms. With the radical right already controlling a quarter of the seats from 1992–96, and no party likely ever to win an outright majority, the right will remain an important political actor, and could even gain significant power with a large plurality of the vote. The radicals could become either fascist, authoritarian, or democratic. Four scenarios are suggested:

TABLE 6.6
RELATIONSHIP BETWEEN ECONOMIC AND ELECTORAL RESULTS

		Establishment victorious	Establishment defeated
	Economy Declines	Right rises Possibility of fascism	Polarization of disloyal opposition
ECONOMIC		Erosion of	Turbulence
	Economy	Right or	and efforts
PERFORMANCE	Improves	uncertainty	to survive

Some economic and electoral factors are more auspicious for the right than others. As suggested by the above table, the right could gradually erode in the unlikely event that the economy improved for the masses as well as for élites, and if free elections were actually held, in which the nominally democratic opposition might win. The first positive economic signals, a moderating of inflation in 1994, a positive savings rate, and modest domestic and foreign investment all occurred for the first time in 1994. This happened in large part because the December 1993 IMF accord insisted for the first time in the four years since the fall of communism that the government stop monetizing its currency and permit real banking institutions to operate. The requirement for real privatization with independent, apolitical stockholders remains to be implemented. Romania's first 'improvement' in 1994 resembled that of many neo-liberal stabilization programmes, beneficial for the élites while leaving behind a pool of more than ten per cent unemployed and 20 per cent underemployed. The latter groups are actual and potential supporters of the right, whether or not gross national product growth is sustained, because they will be poor for the foreseeable future. Free and accountable elections with a formal voter registration and full verification of the results are not foreseeable except under unlikely foreign pressure for electoral reforms.

The only possibility for the lower-left-cell scenario would appear to be if the ruling coalition underwent significant, democratic political learning accompanied by economic growth with privatization. So far, constitutional or legal control of the post-communist regime has been remote. Force has not been used to obtain compliance since the 1992 electoral pact, consistent with what some call the two-millennia-old Romanian national character of 'going along' with those in power.[50] Co-operation of the radical right and Iliescu factions has produced a nascent oligarchy, whose stability is based on neither side becoming dominant and both sharing the spoils of power. Given the right's ideology and terms for the pact, democratic political learning is unlikely. The right will remain a potent actor, either as an uneasy coalition partner or as a rival to obtain power through force, should the economy decline. The suspicious deaths, especially of rightist élites, may have neutralized the latter, but also might prompt acts of vengeance.

The most important variable remains the presidency's control over intelligence agencies, which have, at different junctures, supported or opposed all the parties in the ruling coalition. Iliescu's 1992 electoral pact with the rightists, which was formalized publicly in January 1995, has given the Iliescu presidency a temporary but legitimate monopoly over state coercion. It is difficult to measure how much restraint will be exercised if the right decides that the President's double game should no longer be just for show. It could use violence to prove its anti-Hungarian, anti-Russian, anti-Western/American and/or Jewish credentials, as proof that it practises what it preaches and possibly believes. Possible pretexts could include manufactured or actual Hungarian subversion in Transylvania; Russian failure to withdraw its Fourteenth Army from the Transdniester region by 1998; a Russian rightist electoral victory and/or Russian withdrawal from the NATO Partnership for Peace; entry of Hungary into NATO before Romania; armed Western intervention against Serbia; and/or US failure to deliver adequate trade benefits, foreign aid, or military technology to Romania. In light of what could transpire, it is easy to understand why the West has tolerated the stabilizing incorporation of the radical right into Romania's regime.

Notes

1. I thank Peter H. Merkl and Aurelian Craiuțu for their helpful comments on a prior draft of this chapter.
2. Interview by Leonard Lopate, 'New York and Company' show, WNYC-AM, 5 June 1995. Katherine Verdery explains how intellectuals used nationalism to justify Romania's regime and independence of the Soviet Union in *National Ideology Under Socialism: Identity and Cultural Politics in Ceaușescu's Romania* (Berkeley: University of California Press, 1991).
3. *Modern Times* (New York: Harper Collins, 1991), p. 761. This was similar to the Ottoman Empire's Platonic-type army conscripted by its infamous, but effective mercenary child-tax.
4. Former US Ambassador to Romania, David B. Funderburk, noted that the publication of his PhD thesis in Romanian, *British Policy Toward Romania, 1938–1940*, was halted because he wrote, 'Many of the now Communist leaders were fascists.' *Pinstripes and Reds*, (Washington: Selous Foundation Press, 1987), p. 111.
5. On 24 May 1995 *Ziua* published two letters from General Igor Botnarichuk, Iliescu's teacher in Moscow, which asserted that Iliescu had been a KGB agent since he spent several years studying in the USSR. The often cited letter is somewhat questionable because the editor of *Ziua*, Sorin Roșca-Stănescu, admitted in a 1992 interview published in *22* to having worked for the *Securitate*.
6. 'National Reconciliation and Complicity', Paper delivered to the Bucharest Social Science Centre Conference on National Reconciliation, 3–4 June 1994. Cf, E. Behr, *Kiss the Hand You Cannot Bite: The Rise and Fall of the Ceaușescus* (New York: Villard Books, 1991), p.146.
7. Polls show only 15 per cent support for a constitutional monarchy. Some believe support for a constitutional monarchy is potentially much greater since ethnic Romanians were loyal to their princes and nobles for centuries; democratization was occurring under King Charles II in the 1920s and early 1930s; and his son, King Michael, attracted at least 100,000 spectators in Bucharest at Easter in 1992, during his only permitted visit since he left Romania in 1947.
8. The National Liberals and the National Peasant Christian Democrats were revived by their pre-War leaders. Unlike other Central European countries, Romania has not had a strong civic party because it had so few anti-communists to check infiltrators.
9. Stated by Brucan in 1990 and suggested in his 1992 book *Generație Irostă*. His estimate should be taken as an indicator.
10. A former Romanian Ambassador to the US, Mircea Malița, told me in May 1992 that Mazilu was 'crazy and would have been much worse than Milosevic, had Mazilu taken over the National Salvation Front'. Mazilu was fired by Iliescu on the pretext that he had been director of the *Securitate* school in Băneasa.
11. Larry Watts dates the Iliescu conspiracy to at least 1984, when Iliescu, Militaru, Defence Minister Colonel General Ion Ionița, and General Stefan Kostyal had planned to oppose Ceaușescu's anti-minority line at the Central Committee. 'The Military in a Post-Communist Romania', Draft (Santa Monica, CA: RAND, Dec. 1991), p. 36 (cited with permission of Watts).

12. P. Hockenos, *Free to Hate: The Rise of the Right in Post-Communist Eastern Europe,* (New York: Routledge, 1993), p. 166.

13. Măgureanu had announced the formation of the National Salvation Front on television and had facilitated the coup through contacts in *Securitate*'s anti-terrorism forces.

14. The Iliescu government stated that the former *Securitate* employed about 10,000 agents while Katherine Verdery and Gail Kligman suggest that the real number was closer to 100,000. Cf., 'Romania after Ceauşescu: Post-Communist Communism?' in I. Banac (ed.), *Eastern Europe in Revolution,* Ithaca and London: Cornell University Press, 1992), fn. 19, p. 127.

15. The leading sponsors of these anti-neo-communism protests were the December 21st Group, the December 16–21 Group and the League of Students. None included the date of 22 December, the day when Iliescu took power. Cf., Verdery and Kligman, *Op. Cit.,* pp. 130–40.

16. Iliescu's statement, ROMPRESS, 14 June 1990, pp. 7–8, as reprinted by *România Liberă,* (Free Romania), 13 June 1995, p. 3.

17. M. Rady, *Romania in Turmoil* (London and New York; I.B. Tauris & Co. Ltd., 1992), p. 187.

18. The first two incidents, on 28–29 Jan. 1990 and 18-19 Feb. 1990, were less bloody than the June 1990 and Sept. 1991 missions.

19. D. Uncu, 'Ion Iliescu, Vinovat' (guilty), *România Liberă,* (Free Romania), 13 June 1995, p. 3.

20. President Iliescu had asserted they were of the 'Legionnaire type'. Verdery and Kligman, *Op. Cit.,* fn. 27, p. 133. Martyn Rady concluded that the 'violence of June was the work of the Iron Guard Legionnaires was not entirely inappropriate.' *Op. Cit.,* p. 189. Michael Shafir doubts that the Iron Guard activities were significant. 'Anti-Semitism in the Postcommunist Era', in R.L. Braham, (ed.), *The Tragedy of Romanian Jewry,* (Boulder CO: Social Science Monographs, 1994), pp. 341–2. Those interviewed on the fourth anniversary of the raid on 'Radio Contact' were also dubious.

21. Josif Constantin Drăgan, *Istoria Românilor* (Bucureşti, 1993), p. 284. (Usually his first name is spelled Iosif.)

22. M. Shafir, 'The Congress of the Hungarian Democratic Federation of Romania: Postponed Confrontations', *Sfera Politicii,* (Sphere of Politics), Vol. 1, No. 3, Feb. 1993, pp. 11–12. The Government of Hungary has no territorial claims over Transylvania, though Hungarian ultra-nationalists make irredentist comments.

23. M. Dogan, 'Comparing the Decline of Nationalisms in Western Europe: the Generational Dynamic', *International Social Science Journal,* 1993, No. 136. L. Paul, 'The Stolen Revolution: Minorities in Romania after Ceauşescu', in J. O'Loughlin and H. Van der Wusten, *The New Political Geography in Eastern Europe* (London and Belhaven, NY: Halsted, 1993), pp.161–2.

24. A coalition precursor to the Romanian National Unity Party received slightly more than two per cent in the 20 May 1990 elections. The forerunner to the Socialist Labour Party received less than half of one per cent.

25. H.F. Carey, 'Irregularities or Rigging: the 1992 Romanian Parliamentary Elections', *East European Quarterly,* Vol. XXIX, No. 1, 1995, pp. 43–66. For estimates of true results, H.F. Carey, 'The Art of Rigging: the 1992 Romanian Parliamentary Elections', *Sfera Politicii* (Sphere of Politics) Oct. 1993, pp. 8–9.

26. Cf., Shafir's articles in the March and April 1994 issues of *Sfera Politicii* (Sphere of Politics) on parties of radical revival.

27. Cf., J. Ely and V. Triculescu, 'The Movement for Romania Party,' Student Politics

and National Reconciliation', Paper delivered to the International Sociology Congress, Bielefeld, Germany, July 1994. Only one small article appeared in *România Liberă* (Free Romania) on Munteanu's alleged death during the months that followed.

28. Funar is analogous to Jam Sadiq Ali, who was named Sindh Chief Minister in 1990 to attack and destroy the Pakistan People's Party.

29. H. Pepine, *Sfera Politicii.*, April 1994, p. 4.

30. King Matthew was a Hungarian King and at least partly an ethnic Romanian, 'who should be remembered in public monuments for Romanian–Hungarian co-operation, not for his defeat. The regime is trying to distort history by creating a new monuments commission composed mostly of *nomenklatura*', according to Dinu Giurescu, Interview, Bucharest, 25 March 1993.

31. *Evenimentul Zilei,* (The Event of the Day), 1 Dec. 1994.

32. One Senator from the PDSR ruling party, Simeon Tatus, withdrew his signature under pressure from Iliescu.

33. Telephone interview, 7 Feb. 1995.

34. *Târta* is a colloquial slur against Jews. Quoted in M. Shafir, 'Anti-Semitism in the Postcommunist Era', *Op. Cit.,* p. 336. Cf., Hockenos, *Op. Cit.,* p. 190.

35. Quoted in E. Behr, *Op. Cit.,* p. 203.

36. M. Shafir, 'The Tragedy...', *Op. Cit.,* p. 343. J.G. Pilon, *The Bloody Flag: Post-Communist Nationalism in Eastern Europe* (New Brunswick, NJ: Transaction Publishers, 1992), p. 68.

37. Press conference statement, 2 Oct. 1992.

38. R. Ioanid, 'Anti-Semitism and the Treatment of the Holocaust in Postcommunist Romania,' in R.L. Braham (ed.) *Anti-Semitism and the Treatment of the Holocaust in Postcommunist Eastern Europe* (Boulder, CO: Social Science Monographs, 1994), pp. 171–2.

39. The UDMR memorandum was published in *România Liberă,* (Free Romania) 3 Sept. 1993, p. 9. The Romanian government's response was published in *Adevarul,* (The Truth), 3 Sept. 1993, p. 1.

40. Statement of Corneliu Vadim Tudor, Weekly Press Conference, 24 March 1993. Interestingly, neither Greater Romania nor the other radical parties have attacked women in politics or women.

41. R.L. Braham, 'Anti-Semitism and the Holocaust in the Politics of Eastern Europe', in *Op. Cit.,* pp. 5–7, 14, 16.

42. Generally, only non-critical journalists attend the press conferences of rightist parties. Those from the democratic opposition can be expelled. Livia Săpălacan of *România Liberă* (Free Romania) in 1993 and Diana Georgescu of *Cotidianul* (The Daily) in 1994 have been prohibited from Greater Romania press conferences. The latter reported in *Cotidianul,* 31 Oct. 1994, p. 1.

43. H.F. Carey, 'From Big Lie to Small Lie: Audio-Visual Dominance and Authoritarian Socialization and Legitimation in Romania', *Eastern European Politics and Societies,* forthcoming.

44. I. Bădescu, D. Abraham and S. Chelcea, 'Empirical Patterns and Academic Patterns of Approaching the Situation of Ethnic Groups Living Together in Romania', Paper delivered to the Bucharest Social Science Centre Conference on National Reconciliation, 3-4 June 1994.

45. Crowther and Muntean, 'Electoral Politics and Transition in Romania', Research Monograph of the National Council for Soviet and East European Research. Discussion with Crowther, 15 Jan. 1995.

46. 'The Clash of Civilizations?' *Foreign Affairs,* Vol. 72, No. 3, Summer 1993,

pp. 22–49 and the debates in the next two issues.

47. *Tineretul Liber,* (The Free Youth), 24 Aug. 1993, p. 1.
48. H.F. Carey, 'Institutionalizing Political Polling in Romania', *Sfera Politicii,* (Sphere of Politics), April 1994, No. 14, pp. 21–2.
49. P. Câmpeanu, 'Residual Communist Parties and Radical Capitalization or Internationalization in Romania', Paper delivered to Bucharest Social Science Centre Conference on Internationalization and Democratization, 15 Dec. 1993.
50. This generalization is only true on average. Romanian coup attempts were common during the Second World War. Pressure from the rightist Iron Guard, Ion Antonescu, and popular protests forced King Charles II to abdicate in Sept. 1940. Some argue that the Iron Guard attempted a coup in Jan. 1941, which was suppressed by Marshal Antonescu, whom King Michael overthrew on 23 Aug. 1944.

7

The Radical Right in Post-Communist Russian Politics

Vera Tolz*

The unexpectedly good performance of Vladimir Zhirinovky's extreme nationalist party in the December 1993 parliamentary elections in Russia emphasized the importance of the far right in Russia's post-communist politics.[1] Prior to these elections the majority of Russian and Western observers, with a few exceptions, dismissed as insignificant the extremist right-wing groups which started to openly publicize their views in the official Russian and Soviet media in the late 1980s.[2] But in December 1993, the Liberal Democratic Party, whose leader proposed recreating the Russian empire by reincorporating into it parts of Poland and Finland, and who threatened Russia's neighbours with the use of nuclear weapons, turned out to be the most successful in the elections held on party lists, achieving up to one-half of the seats in the State Duma (the lower chamber of the parliament). Moreover, in many Russian regions Zhirinovsky was followed in the elections by the anti-reformist Communist Party of the Russian Federation, whose platform combines communism with extreme nationalism.

Zhirinovsky and other extreme critics of the post-communist Russian government appealed to those Russians who were 'tired of seeing the children of the *nomenklatura* rising effortlessly to power, the managers of former state-owned factories privatizing their plants and treating them as their own, and former communist bosses stepping nimbly into the role of entrepreneurs', which is what many ordinary Russians regard as the main result of President Yeltsin's economic and political reforms.[3] It has been realized by both the Russian leadership as well as Western observers that Zhirinovsky might be a demagogue, but the popular discontent that he tapped is nonetheless real.

*Vera Tolz is currently a visiting scholar at the Russian Research Center, Harvard University. Prior to that she was assistant director of the Analytic Research Department at Radio Liberty/Radio Free Europe Research Institute (Munich). She received her PhD at the University of Birmingham (England). She is the author of *The USSR's Emerging Multiparty System* (Praeger, 1990) and many other works on Russian politics.

Zhirinovsky's victory in December 1993 did not mean that the far right had come to power in Russia. He and other extremists were quickly sidelined in the Duma and excluded from the most sensitive posts in the parliamentary committees and commissions.[4] Moreover, the parliament's role in today's Russian politics is marginal, because the new constitution, which was adopted in December 1993, vests most of the powers with the executive branch. The parliament does not have the right to form the government, which is a prerogative of the president. However, the far right is playing an important role in Russian politics today by influencing the policies of Yeltsin's government. If economic and political disarray continues, a right-wing candidate has a chance to win in the 1996 Russian presidential elections.

Zhirinovsky's party, and other groups that are the focus of this article, promote ultranationalist extremism, which entails proposals for the territorial expansion of Russia, incitement of racial hatred and prejudice, propaganda of racial superiority and exclusiveness, and encouragement of discrimination against ethnic minorities. Many students of Russian nationalism say that it is difficult to draw a line between extreme and benign nationalism in Russia. Historically, Russian patriotism has often been exploited by radical xenophobic groups, whereas Westernized liberal Russian intellectuals have tended to dismiss patriotism as, using Samuel Johnson's words, 'the last refuge of a scoundrel.' At the turn of the twentieth century there emerged, however, a group of liberal patriots, consisting primarily of professional intellectuals (for instance, university professors), who combined liberal political views with strong Russian patriotism and who criticized other groups of the Russian intelligentsia for their lack of patriotic feelings. These enlightened patriots seemed to have succeeded in liberating themselves from the strong inferiority complex vis-à-vis Western Europe, which had traditionally influenced both the positions of Slavophiles believing in Russia's unique path of development and its messianic mission, as well as the stance of Westernizers, who rejected Russia as a hopelessly backward country. The line between the enlightened patriots at the turn of the century and the radical right-wing groups that became politically active in Russia in the first decade of the twentieth century is clear. The former were cosmopolitan Europeans, who hoped for Russia's future development along the lines of European democracies; they took pride in Russia's achievements in the sphere of culture and science rather than in its military might. The latter, by contrast, were anti-Western isolationists, who saw Russia surrounded by external enemies and crowded by internal evil forces, all trying to achieve its downfall.

The Far Right Emerges as a Political Force

It was in the beginning of Mikhail Gorbachev's *perestroika* that the extreme right-wing groups started to openly hold their meetings, which received coverage in the official mass media. By the late 1980s, these groups began to publish their own newspapers and journals, resurrecting the heritage of Russia's 'Black Hundred' – a conglomerate of extreme nationalist and anti-Semitic organizations that emerged following the October 1905 Imperial Manifesto, giving the Russians limited political liberties, including the right to set up political parties. The pre-revolutionary 'Black Hundred' promoted a theory of Jewish conspiracy against everything Russian. One of its programme documents was 'The Protocols of the Elders of Zion' – a fabrication by the head of Russian intelligence in France – which claimed the Jews' ambition for world domination. The pre-revolutionary far right was also anti-capitalist and anti-Western. Representatives of the far right equated Jews with capitalists on the one hand, and with revolutionaries on the other, thus fearing simultaneous revolutionary influences coming from the West. The 'Black Hundred' was best known for organizing Jewish pogroms in the Russian empire, primarily soliciting support for their activities from among the first generation of urban dwellers, who were insecure in their new status and felt threatened by the social changes of the time.[5] Following the October Revolution of 1917, the activities of the 'Black Hundred' gradually petered out, but extreme right-wing groups continued to exist among the anti-Bolshevik Russian emigration. These groups promoted the idea that the February and October Revolutions were the result of a Judeo-Masonic plot, referring both to the high number of members of Masonic lodges in the Provisional Government of 1917, and to the high number of Jews in the first Bolshevik government. Non-Jewish Bolsheviks were also proclaimed to be Jews trying to conceal their real nationality. As has been demonstrated by Walter Laqueur, the ideas of the Russian far right, which were initially formed under the influence of German and French ultranationalist ideologists of the 1880s, would later have an impact on Adolf Hitler and other Nazi leaders.[6]

In the Soviet Union of the 1920s, these ideas were discussed in some conservative intellectual circles[7] and at times were mentioned with condemnation in the official press, but then they had become gradually forgotten. Nationalism took the form of national Bolshevism (a combination of nationalism with Marxism-Leninism), the most extreme manifestation of which was Iosif Stalin's highly anti-Semitic campaign against cosmopolitanism in the late 1940s and early 1950s.[8]

The late 1960s and the 1970s witnessed the resurrection of Russian nationalism, which found its expression in publications in official cultural journals and which even had an impact on the Communist Party officials at the very top level.[9] Describing the reasons behind this phenomenon, Teresa Rakowska-Harmstone writes: 'The new perception of a threat to their [Russians'] political status in the non-Russian republics combined with a perception of a threat to their biological survival, in view of demographic trends and indicators of environmental destruction. The Russians developed a resentment of the sacrifices they felt they had made in fulfilling their role as an elder brother for which they had been repaid with ingratitude. They felt that they had been exploited by a system based on an alien ideology, which had attempted to destroy the very essence of Russian culture and spiritual values.'[10]

In this period, with the relaxation of Communist Party control over public life, émigré writings of representatives of the extreme Russian right apparently started to enter Russia through underground channels, and were reflected in *samizdat* publications. A few of today's leaders of the far right began as authors of *samizdat*. For instance, in the late 1970s, Valerii Emelyanov, a specialist in oriental studies, wrote a book claiming that the Jewish conspiracy against the Russians began with the Christianization of Kievan Rus in 988, when paganism was abandoned in favour of a religion which was under a strong Judaic influence.[11]

At the same time, the official campaign of anti-Zionism (aimed at the state of Israel, with which the Soviet Union broke off diplomatic relations in 1967) was too highly anti-Semitic. 'Professional anti-Zionists' Begun, Evseev and Romanenko also became ideologists of the far right in Gorbachev's period. Finally, the alleged influence of Masons on politics in pre-revolutionary Russia and on the Provisional government of 1917 started to be depicted in popular novels by the writer Valentin Pikul. In other words, in the same way as many ideas of the leaders of *perestroika* were already discussed by representatives of the liberal Soviet intelligentsia from the 1960s to the early 1980s, the leaders of extreme Russian nationalism were also ideologically prepared to use the relaxation of state control over the media in the late 1980s, their views having largely been formed prior to the advent of *glasnost*.

The first and the best known representative of the far right in the period of *perestroika* was *Pamyat* (Memory). The group was founded in the early 1980s as a literary and historical society attached to the USSR Ministry of Aviation. At the time, its main goal was to restore historical and cultural monuments; it also organized, with official permission, meetings at which Russian cultural and historical issues were discussed.[12] It should be recalled that the first pre-revolutionary extreme

Russian nationalist party, the Russian Assembly (*Russkoe sobranie*), started in 1900 as a group for the study of old Russian culture. Only in 1905, after political activities independent of the state were permitted by the Tsar, did it come up with a political platform, which among other things proposed stricter anti-Jewish laws in the Russian empire. Similarly, as liberalization of the political climate under Gorbachev brought about political activism independent of the state, *Pamyat* began to hold meetings and demonstrations, propagating its main idea of a conspiracy of international Zionism and freemasonry against Russia.

The first meetings of *Pamyat* in premises belonging to the state at which Jews and Masons were blamed for Russia's misfortune started to take place as early as late 1985. At a meeting in December 1985, for instance, its leader, journalist and photographer Dmitrii Vasilev, read aloud excerpts from 'The Protocols of the Elders of Zion', claiming that the subsequent course of history unequivocally proved their authenticity. Quoting from 'The Protocols' that the Jews should sacrifice their own people in order to enslave the gentiles, Vasilev claimed that Adolf Eichmann had been a Jew, and, in supervising the Nazi policy of exterminating the Jews during the Second World War, had acted in accordance with 'The Protocols'.[13] It was not until 1987, however, that the state-run media started to discuss the activities of *Pamyat* and broad segments of the population began to be acquainted with its views. The liberal press criticized the organization and its views, as well as the aggressive behaviour of its members. Only sympathizers of *Pamyat* were welcome at its meetings; others, especially journalists from liberal periodicals, were often harassed or even physically abused by *Pamyat* representatives.[14]

In 1987, a number of official periodicals started to propagate views similar to those expressed by *Pamyat*. The two main journals were *Nash sovremennik*, the organ of the Union of Russian Writers, and *Molodaya gvardiya*, the organ of the Komsomol. The former published works by Russian cultural figures, the majority of whom did not belong to *Pamyat*, but were sympathetic to the organization and expounded similar views, though in a more 'sophisticated' way. *Molodaya gvardiya* became an even more extremist anti-Semitic publication. These and other journals published 'The Protocols of the Elders of Zion' and other pre-revolutionary and Russian émigré anti-Semitic literature.[15] They carried various 'statistics' on the participation of Jews in Bolshevik governments,[16] as well as articles claiming that all major historic events from the French to the Russian revolutions were the results of Judeo-Masonic conspiracies and that many famous Russian political and cultural figures from Tsar Alexander I to the poet Mikhail Lermontov were killed by masons.[17] This irrational ideology combined a devotion to Leninism with the glorification of tsarist Russia. Most of these articles spoke favourably of Vladimir Lenin and especially Iosif Stalin, blaming the terror on their associates of Jewish origin – Trotsky, Sverdlov, and Kaganovich.[18] These magazines also published calls for banning non-Russians, especially Jews, from writing literary works in Russia, and for introducing the so-called proportional representation of Jews in all professions.[19] The adoption in 1990 of the Soviet press law which abolished censorship and permitted virtually everybody to start publishing newspapers and journals resulted in the appearance of a large number of newspapers which were even more extreme than *Molodaya gvardiya*. These publications, which belonged to various unofficial groups, focused almost entirely on the 'Jewish question' and regularly published excerpts from works by Nazi ideologists, including *The Theory and Practice of Bolshevism* by Goebbels.[20] Several magazines, including the monthly of the Defence Ministry, *Voenno-istorichesky zhurnal*, published Adolf Hitler's *Mein Kampf*.

Another important theme of the Russian far right has been the so-called Russophobia. This combines the belief in the malicious hostility of the West towards Russia with the idea that Jews inside the country, inspired by hatred for everything Russian, have been striving for centuries to achieve Russia's downfall. A lot of discussion was provoked by the publication in 1989 in *Nash sovremennik* of the essay, Russophobia, by a member of the Russian Academy of Sciences, Igor Shafarevich, who elaborated on this theme.[21] The discussion was stimulated not so much by the content of the essay, as by Shafarevich's personality. He is a scientist with an international reputation, and in Leonid Brezhnev's period he was a well-known dissident and a close friend of the writer Aleksandr Solzhnetisyn.

The majority of members of *Pamyat* and their supporters in Russia's literary establishment claim adherence to Russian Orthodoxy, and they have sympathizers in the hierarchy of the Church. The attitude of the Russian Orthodox Church towards extreme right-wing groups is similar to that of the Church towards the Black Hundred before the Bolshevik Revolution. Then and now many priests have been more liberal in their views, whereas there have been many reactionaries in the hierarchy. Today, the most notorious is the Metropolitan of St. Petersburg and Ladoga, Ioann, who quotes 'The Protocols' as a credible historic source in his writings. Patriarch Aleksei II, who is a moderate in his political views, is reluctant, however, to take a stand on the question, and extremists in the Church are not taken to task.[22]

Interestingly, some members of the far right have rejected

Christianity as a 'Judaic religion', turning instead to paganism as a 'true Russian faith'. The modern-day Russian pagans echo the idea of the Nazi ideologists who maintained that, being founded by a Jew – Jesus – the Christian religion could not be good and that Germans should therefore return to the religious beliefs of the ancient Germanic tribes. The spiritual father of the pagan branch of *Pamyat* has been the previously mentioned Emelyanov.[23] A boost to the development of politicized paganism with anti-Semitic overtones was given by the publication in 1987 by the prestigious publishing house of the USSR Academy of Sciences of the book by Academician Boris Rybakov entitled *Paganism in Old Russia (Yazychestvo v Drevnei Rusi)*. Rybakov, a well-known but controversial scholar, and at the time the Director of the Institute of Archeology of the Academy, claimed that Christianization had had a negative effect on Kievan Rus, as Christianity was a religion with a strong Judaic influence.

Those publishing and distributing anti-Semitic and often purely fascist literature were not taken to task by the authorities, as they reportedly had many sympathizers in law enforcement organs and in the Communist Party leadership. In a few cases, members of *Pamyat* were put on trial in connection with their involvement in hooliganism, rather than for the distribution of fascist literature. An article of the Russian Criminal Code which forbade distribution of publications provoking inter-ethnic strife had rarely been enforced. On the contrary, according to the liberal Russian press, representatives of the Leningrad City Communist Party Committee and police attended meetings of *Pamyat* in 1987–88, where organizers called for a ban on marriages between Russians and non-Russians and for the deportation of all Jews to 'the place of their historic origin'. On no occasion did these officials make any attempt to protest such statements.[24] Russian liberals also believed that the KGB were closely involved in the far right groups, as had been the case with the tsarist Okhrana and the Black Hundred. In October 1990, for instance, a former close associate of Vladimir Zhirinovsky told a liberal newspaper that Zhirinovsky was a KGB agent, and that the whole idea of setting up his Liberal Democratic Party (which has never been either liberal or democratic) was a KGB plan aimed at discrediting liberalism in the eyes of the Soviet people.[25] The belief that the KGB stood behind *Pamyat* was also stimulated by the fact that its leaders demonstrated a good familiarity with contemporary foreign anti-Semitic literature, primarily with extreme anti-Israeli publications by Palestinians, which was very unusual for an average Russian in the late 1980s.[26]

However, despite the fact that meetings of *Pamyat* and other similar organizations were very noisy and attracted much attention in the media, that a number of Party and KGB officials apparently supported *Pamyat*, that the most extreme fascist publications were sold in public places in major Russian cities, and that *Molodaya gvardiya, Nash sovremennik* and a number of other similar journals were available on subscription in the period of *perestroika*, the impact of the far right on mainstream politics and on the population at large was very limited. Opinion polls demonstrated that liberal, pro-reformist periodicals were far more widely read by Russian citizens than the nationalist ones.[27] In the 1989 and 1990 parliamentary elections, representatives of nationalistic groups lost to members of democratic movements. In the 1990 elections to the Russian parliament only two out of 70 candidates from the joint extreme nationalist-unreformed communist electoral bloc won. These 70 candidates were competing with representatives of democratic groups for the 65 seats (the rest was reserved for candidates of the Communist Party, trade unions and other official Soviet organizations). By comparison, the major democratic alliance, the Interregional Group, won 57 seats.[28]

The reasons for the lack of success of radical right-wing groups in the late 1980s and early 1990s were 1) the absence of a charismatic leader in the movement – such leader being a key element for the success of a populist movement; 2) the right-wing radicals' concentration on plots and conspiracies which sounded rather implausible to average Russians; and 3) their simultaneous neglect of the country's real problems – for instance, the economy. The final blow to nationalists seemed to be made by their alliance with the reactionary communists. While the communist system was becoming ever more discredited, and while the majority of Russians apparently believed in democracy and market economy as the means for solving the country's problems,[29] extreme nationalists decided nevertheless to begin co-operating with the unreformed wing of the Communist Party. The basis for this alliance, which has started to play a major role since the demise of the USSR, was the nationalists' realization of the fact that it was the Communist Party which had been the main force keeping the Soviet Union together. Whereas a few nationalists argued that Russia no longer had the resources to maintain the empire, the majority were imperialists. Even those nationalists who were willing to see the Central Asian or Transcaucasian republics go were still hoping for a tightly-knit union of the three Slavic republics, Russia, Ukraine and Belarus. In addition, both the extreme nationalists and unreformed communists, rejected Gorbachev's reforms. They both viewed these reforms through the prism of conspiracy theories; *perestroika,* for them, was planned by Western intelligence agencies –

above all the CIA – in order to undermine the might of the USSR, and thereby achieve its disintegration.[30]

In sum, there was an inner logic in the emergence of the communist-nationalist alliance, but initially it only further undermined the prestige of the nationalists.[31] Commenting on the obsession with the conspiracy theories on the part of the Russian far right and far left, Walter Laqueur points out that, whereas belief in plots is characteristic for the European far right in general, in Russia this phenomenon is incomparably stronger than in France or Germany.[32] While questioning the sincerity of Hitler's belief in a Jewish-communist conspiracy, Laqueur argues that when Russian extremists of the Gorbachev era accused liberals of serving the Devil, they meant it literally.[33]

The New Situation after the Demise of the USSR

The collapse of communism and the emergence of independent Russia within the borders of the Russian Federation – an artificial creation of the Bolsheviks – resulted in an entirely new political situation that was much more favourable for the proliferation of radical right-wing groups. It can be argued that the existence of Russia/USSR as a multi-national empire in which colonies were separated neither geographically nor politically from the metropolis prevented the central leadership from turning Russian nationalism into an official ideology of the state. Attempts at promoting Russian nationalism by Russian leaders (Alexander III, Nicholas II, and Stalin) were limited and short-lived. The Soviet leaders were also influenced by the anti-nationalist idea of 'proletarian internationalism', although from the 1930s onwards this slogan lost some of its initial significance. With the disintegration of the USSR and collapse of the Communist system, Russian nationalism has obtained more of a chance of influencing the country's policies. Even many of the politicians in the democratic camp began to rethink their attitude to the disintegration of the empire after realizing that more than 25 million Russians found themselves overnight in foreign countries, where titular nationalities were keen to deprive the Russians of the privileged status that they had hitherto enjoyed.

Many of these Russians, especially from Central Asia and the Transcaucasus, where violent inter-ethnic conflicts erupted, have been striving to return to Russia, creating a flood of forced migrants with which the Russian government cannot cope. The Russian forced migrants are, moreover, resented by the population of the Russian Federation as newcomers who compete with the local population for housing, employment, and government social care.[34] (Forced migrants – that is, Russians and other nationalities, who have ethnic autonomy within the Russian Federation, entering Russia from the USSR successor states – are entitled to Russian citizenship.) The decision of the Russian government in 1993 to introduce new laws on forced migrants and refugees, stipulating that forced migrants should get priority in receiving free housing from the state, naturally causes resentment in a country where, in 1992, nine million citizens were officially registered as waiting for the state to provide them with apartments.[35]

Simultaneously, after the demise of the USSR, Russia started to experience an influx of refugees – people from the developing countries as well as citizens of other states of the Commonwealth of Independent States, where armed inter-ethnic conflicts had erupted. The reason was the relaxation of border controls within Russia and other countries of the former Soviet Union. These refugees do not enjoy the privileges allotted to forced migrants, but they often provoke racist feelings on the part of the Russians. Like their counterparts in Western Europe, Russian ultranationalists effectively exploit tensions created by the influx of refugees and forced migrants. The leader of the neo-fascist Party of Russian National Unity, Aleksandr Barkashov, said in August 1993: 'The central regions of Russia are full of emigrants from the Caucasus and Central Asia who are committing acts of violence against Russian people. There will come a time when it will no longer be possible to put up with this and we will have to defend ourselves and our people.'[36]

The humiliation of national and even imperial pride started to play an important role. In an opinion poll, conducted in the summer of 1992, 69 per cent of Muscovites agreed with the statement that 'Russia must stay a great power, even if this leads to worse relations with the outside world.'[37] At this stage, several parties which helped found the main reformist movement, Democratic Russia, left to join forces with nationalists. Those who left Democratic Russia in early 1992 were Viktor Aksyuchit's Christian Democrats, Mikhail Astafev's Kadets, and Nikolai Travkin's Democratic Party of Russia. In February 1992, they organized the Congress of Civic and Patriotic Forces, which once again demonstrated how difficult it is to draw a line between moderate and extreme Russian nationalism, since representatives of Pamyat also participated in the congress.[38]

The Congress was also attended by the then Vice-President Aleksandr Rutskoi, who had already started to co-operate with the nationalist-communist bloc. Several other members of the Russian leadership also followed suit. Manifesting a badly hurt imperial pride, Rutskoi and other nationalists claimed that the borders of Russia could not and should not be equated with those of the Russian Federation, as Russia could not unequivocally give up all the territories it had conquered since the sixteenth century.[39] (Russia's territorial losses after the break-up of the USSR are far more significant than those of Germany following the Versailles Peace Treaty or of France in the 1950s, when it had to withdraw from Algeria – the two countries with which Russia is often compared today.) The most difficult for the Russians was the loss of Ukraine. This loss posed an acute psychological and ideological problem rather than a geopolitical one. Russians became faced with the question of what Russia is without Kiev – the centre of Kievan Rus, regarded by Russians as the 'first Russian state'? And it was only a matter of time before the idea that Russia should enjoy a special role on the territory of the former USSR became a key element of the foreign policy of Yeltsin's leadership.[40]

In sum, whereas non-Russian Soviet successor states realized that they have gained something important as a result of the USSR's demise, that is, independence (although they have been divided over what to do with it) the Russians, found that they had lost the empire at whose centre Russia had traditionally stood. In trying to identify a new concept of Russia's statehood, Russian liberal intellectuals and politicians had virtually no legacy to help them, as their predecessors in the nineteenth and early twentieth centuries did not question the existence of the empire.

Another boost to the proliferation of nationalistic ideas, including extreme ones, was given by the conditions in the country, which resulted from the revolutionary programme of economic reforms that were initiated by the Russian government in January 1992. These economic changes were socially disruptive and resulted in the deterioration of living standards of large groups of the population, whereas the small group of people who benefited from reforms included many members of the old Communist Party *nomenklatura*. This, as well as an increasing crime rate and corruption, stirred up serious discontent among the population and began to discredit the very idea of democracy and market-oriented reforms among many people. As Andrei Sakharov's widow, Elena Bonner, put it in October 1994: 'We have never lived under democracy but we have managed to discredit democracy in the past three years.'[41] As will be shown later, economic hardship, crime, and widespread corruption are currently playing a more important part in enhancing the role of extreme nationalists in politics than the injury to national pride stemming from the break-up of the empire. A joint exploitation of economic hardships strengthens today's alliance between the Russian far right and the far left (various unreformed communist parties that emerged from the disbanded CPSU).

Finally, the emergence of radical groups is encouraged by the fluid nature of Russia's political institutions and by the use of populist methods (that is, disregard for the political, constitutional, and judicial constraints that liberal democracies impose) even by mainstream politicians, including President Boris Yeltsin and members of his team. Part of today's Russian political culture, which has deep historical roots, fosters a more radical political atmosphere stemming from the distrust of any form of opposition to authority – making it harder for moderate parties, critical of President Yeltsin's policy, to make their case, leaving the opposition in the hands of extreme groups and leaders.

The New Ideology of the Far Right

In the early 1990s, the marginal extremists of *Pamyat* were gradually replaced in the political arena by more 'sophisticated' ideologists of the radical right. Although continuing to exist as a small group of activists, *Pamyat* had lost its leadership in the right-wing movement and thereby ceased to attract the attention of the media. The majority of the modern-day right-wing ideologists are also anti-Semites, but the ideas that they are propagating are not reduced to Judeo-Masonic and other conspiracies. They expound imperialist ideas, often aggressively, borrowing lavishly from Russian conservative thinkers of the nineteenth century (the Slavophiles), twentieth-century conservative Russian émigré philosophers (primarily, Eurasians), German thinkers, such as Karl Haushofer and Carl Schmitt, and the contemporary French right (Jean-Marie Le Pen.) Instead of trying to interpret Russian history as a series of plots by Russia's alleged enemies, the ideologists of the Russian right concentrate their efforts on trying to foresee Russia's future, which they picture as an imperial one. As the philosopher Yurii Borodai puts it: 'I can say frankly and openly that I am an imperialist... I believe in the resurrection of the Russian state after Golgotha.'[42] Another nationalist, former émigré writer Eduard Limonov, who has returned to Russia and who is one of the most prolific right-wing publicists of today, states even more boldly that 'since a Russian nationalist does not recognize the unconstitutional liquidation of the USSR' and 'supports the idea of a single powerful state within the borders of Russian civilization...the administrative borders of the communist epoch should immediately be revised according to two criteria: 1. Minimal: Where Russian people live, there is Russian territory... 2. Maximal: where people who regard themselves as belonging to Russian civilization live, there is Russian territory, protected by Russian might.'[43]

Many of the modern-day 'theorists' of Russian imperialism are strongly influenced by the so-called Eurasian movement, which existed among Russian émigré circles in the 1920s. This cultural and political movement began with the publication in Sofia in 1921 of a collection of essays entitled *Iskhod k vostoku* (Exodus to the East). The movement quickly drew support from well-known representatives of the Russian émigré community, whose views were far from being identical. Today's Eurasians are primarily influenced by the writings of the political philosopher Petr Savitsky, who spoke of Eurasia as a unique 'geopolitical civilization'. Savitsky wrote extensively on 'the geographical forces of history, climate, topography, vegetation, and race, which shaped the Russian empire and now Soviet Russia into the continental civilization of Eurasia'. Relying on Savitsky, today's Russian Eurasians also borrowed from Western thinkers of geopolitics the concept of the 'heartland' together with the concept that 'he who controls the heartland controls Eurasia'. One of the main proponents of these ideas in Russia today, Aleksandr Dugin, hopes for a continental empire from Dublin to Vladivostok.[44]

Eurasians of the 1920s were sympathetic towards the October revolution, regarding it as part of 'a global struggle against the imperialism' of the West. They spoke about the revolution as the masses' struggle, rooted in the native Eurasian culture, for liberation from the Europeanized élite of tsarist Russia. As mentioned above, in today's far-right–far-left alliance the devotion to Lenin and Stalin is fantastically combined with the glorification of the pre-revolutionary past. Following this line and echoing his predecessors of the 1920s, one of the modern-day Eurasians hails the October Revolution as 'Russia's purification of the Europeanized (cosmopolitan) intelligentsia.'[45]

The striking feature of the current imperialists, including Eurasians, is their inability to accept reality. They bitterly attack Gorbachev and Yeltsin for having pursued policies that led to the disintegration of the USSR, often referring to the current Russian leadership as 'occupying forces'. The main organ of the imperialist Eurasians is the newspaper *Zavtra* (Tomorrow) – formerly *Den* (Day), whose editor-in-chief is military writer Aleksandr Prokhanov. Prokhanov has often referred to the destruction of Russia and has claimed that in its present form the country has no future.[46] Another contributor to the newspaper, journalist Aleksandr Kazintsev exclaims: 'Look at the great Russian people. In the past the mere mention of their name used to destroy the walls of impregnable fortresses. Now they are defeated by Lilliputians... We have lost our identity; Russians – this word has become an empty sound without any meaning.'[47]

While being very pessimistic about the country's present situation, the imperialists are optimistic about its future, because they firmly believe that Russia will be able to regain its colonies and become 'a model civilization of the twenty-first century'.[48] They claim that the majority of citizens of the former USSR, and not just those living in the Russian Federation, still regard themselves as belonging to one entity – the Soviet people. They also point to the fact that the empire disintegrated at the beginning of the twentieth century but was then pulled together by the Bolsheviks.

Influenced by the Eurasians of the 1920s, the modern-day imperialists insist that, because of its unique geographical location, Russia is bound to remain an Eurasian state and will continue to act as a bridge between Europe and Asia.[49] One of the leading proponents of such ideas is the Tatar writer Shamil Sultanov, who attacks the democrats on the grounds that 'democratic ideology entails the US takeover of the former USSR'. Arguing that the USSR was the natural heir of the Russian empire, Sultanov stresses his belief in the future restoration of the Eurasian state on the territory of the former USSR: 'The state [the Russian and the Soviet empires] was a supranational force that reflected the interests of a multi-national Eurasian community... With all its obvious and hidden shortcomings, it was a definite social, cultural, and geopolitical reality. A Soviet citizen (even if he were a dissident) used to identify himself with it.'[50] Sultanov insists that only through the resurrection of the empire can Russia overcome its current political and economic crisis.

Most imperialists are anti-Western and especially anti-Anglo-Saxon. Commenting on the influence of Eurasianism of the 1920s on today's anti-Western sentiments of nationalists, one scholar says that proceeding from Eurasian geopolitical ideas, Russian nationalists 'view the world as an arena of perennial struggle between two global forces: maritime (Atlanticist) and continental (Eurasian). Atlanticist forces are represented above all by Anglo-Saxon civilization. It is assumed that the Roman-Germanic world is a part of the continental bloc. Thus, the whole concept clearly smacks of anti-Americanism.'[51] This interpretation of East-West confrontation helps the Russian right to justify close contacts with their counterparts in France and Germany. In 1992, the newspaper Den carried an interview with the leader of the French National Front, Jean-Marie Le Pen, several round-table discussions with Alain de Bénoist and Robert Stoikers (representatives of the New Right from France and Belgium respectively), and a conversation between the French nationalist Jean Tiriar and reactionary Soviet communist ideologist Egor Ligachev.[52] In turn, the Austrian and German far right are believed to be supporting financially their counterparts in Russia.[53]

Influenced by the late Slavophiles (Nikolai Danilevsky, Fedor Dostoevsky, Konstantin Leontiev and others), the modern-day ideologists of the right also believe in Russia's unique path of development (the so-called 'third way') and in Russia's messianic role of demonstrating heights of spirituality to the decadent West, which fails to fully appreciate Russia. The journalist Sergei Morozov wrote in 1992, developing this argumentation: 'The Moscow principality, which later became Russia, was designed by its leaders to be a counterbalance to the Catholic West; [its foreign policy was] a rejection of the West, and an indication of Russia's unique path lay in the dogma 'Moscow is the Third Rome.' Russia is a unique civilization; we can become European. But then Russia will lose its place as the first member of Russian civilization and will become the last member of Western civilization.'[54] These views are similar to those expressed by Dostoevsky in 1881: 'What is the need for the future seizure of Asia? What is our business there? It is necessary because Russia is not only in Europe, but also in Asia; because the Russian is not only a European, but also an Asiatic... In Europe we were hangers-on and slaves, whereas to Asia we shall go as masters.'[55]

Commenting on the reliance on Dostoevsky and other thinkers of the nineteenth century by modern-day Russian nationalists, Laqueur convincingly argues that, for all his anti-Western sentiments, Dostoevsky was a product of European culture and belonged to it, whereas today's nationalists do not. He writes:

> The early ideologues of nationalism... were in the tradition of the Enlightenment. Here we touch the basic difference between contemporary right-wing nationalism in Russia (and elsewhere) and its original inspiration: the issue of 'anti-Enlightenment.' To the right-wing nationalists [of today-VT] the philosophy of the Enlightenment is the work of Satan. The idea of being a cosmopolitan citizen of the world and the concept of pan-human values are despicable, the exact antithesis of the values and ideas of a true patriot. It was not always like this. When, in his famous speech about Pushkin, Dostoyevsky claimed that Russia's destiny was incontestably all-European (Western, one would now say) and universal,... he may have been exalted and somewhat woolly, but he was undoubtedly sincere. It is impossible to imagine a contemporary spokesman of the Russian right speaking in the same vein. A break has occurred...[56]

Further emphasizing Russia's uniqueness, today's nationalist ideologists claim that Protestant capitalism and liberal democracy are not suitable for Orthodox Russia, with its tradition of communes and collectivism.

They say that authoritarianism, hierarchy and the primacy of the interest of the nation-state over private interests are essential elements of the 'Eurasian tradition'.[57] The majority of the ideologists of the far right are anti-capitalist – which does not preclude them, however, from being involved in various businesses. Those extreme nationalists, like Zhirinovsky, who claim to support the market, maintain that if they come to power, they will prevent foreign businesses from moving into Russia, and will create conditions in which only Russian businessmen will be able to flourish.[58]

The contemporary Russian far right has also borrowed from Italian fascists the idea of a corporate state. One of the main proponents of 'corporatism' is the above-mentioned Eduard Limonov. In his 'Manifesto of Russian Nationalism' Limonov describes a classical model of a corporate state, envisaging a hierarchical state structure, with associations and unions controlling the lower levels. At the pinnacle of this pyramid should be a national council of corporations, which is to run the country as its 'economic general staff'.[59]

The demise of the USSR added a hitherto little known spectre to the Russian Far Right – an isolationist movement. Isolationist ideologists suggest that ethnic (non-Russian) republics of the Russian Federation should be forced to separate from Russia, and they draw maps of the new, ethnically pure Russia, consisting geographically of the European part of the Russian Federation and parts of Siberia. The most extreme representatives of the isolationists (for instance, the Russian Liberation Movement and the People's Social Party), demand forced deportation of non-Russians from Russia. (Throughout Russian history, however, intermarriage between Russians and neighbouring non-Russians has been a consistent feature, in fact very few Russians could claim purity of blood, but this does not seem to bother the extreme ideologists.)[60] Another branch of isolationists proposes the creation of a 'broader' Russian state, which would unite all Slavs living on the territory of the former USSR, including those in the self-proclaimed Transdniester Republic in Moldova, the northern parts of Kazakhstan, and Narva (in Estonia). The main proponent of this plan is the National Republican Party, which was set up in April 1990. This party proclaims Georgians, Armenians, Azerbaijanis, and the peoples of the North Caucasus, rather than Jews, as 'the main enemies of the Russians'.[61]

Such groups were extremely rare during the existence of the empire and could hardly muster any support. Today, proposals for the creation of a purely Russian republic without ethnic minorities sound more acceptable in the Russian Federation, where the Russians constitute more than 80 per cent of the population, than they could ever have sounded in the USSR, where Russians constituted about half of the population. In addition, economic hardship has strengthened not only traditional anti-Semitism, but also resentment towards Central Asians and people from the Caucasus, who are associated in the minds of many Russians with market traders charging excessively high prices. In addition, the media reports about the active involvement of non-Russians (for instance, the Chechens) in mafia groups influence an increasing number of Russians to support the calls of the extremists for the deportation of Central Asians or Azeris and Georgians from Moscow and other cities.

Inspired by these sentiments, some regional leaders began to adopt policies with clearly racist overtones. For instance, in the aftermath of the October 1993 disturbances, Moscow mayor Yurii Luzhkov ordered the deportation of Central Asians and the peoples of the Caucasus from the Russian capital. Luzhkov's decree was aimed against those who were violating laws, but many innocent people were reportedly mistreated during the campaign. While the campaign was criticized by Russian liberal intellectuals, ordinary people tended to support it.[62] In another example, in the summer of 1994 the Russian media reported that the regional administration in Kostroma demanded that peoples from the Transcaucasus, Central Asia, and the North Caucasian republics of the Russian Federation register with the police when they come to the region, and that they pay for each day of their stay. The policy is aimed at collecting extra money for the regional budget, and also at driving Central Asians and the peoples of the Caucasus out of Kostroma.[63]

One last trend among the radical right-wing groups is monarchist. Monarchists advocate a government by an unelected tsar in the belief that that form of government is the only one possible for Russia. The monarchist movements state that Russia should be governed in accordance with the principle of conciliarity (*sobornost*), whereby the monarch 'interprets the common will of the people and acts as their spiritual father'. Many of these groups are highly anti-Semitic, as is, for instance, the Orthodox Monarchist Concord, which was set up in July 1990 by members of *Pamyat*.[64] The most radical of the monarchist groups is *Zemshchina,* which advocates strict discriminatory laws against ethnic minorities and the imposition of a ban on religions other than Russian Orthodoxy.[65]

Profiles of the Major Extreme Groups in Post-Communist Russia

Radical right-wing groups in today's Russia are very numerous. They are constantly splitting and regrouping, changing their leaderships and reuniting so rapidly that it is not easy to keep track of them. At the same time, most of them consist of only a couple of dozen active members. In addition (as was the case with utranationalist organizations in pre-revolutionary Russia) the same people often participate in and lead several organizations. Today's Russian politics are very personalized; parties and other political institutions play a lesser role than personalities. Yet each strong ultranationalist leader always sets up a group (or groups), whose members he uses to promote his own activities and views. According to Moscow journalist Evgeniya Albats, there were 33 neo-fascist groups publishing their own periodicals in Russia as of September, 1994.[66] Among them, in addition to Barkashov's above-mentioned Party of Russian National Unity, are: the Moscow-based Military Patriotic Centre, 'Patriot', that broke away from Dmitrii Vasilev's *Pamyat* at the end of 1988; another group, also called 'Patriot', that was set up in St. Petersburg (then Leningrad) in 1988 by 'professional anti-Zionist' Aleksandr Romanenko; the Right-Wing Radical Party, a small group that broke away from Zhirinovsky's party in early 1993; and the National Socialist Russian Workers Party, which was set up in June 1994 by Russians living in Tatarstan's capital of Kazan.[67] (The National Socialist Russian Workers Party consists of only 23 members; other fascist groups are also very small.) In turn, in August 1994 the Moscow Anti-Fascist Centre published a list of 50 radical right-wing periodicals that regularly violate the Russian Criminal Code article forbidding incitement to racial hatred. Most of these periodicals, even if closed down by the Ministry of Information, can easily reregister under a new name to continue the publication of highly inflammatory material.[68]

Ultranationalist groups usually have a highly authoritarian internal structure and they impose military-style discipline on their members. Most of them emphasize a pyramidal structure of leadership, calling for 'a national hierarchy headed by a national leader.' The best example of this leadership principle is the Liberal Democratic Party. Set up in 1990, the party is synonymous with its leader, Zhirinovsky. Zhirinovsky's electoral success is the result of his accomplished performance on television rather than the result of a grass-roots activism by his party, most of whose members were not known to the average Russian.

Various radical groups, both left-wing and right-wing, form bigger blocs and alliances. One of the best known is the National Salvation Front (NSF), set up in October 1992 by leaders of nationalist (Mikhail Astafev and Sergei Baburin), communist (Vladimir Isakov), and imperialist (Sazhi Umalatov and Colonel Viktor Alksnis) groups. Following the publication of its programme which called for the overthrow of the existing Russian government, Yeltsin banned the Front by decree. In February 1993, the Russian Constitutional Court relegalized the NFS, however. The chairman of the Front was Ilya Konstantinov, a former activist of the liberal reformist Democratic Russian movement, who in 1992 turned into a bitter opponent of Yeltsin and his policies. The main base of the Front's support was the Russian Unity faction in the Russian Congress of People's Deputies, which Yeltsin disbanded by decree in September 1993. The front called for the recreation of the USSR and advocated the use of force, if necessary, to achieve this goal. The front was again banned by Yeltsin for its participation in the October 1993 disturbances in the centre of Moscow, but a number of its activists were elected in December of the same year to the new Russian parliament.

In the summer of 1993, leaders of the Russian All-National Union (Nikolai Pavlov), of the National Republican Party of Russia (Nikolai Lysenko), of the People's Social Party (Yurii Belyaev), and of the Novosibirsk branch of *Pamyat* (Igor Nikolaev) split from the NSF to set up the so-called National Opposition with the goal of 'fighting against Yeltsin's government and operating separately from the Communists.' Whereas the majority in the NSF were imperialists, the National Opposition promotes the above-mentioned plan of creating a purely Russian or Slavic state. The leaders of the National Opposition criticized the fact that non-Russians, such as Sazhi Umalatova, a Chechen, participated in the activities of Russian ultra-nationalist groups.[69]

Another well-known coalition which includes both ultranationalists and communists is the Russian National Council. Headed by former KGB general Aleksandr Sterligov, the Council was set up in February 1992. The Council's programme, which has strong anti-Semitic overtones, declared the priority of Slavic values above pan-human values, and the interests of the state above those of the individual. The Council combines Barkashov's neo-fascists with Gennadii Zyuganov's communists.[70]

Most extremist parties foster irregular paramilitary formations. Barkashov's party supervises the activities of the Moscow-based military club called the Russian Guard. The National Republican Party of Russia is loosely connected with the paramilitary group, the Russian Legion.[71] These paramilitary formations offer bodyguard services to businessmen, the overwhelming majority of whom are forced to pay protection money to criminal groups, and whose assassinations have become an almost standard feature in Russia's every-day life.[72] These formations reportedly take part in various conflicts in the countries of the 'near abroad', especially in Georgia and Moldova. They also participate on the side of the Serbs in the war in the former Yugoslavia.[73]

There is another branch of paramilitary organizations, gaining strength. It consists of the armed units of the Cossacks that began to revive in Russia in 1990, and which reportedly contains today approximately one million people. President Yeltsin's decree of March 1993 legalized Cossack military formations. Some of them are also participating in armed conflicts in the 'near abroad'. For instance, in the self-proclaimed Transdniester republic of Moldova, the Cossacks participated in the clashes between the Russians and Moldovans on the side of the former. Starting in the seventeenth century as a movement of freedom-seeking peasants, by the turn of the twentieth century the Cossacks gradually turned into the main defendants of the monarchy against revolutionary movements. Many of the Cossacks fought on the side of the White Movement during the Civil War that followed the October revolution of 1917. This provoked the harsh wave of terror against the Cossacks initiated in 1919 by the Bolsheviks, during which most of the Cossacks' settlements were destroyed, their leaders executed, and thousands of Cossack men, women, and even children slaughtered. As a result, the communal existence of Cossacks all but came to an end. The revival of the Cossacks' movement occurred, however, in 1990 with most of the leaders of the movement joining forces with ultranationalists in Russia. Commenting on the ideology of the revived Cossack movement, Henry Huttenbach said: 'On the whole, wherever a coherent ideological identity can be pin-pointed, the overall Cossack message is that of one closer to the spirit of Zhirinovsky than that of the late [Andrei] Sakharov. This should not come as a surprise. Cossack memories of identities rest largely on autocratic *ataman*-led military achievements, either in their own local political interest or in the service of absolutist tsars.'[74]

Prospects

Since December 1991, the influence of the far right on Russian politics has increased considerably. The nationalist idea, that Russia could not give up its influence on the other newly independent states, has in 1993 become a core element of President Yeltsin's foreign policy. The base of support for the right in society at large has also grown. This is reflected in the results of Russia's first post-communist parliamentary elections, and in the mass demonstrations which the right-wing–left-wing coalition is able to organize today. In late 1994, joint communist–nationalist demonstrations attracted tens of thousands of people, whereas in 1990 and 1991 they could hardly gather a couple of dozen.[75] Another important indicator of growing popular support for the far right is the level of youth participation. There are a number of radical right-wing youth organizations, including the Front of Patriotic Youth, set up in April 1993, and People's Social Party–Youth Front, set up in March 1991.[76] Simultaneously, bigger ultranationalist groups are also actively seeking support among disaffected young people by organizing meeting places and activities for them, such as athletic teams and rock clubs.[77]

This author does not subscribe, however, to the view that the replacement of Yeltsin's team by a highly nationalist government is inevitable. The comparison of present-day Russia with Weimar Germany, striking similarities notwithstanding, is in fact superficial, as it does not take into account today's entirely different international climate, which is sympathetic towards Russia, whereas Germany in the 1920s was viewed with suspicion and hostility by France and other European states. The chances of right-wing groups coming to power are usually strongly enhanced by the existence of an external threat to a country. Most Russians understand that no other state seriously threatens Russia's security these days. Therefore, ideologists of the right have to promote fantastic CIA and Judeo-Masonic plots against Russia and describe Yeltsin's government as 'an occupying force'. These ideas are clearly far-fetched, however. In addition, the camp of the joint nationalist–communist opposition still cannot put forward a charismatic leader, and continues to be torn by internal rivalries, which weaken this bloc. As can be said about any party in Russia, including moderate and liberal ones, most of the right-wing groups are very small in their membership, their social base is fluid, and their platforms incoherent. In other words, none of the right-wing groups are full-fledged parties. Although the opposition is very loquacious in criticizing the failures of the present government, it has failed so far to come up with its own coherent consensus plan of reforms.[78] Finally, the extreme methods often proposed by the opposition for the achievement of its goals, and at times employed by Yeltsin's government, are rejected by the majority of the population, as opinion polls conducted in 1994 indicate. For instance, according to *Komsomolskaya pravda* of 4 October 1994, in a survey held in the fall of 1994 in Moscow, 69 per cent of the respondents condemned the use of force by Yeltsin's government against the parliamentary opposition in October 1993. Sixty-two per cent of those polled also said that this use of force had diminished their trust in the government. At the same time, opinion polls have also demonstrated the decrease in interest among Russian citizens in the affairs of the non-Russian successor states to the USSR, and the increase in the belief that the Russian Federation should concentrate on its own internal problems, rather than pursuing an aggressive foreign policy. Interestingly, supporters of Zhirinovsky in the December 1993 elections have stated that it was his promise to restore order and discipline in the country, rather than his ambitious plans to expand Russia's current territory, that made people vote for his party.[79] The reaction in Russia to military actions against Chechnya in December 1994 also served as a confirmation of the same trend. According to several opinion polls conducted by the All-Russian Central Institute of Public Opinion (VTsIOM), one of the most reliable public opinion centres in Russia, up to 80 per cent of those polled throughout Russia opposed the use of force against the rebel republic.[80] Russian citizens felt the war in Chechnya put additional strain on the state budget. They were also opposed to a policy which required Russians to sacrifice their lives in order to preserve control over any territory.

At the same time, if economic conditions continue to deteriorate in Russia, and if leaders in Moscow continue to quarrel about power, paying little attention to strengthening new political and economic institutions, the chances of a victory of a nationalistic leader in the 1996 presidential elections will become more real.

The extreme opposition intends to nominate several candidates for the 1996 elections. One of the candidates will probably be former Vice-President Rutskoi, who, after being released from prison in early 1994, having been pardoned for his role in organizing the October 1993 disturbances in Moscow, set up an extreme nationalist political movement, *Derzhava*, whose main stated aim is to recreate the USSR. In November 1994, the so-called 'irreconcilable opposition' to President Yeltsin, consisting of extreme nationalistic and unreformed communist groups, announced that it intends to nominate Deputy Chairman of the Federation Council, Petr Romanov, as its candidate for the presidential elections.[81] Romanov's ideology combines Russian nationalism with communist beliefs. The third person, discussed in the media as a potential candidate to be supported by nationalists is General Aleksandr Lebed, the commander of the 14th Russian Army, which is stationed in Moldova. In his interviews with the Russian media, Lebed suggests that only a strict authoritarian government, led by an army officer, can solve Russia's problems. His model is General Pinochet of Chile.[82]

It is noteworthy that the right-wing–left-wing coalition is not intending to support the most extreme leaders (it won't support Zhirinovsky), but more 'moderate ones', who would refrain from talking about Judeo-Masonic plots, or from threatening to use nuclear weapons against Russia's neighbours. It also seems that these candidates will emphasize their promises to first establish order and discipline and fight corruption, making Russia's foreign policy ambitions an issue of secondary importance. The results of the 1996 presidential elections will indicate the direction in which Russia is going. Indeed, the new Russian constitution concentrates almost unlimited powers in the hands of the president, whereas democratic institutions (legislatures and independent judiciary), which could safeguard Russia from turning to extremes, are still very weak and ineffective.

Notes

1. M. McFaul, *Understanding Russia's 1993 Parliamentary Elections* (Stanford: Hoover Institution, 1994). Zhirinovsky's party captured 22.9 per cent of the popular vote in the elections to gain half the seats in the lower chamber of the parliament, i.e. 7.2 per cent more than his nearest competitor, the pro-reform Russia's Choice. Only the strong showing of the democratic parties in the highly populated industrial cities such as Moscow, St. Petersburg and Ekaterinburg, pushed Zhirinovsky's overall percentage below 23 per cent. In a number of small and medium-sized towns of the Far East, Siberia, and the North-west of Russia, Zhirinovsky's party received between 30 and 70 per cent. In addition, a number of other extremist leaders, such as Gennadii Zyuganov and Nikolai Lysenko, who will be discussed in this chapter, were also elected to the new parliament.
2. Reviews of W. Laqueur's *Black Hundred. The Rise of the Extreme Right in Russia* (New York: Harper Collins Publishers, 1993) criticized the author for overestimating the role of Russian right-wing extremism in the late 1980s and early 1990s.
3. E. Teague and V. Yassman, 'Who Is Vladimir Zhirinovsky?' *RFE/RL Research Report,* No. 1, 1994, p. 35.
4. W. Slater, 'Russian Duma Sidelines Extremist Politicians', *RFE/RL Research Report,* No. 7, 1994.
5. H.D. Lowe, *Antisemitismus und reaktionäre Utopie.* (Hamburg: Hoffmann und Campe, 1978).
6. W. Laqueur, *Russia and Germany. A Century of Conflict* (Boston: Little, Brown and Company, 1965).
7. T. Emmons (ed.), *Time of Troubles. The Diary of Iurii Vladimirovich Got'e* (Princeton, NJ: Princeton University Press, 1988), pp. 112 and 119.
8. M. Agursky, *Ideologia natsionalnogo bolshevizma* (Paris: YMCA-Press, 1980).
9. J.B. Dunlop, *The Faces of Contemporary Russian Nationalism* (Princeton: Princeton University Press, 1983) and *The New Russian Nationalism* (New York: Praeger, 1985) by the same author. See also A. Yanov, *The Russian New Right: Right-Wing Ideologies in the Contemporary USSR* (Berkeley: Institute of International Studies, University of California, 1978).
10. T. Rakowska-Harmstone, 'A Perspective on Soviet Ethnic Relations', *Journal of International Affairs,* No. 2, Winter 1992, pp. 539–40.
11. Emelyanov's book was published by an extreme Palestinian group in Paris and Damascus: V. Emelyanov, *Dezionizatsiya (De-Zionization)* (Paris: Free Palestine Press, 1979).
12. *Ogonek,* no. 21, 1987, pp. 4–5.

13. *Kontinent,* No. 50, 1986, pp. 211–27 quoted in J. Wishnevsky, 'The Origins of Pamyat', *Survey,* No. 3, 1988, p. 80.
14. *Russkaya mysl,* 27 Feb. and 15 March, 1987.
15. 'The Protocols' were published in *Nash sovremennik,* No. 12, 1991.
16. S. Korolev in *Molodaya gvardiya,* No. 6, 1989.
17. Peter Lanin in *Molodaya gvardiya,* Nos. 7–8, 1991.
18. *Sovetskaya kultura,* 23 July 1987, and *Molodaya gvardiya,* No. 6, 1989.
19. *Nash sovremennik,* No. 8, 1988.
20. These publications include *Russky vestnik, Zemshchina, Puls Tushina, Rossiiskoe vozrozhdenie,* to name just a few of the most extreme.
21. Shafarevich's essay was written in 1982.
22. W. Slater, 'The Russian Orthodox Church', RFE/RL Research Report, No. 20, 1993, pp. 92–5.
23. It should be mentioned that there is a revival of traditional paganism in some non-Russian autonomous republics of the Russian Federation, for instance, Marii-kl and Chuvashia, which has nothing to do with the anti-Semitic political movements in Moscow and St. Petersburg. See O. Antic, 'The Revival of Paganism', *RFE/RL Research Report,* No. 19, 1992.
24. *Moscow News,* No. 32, 1988.
25. *Moskovskie novosti,* No. 45, 1991.
26. J. Wishnevsky, 'The Origins of Pamyat', *Survey,* No. 3, 1988, p. 91.
27. V. Tolz, 'Impact of Glasnost', in Tolz and I. Elliot (eds), *The Demise of the USSR: From Communism to Independence* (Macmillan, 1994).
28. V. Tolz, *The USSR's Emerging Multiparty System* (New York: Praeger, 1990), p. 44.
29. On wide support among the Russians for the concepts of democracy and market economy in the last years of *perestroika,* see A.H. Miller *et al.* (eds), *Public Opinion and Regime Change: The New Politics of Post-Soviet Societies* (Boulder, CO: Westview Press, 1993).
30. J.F. Dunn, 'Hard Times in Russia Foster Conspiracy Theories', *RFE/RL Research Report,* No. 46, 1992.
31. It should be mentioned that although in pre-revolutionary Russia no political alliance between the radical left and radical right seemed possible, Russian liberal intellectuals used to point out that there was a great similarity between radical revolutionary groups and extreme nationalist organizations. See, for instance, R. Pipes, *Struve. Liberal on the Right, 1905–1944* (Cambridge, MA: Harvard University Press, 1980), p. 13.
32. This belief in conspiracies was very strong in the pre-revolutionary far right and then was resurrected in a different form by the Bolsheviks, with their obsession with 'enemies of the people', wreckers, and spies. It should be noted that even representatives of Yeltsin's government at times try to explain their failures, especially in the economy, as a conspiracy of the internal opposition and the West. The proliferation of conspiracy theories in Russia in different periods of its history is to be explained by long-standing political and geographical isolation, bad communications and political naiveté.
33. W. Laqueur, *The Black Hundred,* p. 26. See also Wishnevsky, 'Origins of Pamyat', p. 86.
34. S. Marnie and W. Slater, 'Russia's Refugees', *RFE/RL Research Report,* No. 37, 1993, pp. 51–3.
35. Ibid.
36. *Moskovsky komsomolets,* 4 Aug. 1993. Barkashov has espoused the cult of Adolf

Hitler; he and members of his group call for the establishment of a dictatorship in Russia by 'national-minded military men'.

37. Quoted by P. Rutland in *Arguments and Facts International*, No. 20, 1992, p. 3.
38. *Novoe russkoe slovo*, 14 Feb. 1992 and *Moscow News*, No. 5, 1992.
39. *Pravda*, 30 Jan. and 8 Feb. 1992. For the text of Rutskoi's speech at the Congress of Civic and Patriotic Forces, see *Obozrevatel*, 2–3 Feb. 1992.
40. On the resurrection of neo-imperialist elements in Russia's foreign policy, see B.D. Porter and C.R. Saivetz, 'The Once and Future Empire: Russia and the "Near Abroad,"' *Washington Quarterly*, Summer 1994, pp. 75–90.
41. Bonner in an interview with Ostankino Television, 27 Oct. 1994
42. *Nash sovremennik*, No. 7, 1992, p. 130.
43. *Sovetskaya Rossiya*, 12 July 1992.
44. *Den*, No. 2, 1992. Dugin began his political activities as a member of *Pamyat*.
45. *Den*, 12–18 April 1992.
46. See the dialogue between Prokhanov and the émigré Russian political scientist Aleksandr Yanov, 'Two Views on the Russia Idea', *Literaturnaya gazeta*, 2 Sept. 1992.
47. *Den*, 9–15 Aug. 1992.
48. See the round-table 'Russia after Yeltsin and Gaidar', *Literaturnaya Rossiya*, No. 31, 24 July 1992.
49. N. Narochnitskaya, 'The Tragedy of Disintegration – What Will Happen in the End?' *Literaturnaya Rossiya*, No. 34, 1992.
50. *Den*, 12–18 August 1992.
51. Igor Tarbakov, 'The "Statists" and the Ideology of Russian Imperial Nationalism,' *RFE/RL Research Report*, No. 49, 1992, p. 14. See also V. Tolz 'Westernizers Continue to Challenge National Patriots', *ibid.*, pp. 1–9.
52. Tarbakov, 'The "Statists" and the Ideology of Russian Imperial Nationalism', p. 14.
53. McFaul, *Understanding Russia's 1993 Parliamentary Elections* (Stanford: Hoover Institution, 1994), p. 27.
54. *Den*, 21–7 June 1992.
55. F.M. Doestoevsky, *Polnoe sobranie sochinenii (Complete Works)*, Vol. 21 (St. Petersburg, 1896), pp. 513–23 quoted in M. Hauner, *What Is Asia to Us? Russia's Asian Heartland Yesterday and Today* (Boston: Unwin Hyman, 1990), p. 1.
56. Laqueur, *The Black Hundred*, pp. 285–6. Dostoevsky's speech about Pushkin differs from many other of his writings.
57. A. Gulyga, 'The Formula of Russian Culture', *Nash soveremennik*, April 1992.
58. *Political Program of the Liberal Democratic Party of the USSR* (Politizdat, 1991).
59. *Sovetkaya Rossiya*, 12 July 1992.
60. V. Pribylovsky, 'A Survey of Radical Right-Wing Groups in Russia', *RFE/RL Research Report*, No. 16, 1994, p. 35.
61. Ibid, p. 31.
62. V. Tolz, 'Moscow Crisis and the Future of Democracy in Russia', *RFE/RL Research Report*, No. 42, 1993.
63. M. Obcharov in *Izvestiya*, 10 Aug. 1994.
64. Pribylovsky, 'A Survey of Radical Right-Wing Groups in Russia', *RFE/RL Research Report*, No. 16, 1994, p. 33.
65. Laqueur, *The Black Hundred*, p. 186.
66. Interview with Ostankino Television, 15 Sept. 1994.
67. The first three fascist groups are described in Pribylovsky, 'A Survey of Radical

Right-Wing Groups in Russia', p. 33. The creation of the National Socialist Russian Workers Party was reported by *Izvestiya Tatarstana* (Kazan), 24 June 1994, p. 1.

68. *Novoe vremya,* No. 35, 1994, p. 35.
69. Umalatov, a communist, became known as a bitter critic of Mikhail Gorbachev's reforms in the USSR Congress of People's Deputies, which was elected in 1989.
70. For more information on the National Salvation Front and the Russian National Council, see V. Tolz, W. Slater and A. Rahr, 'Profiles of the Main Political Blocs', *RFE/RL Research Report,* No. 20, 1993, pp. 23–4.
71. *Rech,* No. 1, 1993.
72. *Izvestiya,* 30 July 1993.
73. W. Slater in *The Politics of Intolerance. A Special Issue from the RFE/RL Research Report,* No. 16, 1994, p. 26.
74. H.R. Huttenbach, 'The Cossacks Are Coming! But Who Cares?', Association for the Study of Nationalities (Analysis of Current Events), Sept. 1994.
75. Demonstrations on 7 Nov. 1994, marking the 77th anniversary of the October revolution, whose participants shouted Stalinist and extreme nationalist slogans, took place in more than 100 cities of Russia and were attended by thousands of people (Russian Television, 7 Nov. 1994).
76. ITAR-TASS, 11 April, 1993 and Pribylovsky, 'A Survey of Radical Right-Wing Groups in Russia', p. 30.
77. W. Slater in *RFE/RL Research Report,* No. 16, 1994, p. 27.
78. It should be remembered, however, that the lack of a coherent plan of action is not a serious obstacle to coming to power, as the cases of Hitler and Mussolini demonstrate.
79. Report by the All-Russian Centre for Public Opinion Research (one of the most respected sociological centres in Russia) in *Izvestiya,* 30 December 1993, and Y. Levada's interview in *The New York Times* of the same day. See also other opinion polls, conducted by the Public Opinion Foundation in the summer of 1994, *Delo,* Nos. 26 and 30, 1994. See also, V. Tolz, 'Russia's Parliamentary Elections: What happened and Why?' *RFE/RL Research Report,* No. 2, 1994, pp. 7–8, and E. Pain in *Segodnya,* 22 July 1994.
80. Russian Television, 17 Dec. 1994.
81. *Nezavisimaya gazeta,* 18 Nov. 1994.
82. See interviews with Lebed in *Nezavisimaya gazeta,* 16 Feb. 1994; and *Ogonek,* Nos. 32–34, Aug. 1994, pp. 8–13. See also a report on the general in the German magazine, *Focus,* No. 37, 1994, p. 260.

8

Radical Right Parties and Civic Groups in Belarus and the Ukraine

Taras Kuzio

In the Ukraine and Belarus the influence of radical right groups is very different. Whereas in the Ukraine they are influential to a certain degree, especially in Western Ukraine, in Belarus there is an absence of political movements that advocate either racial superiority or militant action. Ironically, most extreme groups in Belarus are not those advocating Belarusian nationalism but Pan-Slavic integration with Russia.

In the Ukraine there is a larger nationalist constituency than in Belarus but its size and influence upon the country's leadership is far smaller than that in Russia. The growth of right radical Ukrainian groups and political parties has been inhibited by the weakness of Ukrainian national consciousness in Eastern and Southern Ukraine, the lack of strong state traditions, and a widely held concern not to repeat the historical mistakes of previous attempts at achieving independence through radical, revolutionary policies. Two crucial factors in averting ethnic clashes and the resultant rise of nationalism in the Ukraine were the rejection of ethnic, as opposed to territorially-based, citizenship, and the conscious attempt to maintain Russian representation with the ruling élites of the newly independent state.[1]

During the pre-independence period up to December 1991 radical right groups and parties were not popular within the Ukraine. During the Brezhnev era Ukrainian political prisoners were proportionately the largest group in the Gulag, but they were from democratic groups, such as the Ukrainian Helsinki Group, that had good relations with Zionist and other Jewish fellow prisoners.[2] During the Gorbachev era the main three groups in the drive to independence were these former political prisoners, the literary-cultural intelligentsia, and the national communists. Extremist views were anathema to all of these groups.[3] Radical right groups have tended to grow only since 1992–93 and the 1994 elections showed that they were only moving slowly from the margins of society to the mainstream political stage.

This chapter will survey radical right groups and political parties in the Ukraine and Belarus as well as manifestations of extremism and anti-semitism. It does not cover radical left groups in the Ukraine which are far more popular and could also be labelled extremist.

Belarus

With a population of 10.25 million that has a similar ethnic composition to the Ukraine (77.9 per cent Belarusian and 13.2 per cent Russian), the republic became reluctantly independent in December 1991 after the former USSR disintegrated. With a very low national consciousness, a large degree of Russification, and no national communist legacy Belarus has no tradition of political extremism.[5]

In the Gorbachev era the communist party leadership of Belarus accused the various informal groups and the embryo Popular Front of being 'nationalist' and 'extreme', but any cursory glance at their programmes would show that they were far from radical in comparison with similar groups in the Ukraine, Russia, and especially the Baltic Republics. Demands for state support for the Belarusian language, national symbols, open discussion of Stalinist crimes, restoration of banned Orthodox and Catholic Churches, and general democratic liberties were the mainstay of their programme.[6] No overtly fascist or extreme nationalistic groups emerged in the Gorbachev, pre-independence era. The activity of anti-communist groups in the late 1980s and early 1990s obtained their inspiration from three areas: the Chernobyl accident in April 1986, the Belarusian language question, and discovery of the mass graves of Stalinist victims.

Independent Belarus[7]

The slow pace of change in Belarus since 1992 has given it the same air of the five Central Asian states which pay lip-service to independence and reform and maintain the *ancien régime* in power. Belarus has largely remained free from the civil strife seen in many other former Soviet republics that forced the old ruling élites to adopt change. This is possibly due in the Belarusian case to a mixture of political passivity and lack of a culture of extremism, low national consciousness, low international attention, poor domestic resources (which increases

(This chapter utilizes the modified Library of Congress transliteration system for names, place names and endnotes.)[4]

reliance upon Russia), and even possibly a lower resentment of Soviet rule than found elsewhere in the former USSR.[8]

Belarus, with no tradition of national communism, also produced no home-grown version of the former Ukrainian President Leonid Kravchuk, who, through a mixture of appeals to patriotism and personal self-interest, was able to take with him the bulk of the former ruling class in support of independence. The 1994 presidential elections in Belarus brought to power a populist leader, Aleksandr Lukashenko, whose programme rested heavily on demands for reintegration and even unification with Russia.

The lack of ethnic conflict in Belarus can be explained by the following factors:

- lenient legislation on citizenship (especially the law adopted on 15 July 1993);
- a majority of the population's acceptance of the Russian language
- the government's unwillingness to promote Belarusianisation
- lack of targeting of traditional scapegoats (Jews and gypsies)[9]
- no ethnic Russian enclaves that feel threatened by Belarusian nationalism (for example, similar to the Crimea in the Ukraine, Dniester Republic in Moldova, or Narva in Estonia)
- political apathy provides a poor reception to extremist groups
- Western Belarus, although part of Poland (like Western Ukraine) during the inter-war period, has no tradition of integral nationalism.

Political Parties in Belarus

Most political parties in Belarus remain small with the exception of the two main antagonists, the Belarusian Popular Front and the Party of Communists of Belarus, the successor to the banned Communist Party of Belarus. The Belarusian public has largely remained politically apathetic and no political party can therefore claim mass support.[10]

The political passivity of the Belarusian population can be gauged from their support for the former chairman of parliament, Stanislav Shushkevych, which rested not on his association with any ideology or programme but on the fact that he was neither a communist nor a nationalist. Nearly 50 per cent of Belarusians had 'no confidence' in Zyanon Paznyak, leader of the Popular Front and the most visible, but still moderate, nationalist leader.[11]

The relative absence of political extremism in Belarus is reflected in a 1993 poll which, after asking who Belarusians would vote for, gave the following results: the Popular Front (16 per cent), democratic parties (13 per cent – Peasant Party, National-Democratic Party, United Democratic Party, Social Democratic Society, and the Christian Democratic Party), communist parties (17 per cent), others (6 per cent – Slavonic Assembly and the Party of National Accord). The absence of extremism in the programme of the Popular Front could be seen from the proportionately larger number of Poles (who make up 4 per cent of the population) who would vote for it.[12]

Following the decision in February 1993 to lift the ban on the Communist Party in Belarus, 18 like-minded organizations met the following month to launch the People's Movement of Belarus as a 'left centre bloc', a name deliberately chosen to confuse the public because of its closeness to the Popular Front. The new organization included the Belarus Communist Party, the Party of Communists of Belarus, the Movement for Democracy, Social Progress and Justice, and *Slavianski Sobor* (Slavic Assembly). The new bloc therefore unites both communists and national Bolshevik Slavophiles in a manner similar to political alliances in Russia but unlike anything in the Ukraine (with the exception of the minuscule Party of Slavic Unity).

The Slavic Assembly is the most extreme group within the pro-Russian and communist-dominated People's Movement of Belarus. A Belarusian branch of Vladimir Zhirinovsky's Liberal Democratic Party has also been established in the Republic and it is a member of the People's Movement. Its demands for dual state languages (Russian–Belarusian) and unification of the three East Slavic states (Russia, Ukraine and Belarus) are regarded as 'extreme' by the nationalist Belarusian Association of Servicemen and the Popular Front. A leading member of the Slavic Assembly was arrested in Lithuania on charges of inciting the Russian minority, and a number of its members went to Moscow to support parliament in its confrontation with President Yeltsin in Autumn 1993 (of which one was killed, a military officer).

Of the 100 different informal groups and parties in Belarus none of them has established paramilitary groups (unlike in the Ukraine). Officers in the Belarusian armed forces are divided into two groups – the nationalist Association of Servicemen, which demands the Belarusianisation of the armed forces (like its counterpart in the Ukraine, the Union of Officers of the Ukraine) and by the Union of Officers of Belarus, which is pro-Russian and communist. The demands of the former have caused some tension among the largely russified or Russian officer corps. In Ukraine the Union of Ukrainian Officers is not opposed by any other officers' group and between 1991–93 enjoyed a large degree of influence under former Defence Minister Konstantin Morozov.

Ukraine

The radical right in the Ukrainian political spectrum is dominated by three movements – the Union for Ukrainian State Independence (DSU), the Ukrainian National Assembly (UNA – formerly the Ukrainian Inter-Party Assembly, the UMPA) and the Congress of Ukrainian Nationalists (KUN). The UNA is dominated by the highly secretive Ukrainian Nationalist Union which grew out of the nationalist wing of the Association of Independent Ukrainian Youth. KUN was launched in 1992 in the Ukraine as the overt arm of the émigré Organization of Ukrainian Nationalist-Bandera faction (known commonly as OUN revolutionaries, or OUNr).[13]

Of the three radical nationalist movements one of the largest and most influential is UNA, with an authentic, home-grown structure in tune with local conditions. Whereas KUN shares a publication with its émigré financier, OUNr, the DSU also has only one newspaper, but UNA, in contrast, publishes two newspapers in Kiev (*Zamkova Hora* and *Ukrainski Obrii*), a magazine and newspaper in L'vov (*Natsionalist* and *Holos Natsii*), the newspapers *Nasha Sprava* in Rivne, *Cherkasska Zona* in Cherkasy and *Trybuna Narodu* in Vinnytsya. The volume of these publications after the ending of émigré funding from 1992 suggests a large degree of domestic sources of finance and support.

Interestingly, the former chairman of UNA, Lurii Shukhevych, son of the commander-in-chief of the Ukrainian Insurgent Army (national partisans from the 1940s) and a former long-term political prisoner, also gave the UNA a greater degree of legitimacy. UNA is the only one of the three radical right nationalist groups with its own paramilitary structure – the Ukrainian People's Self-Defence Forces (UNSO). There are also reports of the DSU and KUN attempting to establish their own paramilitary structures, but these are in their embryo stage of development. All radical right groups have camps for young people where political and military-sports training is undertaken. The DSU have appealed to the Ministry of Defence to help young people prepare for conscription by attending training camps of their 'sports' section, the DSU *'Varta'* (Guard).[14] Other organizations, such as the Association of Ukrainian Youth, increasingly adopted 'revolutionary nationalism' as their ideology in 1990–91, with nationalists propagating a 'youth cult' to attract the younger generation (both for membership and intellectual support). It is also often pointed out that Ukrainian nationalism will have a large appeal among the youth of tomorrow, although the bulk of young people in Ukraine remain politically apathetic.

Other nationalist groups, though smaller, have also emerged. These

include the Ukrainian National-Radical Party and the Organization for
the Liberation of Ukraine, but they have remained largely insignificant.
The Ukrainian National-Radical Party was established at the end of
1990 in L'vov, joined the Ukrainian Inter-Party Assembly, but remained
underground. Its leader, Mykhailo Stasiuk, launched the nationalist and
widely-read journal *Derzhavnist* in 1991, claiming a highly inflated
membership figure of 500 members.

The Ukrainian Conservative Republican Party and the Ukrainian
National Conservative Party are both small and straddle the centre-right
and radical right spectra. The former is composed of the small number
of members, grouped around Stepan Khmara, who were expelled from
the Ukrainian Republican Party in Spring 1992 for their 'radicalism' and
their hostility to co-operation with the Ukrainian National Party and the
Ukrainian People's Democratic Party in 1992 who were the two
founding organizers of the UMPA.

At the end of 1991 a Social-National Party of Ukraine was founded
in L'vov headed by Yurii Kryvoruchko, former member of the L'vov
region 'Varta' (Rukh Guard). Members of this small party, which has
already earned a reputation for engaging in violence, have apparently
attracted some members from the Student Brotherhood. They wear
black-shirt uniforms and use a swastika-like variation of the Ukrainian
national symbol (the trident). But, during the 1994 elections their leader
obtained only five per cent of the vote in L'vov, the highest of anybody
from his party.

Finally, the communist-Bolshevik Party of Ukraine, which is further
to the left than the officially registered Communist Party of Ukraine with
80 members of Parliament, endorsed violence by its backing for the
armed revolt against President Boris Yeltsin in Moscow in Autumn
1993. Thirty members of the youth branch of this party travelled from
Kiev and Kharkov to Moscow to support the Russian parliament in the
conflict.

'Romantic Nationalists'

The DSU represents the most extreme wing of the radical right in
Ukraine, which has inherited the traditional, ethnically based,
authoritarian nationalism of the émigré-based Bandera faction of the
OUN. It was established on 7–8 April 1990 in L'vov where the inaugural
congress was attended by 66 delegates who elected Ivan Kandyba as
chairman. A number of resolutions were adopted dealing with the
Ukrainian diaspora, the Law on Ukrainian as the State Language,
separate armed forces, and Lithuania. 'To avoid dissipating patriotic

forces, we have reached the conclusion that it is necessary to establish the Union for Ukrainian State Independence, whose task would be to mobilize the people for the establishment of an independent state...', the statement read.[15] A programme and a statute were ratified.[16] The DSU then launched the publications *Poklyk Voli* (L'vov), *Zahrava* (Stryi) and later *Neskorena Natsiia* (Kiev).

At its second congress on 22 December 1991 the DSU ratified amendments to its programme and continued to call for the establishment of an 'All-Ukrainian Political Co-ordinating Centre', which would unite Ukrainian nationalists in a broad movement and be led by the DSU and its émigré OUNr supporters (whose leaders resided full-time in Ukraine from mid-1992).[17] In contrast to the more 'pragmatic' UNA, the DSU's new programme called for the banning of former Ukrainian KGB employees from employment in the Security Services and other state positions, while placing them on trial for 'criminal activities'. Former 'communist party activists' should also be put on trial and prevented from holding state posts.

The third congress of the DSU was held in December 1992 and attended by 102 delegates from 16 *oblasts* representing only 530 members. The congress speakers attacked not only communists but also, with equal venom, democratic groups such as Rukh. Calls were made for Ukraine to possess a million-strong army and to keep hold of its nuclear weapons. DSU created an internal counter-espionage department entitled 'The Information Service'. Kandyba stepped down as leader to work on the revival of OUN in Ukraine and was replaced by the 37-year-old Volodymyr Shemka with Koval as his deputy. The congress was greeted by like-minded groups such as Stepan Khmara (leader of the Ukrainian Conservative Republican Party), Association of Ukrainian Youth, E. Konovalet's Military Organization, Club of Ukrainian Young Elite and the L'vov nationalist wing Rukh. DSU was finally registered in March 1993 as a nationalist movement which only accepted ethnically pure Ukrainians as members.[18]

Many former members of OUN from the 1940s such as Petro Dushy, and former members of the Ukrainian Insurgent Army, Mykhailo Zelenchuk, joined the DSU (although they later left for KUN). Indeed, on numerous occasions the DSU stressed that it (as the Ukrainian National Front of the 1960s) continued in the traditions of OUNr (in actual fact, the DSU programme differed little from that of OUNr at that stage). The DSU began to re-print the London-based émigré OUNr journal *Vyzvolnyl Shliakh* beginning with the December 1991 issue. Zinovyl Krasivskyi[19], deputy head of DSU until his death in September 1991, was also 'head of OUNr' in Ukraine.[20]

The DSU did not call itself a 'party' because this word was discredited in the eyes of the population, and it could not use the word 'organization', as this already existed in OUN. A major difficulty with the DSU was its lack of a programme on how to achieve independence. If it followed in the path of OUNr as a conspiratorial group but rejected violent methods, while, at the same time, rejected the parliamentary path, then it was left with few options on how to achieve power. At least UMPA (now UNA) had a clear programme prior to August 1991; namely, to elect a National Congress after signing up over 50 per cent of Ukrainian citizens, and then to declare independence.

Until Summer 1991 the émigré OUNr had close relations with both the DSU and UNA. Slava Stetsko, leader of the émigré OUNr, attended the fifth session of the UMPA in late June 1991 on the last occasion. The DSU consistently refused to join the Ukrainian Inter-Party Assembly/Ukrainian National Assembly. The differences between the DSU and UNA could be seen in their attitudes towards participating in the December 1991 Ukrainian presidential elections. Whereas the UNA promoted their chairman, Shukhevych (who failed to obtain the 100,000 signatures necessary for registration), the DSU was opposed to taking part and believed, like OUNr at that time, in the necessity of boycotting official structures.

The failure to attract the DSU (which had also called for a boycott of the March 1990 republican elections) to the UMPA led in 1990 to calls for the establishment of a nation-wide National Revolutionary Front. This was planned so as to include the UMPA, DSU and the Ukrainian Christian Democratic Party, but it failed to unify nationalist groups into one bloc, as did a similar call to create a Ukrainian National Front in 1993. With the increasing radicalization of the UMPA, Kandyba was proposed as head of the executive committee of the UMPA, with Pryhodko head of the National Council and Shukhevych overall head of the UMPA. But these proposals did not come to fruition. The DSU and UMPA/UNA have since remained in conflict.

Krasivskyi believed that former prisoners of conscience, such as Viacheslav Chornovil and Levko Lukianenko, had been calling since the 1960s for participation in the Supreme Council and local councils. Since 1988 their big mistake, in his view, was not to put forward the demand for independence immediately (until late 1989 only small nationalist groups in Western Ukraine advocated independence) and create an alternative to the existing regime. Instead, they worked within the then existing Soviet system.

In the course of the Ukrainian Republican Party's existence it had constantly suffered from internal struggles against its radical wing.

These radicals had either been expelled or had resigned; some had joined the DSU (Koval, Hryhorii Hrebeniuk and Anatoly Sherbatiuk), while others had formed new parties (Khmara), such as the Ukrainian Conservative Republican Party. In certain regions, such as Rivne and Zaporozhye, entire local branches of the Ukrainian Republican Party had defected to the DSU. Koval edited the DSU publication *Neskorena Natsiia* during 1992–93 and went on to replace Kandyba as current leader of DSU.

Many young defectors from the Ukrainian Republican Party joined the DSU because of the leadership's decision to co-operate with national communists (such as former President Kravchuk) from 1991 onwards in its 'statehood-first' policy. Stepan Khura, formerly head of the Ukrainian Republican Party in Kerson oblast, argued that any agreement between the communists and the People's Council in the Supreme Council, 'was always a risky path; collaborating with the occupier never ensured the path to liberty.'[21]

The DSU's main ideologist and head is Koval and therefore a closer look at his essay 'What Kind of Ukraine Do We Want?', written when he was deputy chairman of DSU, will provide an insight into his ideological profile.[22] The essay begins by stating that with the decline of Russian imperialism, which therefore presents less of a threat to the Ukraine, a new threat has grown – that of international liberalism with its campaign for 'human rights'. Support for individual over national rights at a time when the state is developing harms the establishment of a Ukrainian state. The independent state will be irreversible only when 'the idea that the priority of state rights is higher than individual rights will become dominant in Ukrainian society'. The nation, Koval believed, is the highest form of good and it, in itself, guarantees human rights.

The unification of all ethnic Ukrainian territories is a 'fundamental principle of the ideology of Ukrainian nationalism'. On the other hand, 'Ukrainian liberals and socialists understand unity only within the existing borders of the former Ukrainian SSR'. But Ukrainian nationalists regard 'the question of ethnic Ukrainian lands which are outside the state as remaining open for dispute'. In that context Ukrainian nationalists also stand for the liquidation of Crimean territorial autonomy. Ukrainian nationalists are in favour of 'determined state actions in defense of national interests'. 'We do not want peace in exchange for our territory', Koval stated.

Ukrainian nationalists stand for 'the cult of strength–spiritual, physical, economic and military – because they know that strength is everything. If we stand on our own two feet we will learn how to dictate and we will get allies; if we kneel we will receive only humanitarian aid', Koval argued. Therefore, they are in favour of strong borders, a strong army and nuclear weapons. 'We need a GREAT UKRAINE. We are not only statists – we are great statists'.

A major difference between nationalists and liberals is over the question of 'enemies'. Liberals are afraid of saying who the enemy of Ukrainian independence is – namely, imperialist Russia. Hence, 'the question of an "enemy" is one of the central concerns in our philosophy. The enemy and hatred for him is a great integrating element', because, 'when a nation "loses" the image of the enemy she becomes disorientated. A neutral Ukraine today is a colonial Ukraine tomorrow', Koval believes.

Pluralism only divides society whereas nationalists want unity and therefore they are in favour of 'democracy within certain boundaries'. The state sets these boundaries in order to control the ambitions of parties and individuals while the state has 'the right to neutralize actions harmful to its existence. Until we become a nation state, until we solve our national problems and aims, we cannot blindly be led by the basics of the Universal Declaration of Human Rights', Koval argued. For example, the state has both the right to halt migration into the country and the right to ensure that Russians living in the Ukraine learn the state language and to prevent them from forming autonomous regions.

A person's liberty, 'is not absolute but is only relative. Citizens of Ukraine have to be responsible about their state'. Because Ukrainian nationalists regard the state as being higher than the individual, there is a need for a 'permanent politicization and ideologization of society'. In addition, the question of 'order' is paramount with a hierarchical structure for society because 'inequality is a fundamental principle of the law-based society'. The state should first and foremost help the 'strong and talented'.

The question of security will remain an important question for the Ukrainian state for the foreseeable future. Liberals are unable to ensure the defensive capability of the country. 'And is this not why the West supports Ukrainian liberals? And is this not why America implants into the Ukraine, liberalism which disarms the young Ukrainian state. It is obvious that America is not interested in the entry on to the geopolitical arena of the new super-state Ukraine, which in the near future could become a serious opponent of American hegemony', Koval argued. Hence why are the Americans supporting those political groups which stand for nuclear disarmament, which place 'American values' over the Ukrainian state and are in favour of open borders.

The Ukraine should earnestly search out allies abroad, in particular in Central Europe, the Baltic Republics and Turkey. In addition, good relations should be cultivated with Germany, Italy, Austria, and Scandinavia. The axis that the Ukraine could develop should rest upon a connection of 'Kiev–Berlin–Vienna–Budapest–Rome'. Finally, the conservative basis of Ukrainian nationalism is based on the following principles: 'national interests, unity of all Ukrainian lands, militarism, hierarchy, order, superiority of the nation-state, anti-communism, anti-liberalism, and responsibility before the nation'. Ukrainian nationalism is 'state creating and nationalists are striving that it may become the state ideology of the Ukrainian revival'.

The only political groups close to the ideals of DSU were the Ukrainian National Party, the Ukrainian Christian Democratic Party, Ukrainian Conservative Republican Party, and the Association of Ukrainian Youth.[23] In terms of economic policy though, there is little to differentiate all of these groups on the fringe of the centre-right or in the radical right camp from the socialists and communists. The antipathy of the socialist chairman of parliament, Oleksandr Moroz, towards privatization is backed by the DSU which is opposed to allowing foreign control of Ukrainian resources and in favour of state regulation of prices. The DSU have therefore condemned 'American' pressure to privatize which they believe would only benefit Russian and Western capital.[24] These parties are therefore as anti-American as they are anti-Russian.[25] All radical right groups are critically disposed towards the IMF which would 'bring nothing good to Ukraine', according to UNA. Economic reforms and privatization would only benefit the West, UNA believed.[26]

Like other nationalist groups, they believed that the DSU should not strive to become a mass organization – although whether it could do so was open to question. At the time of its foundation the DSU had 300 members, which by December 1991 had increased to only 650 (less than that given at the previous congress). At the DSU inaugural congress, 75 per cent of the members were reportedly from L'vov *oblast*. The DSU, like OUN previously, should be a vanguard, élitist organization which enjoyed great influence over the masses, it argued.

By the fifth congress of the DSU, between 29–30 October 1994, of the 168 delegates in attendance they represented 1,344 members,[27] a proportionately large increase over the previous congresses but still representing only a relatively small political movement in comparison with its other two nationalistic rivals. The DSU leader, Koval, admitted that, 'not a single point of the DSU programme has been achieved, the Ukraine has not moved even one step ahead'. The DSU had not 'turned into an organization capable of influencing events on an all-Ukrainian scale', admitted Koval. On the positive side, Koval claimed that its sympathizers had grown to 'one and a half million'. It had broken the information blockade and established close contacts with like-minded parties and groups. The DSU launched its own newspaper *Nezboryma Natsiia* in January 1994 after *Neskorena Natsiia* had become the organ of the OUN in Ukraine, led by the former leader and founder of the DSU, Kandyba.

Congress of Ukrainian Nationalists (KUN)

In the Ukrainian diaspora, OUNr, as the leading force in the open Ukrainian Liberation Front, was on the extreme right. Slava Stetsko was also the leader of the Anti-Bolshevik Bloc of Nations which is a long-time member of the World Anti-Communist League based in Taiwan.

KUN was launched in the Ukraine in March 1992 by the émigré OUNr and held its inaugural congress in Kiev in October of the same year. Throughout summer 1992 *oblast* conferences of KUN were held to establish local chapters. Its ties to OUNr can be seen in the fact that the leader of both organizations is Slava Stetsko (who was in exile in Munich until 1991). The organ of both KUN and OUNr is the weekly newspaper *Shliakh Peremohy*, which moved its editorial offices from Munich to L'vov after independence.

Three hundred delegates from 14 *oblasts* attended the inaugural congress of KUN with the largest delegations from Donets'k, Luhans'k, L'vov, Kharkov, and Ivano-Frankovsk. Again, as with the DSU, many of its activists came from the ranks of the Ukrainian Republican Party, such as Maria Oliinyk from Donets' k who, like Khmara, had been expelled from the party in 1992 for her 'radicalism'.

Whereas DSU rejected outright any co-operation with democratic groups and is a *de facto* political party, KUN claimed its readiness to co-operate with national democrats on the centre-right, and declared itself as a unifying umbrella group for nationalist bodies (in this quest it came into immediate competition with DSU and UNA for the vanguard nationalist mantle). Although KUN is willing to co-operate with national-democrats in parliament it remains a 'nationalist force'. According to the head of the KUN Secretariat it did not recognize the current Ukrainian state because members of the 'procommunist *nomenklatura*' remained in power.[28] Like Rukh, DSU and the Ukrainian Conservative Republican Party, consequently, KUN opposed co-operation with the national communists and refused to work with former President Kravchuk. This is in contrast with the 'statehood-first' position of the UNA and the centre-right Congress of National Democratic Forces, which championed co-operation with the national communists as a pragmatic policy.

KUN was registered as a new political association in January 1993.[29] In early July 1993 a world Congress of Nationalists was held in Kiev with 500 delegates from the diaspora. The evolving split between UMPA/UNA and OUNr from late 1991 also led to poor relations with KUN. The UNA described KUN as 'uniting former democrats from the URP (Ukrainian Republican Party), since Rukh was coupled with a section of the diaspora which tied itself to the activities of OUN, but they had no relation to the armed struggle of the 1940s and 1950s...'.[30] The entry of KUN from the diaspora on to the Ukrainian political arena in 1992 therefore only served to divide further the radical right in the Ukraine.

Pragmatic Nationalists

The Ukrainian Inter-Party Assembly (UMPA) was established on 1 July 1990 as an alternative to those political groups who were in favour of taking part in official structures, such as the Supreme Council. But it never united all of the nationalist groups that had called for a boycott of the March 1990 elections, notably the DSU and the Ukrainian Christian Democratic Party. Many of the members of the UMPA were small or still in the process of formation. These included the Ukrainian National Radical Party, Association of Independent Ukrainian Youth-nationalists (who later renamed themselves the Ukrainian Nationalist Union), the Dmytro Dontsov Supporters Club and the Ukrainian Catholic Youth Committee. The two main groups which launched the UMPA were the Ukrainian National Party and the Ukrainian People's Democratic Party. Both of these were eventually forced out by the increasingly dominant Ukrainian Nationalist Union. The Ukrainian People's Democratic Party had limited its involvement in the UMPA to the Citizen's Committees due to ideological differences with the Ukrainian National Party.

The Club of Supporters of Dmytro Dontsov, the pre-eminent pre-war Ukrainian integral nationalist thinker, was established in L'vov on 17 December 1990 and it began to publish the journal *Nationalist*. It grew out of former members of the Association of Independent Ukrainian Youth – a nationalist faction, which later transformed itself into the Ukrainian Nationalist Union. Dontsov is regarded as the main source of inspiration for contemporary integral nationalists in the Ukraine, both of the moderate and radical varieties.

The first session of the UMPA was attended by 'observers' from the Ukrainian Republican Party and Rukh, but the relations between national-democrats (elected to the Supreme Council in March 1990) and nationalists (based in the UMPA) became increasingly bitter and have remained so. Although the UMPA established itself as an alternative to the Supreme Council, Petro Kahui, head of the UMPA executive committee, initially claimed that the UMPA never regarded itself as an alternative to Rukh, although their aims coincided after Rukh's second congress when they both stood for full independence. The UMPA merely believed that the parliamentary path was insufficient to gain independence. 'The very activities of the deputies of the Democratic Bloc promoted a quick recognition by a large mass of the population of the Ukraine of the ineffectiveness of the parliamentary path to achieve independence...', in the view of Anatoly Lupynos.[31]

Indeed, initially many groups had overlapping memberships of both Rukh and the UMPA (such as the Ukrainian Peasant Democratic Party), 'the...Assembly is directing its efforts at the implementation of an entire range of complex practical issues which will be an important addition to the activities of Rukh',[32] one commentator pointed out. On a visit to the West, Pryhodko, then a leader of the Ukrainian National Party and a leading member of UMPA, argued that, 'in the near future it will be possible to create a joint national liberation front' with the 'patriotic forces of the Democratic Bloc' in the Supreme Council.[33]

Yet, Pryhodko also called the Supreme Council and UMPA 'two antagonistic structures', condemning the view of Lukianenko, then leader of the Ukrainian Republican Party, that 'there was nobody to co-operate with in the UMPA'. In Pryhodko's view, the UMPA had 'forced the leaders of the Ukrainian Helsinki Union to abandon the idea of confederation' in support of at least a declaration in favour of independence. But, at the local level, some members of the Ukrainian Republican Party helped organize the registration of Ukrainian citizens.

The first session of the UMPA created the National Council on the Rebirth of Ukraine's Statehood and the Executive Committee, which registered citizens on the basis of the March 1918 Ukrainian People's Republic citizenship law. The first action of the National Congress after it had collected more than 50 per cent of registered citizens would be to declare independence, take power unto itself and dissolve the Ukrainian SSR structures. Then it would ensure defence of its borders, establish diplomatic relations, and conduct negotiations with Ukraine's neighbours. The head of the National Council elected at the first session was Pryhodko, while Arcady Kiryiev (leader of the Ukrainian People's Democratic Party) was elected head of the Co-ordinating Council of Committees of Ukrainian citizens.

At the second session of the UMPA on 6–7 October 1990 the Ukrainian People's Democratic Party refused to put forward candidates for the National Council because the ideological views that the UMPA propounded were 'undemocratic' and therefore in conflict with the programme of the Ukrainian People's Democratic Party. A certain section of the Ukrainian People's Democratic Party, led by Kiryiev, attempted to split the Citizens Committee away from the UMPA.

The UMPA had registered 729,000 people as citizens of the 1918 Ukrainian People's Republic by its second session. The largest number of registrations were in L'vov and Kiev *oblasts* and the lowest in Odessa and Chernigov. At the second session it was proposed to establish a Constitutional Committee to draw up a draft constitution for an independent Ukrainian state, a law on citizenship, and other draft laws. The second session also called upon 'all patriotic forces in the Ukraine' to co-ordinate their activities with the UMPA, something that never materialized.

The second session of the UMPA sent an appeal to the émigré OUNr government-in-exile, which it increasingly leaned towards.[34] This disconcerted the Ukrainian People's Democratic Party which was closer to the more moderate Ukrainian People's Republic (*Ukrainska Narodna Respublika*) government in exile from 1917–21 and dominated by the OUN-Melnyk faction. To which government-in-exile should UMPA owe its allegiance? Although UMPA registered citizens with the citizenship law of the Ukrainian People's Republic, that government-in-exile nevertheless refused any dealings with it because of its domination by radical right elements that leaned towards its arch opponent, the other main branch of OUNr (Bandera faction). Therefore, only *Derzhavne Pravlinnia* ever co-operated with UMPA and even that ceased in late 1991.

At the third session of the UMPA on 21–22 December 1990 the Ukrainian People's Democratic Party issued a statement outlining that it could no longer take part in the UMPA because of ideological differences which contradicted its programme. It would continue to function solely through the Citizens Committees where it could propagandize the traditions of the UNR, pointing out that it had first proposed the idea of registering citizens as early as January 1990. In addition, Pryhodko also walked out of the session with a section of the Ukrainian National Party, which led to its split into two groups. Pryhodko was criticized for his personal ambitions and 'dictatorial, destructive activities'.[35]

Shukhevych was then elected chairman of the UMPA. The UMPA outlined its main goals as the creation of Ukrainian armed forces, a boycott of the March 1991 referendum on the Union Treaty and the organization of a political strike in defence of Khmara who had been arrested a month earlier. Pryhodko's proposal to begin organizing a National Conference was voted out.

On 30 March 1991 the fourth session of the UMPA was held in Kiev which was still marred by conflict between Pryhodko and the Executive Committee, as well as by the announcement of the Ukrainian People's Democratic Party that it was resigning completely from the UMPA. In the appeals issued by the fourth session they repeated the call that only through the registration of citizens would the Ukraine be able to hold genuinely free elections to a Ukrainian National Congress which would lead to Ukrainian independence.

After the declaration of independence by the Ukraine on 24 August 1991 the UMPA changed its name to the Ukraine National Assembly (UNA) and halted the registration of citizens. The UNA then began an unsuccessful campaign to collect 100,000 signatures to register Shukhevych as a presidential candidate for the December 1991 elections. The fifth session of UNA was attended by the same organizations as before, as well as the Ukrainian Conservative Republican Party, which had only just been created out of those who supported Khmara and had been expelled from the Ukrainian Republican Party. The session stated that in Ukraine there were only three political forces. The first two, the Socialist Party of Ukraine and the New Ukraine bloc were oriented towards Moscow and Washington and would gamble away Ukrainian independence. Only the third – UNA – would guarantee reform and statehood through the establishment of 'order'.

UNA also claimed as its success the change in former President Kravchuk's attitudes towards the Dniester Republic of Moldova in June 1992, after members of the Ukrainian People's Self Defence Forces had undertaken combat operations there. By the time of UNA's registration in May 1992, it claimed a total of 16,000 individual, association and collective members,[36] although at the first UNA republican conference the following year this figure was dropped to between 3,000–4,000.[37] The Ukrainian Nationalist Union, though maintaining its conspiratorial organization, refused to request official registration. The Ministry of Justice refused registration to the paramilitary Ukrainian People's Self Defence Forces.[38] In December 1994 UNA was officially re-registered by the Ministry of Justice, claiming it had 10,000 members. 'I would like to say to those who still have doubts about registering with UNA – this is not a political error. This is a well-founded decision. A democratic country based on law must accommodate divergent political views', Justice Minister Vasyl Onopenko said.[39]

UNA's adopted slogan was 'Order, Strength, Well-Being'. It called for strong armed forces, the maintenance of a nuclear arsenal, a 'vigorous national policy', rapid establishment of state structures and support for Ukrainian industry until it was in a position to compete with foreign enterprises. The fifth session of UNA on 8 September 1991 outlined the continued threat to this Ukrainian declaration of independence from Russia, and criticized Ukrainian democrats for struggling against the national communist élite in the Ukraine (which was helping to build an independent state), while, at the same time, looking for allies among Russian democrats. By the second half of 1993 UNA's support for the national communists had waned due to the economic crisis, corruption, and their inability or unwillingness to combat growing separatism.

The cultivation of the need for a strong state moved the UNA closer to the national communists, such as Kravchuk, after they had voted for independence in December 1991. During the December 1991 presidential campaign the UNA gave instructions to its members to vote for Kravchuk, the only candidate not supported by the democratic parties. As Kovalenko, editor of *Zamkova Hora*, noted 'the people have become tired of democratic anarchy', and former President Kravchuk's supporters from the *nomenklatura* were more likely, they wrongly believed, to move to the nationalist than the democratic camp.[40]

So far democrats have not been able to organize the population, while the nationalist are still weak. The UNA claimed that the Ukraine therefore will be led to independence and beyond by those in power: 'The enemy of the Ukrainian administration is Russian democracy. The only weapon for it is state independence.' Hence the UNA believed that Kravchuk's anathema for Russian democracy would transform itself into support for authoritarianism and nationalism within an independent Ukraine. An alliance between the UNA and the national communists could be forged if the economic crisis and the hyperinflation worsened, particularly in response to the growth of strikes and social-ethnic unrest in the Ukraine. Democratic political parties and civil society are still weak and developing. This was the hope pinned by the UNA upon an alliance with the national communists in 1992–93 which failed to materialize.[41]

The UNA elaborated strong arguments in favour of the national communists because of their anathema for democrats and support for its state-building policies. In this respect they were close to the Congress of National Democratic Forces (also staunch supporters of Kravchuk). Viktor Melnyk, head of the UNA executive, claimed:

The vote in favour of independence, which was made by the population of the Ukraine, was not the result of the activity of the so-called 'democratic forces' (apart from possibly the territory of

Western Ukraine), but was the result of the turn towards independence of the higher organs of power in the Ukraine, as was seen in the election of Kravchuk as president of the Ukraine. The state can be governed only by those able to take upon themselves this function. Therefore, until a new generation of administrators, managers and academics appears, the former 'apparatchiki' remain 'the only real, ruling layer'. Yes, they govern the state poorly but the 'democrats' (which is evident from the L'vov *oblast* council) cannot govern in any manner whatsoever. The movement from bad to worse governance of the state, which the 'democrats' are proposing at the moment (by taking power into their own hands), would signify a quickening of the arrival of a catastrophe'.[42]

In a statement released on the eve of the sixth session of the Supreme Council in 1993, the UNA admitted that both the government and parliament are not those 'which Ukraine needs today'. But a government created by New Ukraine, Rukh, or the congress of National Democratic Forces would be far worse, UNA believed. Any new elections would merely increase the number of (democratic) 'demagogues' in the Ukrainian parliament. Although the democrats know this, their ambitions nevertheless will lead to greater chaos in society. Only the UNA could guarantee the social stability necessary to undertake economic reform, maintain law and order, and provide the base for Ukrainian statehood. The UNA therefore also opposed the more reformist government of former Premier Leonid Kuchma (October 1992–September 1993), and called for the president to head the government.

The ideological profile developed in 1993 away from older Ukrainian nationalistic thinkers, such as Dontsov (who continued to dominate the DSU and KUN), to encompass challenges to Russia as the dominant nation of the Eastern Slavs. Korchynsky argued that the UNA must propose that Ukraine be 'the main defender of Slavonic interests and the kernel of Slavic unity', as well as 'the best friend of the Turkic peoples'.[43] Ukraine should propagate the idea of Pan-Slavism and 'Ukrainian Imperial Spirituality' where Ukrainian national interests could be defended by going on the 'attack'.[44] 'Our citizens are used to living in a great state. We will ensure that they will not have to renounce their traditions', a leading UNA ideologist argued.[45]

The UNA and its paramilitary offshoot appealed to Cossack groups in Russia, with whom they had jointly fought against Moldovans in the Dniester Republic, for a 'confederation of Cossack republics' which would replace the former USSR and the Commonwealth of Independent States with Ukraine as its core.[46] This change in orientation was coupled with growing hostility towards the USA for interfering in Ukrainian internal affairs by encouraging strikes[47] and cajoling it to de-nuclearize.

The resignation of Shukhevych as UNA leader in September 1994 brought out further divisions within that organization on ideological questions.[48] He complained that the UNA was moving away from integral nationalism and opposed the growth of *vozhdism* (cult of individual leaders).[49] Shukhevych also disagreed with UNA's Pan-Slavism, a radical departure from traditional integral nationalistic thinking, although one which attracted support in Central Eastern Ukraine and the capital city, Kiev.

Vitovych, the new UNA leader, told a meeting of its party that, 'the current political situation in the Ukraine is reminiscent of the quiet before the storm' and that it was time to take up 'harsher fighting methods'.[50] At the tenth session of the UNA in October 1994 over 200 delegates listened to Korchynskyi, the organization's chief ideologue, saying that they were 'waiting with impatience for changes in the state for which these changes would be advantageous'. 'We are waiting for revolution and we are ready for it', he added.[51]

Growing Divisions among Radical Right Groups.

The dispute betweeen the DSU and the UNA has grown considerably since 1991. The editor of the Ukrainian Nationalist Union newspaper *Zamkova Hora*, Kovalenko, has pointed out that, 'The UNA–Ukrainian Nationalist Union, in contrast to the small nationalist groups of 'romantic nationalist' (that is, KUN and DSU), does not stand on a position of ethnic nationalism. We are nationalist pragmatists, statists. But this does not mean in any way that we reject the slogan "The Ukraine for Ukrainians".'[52]

Another aspect of the dispute is that the DSU is still primarily a Galician nationalist movement which follows in the traditions of the OUNr (and the Ukrainian National Front of the 1960s), whereas the UNA has support outside Western Ukraine, which, although respecting the integral nationalistic traditions and writers of the pre-Second World War era, has evolved its own ideology along more clearly defined fascist, statist lines. The UNA's 'ultra-pragmatism' has earned it greater popularity and visibility because it has led to policies and slogans which find favour with the man in the street (such as its populist campaigns against the mafia). The UNA's main aim is to come to power and it is ready to promise anything to achieve this goal, even at the expense of rejecting ideological purity.

Other right radical groups criticized the UNA for sending paramilitary volunteers to the Dniester Republic of Moldova. Although it was claimed that they were there to support the Ukrainian minority, their presence also gave backing to the separatist, pro-Russian communist region in its struggle against Moldova. In addition, KUN also criticized the sending of UNA volunteers to Georgia, where they fought against the separatist Abkhaz, because, by so doing, they gave political support to President Eduard Shevardnadze, who, as the former communist leader of Georgia, was highly suspect in the eyes of anti-communist groups in the Ukraine. The dispatch of 200 UNA volunteers to support the Chechens in December 1991 against a Russian invasion is unlikely to be criticized, though, by other nationalistic groups.

Between 1990–91 the émigré OUNr supported both DSU and the UMPA, even though they refused to co-operate with each other. After the aborted Soviet August 1991 *coup d'état*, the OUNr and the renamed UNA went their separate ways. By early 1993 KUN and DSU also took separate paths.

In both cases the conflict between KUN, on the one hand, and DSU and UNA, on the other, was partly connected to the perennial problem of whether an émigré group should control (or merely cooperate with) a group based in *kraj* (homeland), as well as to questions of ideology, ways of operating (underground or openly), and attitudes to the current situation. This was coupled with KUN's attempt to re-portray itself in 'democratic' colours in order to make itself attractive to the electorate and its support for co-operation with national democratic groups. Chornovil, leader of Rukh, told the inaugural congress of KUN that there were little divergences between the ideological platform of the Organization of Ukrainian Nationalists and that of Rukh. For both there was the primacy of the national state. But KUN's attempts to portray a more 'democratic' image were a façade as shown in the undemocratic expulsion of Roman Zvarych, its former deputy head, who had attempted to democratize its programme and gone too far.[53]

In reality KUN has increasingly aligned itself with traditional national democratic parties in Parliament and appeals, although the relationship never came as close as Chornovil hinted it might. The attempt to gain 'respectability' on the part of KUN proved to be the prime factor in its split with the second radical right group it had originally funded and supported, the DSU. Leading members of DSU, such as Koval, accused KUN and its émigré backers of 'selling out' their nationalist ideology to gain respectability and votes.[54]

In January 1993 in L'vov former members of OUN from the 1940s together with the DSU organized a congress to revive the OUN as an official structure in the Ukraine (in contrast to the importation of three branches of OUN in the diaspora).[55] Both the UNA and the DSU had long held the view that in an independent Ukraine nationalist movements should not remain underground, but operate openly. This view was in contrast to that of OUNr which continues to believe in the need for underground cells and the use of a 'front' structure, KUN (as it had always in the West through the public profile Ukrainian Liberation Front). The initial aim was to revive the OUN in Ukraine as an official organization which would not be plagued by the three-way division found in the diaspora. Then the DSU would be renamed the OUN.

OUNr, therefore, condemned the organizers of this congress as acting without their mandate and 'illegally', further placing them into conflict with the DSU and its former leader and long-term politicial prisoner, Kandyba, the prime organizer of the congress.[56] These criticisms from OUNr only served to further aggravate relations between the DSU and KUN.[57]

Although the resulting relations between the three main radical right parties are poor, they are still willing to unite against their two political 'enemies' – the democrats and communists.[58] To oppose Rukh's candidate for chairman of Ternopil *oblast* council KUN, UNA, the OUN-UPA (Organization of Ukrainian Nationalists–Ukrainian Insurgent Army) Brotherhood, the Ukrainian Christian Democratic Party, and the Ukrainian Conservative Republican Party formed a Conference of United Nationalist Organizations in June 1994.

Racialism and Anti-Semitism

All three radical right political parties are intrinsically hostile towards Russians and Russia, whom they perceive as imperialistic, chauvinistic, and the major threat to Ukrainian independence. This hostility towards Russia has not been translated into anti-Russian ethnic violence in the Ukraine, and many Ukrainian groups distinguish between 'our Russians' and those 'Muscovites' (who actually live in Russia proper). Of course, this distinction could evaporate in the event of a Yugoslav-style conflict between Ukraine and Russia.

The only exception to this rule is in the Crimea whose ethnic Russian inhabitants are 'Muscovites' brought to repopulate the peninsula after the deportation of the Tatars in 1994. Thus far the majority of violence in the Crimea has been localized. Although political in nature at times it has also been interconnected with the area's thriving world of organized crime.[59] Hostility to Russian autonomy, dual state languages (Russian–Ukrainian), dual citizenship, and membership of the CIS transcends the division between the centre-right and radical-right political camps from Rukh to DSU. Centre-right political parties might not go as far as UNA demands on the Crimea but they would back any move to abolish its autonomy.[60]

The Ukraine has largely remained free of anti-semitic outbursts or pogroms, while the notorious Russian anti-semitic organization *Pamyat* has been unable to establish a presence in the country. Jewish community leaders have applauded the tolerance shown towards Jews in the Ukraine as exemplary and one of the best in the former USSR.[61] The main focus of attention therefore of nationalists in the Ukraine remains on the communists and Russia, representing the two main threats to independence. By contrast in Russia, communists are in alliance with nationalists in the preservation of the Russian state and its expansion to Tsarist and Soviet borders. Therefore, the focus of hate in Russia is directed against 'Blacks' – i.e., Caucasians and Muslims (particularly Chechens), Jews, and Freemasons. Some radical right publications in Ukraine have accused the Jews of playing a large role in organizing the 1933 artificial famine in Ukraine, which led to the death of over seven million Ukrainians, due to their disproportionate numbers in the security police (NKVD).

The 'pragmatism' of the UNA in relation to the recruitment of members deliberately does not depend on racial purity (unlike the DSU), which reflects their acceptance of the reality of low national consciousness, mixed marriages, and large numbers of Russian-speakers in the Ukraine.[62] The UNA has distanced itself from the KUN and DSU in South-eastern Ukraine by approaching Ukrainianization through economic issues, an approach which has brought them greater success in linking up with Russian-speaking coal miners, for example.

Nevertheless, there have been some anti-semitic undercurrents within the UNA and especially the DSU. Mass rallies held in Vinnytsya against the mayor in 1993 organized by both groups played on his Jewish ethnic background. Anti-semitic articles have tended to appear in the DSU press, but not in UNA or KUN publications.[63] UNA publications have also called for the expulsion of Armenians, Jews, and Gypsies, 'who do not live permanently in Ukraine'.[64]

In Autumn 1993, the DSU published an outline of its aims that advocated 'Ukraine for the Ukrainians!', hostility towards mixed marriages and the inflow of non-Ukrainians into the Ukraine. 'We are for returning Russians and Jews to their historic fatherland', the declaration continued. Sherbtiuk, a leading DSU ideologist, has proposed that it back a 'national revolution' through 'terror' against 'racial impure elements'.[65]

The DSU has marked out for itself the most extreme position on the political spectrum as a well-known political party. At the fifth congress of the DSU in late 1994, Koval openly declared that 'When we take power we shall above all square accounts with internal enemies...The Ukrainian woman will be protected against the criminal encroachments of Russian pimps and the propaganda of American pornography. The DSU should romanticize 'confrontation' by 'sanctifying feelings of revenge and inevitable retribution'. The struggle against Russia on the domestic front, he warned, would not be, 'by parliamentary methods alone'. It will 'mean a merciless fight against everything Russian brought into your homes: villainy, lechery, depravity, dissoluteness of young people... filth in the streets, corrupt Russian literature and the Russian language.'[66]

Conclusions

Extremist and racialist groups do not exist in Belarus. The weakness of Belarusian national consciousness, lack of state traditions, and a large degree of Russification give no popular base for radical-right political parties and civic groups. Some friction has taken place within the officer corps over the degree to which Belarusian should be made compulsory as the language of the armed forces. In addition, a small number of Slavophile-National Bolshevik groups are allied to communist parties that promote unification with Russia, policies which, if pursued, might lead to ethnic and political instability.

Although the Ukraine has witnessed the growth of numerous nationalist parties and groups, they tend to be divided by personalities, by historical disputes, émigré influence, and ideological tendencies. All three radical-right groups in Ukraine – DSU, KUN, and UNA – are split and their unification into one alliance is unlikely except in crisis situations against external or domestic enemies (Russia and/or communists).

The UNA is more broadly based throughout the Ukraine. While not looking to the past as a guide to its policies, it is also the most influential one in terms of its paramilitary structure, large membership, and range of publications. In a similar manner UNSO (Ukrainian People's Self-Defence Forces) work together. In times of crisis UNA is transformed into UNSO. In 'quieter times' the UNA carries out political tasks while

UNSO 'engages in such general activities as physical education, leadership training and propaganda'.[67]

In contrast, both the KUN and DSU, which until the end of 1992 co-operated closely, look backwards to OUNr for ideological inspiration and are more ethnically oriented. Both the KUN and DSU are more concentrated in Western Ukraine. Undoubtedly, KUN's association and control by the émigré OUNr has, and will continue to prove to be , a handicap to its performance in the Ukraine. The KUN and OUNr are in competition with the other two branches of the émigré OUN for the allegiance of Ukrainians to the historical ideals of the OUN.[68]

In the event of a breakdown of law and order, or an acute crisis in relations with Russia, the UNA is the most likely of the three nationalist movements to organize its paramilitary forces. The 1994 elections reflected the weakness of the DSU, the most extreme of the three radical-right parties, which failed to win any seats. Only the UNA and its paramilitary arm are large enough to warrant concern by the authorities, including particularly the Security Service. Although the KUN won more seats than the UNA in the new parliament, it is preoccupied in its attempt to garner 'respectability'. The UNA may have won only three seats but it came a close second in Kiev as well, an indication that it is entering the mainstream and could be more successful in the next elections. The election of only three UNA deputies still confers legal privileges, publicity, and the ability to exert influence on state policies.

The DSU and KUN largely remain confined to their traditional West Ukrainian strongholds where the growth in their popularity has only come about at the expense of national democratic groups, such as Rukh (and not by recruiting previously unaffiliated voters or members). In contrast, UNA's pragmatism has proved to be sufficiently versatile to attract support outside Western Ukraine and it is therefore potentially the most likely of the three to grow in popularity. 'On the contrary, while communists talk about the "socialist utopia", nationalists struggle for the language, and centrists for the constitution, the UNA remains the only organization which talks to citizens about subjects in which they are interested. If this is indeed the case then its slogan from its election leaflet "Vote for UNA and you will not have to go to elections again!" might come true', one commentator believed.[69]

TABLE 8.1
THE RADICAL RIGHT IN THE 1994 UKRAINIAN PARLIAMENT

Party	Seats (total 450)
Ukrainian Conservative Republican Party (UKRP)	1
Ukrainian National Assembly (UNA)	3
Congress of Ukrainian Nationalist (KUN)	7

TABLE 8.2
NUMBER OF VOTES FOR POLITICAL PARTIES IN L'VOV *OBLAST* IN
THE 1994 PARLIAMENTARY ELECTIONS[70]

Party	Number of Votes
Rukh	230,000
New Wave (liberal/reformist)	150,000
KUN	150,000
Ukrainian Republican Party	120,000
UNA	100,000
Social-National Party of Ukraine	50,000
Communist and Socialist Parties	35,000

Notes: Three radical right parties obtained a total of 30,000 votes or nearly a third of the votes cast in L'vov *oblast*.

Notes

1. A good argument could be made that ethnic conflict and tension in Moldova and the three Baltic Republics resulted from the displacement of their large Russian and Russian-speaking minorities, who had held a large degree of influence in the Soviet era, from the élites of the newly independent state. In contrast, in Ukraine, of the three prime ministers between 1992–94, one was Russian, another a Russified Ukrainian, while the third was Jewish.
2. See I.L. Rudnytsky, *The Political Thought of the Soviet Ukrainian Dissent* and V. Haynes, 'Postmortem of the Ukrainian Helsinki Group', *Journal of Ukrainian Studies*, No. 11 (Fall 1981), pp. 3–16 and No. 15 (Winter 1983), pp. 102–13.
3. See T. Kuzio and A. Wilson, *Ukraine. Perestroika to Independence* (London: Macmillan and New York: St. Martin's Press, 1994).
4. See also the map supplement 'Russia and the Newly Independent Nations of the Former Soviet Union', *National Geographic*, March 1993 for correct transliteration of Ukrainian and Belorusian place names. The only exception I have made is for Kiev (in Ukrainian Kyyiv).
5. See C. Rosett. 'Finally Free. Belarus Finds that Statehood is a Lonely Business', *The Wall Street Journal*, 20 June 1994.
6. See B. Nahaylo, 'A Profile of Informal Patriotic Youth Groups in Belorussia', RL

318/88, *Radio Liberty Research*, 14 July 1988. R. Solchanyk, 'Belorussan Informal Groups Criticized for Nationalism', RL 491/88, *Radio Liberty Research*, 3 Nov. 1988 and *The Independent*, 19 Nov. 1988.

7. See J. Zaprudnik, *Belarus: At a Crossroads in History* (Boulder, CO: Westview Press, 1993)

8. D.R. Marples, 'Belarus: The Illusion of Stability', *Post-Soviet Affairs*, Vol. 9, No. 3, p. 256.

9. U. Markus, 'The Politics of Intolerance, Belarus', *RFE/RL Research Report*, Vol. 3, No. 16 (22 April 1994).

10. A. Lukashuk, 'Belarus: A Year on a Treadmill', *RFE/RL Research Report*, Vol. 2, No. 1 (1 Jan. 1993).

11. K. Mihalisko, 'Politics and Public Opinion in Belarus', *RFE/RL Research Report*, Vol. 2, No. 41 (15 Oct. 1993).

12. *Op. cit.*, Ref. 11.

13. For further information about the historical legacy of Ukrainian nationalism see A.J. Motyl, *The Turn to the Right: The Ideological Origins of Ukrainian Nationalism* (Boulder, CO: East European Monographs, 1980); J.A. Armstrong, *Ukrainian Nationalism* (Littleton, CO: Ukrainian Academic Press, 1980) and P.J. Potuchnyj and Y. Shtendera (ed.), *Political Thought of the Ukrainian Underground, 1943–1951* (Edmonton: Canadian Institute of Ukrainian Studies, 1986).

14. See the report on the UNA camp for young people in Ternopil *Holos Natsii* [L'vov] Nos. 6 and 17, 1994.) The DSU 'Varta' is small and not well known in the Ukraine (*Visti z Ukrainy* [Kiev], No. 46, 10–16 Nov. 1994).

15. *Shliakh Peremohy* (Munich), 22 and 29 April 1990, *The Ukrainian Review*, Vol. 38, No. 2 (Summer 1990), pp. 71–9.

16. *Prohrama Vseukrainskoho politychnoho obiednannia Derzhavna Samostiinist Ukrainy* (Kiev–L'vov, DSU, 1990).

17. *Status I Prohrama DSU* (Kiev–L'vov, 1992). See also the appeal dated April–May 1991 in *Shliakh Peremohy*, 11 Aug. 1991.

18. *Vechirnyi Kiev* (Kiev), 30 March 1993.

19. Krasinskyi was imprisoned in the Brezhnev era as an organizer of the Ukrainian National Front established in the 1960s to continue the traditions of the Bandera wing of the OUN which had ceased to exist in Ukraine by the early 1950s.

20. See the interview with Kandyba in *Za vll ukrainu* (L'vov), 16 May 1991 and 'Who are We?' in *Neskorena Natsiia* (L'vov), No. 2, 1992.

21. *Neskorena Natsiia*, No. 11 (June 1992).

22. *Neskorena Natsiia*, No. 1 (Jan. 1992) and *Derzhavnist*, (L'vov), No. 2 (April–June 1992)

23. See interview with Zelenchuk in *Halychyna* (Ivano-Frankovsk), 22 July 1990 and the speech by Kandyba at the inaugural congress of the Ukrainian Conservative Republican Party in *Neskorena Natsiia*, No. 11 (June 1992).

24. *Vechirnyi Kiev*, 1 July and *Holos Ukrainy* (Kiev), 2 Sept. 1994.

25. See the report on the second congress of the Ukrainian Conservative Republican Party entitled 'S. Khmara does not like either Moscow or Washington'. *Visti Ukrainy*, No. 38 (15–21 Sept. 1994).

26. *Interfax news agency*, 30 Oct. 1994

27. *Informatsiinyi Biuletyn Presluzhby* URP ta KNDS (Kiev), No. 45 (8 Nov. 1994).

28. *Informatsiinyi Biuetyn Presluzhby* URP ta KNDS, No. 42 (18 Oct. 1994).

29. *Kievska Pravda* (Kiev) 29 Jan. 1993.

30. *Holos Natsii*, No. 6 (Feb. 1993).

31. *Visti UMA* (Kiev) No. 4 (Oct. 1990).
32. *Visnyk Rukhu* (Kiev) No. 6.
33. *The Ukrainian Weekly*, 21 Oct. 1990.
34. The government-in-exile *Derzhavne Pravlinnia* was based on the declaration of independence of 30 June 1941 in L'vov by the OUNr as the Germans attacked the USSR. OUNr leaders were then arrested by the Germans for refusing to renounce this act.
35. See *Ratusha* and *Moloda Haluchyna* (L'vov). 10 Jan. 1991.
36. *Vechirnyi Kiev*, 14 May 1992.
37. *Vysokyi zamok* (L'vov), 16 Feb. 1993
38. On the paramilitary arm of UNA see my two articles 'Ukrainian Paramilitaries' and 'Paramilitary Groups in Ukraine', *Jane's Intelligence Review*, Dec. 1992 and March 1994.
39. *Reuters*, 30 Dec. 1994.
40. *Natsionalist*, (L'vov) No. 2, 1992.
41. See the comments by D. Korchynskyi, a leading UNA member, in Neskorena *Natsiia*, No. 2 (Sept. 1991).
42. *Natsionalist*, No. 7, 1992.
43. *Holos Natsii*, No. 7 (Feb. 1993).
44. *Za vilnu ukrainu*, 16 Feb. 1993.
45. *Visti z Ukrainy*, No. 46 (10–16 Nov. 1994).
46. *Trudovoi Tyraspol* (Tyraspol) 17–23 Feb. 1993. This new Pan-Slavism of UNA was sharply criticised by both DSU and KUN.
47. The Free Trade Union Institute of the AFL-CIO financed independent trade unions in Ukraine with grants from the US Congress-funded National Endowment for Democracy, including the newspaper *Most*. They were blamed for strikes, especially the successful transport strike in early September 1992.
48. See 'UNSO is Threatened by a Split', *Vechirnyi Kiev*, 1 Nov. 1994.
49. *Holos Ukrainy*, 29 Sept. 1994.
50. UNIAN news agency (Kiev), 18 Aug.1994.
51. UNIAR news agency (Kiev), 29 Oct. 1994.
52. *Zamkova Hora* (Kiev), No. 10, 1992 and *Visti z Ukrainy*, No. 35, 1992.
53. The undemocratic expulsion, which could only have legally occurred at the next KUN congress, was actually undertaken by KUN's Political Council, a fact reported gleefully by DSU (*Vechirnyi Kiev*, 14 May 1994).
54. See the draft constituion prepared by KUN experts in *Shliakh Peremohy*, 22 Oct. 1994.
55. *Samostiina Ukraina* (Kiev), No. 5 (10 Feb. 1993)
56. *Za vilnu ukrainu* 24 April 1993.
57. The First Great Assembly of OUN in Ukraine is covered in *Neskorena Natsiia*, No. 10 (June 1994).
58. In Summer 1994 KUN held a press conference devoted to the current political situation in the Ukraine that announced that it would be concentrating the main directions of its work on stopping the offence of pro-communist forces ... uniting all patriotic forces around the national state-building idea ... capable of bringing healthy and vigorous national forces to power in the state (UNIAR news agency, 10 July 1994).
59. Violence in Crimea, *Foreign Report*, 13 Jan. 1994.
60. The draft parliamentary resolution by UNA on the Crimea included the abolishing of its autonomy, declaration of martial law and placing the area under the administrative control of the Ministry of Defence, arrest and sentencing of its

leaders, and bringing in of additional security units (*Holos Natsiia*, Nos 16–17 (May 1994).

61. See the statement by Rabbi Yaakov Dov Bleich, chief rabbi of Kiev and Ukraine, in response to a CBS 60 Minutes programme on alleged widespread antisemitism in Ukraine (*The Ukrainian Weekly*, 6 Nov. 1994).

62. See Sergei Tikhy, 'Is a new terorist movement emerging?' *Moscow News*, 9–15 Sept. 1994 and *The Times*, 30 Aug. 1994.

63. See interview with Iosef Zisses, president of the Association of Jewish Organizations and Communities of Ukraine, in *The Ukrainian Weekly*, 11 Dec. 1994.

64. Bohdan Nahaylo, *The Politics of Intolerance*, Ukraine. *RFE/RL Research Report*, Vol. 3, No. 16 (22 April 1994), p. 46.

65. *Visti z Ukrainy*, No. 46 (10–16 Nov. 1994).

66. Radio Ukraine, 30 Oct. 1994.

67. See interview with Vitovych in *The Ukrainian Weekly*, 23 Oct. 1994.

68. The other two branches of OUN have democratized themselves in the diaspora and co-operate with the two leading parties in the Congress of National Democratic Forces (the Republican and Democratic Parties of Ukraine).

69. *Visti z Ukrainy*, No. 46 (10–16 Nov. 1994).

70. *Op. cit.*, ref. 64, p. 47.

9

The American Radical Right in Comparative Perspective

Leonard Weinberg

I.

In 1955 Louis Hartz published his landmark volume on *The Liberal Tradition in America.*[1] There is a largely overlooked irony concerning the link between the book's central contention and the year of its publication. Hartz asserts that American political history has been dominated by a liberal consensus. Largely because American society never went through feudalism, an *ancien régime*, and the revolutionary and reactionary responses that that form of social organization elicited in Europe, the country's political life never experienced the bitter conflicts between left and right that characterized politics in France, Germany, Italy, and so on in modern times. While Europe offered extremism, America provided a politics of consensus and moderation structured around the values of John Locke. *The Liberal Tradition* appeared in the same year – 1955 – in which the United States Senate voted to censure Senator Joseph McCarthy, a man whose name had become associated with the 'Great Fear', the anti-communist hysteria of the post-war era. The period of McCarthyism, a time when state legislative and congressional committees sought to uncover 'subversion' and 'un-American' activities in almost all areas of public life, was coming to an end just as Hartz's celebration of the American consensus appeared in the bookstores.

Why the myopia? Didn't the existence of a radical right movement led by McCarthy constitute something more than the minor 'irritation' Hartz calls it?[2] One explanation for the inattention of Hartz and others to the role of right-wing extremism in American politics has to do with their preoccupation with the left and the question of socialism. *The Liberal Tradition* itself and much of the discussion surrounding it concerned the fact that the United States was unique among the industrialized democracies because it lacked a major socialist movement. For Hartz and his followers the reason for the absence of a mass socialist movement was the absence of a feudal past against which a popular revolution would be mounted.

During these Cold War years Hartz was hardly alone in emphazing the uniqueness of the American experience or, at a minimum, its dissimilarity from the European one. And reasons other than the influence of Lockean liberalism were adduced to explain it. The social consequences of material abundance competed with 'natural right' as a leading explanation. In most cases, however, those who emphasized American exceptionalism and the absence of a coherent socialist movement paid very little attention to the right side of the political spectrum.[3]

If American politics seemed so un-European because there was no significant political force comparable to the British Labourites, German Social Democrats or the Italian Communists, was it also unlike Europe when it came to the right? Were there certain things about right-wing politics, especially right-wing extremist politics, that distinguished the United States from its European counterparts? The answer appears to be that, indeed, there were such differences.

First, rightist politics in the United States has been shaped by the issues of slavery and race in ways dramatically unlike those in Europe. Since the Civil War a long list of right-wing organizations, the various Ku Klux Klans most obviously, have secured popular support based on the presumption of black racial inferiority and the threat posed by efforts to achieve equality among the races.[4] A second way in which the American right has differed from its European counterparts concerns the matter of national identity, an issue of particular sensitivity for rightists on both sides of the Atlantic. America has been a nation of immigrants and this fact has had important consequences in affecting the meaning of nationality. In general, one becomes a German or a Greek by birth while, given the nature of the situation, becoming an American has come to be associated with the adoption of a set of beliefs and various forms of personal conduct. To be sure over the course of the nineteenth century nativist organizations seeking to represent earlier immigrant groups resorted to the application of ascriptive standards in excluding newer immigrants, especially Catholic ones, from the American community.[5] In general however conduct and life-style became more salient than blood in determining national identity. For McCarthy, unlike Enoch Powell in Britain for example, one could be authentically American irrespective of background so long as one possessed the appropriate outlook.

Third, for almost all of its history the United States never experienced the kind of national humiliation that Roger Griffin among others identifies as a prerequisite for the emergence of a kind of right-wing extremism to which the term fascism is often applied.[6] After the First World War, for example, the United States was not compelled to admit its guilt for beginning the hostilities nor did it experience a 'mutilated victory' for want of territorial aggrandizement. It is true that during the 1930s a number of fascist-like groups emerged in the United States of which the National Union for Social Justice led by the radio priest Father Charles Coughlin was the most significant. But Coughlin's initiative and others like it, the German-American Bund or the Silver Shirts of William Dudley Pelley for example, were essentially mimetic organizations whose style and structure were shaped by more successful models on the other side of the Atlantic.[7]

Fourth, to an extent substantially greater than the European case(s), right-wing politics in the United States has been shaped by a religious outlook informed by evangelical protestantism. Of course no one should doubt for a moment the important role religion played in stimulating various rightist movements in Europe, ones ranging geographically from Franco's followers in Spain to the followers of the Archangel Michael in Romania, but America's experience still seems rather different. In the United States the kind of moralism ('moral indignation') and spiritual crusades often directed by rightist groups against their political targets, the Christian Anti-Communist Crusade for example, derive from the country's distinctive religious roots.[8] No doubt the journalist H.L. Mencken was writing tongue-in-cheek when he referred to the Ku Klux Klan as the secular wing of the Methodist Church in the South but he was calling attention, nonetheless, to an authentic tendency in American rightist politics.

Finally, the American right's long-term preoccupation with the danger of socialism or the communist threat seemed rather curious when placed in a European context. The rise of Fascism in Italy, Nazism in Germany and other less successful right-wing extremist groups in other parts of inter-war Europe were stimulated by the Russian Revolution and the appearance of large revolutionary socialist or communist parties in those countries in which these rightist movements took hold. In the United States, on the other hand, the danger posed by a domestic communist movement, for reasons Hartz and others emphasized, represented an optical illusion because no such threat existed. This fact did not inhibit the American radical right, the John Birch Society for example, from acting as if the country were in mortal danger. As a result the rightist search for communist subversion managed to display what Richard Hofstadter referred to as 'the paranoid style in American politics'.

II.

Despite the divergent experiences in the past described above the current situation is one of *convergence*. Today the conditions that promote radical right activity in Western Europe appear similar to those at work in the United States. Further, there seems to be a growing cultural and political affinity between right-wing extremist groups on both sides of the Atlantic together with an increasing exchange of ideas, perspectives, forms of organization and so on, between radical right groups presently active on the two continents.

The end of communism and of the Soviet Union itself may be playing roles in the convergence of American and European right-wing extremism. Not all that long ago American rightist groups even stood out in a numerical sense. *The Radical Right: A World Directory*, a collection compiled by Ciaran O'Maolain and published in 1987, classified radical right groups under three categories.[9] The first category included libertarian, militarist and moralist (religious) groups; the second covered neo-nazi, neo-fascist and racist organizations; and the third category was composed of anti-communist groups. For the purposes of this paper this writer counted all the radical right groups falling under each of these three categories that were identified as active in the 21 democracies of Western Europe and North America. The results (see Table 9.1) of this rudimentary calculation point to a distinctive American pattern.

TABLE 9.1
RADICAL RIGHT GROUPS IN THE WESTERN DEMOCRACIES

	Libertarian, etc. Anti-Tax- Religious	Racist Neo-Nazi Neo-Fascist	Anti- Communist	Total
Non-USA	44 (19.1%)*	175 (76%)	21 (9%)	230
USA	37 (25%)	68 (45%)	43 (30%)	150
	81	243	66	380

Source: The Radical Right: A World Directory, compiled by Ciaran Maolain (Santa Barbara, Ca: ABC-CLIO, 1987).

* Percentages are based on raw totals

The most dramatic aspect of the distribution is the exceedingly high percentage of American groups devoted to the anti-communist cause. While neo-nazi, neo-fascist and racist groups were the most common type of radical right group for the other western democracies, the most numerically common type of American radical right group was one given over to the struggle against communism. It seems likely, although it cannot as yet be demonstrated empirically, that the number of such groups has dwindled (anti-communist emigré organizations for example) as the 'communist threat' as an issue has become less salient. If this is the case, then it follows that the distribution of American radical right groups should come to resemble more closely that of the other western democracies.

There are other factors at work that appear to promote a convergence between American and European right-wing extremism. The prosperous nations of Western Europe are now the recipients of large numbers of immigrants whose origins are outside the European Union. Their presence has served as an important stimulus to the kind of backlash politics long associated with right-wing groups in the United States.[10] Approximately the same may be said with respect to the issue of race. Long regarded as quintessentially an American problem, the appearance of immigrants and would-be political refugees from North and Sub-Saharan Africa and South Asia has stimulated sufficient popular fear so that major cities all over Western Europe are now the sites of the kind of racial violence long identified with the American South.[11] And right-wing politicians from Franz Schönhuber to David Duke have sought to exploit these backlash sentiments through the ballot box as well. In these cases explicitly racist and xenophobic appeals are often partially submerged by expressions of concern about the threat to jobs posed by the immigrants and by the public costs involved in providing them with social services.

The economic circumstances in which the United States and Western Europe find themselves may also contribute to a radical right convergence. These circumstances involve the competitive challenges posed by Japan and the Newly Industrialized Countries (NICs) of East Asia along with the drying up of jobs in the manufacturing sector brought on by automation and the tendency of the multinationals to have much of their production done 'offshore', in low wage countries. One effect of these developments, on both sides of the Atlantic, is a large pool of workers who feel their jobs are put in jeopardy by foreign competition or, after facing unemployment, have taken jobs in the service sector at salaries and wages well below their previous earnings. In short there now appear to be large numbers of Western European and American workers experiencing downward social mobility and the kind of status anxiety observers such as Daniel Bell have associated with support for radical right causes.[12]

III

Beyond these structural factors, and perhaps deriving from them, there are a number of signs that right-wing extremist groups are coming to share a common culture and a common outlook. We may be at a point when it makes sense to refer to a 'Euro-American' radical right. The religious realm offers an interesting case of reciprocal influence. There is, first, the explicitly anti-Christian and violently anti-Semitic Church of the Creator. Founded by the late Ben Klassen, a Ukrainian immigrant to Canada and then later the United States, the Church promotes worship of the old Nordic gods and the supremacy of the white race.[13] It advocates a racial holy war on a world-wide basis in an effort to re-establish Aryan supremacy. In some instances the Church's followers have sought to implement these ideas by planning to assassinate prominent blacks and bomb various churches and synagogues in the United States (several were arrested in the Los Angeles area by the FBI in 1993) and to develop similar schemes among other Creators in South Africa.[14] In addition to South Africa, the Church of the Creator has now become active in Canada and Sweden as well.

It is Identity theology, however, that offers the most prominent and widespread religious manifestation of the convergence between American and European right-wing extremism. Originally based on a nineteenth-century English doctrine, 'British Israelism', which asserted Britons were the literal descendants of the ten lost tribes, Identity theology was modified and translated for twentieth century American audiences by the Rev. Wesley Swift. Unlike Creativity, with its explicit rejection of Christianity as a Jewish phenomenon, Swift and his successors, William Potter Gale and Richard Butler, offer a synthesis of nazi-like biological racism with an exotic biblical interpretation.[15] A full explication of the religious ideas associated with the Identity teaching is beyond the scope of this paper; suffice it to say the principal Identity ideas involve the assertion of a satanic Jewish conspiracy pursuing world domination (from Israel) via the control and manipulation of racially inferior segments of the population. Racially superior Aryans, God's Chosen People properly understood, are the major targets and victims of these diabolical developments.

Identity theology has influenced a variety of radical right aggregations in the United States and Canada including such violent groups as the Covenant, Sword and Arm of the Lord, the Order, and the Posse Comitatus.[16] But from this paper's perspective it is important to note that Identity ideas have crossed the Atlantic once again and now constitute one of the ideological pillars of Sweden's White Aryan

Resistance (*Vitt Ariskt Mostand*).[17] Just as their counterparts in the United States believe that Washington is under the control of ZOG (the Zionist Occupation Government), so, too, Identity adherents in Sweden perceive Stockholm as having fallen under the sway of the same Tel Aviv-based conspiracy. Likewise, there is a tendency for some Identity followers in Europe and America to deify Adolf Hitler by, among other things,regarding his birthday as an event fraught with religious meaning.

Holocaust denial or Holocaust 'revisionism' has become another ideological perspective shared by American and Western European radical right groups along with various rightist writers and publicists.[18] In some instances denying the Holocaust, as in the case of Hans Schmidt and his German-American National Political Action Committee based in Santa Monica, California, and Ernst Zundel of Toronto, Canada, together with a long list of individuals in the Federal Republic itself, the motivation seems to be largely German nationalism. Accounts of the Holocaust constitute defamations of German culture and society, and consequently the accounts by their very nature must be spurious. A similar nationalist outlook appears to be at work among deniers of the Holocaust in Croatia, Slovakia and Lithuania. More commonly though the motivation for Holocaust denial involves the legitimation of fascism. To the extent that the Holocaust is associated with Nazi Germany or with the fascist movements of the inter-war period more generally, it constitutes a barrier for those who wish to promote a fascist revival. If the Holocaust can be discredited, it makes the neo-fascist project that much easier to accomplish. The United States has become a beehive of Holocaust denial activity. Among the most prominent initiatives is the California-based Institute for Historical Review and its 'scholarly' *Journal of Historical Review*. The latter's editorial advisors include John Bennett, an Australian neo-nazi, Robert Faurisson and Henri Roques, the former French academics, and Wilhelm Staeglich, a retired German judge and author of *The Myth of Auschwitz*, a book banned in Germany but readily available in the United States. The international composition of the *Journal's* editorial board is symptomatic of the linkage between Holocaust revisionists in the United States and Europe.

Holocaust denial may be seen, at one level, as a recondite literary tendency, perhaps as the neo-fascist equivalent of deconstructionism. The skinhead phenomenon, on the other hand, clearly belongs to the realm of mass youth culture and the politics of the street. As is well known by now, 'skinhead nation' evolved in Britain as an outgrowth of a white working-class youth reaction against the manner and style of the Vietnam era long-haired hippies. Originally the English skinheads were apolitical and not especially racist (there was some Jamaican influence in the music to which they became attached).[19] Things changed by the early 1970s so that white youth affecting the skinhead style and listening to the distinctive skinhead music began assaulting Pakistanis, gays and blacks. Skinhead culture and music spread to the Continent and to the United States. In this context some of the skinhead groups became attracted to various radical right groups. Nazism or what they perceived to be nazism held a fascination for many of the skinheads. In Italy the Nazi-Skins emerged.[20] In Los Angeles the Reich Skins, an outgrowth of the White Aryan Resistance, put in an appearance. And in Germany a variety of neo-nazi groups courted the participation of the skinheads in their anti-foreigner campaigns.[21]

Racist skinhead gangs have found the United States to be a congenial locale for their adventures. One effort to calculate their numbers reports that in 1988 there were approximately 1500 members of such gangs present in 12 states; but by 1993 their numbers had more than doubled and now such groups were present in a total of 40 states.[22] In addition to various acts of intimidation and vandalism, in recent years skinhead gangs have carried out more than two dozen homicides based on racial motivations. African-Americans, the white friends of African-Americans, gays and Asians seem to be their most common victims; the perceived helplessness of the victim appears to be an important stimulus for attacks by skinhead gangs. In any case, the dispersion of skinhead culture, with its emphasis on racism and violence, throughout Western Europe and the United States provides another example of the increasing similarity of radical right phenomena.

Approximately the same may be said with respect to neo-nazism. In the United States the first post-war effort to form an American Nazi Party was undertaken by George Lincoln Rockwell in 1958. Rockwell's none-too-subtle propaganda slogans, 'Gas Red Jew Spys' (*sic*) and 'Fight Race Mixing', left little doubt about his party's objectives.[23] In the context of the struggles over racial integration of the schools and other public facilities, the American Nazis were able to capture some public attention. The party, though, laboured under a worse handicap than its pre-war predecessors. Not only was it perceived as alien and mimetic of the German original, but the party was associated with the events of the war itself, a war in which the United States had committed itself to the annihilation of nazism.

With the passage of time and despite these problems, neo-nazism has managed to adapt itself to the American situation. By 1989 Klanwatch (a project of the Southern Poverty Law Center) was able to identify 26 independent neo-nazi organizations active in approximately the same number of states.[24] In some cases the neo-nazi groups have absorbed ideas from one or another of the various Ku Klux Klan organizations, as with David Duke's initiatives in Louisiana; in others instances skinhead or Identity ideas have meshed with nazi ones to create hybrids. Nazi paraphernalia and slogans seem to hold a fascination for a variety of people. At one time there was even a group exclusively for gay neo-nazis, the National Socialist League, located in San Diego, a tribute to American pluralism if ever there was one.

In addition to their cultural adaptation, American neo-nazis now find themselves in a position to furnish assistance to their German counterparts. Since German law bars the publication and distribution of nazi propaganda material, German neo-nazi groups have been able to acquire this material surreptitiously from American suppliers. Thus, Gary Rex Lauck of Lincoln, Nebraska, head of the *National Sozialistische Deutsche Arbeiter Partei – Auslands Organisation* branch in the United States has been able to print and smuggle into Germany the periodical *Kampfruf* for distribution among neo-nazi enthusiasts in that country.[25] The latter case is one example of a growing phenomenon involving the co-operation of European and American neo-nazi and other types of racist organizations. American Ku Klux Klan leaders now make periodic tours of Western Europe, while European radical rightists attend Aryan Nations Congresses at Hayden Lake, Idaho.

In the context of what this writer perceives to be a tendency towards convergence, it now makes some sense to compare the level of support for and actual manifestations of radical right activity in the United States with the European.

IV

In the Western World in general right-wing extremism is associated with attitudes of racism, xenophobia and religious bigotry, anti-Semitism especially. How much popular support for these views exists in the United States? Two recent nationwide surveys may help provide some answers. The first was conducted for the Anti-Defamation League (ADL) in 1992, while the second was performed by Louis Harris for the National Conference of Christians and Jews (NCCJ) in 1993.[26]

Both surveys confirm generalizations based on earlier work in the field; namely that racial bias, xenophobia and anti-Semitism tend to go together. The same kinds of people who dislike blacks also tend to be intolerant of foreigners and anti-Semitic. Furthermore, it is older people and the least educated who display the highest levels of prejudice. The NCCJ study also reports that bigoted attitudes are unevenly distributed

TABLE 9.2
AMERICAN STEREOTYPES OF BLACKS, JEWS, AND MUSLIMS

BLACKS

% saying "probably true"

Complain too much abour racism	62%
More prone to violence than people of other races	38%
Prefer to accept welfare rather than work for a living	35%
Less ambitious than people of other races	29%
Too loud and pushy	27%
Do not take care of their children as well as people of other races	21%
Less native intelligence than people of other races	13%
Too much power in U.S.	13%

JEWS

% saying "probably true"

Stick together more than other Americans	51%
Always like to be at the head of things	39%
More loyal to Israel than America	35%
Too much power in the U.S. today	31%
Too much control & influence on Wall Street	27%
Too much power in the business world	24%
Lots of irritating faults	22%
More willing to use shady practices	21%
Businessmen so shrewd	19%
Don't care what happens to anyone but own kind	16%
Just as honest as other businessmen (% saying "false")	16%

MUSLIMS

% agree

Take pride in their cultural and religious heritage	83%
Are anti-Western and Anti-American	43%
Are a deeply religious people and follow a strict code of personal behavior	79%
Segregate and suppress women	62%
Are strongly committed to the welfare of their own people and communities	73%
Belong to a religion that condones or supports terrorism	42%
Really suffer from discrimination	38%

Source: *Highlights from an Anti-Defamation League Survey On Anti-Semitism and Prejudice in America* and *Highlights from an Anti-Defamation League Survey on Racial Attitudes in America* (New York: ADL, 1992 and 1993); and *Taking America's Pulse: The National Conference Survey on Inter-Group Relations* (New York: NCCJ, 1994).

among ethnic groups and regions of the country. With other variables held constant African Americans and Hispanics are more intolerant of Asians and Jews than is the general population. (This pattern has been the subject of intense debate in recent years.) Regionally, intolerance is highest in the South and Midwest and lowest in the East and West.

Both surveys yield a mass of responses about popular stereotypes concerning various minority groups. On balance the stereotypes are more positive than negative. For example, far more respondents in the NCCJ study believe that 'African Americans have made valuable contributions to American society' and that Jews 'are charitable and supportive of social justice for others' than hold negative beliefs about these traditional targets of bigotry. Given this paper's concern with the radical right and the welter of information available, it is appropriate to accentuate the negative and narrow the focus.

Table 9.2 records data concerning negative attitudes towards blacks, Jews and Muslims. As may be seen, in the cases of blacks and Jews only one item wins majority support. Over 60 per cent of respondents agree that blacks 'complain too much about racism', while a narrow majority (51 per cent) holds the view that Jews 'stick together more than other Americans'. No other item succeeds in winning the endorsement of more than 40 per cent of the sample. The traditional stereotype of blacks as less intelligent than people of other races receives comparatively little endorsement. On the other hand, close to a third of the sample agrees that Jews have too much power in the United States, another traditional negative stereotype, support for which has actually increased over the last few decades.[27]

Muslims constitute a growing minority religious group in both Western Europe and the United States. In the latter country, according to the NCCJ survey, followers of Islam elicit considerably higher levels of negative stereotyping than blacks and Jews. As the reader may see, more than 40 per cent of those questioned believed that Muslims belonged to a religion that condones or supports terrorism and one which is anti-western and anti-American. Particularly damaging in a country increasingly sensitive to the rights of women is the fact that approximately two-thirds of the sample agrees that Muslims segregate and suppress women. One suspects that events in the Middle East rather more than personal interaction with American Muslims contribute to these widespread negative perceptions.

How do these results compare with European distributions of public opinion? There is of course considerable difficulty in making such transatlantic comparisons and the information available to this writer is at best fragmentary, but a few observations are possible.

First, studies of post-communist Eastern Europe indicate a revival of anti-Semitic sentiment. In countries like Poland, where Jewish populations have virtually disappeared, there are significant perceptions that Jews play too powerful roles in their national lives.[28] In addition to ghosts and phantoms, the Gypsy or Roma community has become the target of high levels of animosity in a number of Eastern European nations.

Next, in Western Europe one finding about support for bigotry is clearly consistent with American results: namely, those with less education and older people are most likely to exhibit the highest levels of racial or religious intolerance.[29] Third, according to a *Eurobarometer* survey of public opinion in the European Union's 12 member states conducted in 1988 slightly more than 50 per cent of those questioned believed there were too many 'others' (defined in terms of race, religion, culture, nationality and social class) residing in their countries. In general, there was less prejudice towards minorities reported in the countries of southern Europe and Ireland than among the other member states. Countries such as France, Belgium and the United Kingdom ranked particulalrly high (more than 40 per cent) in terms of the belief that racial minorities were too large a presence. Nationality rather than religion seemed to elicit the greater degree of intolerance. And the greater the presence of minority nationalities from outside Europe, the more widespread was the prejudice against 'others'.[30]

Based on this limited amount of information it requires a substantial amount of guesswork to compare levels of prejudice in the United States and Western Europe. This writer's best guess is that the level of racial and religious prejudice in the United States falls somewhere between the high- and low-ranked members of the European Union. If the relative size of a minority population is treated as an independent variable, a factor that predicts a high level of prejudice, it does not seem unreasonable to believe that the level of bigotry in the United States is lower than it should be, given the size of the country's racial and religious minorities. Or, put another way, it seems to require a proportionately smaller minority presence to elicit comparable levels of racial and religious prejudice in Western Europe.

Another and perhaps more meaningful indicator of racism, religious bigotry and xenophobia on which right-wing extremist groups feed is the volume of violence directed against members of various minority groups; what in the United States have come to be known as 'hate crimes'. To what extent are members of minority groups as individuals along with their property and their institutions targeted for attack simply on the basis of prejudice?

In the United States, Congress enacted a Hate Crime Statistics Act in 1990.[31] This legislation requires the attorney-general to compile and publish statistics on an annual basis about crimes motivated by prejudice against members of racial, religious or ethnic groups. Further, crimes committed against individuals because of their 'sexual orientation' are also covered.

One problem in providing an accurate assessment of the magnitude of 'hate crimes'was that only 32 of the 50 states had bias or 'hate crime' statutes at the time the federal legislation went into effect. Thus the first report published by the FBI in 1991 is necessarily limited in its scope. This document reports a total of 4,755 'hate crimes' over the 1991 calender year.[32]

Race was far and away the most common basis for attack (62.3 per cent of the total) followed by religion, ethnicity and sexual orientation. More specifically, the most frequently attacked groups, in order, were blacks, Jews, whites and homosexuals. The one group whose appearance among the leading targets seems odd is 'whites', traditionally and stereotypically the dispensers rather than the victims of violence. When the appearance of whites among the leading victims of 'hate crimes' is coupled with the fact that blacks represented the second highest category of perpetrators of such offences, a picture emerges that must seem curious to European eyes. Racist violence in the United States is now a reciprocal endeavour in which blacks participate as offenders. One trouble with this finding, as with the others made available through the FBI report, is that it is impossible to determine if it represents a secular trend or just a short-term oddity. Are there any databases available which would permit such longitudinal evaluations?

The ADL has been conducting an annual audit of anti-Semitic incidents since 1980 on a nationwide basis. But these audits of course have been limited to acts directed against Jews.[33] Fortunately, Klanwatch has sought to monitor the occurrence of hate crimes and bias incidents since 1980. Its coverage includes all the groups identified by the federal legislation as likely targets of hate crimes. Some comparisons then become possible.

The review of Klanwatch's data was limited to the most serious hate crime/bias incidents, ones involving murder, bombing/arson and shootings/assaults. As may be seen in Table 9.3 the trend over the 12-year period recorded by Klanwatch is towards an escalation in the volume of serious hate crimes. The years 1992 and 1993 show especially dramatic increases in the incidence of murder and shootings/assaults.

These observations do not disclose where the attacks occurred nor who committed them nor whom were their victims. This writer made use of the Klanwatch data to bring these variables under consideration. In addition to identifying the perpetrators and victims by the social category to which they belonged, it was possible to determine whether or not the perpetrators belonged to some organized group and where their attacks occurred; in which region of the country the event took place and if it occurred in a city or small town setting. Calculations were made for each of three years, 1980, 1985 and 1993. There are some missing data, most commonly when the identity of the perpetrator remains unknown.

TABLE 9.3
HATE CRIMES/BIAS INCIDENTS
(1980-1993)

Year	Murder	Bombing/Arson	Shooting/Assaults	Total
1980	6	7	14	27
1981	3	5	3	11
1982	4	3	7	14
1983	7	10	5	22
1984	7	12	10	29
1985*	11	11	10	32
1986	4	8	10	22
1987	3	5	15	23
1988	7	13	44	64
1989	5	16	52	73
1992	24	18	207	249
1993	25	21	182	228

Source: *Hate, Violence and White Supremacy* (Montgomery, AL: Klanwatch, 1989); and *Klanwatch Intelligence Report* 65 (February 1993) pp. 16-29; *Klanwatch Intelligence Report* 71 (February 1994) pp. 17-31.

The most significant findings (see Table 9.4) are these. First, only a small proportion of hate crimes are committed by members of organized groups (skinheads most commonly). It may be true that the Order launched a campaign of right-wing terrorism in the 1983–84 period and that followers of the Church of the Creator developed a scheme to attack blacks and Jews in Los Angeles in 1993, both in an effort to spark a race war, but these aborted operations are unrepresentative of hate crimes in general. Second, there are significant changes in the identity of perpetrators and victims between 1980 and 1985 and those from the 1993 period. In the earlier years the victims are largely blacks and the perpetrators almost exclusively whites. In 1993 however the pattern is significantly different. Gays and whites have become frequent targets of hate crimes, murders and assaults in particular. And blacks are by now

TABLE 9.4
HATE CRIMES/BIAS INCIDENTS: VICTIMS, PERPETRATORS, LOCATION
(1980, 1985, 1993)

1980

	Murder	Bombing/Arson	Shooting/Assault
Victim			
Blacks	5	4	14
Hispanics	1		
Perpetrator			
Whites	6	4	14
Organized Group			
Involvement			
yes	0	1	5
no	6	3	8
		Region	
East	1	1	2
South	2	1	8
Midwest	1	2	2
Southwest	0	0	0
West	2	0	2
		Community	
City	4	4	8
Town	2	0	6

1985

	Murder	Bombing/Arson	Shooting/Assault
Victim			
Blacks	6	9	5
Jews	1		1
Asians	2	1	1
Whites	2	1	3
Perpetrator			
Jews		1	
Whites	10	11	9
Organized Group			
Involvement			
yes	4	1	2
no	7	10	7
		Region	
East	1	4	2
South	2	6	3
Midwest	3		3
Southwest	1		
West	4	1	1
		Community	
City	6	7	4
Town	5	4	6

1993

	Murder	Bombing/Arson	Shooting/Assault
Victim			
Blacks	8	4	60
Jews		3	
Hispanics	1		17
Asians	1	4	5
Gays	10	4	31
Whites	6	2	41
Perpetrator			
Blacks	5		47
Jews			2
Hispanics	2	1	6
Asians			4
Whites	17	2	106
Organized Group			
Involvement			
yes	4	0	18
no	22	1	139
		Region	
East	4	2	33
South	7	6	39
Midwest	6	2	25
Southwest	1	2	7
West	7	4	53
		Community	
City	14	8	92
Town	12	9	72

Sources: same as Table 9.3.

responsible for the commission of a relatively high proportion of serious hate crimes, a finding consistent with the FBI's 1991 report. Neither Asians nor Jews appear as frequent victims or perpetrators of these deeds. It seems likely that members of these groups are not uncommonly the targets of vandalism and other types of abuse that fall short of the serious crimes recorded here. Third, hate crimes are hardly confined to one region of the country. The West and Midwest are as common locations as the South. Cities are more commonly the sites of hate crimes than small towns but given the obvious disparity in the population's distribution this is hardly astonishing.

It is not all that easy to make comparisons between American hate crimes and acts of racist violence in Western Europe. Among other things the criteria concerning the nature of the criminal act may differ. For example, the dissemination of anti-Semitic propaganda may be regarded as a crime in Germany but is extended constitutional protection in the United States. In the former country, the Federal Office for the Protection of the Constitution records crimes carried out by right-wing extremists but, of course, one need not be a right-wing extremist or politicized at all to be defined as a perpetrator of a hate crime by Justice Department standards in the United States.[34] According to Bjorgo and Witte, there are also measurement problems based on the different criteria local police forces employ in identifying racially-motivated crimes from one region of a country to another.[35]

With these reservations in mind, a few observations seem worthwhile nevertheless. In Britain, France and Germany, despite year-to-year fluctuations, the number of hate crimes now number in the thousands on an annual basis. It may be trite but worth stressing nonetheless that the surge in hate crimes in the 1990s is not an optical illusion generated by the mass media but an authentic problem for the Western democracies, the United States included. On both sides of the Atlantic people who seem odd and defenceless, Turkish grandmothers, gay passers-by, the homeless, Hassidic Jews, Pakistani shopkeepers, and so on, seem to provide the most tempting targets for violent attack. There are cross-national differences in terms of the groups that have become the principal victims: Algerians in France, Turks in Germany, South Asians in Britain, blacks in the United States. The latter country appears to stand apart from the others in the low percentage of hate crimes committed by organized right-wing groups and by the fact that racist violence has become a two-way street, with blacks in many cases acting as perpetrators as well as being the victims.

Racist, xenophobic and anti-Semitic attitudes in the public and acts of racist violence on the streets furnish the context or the boundaries within which organized right-wing extremism may operate. As an organizational presence how does the American radical right compare to its counterparts in Western Europe. The first thing one may say is that as a party political factor, right-wing extremism is a neglible force in the United States. The neo-Fascist Italian Social Movement, transformed into the National Alliance, has become part of the ruling coalition in Italy. In France, the *Front National* has been a significant electoral force for some years now. About the same may be said for Jorg Haider's Freedom Party in Austria. In Germany one or another of the ultra right parties seems poised to enter parliament after the next general election.

By contrast, unless one is willing to define the right-wing of the Republican party, with its links to the Christian evangelicals of the Rev. Pat Robertson, as constituting an extremist presence, the American radical right's partisan political fortunes seem comparable to Britain's.

From time to time there have surfaced radical right luminaries who have wished to create a coherent right-wing extremist alternative for the electorate. Willis Carto, Lyndon LaRouche and David Duke have either sought to become influential figures inside the Republican and Democratic parties or to form their own party organizations. But their initiatives have amounted to little in the final analysis. In fact, the outstanding organizational attribute of the American radical right is its fragmentation. America abounds with radical right groups. According to Maolain's 1987 compilation the United States is home to close to 40 per cent of all the radical right groups present in the Western democracies. But this profusion is probably symptomatic of weakness rather than strength.

According to information, supplied once again by Klanwatch, there were slightly more than 200 'white supremacist' groups active in the United States in 1989 and 1993. Numerically, the skinhead gangs were the most common type followed by the various Klans (see Table 9.5).

As may be seen, the different types of groups are not randomly distributed around the country. They seem to appeal to different constituencies. The Klan is basically a small town and Southern phenomenon. About the same may be said with respect to the supporters of the Identity religious teaching, although Identity groups frequently appear in the West as well. The skinheads and groups identified by Klanwatch as neo-nazi in character are basically urban phenomena. Modally, the neo-nazis emerge most often in the Midwest, while the skinheads have become nation-wide in scope, about as common on the East as on the West Coast. In view of these distinctions, one might hypothesize the existence of two separable varieties of right-wing extremism active in the United States, with the Klan, Posse Comitatus and Identity groups appealing to more tradition-bound segments of the population, while the neo-nazis and the skinheads present themselves as exemplars of the new and trendy.[36]

What means are available under the law to counter the activities of radical right groups present in the United States and Western Europe? To the extent that such groups seek to incite racial or religious hatred via public discourse, Great Britain, France, Germany and indeed most of the other western democracies have statutes, which, to varying degrees, criminalize this type of commentary, written or oral.[37] Because of First Amendment protection of 'free speech', the United States has long been

TABLE 9.5
WHITE SUPREMACIST GROUPS – 1989 AND 1993

TYPE

1989

Klan	Neo-Nazi	Identity	Posse Comitatus	Skinhead	Other	Total
53	26	38	6	70	12	205

1993

	Klan	Neo-Nazi	Tax Protest	Skinhead	Other	Total
	60	34	8	76	25	203

LOCATION OF WHITE SUPREMACIST GROUPS–1989

Region

	Klan	Neo-Nazi	Identity	Posse Comitatus	Skinhead	Other
East	6	1	2	1	8	1
South	32	5	15	1	11	9
Midwest	7	12	7	1	16	
Southwest	4	1	3		8	
West	5	7	11	2	24	2

Community

	Klan	Neo-Nazi	Identity	Posse Comitatus	Skinhead	Other
City	13	15	7	2	55	3
Town	38	11	31	3	12	9

LOCATION OF WHITE SUPREMACIST GROUPS – 1993

Region

	Klan	Neo-Nazi	Tax Protest	Skinheads	Other
East	5	6	1	15	1
South	36	9		17	11
Midwest	15	13	3	17	2
Southwest	4		1	10	4
West	2	6	3	16	6

Community

	Klan	Neo-Nazi	Tax Protest	Skinheads	Other
City	20	18	7	46	11
Town	40	16	1	24	14

Sources: same as Table 9.4

considered something of an exception in this regard. In fact, Supreme Court rulings have changed over the years. By the early 1950s the Court had upheld the constitutionality of 'fighting words', racial incitement and group libel as appropriate standards in restraining hate speech. With the civil rights movement of the 1950s and the anti-Vietnam War movement of the 1960s, the climate changed and the Court became far more reluctant to restrict speech of any kind. In more recent years the pendulum has swung the other way so that now the Court has been willing to uphold the constitutionality of laws that criminalize 'performative speech'; for example, speech that encourages or incites individuals to commit violent acts. The legal status of speech that is merely insulting or does not focus on a specific individual is far more ambiguous.[38] In the era of 'political correctness', speech that appears to harass members of some minority groups as well as women has been upheld as being criminal.

In addition to the matter of speech many states have enacted legislation directed against other 'hate crimes'. These laws typically provide more severe sanctions, longer prison terms for example, for individuals who commit crimes where racial, religious or gender bias has been a motive for their commission. And at least on one occasion the Court has held this practice to be constitutional.

In Italy, Germany, France and elsewhere the government has the authority to order the dissolution of organizations of a neo-fascist or neo-nazi nature. Because of the 'free association' protection of the First Amendment such actions are more difficult to accomplish in the United States. At the height of the Cold War the Court came close to treating membership in the Communist Party, in and of itself, as a criminal act. The atmosphere and the Court's attitude changed as the McCarthy era passed. In recent years the Justice Department has employed the RICO Act, federal legislation originally intended for use against racketeering in interstate commerce, as a means for prosecuting members of such violent radical right groups as The Order or *Bruders Schweigen*.[39]

On the surface the democracies of Western Europe appear to have a wider array of legal measures that they can bring to bear against right-wing extremism, particularly to the extent that it is manifested in the incitement of racial or religious hatred and the use of violence, than is now available in the United States. On closer view however, the differences do not appear to be all that wide. In recent years the United States has brought itself into closer conformity with European legal practices.

V

The United States experienced no monarchy, no established church, no landed aristocracy, no peasantry. The right of political participation, the franchise, was extended early, at least to white males, in the course of the country's history. And at least until the Vietnam War, the United States suffered no humiliating military defeat. Capitalism, for the most part, was not seriously challenged as the most appropriate form of economic organization. The revolutionary left did not constitute a menace to the established order. In short, the United States lacked almost all the ingredients necessary to constitute European-like right-wing extremism. Mass immigration and the effects of slavery provided the bases for a distinctively American radical right.

As this paper has sought to demonstrate however, social and political conditions on both sides of the Atlantic have recently changed in such a way as to promote a convergence of the radical right-wing activity. The various groups involved have reacted to increasingly similar stimuli and have begun to look and sound, if not identical, then at least very similar. There are increasing personal contacts between activists on both sides of the Atlantic. If a Euro-American radical right has not emerged as yet, one certainly appears to be on the horizon.

Notes

1. L. Hartz, *The Liberal Tradition in America* (New York: Harcourt, Brace and World), 1955.
2. *Ibid.,* p. 12.
3. E. Shils, *The Torment of Secrecy* (Glencoe, IL: The Free Press, 1956) is a notable exception.
4. For a brief summary see S. Bullard (ed.), *The Ku Klux Klan: A History of Racism and Violence* (Montgomery, AL: The Southern Poverty Law Center, 1991).
5. See for example, D. Bennett, *The Party of Fear* (Chapel Hill, NC: University of North Carolina Press,1988) pp. 61–155.
6. R. Griffin, *The Nature of Fascism* (New York: Routledge, 1991) pp. 26-53
7. See for example O.J. Rogge, *The Official German Report* (New York: A.S. Barnes, 1961) pp. 113–299.
8. See for example R. Hofstadter, *Anti-Intellectualism in American Life* (New York: Alfred Knopf, 1963); and R. Liebman and R. Wurthow (eds), *The New Christian Right* (Hawthorne, NY: Aldine, 1983).
9. *The Radical Right: A World Directory* compiled by C. O'Maolain (Santa Barbara, CA: ABC-CLIO, 1987), pp. vii–ix.
10. See for example, P. Hainsworth (ed.), 'The Extreme Right in Post-War Western Europe and the USA,' in *The Extreme Right in Europe and the USA* (New York: St. Martin's Press, 1992) pp. 7–9.

11. See for example, T. Bjorgo and R. Witte, *Racist Violence in Europe* (New York: St Martin's Press, 1993) pp. 1–16.
12. See for example, D. Bell, 'The Dispossessed – 1962,' in *The Radical Right* edited by D. Bell (New York: Doubleday, 1963), pp. 1–38.
13. *The Church of The Creator: Creed of Hate* (New York: Anti-Defamation League, 1993), pp.1–15.
14. *San Francisco Chronicle* (13 August, 1993), p. 1.
15. See for example, J. Aho, *The Politics of Righteousness* (Seattle: University of Washington Press, 1990), pp. 83–113; and M. Barkun, 'Millenarian Aspects of 'White Supremacist' Movements,' *Terrorism and Political Violence* 1:4 (1989), pp. 409–34; and J. Kaplan, 'The Context of American Millenarian Revolutionary Theology: The Case of the 'Identity Christian Church of Israel," *Terrorism and Political Violence* 5:1 (1993), pp. 30–82.
16. See for example, J. Corcoran, *Bitter Harvest* (New York: Penguin Books, 1990), pp. 24–42.
17. T. Bjorgo, 'Militant neo-Nazism in Sweden', *Terrorism and Political Violence* 5:3 (1993), pp. 28–57.
18. See for example, D. Lipstadt, *Denying The Holocaust* (New York: The Free Press, 1993), pp. 103–21: *Hitler's Apologists* (New York: Anti-Defamation League, 1993); and R. Eatwell, 'The Holocaust Denial: A Study in Propaganda Technique', in *Neo- Fascism in Europe*, edited by L. Cheles, R. Ferguson and M. Vaughan (London and New York: Longman, 1991), pp. 120–146; G. Seidel, *The Holocaust Denial* (Leeds: Beyond the Pale Collective, 1986).
19. See for example, M. Hamm, *American Skinheads* (Westport, CT: Praeger, 1993) pp. 15–36.
20. *The New York Times* (1 June 1994), p. 3.
21. See for example, R. Lewis, *A Nazi Legacy* (Westport CT: Praeger, 1991) pp. 95–9.
22. *Young Nazi Killers: The Rising Skinhead Danger* (New York: Anti-Defamation League, 1993), p. 5.
23. G. Thayer, *The Farther Shores of Politics* (New York: Simon and Schuster, 1968), pp. 13–33.
24. *Hate, Violence and White Supremacy* (Montgomery AL: Klanwatch, 1989), pp. 25–6.
25. E. Jensen, 'International Nazi Cooperation: A Terrorist Oriented Network', in *Racist Violence in Europe*, pp. 86–7.
26. *Highlights from an Anti-Defamation League Survey on Anti-Semitism and Prejudice in America* and *Highlights from an Anti-Defamation League Survey of Racial Attitudes in America* (New York: ADL, 1992 and 1993); and *Taking America's Pulse* (New York: National Conference, 1994).
27. See for example, G. Selznick and S. Steinberg, *The Tenacity of Prejudice* (New York: Harper Torchbooks, 1969) p. 6.
28. R. Cohen and J. Golub, *Attitudes toward Jews in Poland, Hungary and Czechoslovakia* (New York: American Jewish Committee, 1991); and Robert Wistrich, 'Once Again, Anti-Semitism Without Jews', *Commentary* 94:2 (1992), pp. 45–9.
29. *Eurobarometer: Racism and Xenophobia* (Brussels: Commission of the European Communities, 1989), p. 46.
30. *Eurobarometer* pp. 35–50.
31. J. Levin and J. McDevitt, *Hate Crimes* (New York and London: Plenum Press, 1990), pp. 247–9.

32. US Department of Justice, Federal Bureau of Investigation (GPD J1.14/2:C86/17X c.3).
33. See for example, *Audit of Anti-Semitic Incidents 1993* (New York: Anti-Defamation League, 1993).
34. *The Week in Germany* (21 January 1994) p. 6.
35. Bjorgo and Witte, *Racist Violence in Europe*, pp. 4–5.
36. See for example, M. Jay, 'Postmodern Fascism: Reflections on the Return of the Oppressed,' *Tikkun* 8:6 (Nov./Dec. 1993), pp. 37–41.
37. S. Roth, 'The Laws of Six Countries: An Analytical Comparison,' in *Under The Shadow of Weimar*, edited by L. Greenspan and C. Levitt, (Westport, CT: Praeger, 1993), pp. 177–203.
38. D. Downs, 'Racial Incitement Law and Policy in the United States,' in *Under the Shadow of Weimar*, pp. 107–30.
39. See for example United States of America v. Bruce Carroll Pierce et. al., *Second Superseding Indictment*, United States District Court, Western District of Washington at Seattle, No. CR85-001M.

10

The Quiet Dog: The Extreme Right and the South African Transition

Adrian Guelke

"Is there any other point to which you wish to draw my attention?"
"To the curious incident of the dog in the night-time."
"The dog did nothing in the night-time."
"That was the curious incident," remarked Sherlock Holmes.[1]

Even with the gradual fading of the euphoria that surrounded Nelson Mandela's inauguration as president of South Africa on 10 May 1994, there remains a broad consensus that the South African transition to democracy was miraculous[2] and 'against the expectations'.[3] One aspect of South Africa's transformation which has been particularly surprising has been the relatively small scale of violence that has emanated from the extreme right-wing opponents of reform, especially in the context of the high level of violence that occurred in the period between the unbanning of the African National Congress (ANC) in 1990 and South Africa's first democratic elections in 1994. The puzzle of why South Africa's ultras did not offer greater resistance to the establishment of a government dominated by the ANC is related to another larger issue, the acquiescence of the White community as a whole in the transfer of power, contrary to all indications of white opinion prior to 1990. Before these questions are tackled, a brief history of the extreme right in South Africa is needed to explain why it seems at the outset of South Africa's transition such a potent threat to the process of reform.

The zeal with which Hendrik Verwoerd, South Africa's Prime Minister between 1958 and 1966, pursued the policy of apartheid left little room on the far right of the political spectrum. It was only after his death that the government started to be criticized from the right. By the late 1960s, the policies of the South African government were becoming increasingly offensive to opinion in the West. The evolution of attitudes on race in the United States and in former colonial powers such as Britain and France created the danger that South Africa would become isolated. In fact, that was already happening in the symbolically important field of sport. To avert the danger of further isolation, Verwoerd's successor, B.J. Vorster modified his predecessor's rigid policies. The change of direction resulted in a minor split in the ruling National Party. The break came over the government's decision to allow a New Zealand rugby team containing Maoris to visit South Africa. The alternative would have been no tour at all as the New Zealand Rugby Union was no longer prepared to accept racial restrictions on its choice of players for tests against South Africa.

Those who continued to oppose the new policy were expelled from the National Party in 1969. They formed the *Herstigte Nasionale Party* (HNP – refounded National Party). The party's candidates fared poorly in the 1970 general election. However, the failure of the HNP did not put an end to political conflict in the Afrikaner community. It was encapsulated by the use of terms, *verligtes* and *verkramptes*, to describe respectively progressives and traditionalists in and outside the ranks of the ruling party.[4] During the 1970s these divisions spawned a number of organizations, particularly among traditionalists alarmed at the gradual erosion of social segregation as a result of further adjustments of the government to external pressures. The most significant of the new organizations was the *Afrikaner Weerstandsbeweging* (AWB – Afrikaner resistance movement). According to the founders of the movement, it was formed by seven worried Afrikaners in 1973. Its leader was Eugene Terre Blanche. He was a former policeman whose duties had included acting as a bodyguard for Prime Minister B. J. Vorster. He stood for the HNP in the 1970 general election after resigning from the police force.

The AWB remained a secret organization until 1979 when it achieved instant notoriety after members of the organization tarred and feathered a distinguished Afrikaner nationalist historian, Professor F.A. Jaarsveld. His offence in the eyes of the AWB was that he delivered a lecture in which he questioned the basis for treating as a holy day the Day of the Vow, which celebrated the victory of the voortrekkers over the Zulus at the battle of Blood River as a God-given deliverance. Terre Blanche and 13 of his followers faced a number of charges over the incident and were heavily fined. In 1980 the AWB published a political programme, outlining its commitment to the creation of a *Blankevolkstaat* (White people's state). At the same time, it adopted a three-legged swastika as its emblem. But, while the AWB drew some of its inspiration from European fascism, Afrikaner nationalism remained the foundation of its appeal. For example, the suggested boundaries for the *Blankevolkstaat* were those of the nineteenth century Boer Republics that had fought to maintain their independence from incorporation in the British Empire. The organization also stood for the strict maintenance of racial separation. In the past, such a commitment would hardly have distinguished the AWB from the National Party.

However, with the election of P.W. Botha as Prime Minister in 1978, the ruling party had embraced reform and had started to distance itself ideologically from apartheid as conceived by Verwoerd. While Botha's predecessor, B.J. Vorster, had presided over the erosion of segregation in a number of fields, he had justified the changes as compatible with apartheid ideology by using the rubric of multinationalism. Thus, permission had been given to 'international' hotels to admit guests of different races. Botha's abandonment of fundamental aspects of the ideology transformed the political prospects of the extreme right. The HNP achieved a breakthrough in the 1981 general election, securing 14.1 per cent of the vote compared to 3.3 per cent in 1977. A smaller right-wing party picked up another 2.5 per cent of the vote.

That was followed in 1982 by a further split in the National Party over the issue of constitutional reform, leading to the formation of the Conservative Party under the leadership of the former leader of the National Party in the Transvaal, Andries Treurnicht. The Conservative Party quickly became the dominant force on the extreme right of the political spectrum. The government presented its constitutional proposals as a step towards power-sharing with the Coloured and Indian communities, who were to be represented in separate chambers of a tricameral parliament, though in fact they ensured continuing White control of the political system. However, a few people on the extreme right took the government at its word and saw the new constitution as an irreversible step justifying a resort to violence. In 1983 two former members of AWB were convicted under the Internal Security Act of planning bombing attacks on multiracial hotels and, more significantly, the offices of the President's Council, the embodiment of 'power-sharing' under the new constitution. In the same year Eugene Terre Blanche and a number of other AWB leaders were convicted of terrorism on the basis of illegal possession of arms and received suspended sentences, while the government announced an inquiry by the Ministry of Law and Order into the activities of the AWB.

By this time the AWB was acquiring paramilitary trappings with a uniformed bodyguard, the *Blitzkommando*, accompanying the leader in his public appearances. This was the first of many paramilitary units to be established by the AWB. The *Blitzkommando* gave added menace to the increasingly virulent rhetoric Terre Blanche employed after the passage of the new constitution. Nonetheless, the threats of blood flowing in the streets remained couched in the future conditional tense. This was partly because it was still possible for the government to be defeated by constitutional means. Thus the White electorate still had the power to throw the government out and to reverse the process of change. While Terre Blanche complained that the new constitution meant that the White nation had lost sovereignty without a shot being fired, in fact, the principle of white self-determination remained largely intact. At the same time, the success of both the Conservative Party and the HNP in by-elections in the mid 1980s lent practical weight to a constitutional approach. The government tried to embarrass the Conservative Party over its close links with AWB, but these ties were more a reflection of the faith of AWB members in the continuing potency of the ballot box than evidence of the revolutionary intent of the Conservative Party. Furthermore, with the upsurge in Black political violence after 1984, it became possible for paramilitary posturing to be presented in a defensive light.

The growing strength of the AWB within the extreme right became evident in the course of 1986, fuelled by a White backlash over the possibility of negotiations between the government and the ANC as a result of a Commonwealth mission to South Africa. AWB members took over a public rally for the National Party in Pietersburg in May that was to have been addressed by the Minister of Foreign Affairs, while the police looked on indifferently. Concern over AWB influence in the security forces had already led to the imposition of a ban on members of the South African Police (SAP) or South African Defence Force (ASDF) joining the AWB. At the end of May, an AWB rally at the Voortrekker Monument outside Pretoria to celebrate Republic day attracted a crowd of 50,000, the largest gathering at the Monument since 1960. These signs of dissent prompted a change in direction by the government, which reimposed the state of emergency lifted earlier in the year and made it clear that there was no prospect of negotiations with the ANC. This was still the government's posture in May 1987 when elections to the white House of Assembly took place. However, the tough stance of the government did not prevent a large swing to the extreme right, with the Conservative Party and the HNP picking up almost 30 per cent of the vote. The election clearly established the dominant position of the Conservative Party within the extreme right. Among the Conservative Party's successful candidates were three members of the AWB. At the same time there was a sharp fall in the vote for the liberal Progressive Federal Party.

The electoral success of the extreme right was reflected in a further proliferation of extreme-right pressure groups. The most radical of the new groups to emerge in 1987 was the *Blanke Bevrydingsbeweging* (White freedom movement) (BBB). It stood for 'the removal of all non-whites from white South Africa'.[5] However, in the first instance the organization threatened that its members would enforce residential segregation in areas where the government had turned a blind eye to infringements of the Group Areas Act, so-called 'grey' areas such as Mayfair in Johannesburg. A number of incidents resulted in the government's warning to the BBB on more than one occasion that it would not be allowed to take the law into its own hands over enforcement of the Group Areas Act. However, in the event the incident that prompted the Government to take action against the BBB did not even involve a member of the organization.

In November 1988, Barend Strydom, a member of the AWB and a former policemen, opened fire on a lunchtime crowd of blacks in central Pretoria. Seven people died as a result of the attack. While White vigilantes were suspected of responsibility for a number of other random killings of Blacks in 1988, this was the single most serious instance of right-wing vigilante violence during the 1980s. Strydom claimed that he was the leader of the *Wit Wolwe* (White Wolves). There was speculation in the press at the time about *Wit Wolwe*, after a claim of responsibility was made in the group's name for a bombing attack on the headquarters of the South African Council of Churches. However, it is now known that the bombing of Khotso House was, in fact, a covert police operation.[6] Strydom described his actions as the start of the *Derde Vryheidsoorlog* (third freedom war), a reference to the fact that Afrikaners commonly referred to the wars between Britain and the Boer Republics before the establishment of the Union of South Africa as the first and second freedom wars. In the aftermath of the incident the government banned the BBB.

A general election of all three houses of the tricameral parliament took place in September 1989. By this time, F.W. De Klerk had succeeded P.W. Botha both as leader of the National Party and as head of government. The National Party fought the election on the basis of a five-year Plan of Action, the aim of which was the creation of a new South Africa through negotiations leading to a political dispensation, in which there would be participation by all, with group rights providing a safeguard against domination.[7] This vague formula was accompanied by the promise that any new constitutional principles would be submitted to the (White) electorate before implementation. Furthermore, any changes would then have to be approved by the tricameral parliament. The government lost ground to both the extreme right and to the liberal opposition in the election, but retained its overall majority in the white House of Assembly.

While the tone of the National Party's 1989 campaign differed from that of 1987, there was little hint of the racial change to come, culminating in the package of measures announced by President De Klerk on 2 February 1990. The unbanning of the ANC, Pan Africanist Congress and the South African Communist Party and the promise of Nelson Mandela's imminent release was a considerable shock to the extreme right, which was not mollified in the least by the simultaneous lifting of the ban on the BBB. The tone of the extreme right's response to De Klerk's dramatic initiative was set at a rally in Pretoria on 15 February, four days after Mandela's release, at which the two most prominent slogans on display were Hang Mandela and Free Barend.

To many on the extreme right, the unbanning of the ANC and the release of Nelson Mandela represented the point of no return. There seemed to be good reasons for taking the threat of extreme right-wing violence seriously. Firstly, the opponents of reform represented a substantial section of the White electorate with the support of close to half of the Afrikaner community. Secondly, there were a number of precedents for resort to violence by radical Afrikaner nationalists. In particular, South Africa's participation in support of Britain in the First World War had prompted a rebellion within the Afrikaner community. Rebel commandos took to the field led by three generals from the Anglo-Boer War at the turn of the century. They were rapidly defeated by government forces, but a total of 332 people died in the rebellion. There was also violent opposition from within the Afrikaner community to the country's participation in the Second World War. This took a variety of forms from street brawling to bombing. Most of the violence was carried out by members of the *Ossewabrandwag* (ox-wagon sentinel), which was formed as a result of Afrikaner nationalist enthusiasm engendered by the celebration of the centenary of the Great Trek in 1938. Thirdly, while De Klerk's bold action had initially attracted White support, in part because they held out the prospect for an end to international economic sanctions against South Africa, disillusionment grew as it became clear that in the short term liberalization of political activity had increased rather than reduced the level of disorder. The extent of the disillusionment was underscored by a by-election in June 1990 in Natal in which there was a massive swing among White voters to the Conservative Party.

The level of violence from the extreme right after the unbanning of the ANC did not match the virulence of its rhetoric. In April 1990 a number of weapons were stolen from an Air Force arsenal in Pretoria. Piet Skiet Rudolph of the small *Boerestaat* (Boer State) party claimed responsibility for the raid when he released a series of videos calling for the violent overthrow of the government. This was followed by a spate of bombing attacks on the offices of the National Party and the Democratic Party attributed to the underground organizations Rudolph founded, *Orde Boerevolk* (Order of the Boer People). Other targets of extreme right-wing bombers during the year were the British embassy, trade union offices, the homes of Johannesburg city councillors, and newspaper offices. A variety of organizations were involved in White vigilante violence, including the *Orde van die Dood* (Order of Death), which lived up to its name through the random killings of Blacks, and the inevitable *Wit Kommando* (White Commando). Rudolph was arrested in September and, after calling on his followers to return the stolen weapons, announced that he intended to apply for indemnity under the programme agreed between the government and the ANC to bring an end to the armed struggle .

In addition to covert violence, the extreme right was involved in a number of ugly racial confrontations at a local level. The most serious of these took place in the mining town of Welkom in May. It was precipitated by an attempt of the local White vigilante organization, *Blanke Veiligsheid* (BV – White Safety), to impose a 'White at night' curfew on the town by force. The confrontation spread to the mines themselves, leading at one mine to the deaths of two Whites and injuries to 14 Blacks. Following the repeal of the Separate Amenities Act, in October, ending the legal basis for the segregation of public facilities, there were a large number of incidents of assaults on Blacks attempting to use such facilities, particularly in small towns that had elected Conservative councils. According to the Human Rights Commission, the right-wing was responsible for 26 deaths between July and December 1990. However, that was out of a total of 1,811 deaths from political violence.[8]

The relatively small scale of extreme right-wing violence in comparison with other sources of violence remained the pattern throughout the transition. For example, the Human Rights Commission attributed 20 deaths to the right-wing in 1993 out of a total of 4,364 fatalities due to political violence in that year.[9] The main exception to this pattern was the state of extreme right-wing bomb attacks on the eve of South Africa's first non-racial general election in April 1994, in which 21 people died. Even this did little to disturb the elections which otherwise generally passed off remarkably peacefully. But despite its small scale, fear of extreme right-wing violence persisted throughout the transition. This was partly because of the high profile of some of the incidents involving the extreme right. It was also partly because of continuing threats by leaders of the extreme right to plunge the country into a civil war. Despite their repetition, these threats retained their credibility because of the fragility of the political situation. A further and substantial reason for the perception of the extreme right as a threat to the transition was its links with other groups involved in violence.

The extreme right dubbed 2 February 1990, when President De Klerk announced the unbanning of the ANC and his intention to release Nelson Mandela, 'Red Friday'. But even though De Klerk's initiative was seen as a watershed, it did not resolve the extreme right's dilemma over how it should act. In particular, his promise to consult the (White) electorate held out the possibility that the process De Klerk had set in train might yet be defeated through the ballot box. Consequently, a large section of extreme right-wing opinion continued to argue that the best strategy was to rely on constitutional means to defeat the government. Violence, except when it could be presented in a defensive light, was seen as an obstacle to this strategy because it alienated White voters. But not merely were there divisions within the extreme right over means, they were also divided over policy. An increasingly influential section of the extreme right argued that it was no longer realistic to advocate the restoration of apartheid and that the plans the extreme right formulated for the future had to take into account the shift that had taken place in the balance of political forces in the country.

This was an acknowledgment of an important aspect of the dynamic of the reform process. The South African government had faced a crisis of governability since 1976 when the brutal suppression of a protest by schoolchildren in Soweto had sparked off nation-wide unrest. Social and economic reforms followed as the government accepted that repressive measures alone were not sufficient to quell the unrest. However, the government found that the reforms it had introduced produced a shift in the balance of power in the society, which forced the government to make further concessions to the subordinate communities. Adding to the pressure on the government for reform was an accompanying demographic shift in the country's population. During the first 50 years of the country's existence, the White ratio of the population had remained at approximately a fifth of the total. By 1991, the White ratio had fallen to 14.1 per cent and was projected to fall to 11.4 per cent by the year 2000.[10] Another complicating factor in the extreme right's response was uncertainty over the government's intentions. At the time of Mandela's release, the government was still insisting that any further dispensation would have to incorporate the concept of group rights. As the ANC rejected the notion of group rights out of hand, the government's commitment to the concept seemed hard to reconcile with its hopes for a negotiated settlement.[11]

At the start of 1991, the position of the extreme right seemed relatively strong. It enjoyed widespread support among Whites. At the same time, the launch of the Inkatha Freedom Party (IFP) in August 1990 presented a challenge to the ANC's domination of the townships. Further, the extreme right claimed persuasively that there was widespread support for its position among Whites in security forces, and especially in the police. By the end of the year, its position had weakened considerably. In February 1991 De Klerk had announced that racially discriminatory legislation would be repealed, maintaining the momentum of reform. In August the AWB announced its intention to confront President De Klerk when he addressed a meeting in Ventersdorp, a stronghold of extreme right-wing opinion. The AWB mobilized over 2,000 of its members for confrontation. They were met by a large contingent of police. Three AWB members were killed and 58 people were injured in the ensuing conflict between the police and AWB paramilitants. The readiness of Afrikaner policemen to open fire on the extreme right undermined a widespread assumption that the extreme right could count on, at the very least, the passivity of the security forces in any conflict with the state. Finally, in December, negotiations began among 19 political parties on the future political orientation of the country. The Convention for a Democratic South Africa (CODESA) proceeded despite a boycott by the extreme right-wing parties, which stated that the talks were doomed to failure because of the absence of parties that, they claimed, enjoyed the support of a majority of Whites.

The Conservative Party's capture of a seat from the National Party in a by-election in February 1992 appeared to provide a measure of support for that claim. In response President De Klerk called a referendum on the reform process among White voters, staking the whole future of the process on its outcome. While the ANC objected, it did nothing to obstruct the referendum and indeed urged Whites to vote 'yes' to the continuation of the reform process. The government in its campaign made a great play of the threat of a resumption of international sanctions against South Africa in the event of a 'no' vote and of the link between the extreme right-wing parties and violent paramilitants. Its tactics were successful. The government won the backing of 69 per cent of those who voted, a result further underpinned by a very high turn-out.

The outcome of the March 1992 referendum was a divesting blow to the extreme right. It had always attacked the legitimacy of the reform process on the grounds that it conflicted with White self-determination. White endorsement of the process undercut this position. The parties at CODESA in December 1991 had signed a Declaration of Intent establishing parameters for their negotiations. This included a commitment by all parties to universal adult suffrage on a common roll of voters in an undivided South Africa. While the government continued to emphasize the importance of minority rights and of the principle of power-sharing during the referendum campaign, the CODESA Declaration of Intent left little doubt that Whites had endorsed a major shift in power to the previously voteless African majority. This presented the extreme right with a further dilemma as to the country's future dispensation.

In the event, there was deadlock in the negotiations at CODESA in May 1992 and a breakdown in relations between the government and the ANC, partly prompted by continuing political violence in the townships and in Natal. In particular, there was the deep suspicion within the ANC that the violence was directed towards the weakening of the ANC and enjoyed the support of elements both of the security forces and of the government. The ANC launched a campaign of mass action to put pressure on the government, but it threatened to spiral out of control. In September the government and the ANC stepped back from the brink, signing *The Record of Understanding*. This signalled the determination of the two sides to reach a political accommodation. It infuriated Chief Buthelezi of the IFP since it clearly indicated that the government had abandoned the strategy of seeking to promote a leading role for Buthelezi and his party.

Even before *The Record of Understanding*, the prospect of the resumption of multiparty negotiations had precipitated division within the ranks of the extreme right over the issue of negotiations with the ANC. In August *Afrikaner Volksunie* (AVU – People's Union) under Andries Beyers broke from the Conservative Party in order to be able to negotiate with the ANC, which it recognized as representing most Blacks. Such realism was a minority position, but an indication of the shift of opinion occurring within the extreme right. It was followed by a change in the approach of the principal organization on the extreme right, the Conservative Party. Its leader, Andries Treurnicht, persuaded the party that it could not stand aside from negotiations on a new dispensation. As a first step the party participated in a conference to prepare the ground for multiparty negotiations. That paved the way for the party's participation in the Multi-Party Forum that got under way in April 1993 at the World Trade Centre outside Johannesburg. At the same time, the breach that had occurred between the National Party government and the IFP as a result of *The Record of Understanding* created new possibilities for the extreme right. They were reflected in the establishment in the Concerned South Africans Group (COSAG) in October 1992. It included the IFP, the leaders of two of the country's independent homelands, President Lucas Mangope of Bophuthatswana and Brigadier Oupa Gqozo of Ciskei, the Conservation Party, and the AVU. Another indication of changing alignments was De Klerk's suspension or retirement in December of 23 senior officers of the South African Defence Force accused of involvement in efforts to sabotage negotiations.

Throughout this period of tumultuous political change, violence continued to be a significant component of extreme right-wing political activity. For example, there was a spate of bombing attacks attributed to the extreme right during the referendum campaign in 1992. However, the impact of extreme right-wing violence remained slight until 10 April 1992. On that day a Polish immigrant with extreme right-wing sympathies and connections shot dead an immensely popular Black political leader, Chris Hani, at his home in Boksburg near Johannesburg. The assassination of Hani, general secretary of the South African Communist Party, provoked a wave of anger among Blacks that threatened to engulf the country in further violence. The political impact of the assassination is described well by Allister Sparks:

> As with all the previous crises, this national trauma strengthened rather than weakened the political centre and spurred the negotiating parties to speed up their work. It also enhanced Mandela's stature as a national leader. As the crisis swelled, there was little that De Klerk could do to calm the nation; but Mandela could, for they were his people who were aggrieved. He went on national television at the height of the furor and issued a moving appeal to whites and blacks to close ranks and prevent their emotions from destroying their joint future.[12]

In short, the assassination of Hani proved politically counter-productive from the perspective of the extreme right.

The spur given by the crisis to the negotiating process was reflected in the setting of a provisional date (27 April 1994) for the country's first non-racial democratic elections. This was despite protests from COSAG. The prospect of the date's confirmation by the Multi-Party Forum prompted a further high-profile act of political violence by the extreme right. On 25 June, over 3,000 members of AWB, some in khaki, others in the black uniforms of the AWB's élite paramilitary unit, the *Ystergarde* (Iron Guard), invaded the World Trade Centre, venue for the Multi-party Forum. They used a yellow armoured vehicle to smash their way into the building through its plate glass frontage. The protesters took over the negotiating chamber, hurling abuse at any delegates to the talks they encountered, but most especially Black delegates regardless of their political affiliation. The police charged with guarding the talks did not intervene, justifying their inaction on the grounds that any attempt to arrest protesters would have endangered lives, since the AWB paramilitants were heavily armed. After having disrupted the proceedings of the Multi-Party Forum for the day, the protesters eventually withdrew.

The protesters achieved massive publicity. The pictures of their dramatic entry into the World Trade Centre were relayed around the world. However, in other aspects, they achieved relatively little. They did not prevent the confirmation of the election date. Further, their actions strained relations within COSAG, due to the overtly racist behaviour of many of the AWB protestors. But a troubling aspect of the incident for the government and the ANC was the behaviour of the police, notwithstanding the case that could be made for the tactics they adopted. It reinforced the need for ways to be found to defuse the threat posed by the extreme right, especially in the light of its tactical alliance with the IFP and two of the independent homelands. The persistence of that alliance, despite strains, was underscored by the launch of the Freedom Alliance in October 1993, a repackaging of COSAG designed to enhance its popular appeal.

An important development in extreme right-wing politics preceded the dramatic events at the World Trade Centre. This was the formation in May 1993 of the *Afrikaner Volksfront* (AVF – people's front). Headed by four generals, the AVF provided an umbrella for a multitude of extreme right-wing organizations. The formation of the AVF was partly due to the polarization that occurred as a result of the unrest that followed Hani's assassination. It also reflected a crystallization of the objectives of the extreme right into demands for the creation of a *volkstaat* or Afrikaner homeland. This approach chimed in well with the regionalist demands for self-determination of the members of the Freedom Alliance. These demands were backed up by the threat of a boycott of the country's first non-racial elections that would have been damaging to the legitimacy of the whole process.

Potent though the weapon of an election boycott was, it had two major disadvantages. Firstly, it alienated international opinion sympathetic to the case for federalism, which provided the most moderate gloss on the demands of the extreme right. Secondly, it ran counter to the strong desire of Blacks in every region of the country to participate in the election. Indeed, the attempt of President Lucas Mangope to prevent the people in Bophuthatswana from taking part in the election brought about a revolution. After Mangope announced that Bophuthatswana would not be taking part in the election, civil servants in the independent homeland went on strike. When the police joined in the strike, conditions became increasingly chaotic. Mangope then appealed for assistance from his allies in the Freedom Alliance. Had the effort to help Mangope been entirely channelled through the generals of the AVF, a revolution might have been averted. It was the intervention of the AWB that doomed it. A force of several hundred AWB paramilitants entered Bophuthatswana after they had been mobilized in response to appeals for assistance for the Mangope government broadcast over the radio station run by the extreme right, Radio Pretoria. The racism of the AWB members proved their undoing. When AWB members opened fire at random on Black civilians in Mabatho, the capital of Bophuthatswana, this proved too much for the hitherto loyal members of the Bophuthatswanan Defence Forces. They mutinied, turning their guns on the paramilitants of the AWB. That prompted their rout. In the AWB's retreat from Bophuthatswana, two of its members were shot in cold blood by Bophuthatswanan policemen in full view of the world's media. The impact was immense. An influential section of the extreme right treated these events as proof of the disutility of violence as a means for furthering the cause of a *volkstaat*. Immediately after the confrontation in Bophuthatswana, General Constand Viljoen in defiance of the majority of the AVF registered for the election in the name of the Freedom Front. His action quickly won the support of many of the leading figures on the extreme right.

The overthrow of Mangope put pressure on the other members of the Freedom Alliance. Brigadier Gqozo of Ciskei voluntarily gave up power after civil servants there went on strike. That left Buthelezi and the IFP. Their resistance to the election lasted longest. In fact, the IFP's agreement to participate only came in the week before polling began. The achievement of an inclusive election was not simply the product of the negative pressures on the parties attempting to disrupt the process, it was also the product of positive incentives to participate. Both the National Party government and the ANC felt sufficiently confident about the basis of their own agreement, providing for power sharing for a period of five years after the election, that they were willing to explore all avenues to secure the participation of the other parties.

In the run-up to the election, a series of concessions were made to the other parties. In the case of the extreme right, the ANC and the National Party agreed to an accord with the Freedom Front in early April to ensure its full commitment to the election. The accord provided for the formation after the election of a *volkstaatsraad*, a statutory council consisting of 20 members. In addition, there was provision for an advisory body consisting of 25 elected representatives of the local communities from areas where the general election showed there was support for the concept of a *volkstaat*. The two bodies were to report to the Constituent Assembly charged with drawing up the constitution on the feasibility of setting up a *volkstaat*, bearing in mind references in the interim constitution to the principle of self-determination within the context of a united South Africa. What this amounted to was the promise that if the extreme right was able to demonstrate widespread support within the white community, serious efforts would be made to accommodate its demands. However, this impressed neither the Conservative Party nor the AWB, both of which denounced the accord as worthless. They continued to urge a boycott of the election.[13]

The election campaign consequently was a battle for influence over the extreme right between the Freedom Front and the Conservative Party. The defection of nine Conservative MPs to the Freedom Front was an indication of its success in this contest. In the election itself, the Freedom Front polled 2.2 per cent of the national vote. It did substantially better in the elections to nine regional parliaments, with 3.2 per cent of the total votes cast. Ironically, in view of the image of right-wing Afrikaners as farmers, it achieved its best results in the overwhelmingly urban province of Pretoria–Witwatersrand–Vereeniging, where it polled 6.2 per cent of the vote in the regional elections.[14] While the total number of votes cast for the Freedom Front in the national elections was less than half that of the 'no' vote in the 1992 referendum, the previous benchmark of support for the extreme right, its relatively small share of the vote was fundamentally a reflection of the fact that the overwhelming majority of the electorate was Black. Thus, it has been estimated that in the regional elections, the party polled 41 per cent of the votes of White Afrikaners.[15]

A bomb placed near the ANC regional office in the city centre of Johannesburg on 24 April killed nine people and injured approximately a hundred people. The following day there were bomb attacks on a restaurant in Pretoria, which killed two people and injured 29, and on a taxi rank in Germiston, which killed ten people and injured 41. There were also other bomb attacks mainly directed at property, including two polling stations. However, none of the attacks had any discernible impact upon the process of polling. Reassurance to the public was provided by the early arrest of a number of AWB members in connection with the blasts. From a political perspective, the threat of extreme right-wing violence reinforced the dominance of peace as an election issue. The party that may have been damaged by that was the Pan-Africanist Congress, with its association with the slogan 'one settler one bullet' contributing to the party's dismal result.

Neither the constitutional nor the violent wing of the extreme right has made much of an impression on South African politics since the election. Negotiations over a *volkstaat* appear to have made little progress. The fundamental problem for the constitutional extreme right is that the size and nature of the territory that could realistically be demanded for an Afrikaner homeland has little appeal in practice to most Afrikaners, including even the supporters of the extreme right. Extreme right-wing violence has not ceased, but threats of civil war have lost their potency, along with their credibility. The main incident attributed to the extreme right was the assassination in November 1994 of a former leader of the main Dutch Reformed Church, Professor Johan Heyns. The threat of further extreme right-wing violence was underlined by the interception by the police of weapons destined for the extreme right. The arms had been sent to South Africa by American extreme right-wingers.[16]

South Africa has often been compared to other deeply divided societies such as Northern Ireland and Israel. It is possible to make the comparison at a number of levels. In particular, there are a number of parallels between the violence of the extreme right in South Africa and Loyalist violence in Northern Ireland during the province's latest troubles between 1968 and 1994. In both situations, right-wing violence was a response, in the first instance, to reform measures initiated from within the dominant community as well as to the erosion of segregation between the communities. In both cases there were numerous instances of violence being directed in a totally indiscriminate manner against members of the subordinate community. Another similarity between the paramilitaries in the two cases was their links with elements in the security forces, especially in the lower ranks of those drawn from the dominant community. In both, there were allegations of collusion between the security forces and right-wing paramilitaries that led to suspicion being cast on the role and attitude of government, though the most common charge against government was one of failure to control rogue members or elements of the security forces.

But for all the similarities between the two cases, there was a very substantial difference between them. The scale of extreme right-wing violence during South Africa's transition never reached the level or intensity of Loyalist violence during Northern Ireland's troubles. There are a number of possible explanations that can be given for the differences. Firstly, the historical experience of vigilantism in the two societies was different. In Northern Ireland the threat of force in the form of the Ulster Volunteer Force helped to stave off the imposition of Irish home rule before the First World War, establishing a precedent for the successful use of violence by the dominant community. By contrast, the National Party rejected the use of such tactics by Afrikaners during the Second World War and its insistence on following a constitutional road to power was vindicated by its electoral victory in 1948. Secondly, the numerical preponderance of the subordinate community in South Africa meant that indiscriminate violence against members of the subordinate community appeared (and was in practice) more obviously self-defeating than in a situation where the subordinate community was a minority. Thirdly, the fact that agencies of the South African state were so active over the years in conducting covert warfare against the government's political adversaries provided a further reason for restraint by the White extreme right. Fourthly, although the process of reform was much more far-reaching in the South African case, every step on the way was carried through by a government elected by Whites. In Northern Ireland, the dominant community lost its veto on reform within the province when the British government imposed direct rule in March 1972. This provoked a sharp escalation in the level of Loyalist violence. The primary agency for political change in South Africa was the realization among Whites that they had to come to terms with the shift in power that was taking place in the country as a result of demographic and economic change. Such pressure was not present to the same degree in Northern Ireland. In South Africa, even the extreme right was influenced by the power realities. This was not unprecedented. A similar process of change had taken place in other African societies where a White minority had wielded power over an African majority. However, as the Algerian case shows, the potentiality did exist for a catastrophic ending. A variety of factors contributed to the relative smoothness of the change in the South African case, including a favourable international climate for such change. Among the most important internal factors were the tactics employed by the ANC to defuse the threat from the extreme right, most particularly the encouragement the ANC gave to the pursuit of a constitutional option by the extreme right.

Notes

1. Sir Arthur Conan Doyle, *The Memoirs of Sherlock Holmes* (Penguin, Harmondsworth 1950), p. 28.
2. See, for example, S. Friedman and D. Atkinson (eds), *The Small Miracle: South Africa's Negotiated Settlement (South African Review 7)* (Ravan Press, Johannesburg 1994).
3. Hermann Giliomee, 'Consolidating South Africa's New Democracy', *South African Foundation Review* (Johannesburg), Sept./Oct. 1994.

4. See J.H.P. Serfontein, *Die Verkrampt Aanslag* (Human & Rouseau, Kaapstad en Pretoria, 1970).
5. Quoted in C. Cooper (ed.), *Race Relations Survey 1987/88* (South African Institute of Race Relations, Johannesburg 1988), p. 718.
6. See, for example, Mduduzi ka Harvey, 'How Khotso House was Bombed', *The Weekly Mail and Guardian* (Johannesburg), 16–22 Dec. 1994.
7. *Five-year Plan of Action of the National Party 1989–94*, (National Party, Cape Town, 1989).
8. *Back to the Laager: The Rise of White Right-Wing Violence in South Africa* (Legal Foundation Education Project, Institute of Criminology, University of Cape Town, Cape Town 1991), p. 12.
9. The figures are given in the year-end review in *Monthly Repression Report: December 1993*, Human Rights Commission, Braamfontein.
10. The figures are cited in *South Africa 1993*, South African Foundation, Johannesburg 1992, p. 9.
11. See, for example, Nelson Mandela, *Long Walk to Freedom* (MacDonald Purnell, Randburg 1994), pp. 544–5.
12. Allister Sparks, *Tomorrow Is Another Country: The Inside Story of South Africa's Negotiated Revolution* (Struik, Sandton 1994), p. 189.
13. A. Reynolds (ed.), *Election '94 South Africa: The Campaigns, Results and Future Prospects* (David Philip, Cape Town 1994), p.47.
14. *Ibid.*, p. 208.
15. *Ibid.*, p.104.
16. *The Star* (Johannesburg), 22 Nov. 1994.

Conclusions

Leonard Weinberg

In theory, or at least according to some theories, right-wing extremism should no longer exist. Over the course of this century many observers have linked the appearance of ultra-right movements and parties, fascist ones in particular, to social or political conditions that seem to have disappeared in recent years. There is, in short, a body of theoretically informed writing on the subject, which would lead readers to the conclusion that in Europe and America, at least, right-wing extremist organizations, rather like monarchist ones, are atavistic, left-overs from a bygone area whose contemporary relevance is hard to discern.

One widely known interpretation links right-wing extremism to anti-communism. For any number of analysts radical and violent oppositon to the communist cause constitutes its *raison d'être*. For instance, during the 1950s and '60s in the United States the McCarthy phenomenon, the John Birch Society, Christian Anti-Communist Crusade and a long list of like-minded individuals and groups were able to arouse popular fears of a pervasive domestic communist conspiracy in order to advance their political interests.[1]

During the inter-war period in Europe, left-wing observers saw the rise of fascism as an outgrowth of the class struggle. Particularly for Marxists, the appearance of fascist movements in Italy, Germany and elsewhere was interpreted as an attempt by capitalists violently to repress the revolutionary aspirations of the working class. No revolutionary working class under communist auspices, no fascist movement, at least not one of any signifance.[2]

In recent years the Soviet Union has disintegrated and the communist threat has virtually disappeared (an unreconstructed communist party continues to do well at parliamentary elections in Nepal). Despite these developments, parties, movements and individual politicians espousing right-wing extremism have not become extinct. In the United States, for example, David Duke, a man whose biography includes positions of leadership in neo-Nazi and Ku Klux Klan organizations, came close to being elected governor of Louisiana. The Rev. Pat Robertson continues to be an influential force inside the Republican party. At the 1994 Italian national elections, the National Alliance, the re-named successor of the neo-Fascist Italian Social Movement, received a higher percentage of the vote than it had at any time since the end of the Second World War, including periods when it seemed as if Italy's Communist Party was on the verge of coming to power. In France Le Pen's *Front National* became a significant electoral force long after the once formidable French Communist party slipped below the waves.

Another widely discussed interpretation of the fascist version of right-wing extremism, Italian Fascism in particular, reverses the Marxist understanding. According to this line of reasoning classical fascism was not a reactionary but a progressive force.[3] Among other things, it represented a strategy for promoting national economic development in countries that were latecomers to the industrialization process. Mussolini's regime, properly understood, was the first twentieth-century example of a 'mass-mobilizing developmental dictatorship'. A. James Gregor and the other scholars who see fascist movements as promoting social solidarity, enhanced economic productivity and national glory believe that such movements continue to exist as we approach the end of the twentieth century. They have not disappeared but merely changed location. Most countries in Europe have long since passed the stage of economic and political development when fascist movements had any chance of gaining mass support. Such movements and some regimes on which they are based are presently to be found in the Third World. The Baathist dictatorship of Saddam Hussein in Iraq comes to mind.[4]

In sharp contrast to those who see it currently at work in parts of Africa, the Middle East and Latin America, there are other observers who stress fascism's historical particularity. The historians Renzo de Felice and H.R. Trevor-Roper, among others, maintain that fascism was the short-term consequence of a general crisis that Europe experienced in the aftermath of the First World War. From this perspective fascism began in 1919 and ended in 1945 with the defeat of the Axis.[5] That's that. Virtually by definition then the idea of 'neo'-fascism becomes an impossibility.

It seems clear that none of the above interpretations is especially helpful in aiding our understanding of the emergence or, arguably, re-emergence of strong right-wing extremist forces in the 1980s and '90s. There is a need for new theories and new interpretations – along the lines suggested by some of the contributors to this volume. However, before commenting on these suggestions and perhaps some other lines of inquiry, it may be helpful to all concerned if we attempted to judge the magnitude of the problem. Just how powerful is the current manifestation of right-wing extremism? After all, not all the contributors to this volume have been persuaded that right-wing extremism poses all that serious a challenge to democratic politics. Illustratively, Adrian Guelke is struck by the 'dog that did not bark', the inability of extreme defenders of apartheid to muster much support during South Africa's transition to majority rule. In reporting *Eurobarometer* data, Lauri Karvonen expresses uncertainty about the extent to which there has been a serious increase in anti-foreigner attitudes among West European publics in recent years. And Taras Kuzio notes the absence of any significant radical right activity in Belarus.

Perhaps the best way to measure the level of popular support for political parties of the extreme right in the countries on which this collection of essays is focused is to use recent national electoral returns and place them in historical context. So far as the latter is concerned, an obvious benchmark is the electoral performance of fascist parties during the 1920s and '30s, fascism's 'golden age'. Or, in other words, how well do contemporary parties of the extreme right perform at the polls compared to their fascist predecessors of the inter-war period?

The effort to answer this question is fraught with difficulties. In the case of Eastern Europe and the new European republics of the ex-Soviet Union we are dealing with nations whose experiences with open competitive elections is highly uneven, to say the least. Thus, Zhirinovsky's Liberal Democrats may have taken approximately one-quarter of the vote in Russia's 1993 parliamentary election but there is no standard with which to compare its recent performance. Despite the existence of various pro-fascist exile groups, and so on, during the inter-war period, the Communist Party of the Soviet Union monopolized the voting process in that era not only in the Russian Republic but also in the Ukraine and Belarus.[6]

All things considered, the most sensible way to measure the electoral strength of contemporary parties of the extreme right is to restrict the analysis to countries that had both open competitive elections during the 1920s and 1930s and fascist parties contesting them. Further, given the differences in historical experiences (for instance, was the country part of or occupied by the Soviet Union?), it also makes sense to keep the new post-1989 democracies of Eastern Europe, the old Warsaw Pact, separate from the longer-lasting ones of Western Europe.

Electoral data on the performance of fascist parties in the inter-war period were drawn from Juan Linz's well-known essay on the 'Comparative Study of Fascism'.[7] For Western Europe, both the identity of parties of the extreme right and their level of voter support during the 1980s and early 1990s were drawn from the work of Piero Ignazi.[8] Since Linz reports fascist parties contesting elections in Romania, Hungary and Czechoslovakia, this analysis only compares their inter-war electoral results with those of contemporary extreme-right parties active in the same countries (the Czech Republic and Slovakia are treated separately) as described in the contributions to this volume by Thomas Szayna and Henry Carey.

TABLE 1
AVERAGE* OF FASCIST AND EXTREME RIGHT VOTE:
INTERWAR PERIOD AND 1980s – 1990s

Country	Interwar	1980s-1990s
Austria	5.46%	10.77%
Belgium	7.49	3.00
Denmark	0.64	4.72
France	-.---	8.01
Germany	16.67	0.95
Italy	19.24	7.90
Netherlands	4.06	0.74
Norway	2.02	6.88
Spain	0.70	-.--
Sweden	0.44	6.70
Switzerland	1.47	4.40
United Kingdom	0.16	0.00
Average	5.22	4.92

* In those countries where the fascists competed in only one election, the percentage of the vote garnered by the fascist parties is used in lieu of the mean.

Western Europe

Table 1 reports the average (mean) level of electoral support, by country, received by fascist and right-wing extremist parties in the two periods. Obviously at the national level there is some significant year-to-year variation. Although a number of fascist parties contested elections in France's Third Republic, none achieved much support at the polls. That is decidedly not the case with Le Pen's *Front National,* which has. In Germany the situation is reversed. The Nazis were a major electoral force, especially after Germans felt the impact of the world-wide Depression. But today, despite considerable apprehension, the extreme-right parties are a negligible factor, at least when it comes to voting at recent *Bundestag* elections.

Despite these and other national variations, there are two observations that seem striking. First, despite the enormous historical differences between the two eras under scrutiny, there is very little difference in the overall magnitude of popular support enjoyed by fascist and contemporary extreme-right parties. On average the fascist parties of the 1920s and 1930s fared only slightly better, less than one quarter of one per cent, than their counterparts of the 1980s and 1990s. In other words, in purely electoral terms today's extreme right in Western Europe is about as formidable as fascism during its 'golden age'.

The second observation that stands out is the very limited appeal right-wing extremism had for West European voters in both periods. In the 1980s and 1990s, as in the 1920s and 1930s, we are dealing with parties whose average level of electoral support congregates around five per cent. The Italian Fascist and German Nazi cases are clearly aberrant. To the extent Mussolini's party enjoyed widespread popular support, it was as the result of the crisis that Italy experienced immediately after the First World War. In Weimar Germany it should not be forgotten that the Nazis won precisely 2.8 per cent of the vote in the 1928 *Bundestag* elections, that is in the last national balloting before the Depression hit. As in Western Europe so too in the United States, the inter-war decades are widely believed to have been a time when fascist and various other types of extreme right-wing movements flourished. During the 1930s especially such pro- or quasi- fascist political figures as Father Charles Coughlin, the radio priest, and Louisiana Senator Huey Long won or allegedly won millions of followers on the bases of their demagogic appeals. Further, historians of the 1930s call attention to the visibility of such mimetic fascist groups as the Silver Shirts, Black Legion, Christian Front and German-American Bund in these years.

But if we measure strength in electoral terms, fascism or right-wing extremism does not appear to have been particularly formidable. In the 1936 presidential elections Father Coughlin's candidate, the North Dakota congressman William 'Liberty Bell' Lemke, won less than one per cent of the popular vote.[9] (Of course if Huey Long had not been assassinated in 1935 he would most likely have made a more impressive showing.)

The situation in the United States during the 1980s and 1990s is not strikingly different. There are an abundance of right-wing extremist groups which are opposed to the constitutional order for a variety of religious or secular reasons. Some advocate or even practise violence to advance their political objectives. Yet if we apply the same electoral test as in the 1930s the result is about the same. In recent years, the extreme right-wing Populist party, a creation of the long-time antisemitic activist

Willis Carto, mounted presidential campaigns on behalf of several aspirants.[10] None of the latter, ranging from the former Olympic pole-vaulter the Reverend Bob Richards to the ex-Green Beret officer Charles 'Bo' Gritz, came close to gaining one per cent of the popular vote. The same may be said about the outcomes of the multiple presidential campaigns of cult leader Lyndon LaRouche.[11]

TABLE 2
AVERAGE OF FASCIST AND EXTREME-RIGHT VOTE:
INTERWAR PERIOD AND 1990s FOR EASTERN EUROPE

Country	Interwar		1990s
Czechoslovakia	27.30	Czech	3.70
		Slovakia	9.70
Hungary	13.90		1.60
Romania	5.71		11.60
Average	15.60		6.60

Eastern Europe

The electoral performance of the extreme right improves as we turn from the Western democracies to the countries of Eastern Europe. Compared to Western Europe and the United States, fascist parties did relatively well at the polls (see Table 2) at competitive elections in Romania, Hungary and Czechoslovakia during the inter-war period. The average for all three countries is over 15 per cent. To the extent that it can be measured by voter preference, fascist parties, on average, were more than twice as popular in Eastern than in Western Europe.

The relationship today is somewhat different. Based admittedly on a comparative handful of national elections since 1990 in Romania, Hungary, the Czech Republic and Slovakia, parties of the extreme right perform better than their counterparts on the other side of the old 'iron curtain'. But the difference on this occasion is only a few percentage points. Furthermore, unlike the situation in the West, where average voter support for contemporary extreme-right parties approximates to that obtained by their fascist predecessors, the East European extreme right has been, so far, less than half as successful as the old fascist groupings. These results seem rather surprising. Since 1989 much popular commentary concerned with the dangers of a revived right-wing extremism has focused on the situation in Eastern Europe. The emphasis has been on the susceptibility of new fragile democracies to the old prejudices and unreconstructed fascists of the pre-communist era.[12] Proportionately speaking however, the new right-wing forces in Eastern Europe are much weaker today than were the fascists, while in the West the new extreme right is about as popular as the old.

One problem with this attempt to evaluate the seriousness of the challenge posed by the contemporary extreme right is the unit of measurement: the vote. Fascist movements often sought to make their weight felt and to arouse mass support by means other than electoral campaigns. In Italy, Germany and elsewhere these movements employed paramilitary parades, mass public rallies, street corner brawling, 'punitive expeditions' and any number of other primitive theatrical displays to create the impression of dynamism and widespread popular support. Furthermore, there is the elusive but not insignificant matter of atmospherics. In the 1920s and 1930s the anti-democratic fascist world-view was able to win adherents among many influential intellectuals, writers, artists, scientists, journalists and other public figures. The effect was to amplify the significance of fascist movements far beyond the magnitude of their electoral support. Also, in the earlier era democratic politicians, government leaders and proponents of constitutional order were far less secure in their defence of democratic institutions than is the case with their counterparts in the 1980s and 1990s. And, perhaps most important of all, there were the two functioning dictatorships in Italy and Germany to serve as centres of power and poles of attraction for fascists all over Europe and beyond.

To say that today's extreme right does not represent as formidable a threat to democratic political systems as inter-war fascism should not lead us however to minimize its significance. As suggested by some of the earlier accounts in this volume, there are a number of nations in the West – Austria, Belgium, France, Italy – where the extreme right appears to be exceptionally dynamic. In the East, someone would have to be truly myopic not to see the dangers that Russia faces from ultra-right forces. And while it is easy to use the term 'fascist' promiscuously, its application to the forces at work in Serbia and Serbian-controlled Bosnia does not seem all that far off the mark.[13]

As a consequence there is a need for some interpretation, some theorizing, as a means for getting a purchase on these developments. In this writer's judgement the best approach requires that we employ a few old ideas in combination with some new ones.

Although it would be hard to imagine them agreeing on much else, both Renzo de Felice and H.R. Trevor-Roper see fascism as consisting of two distinct strands.[14] For de Felice the distinction is between Fascism as 'movement' and Fascism as 'regime': the one dynamic and revolutionary, the other conservative and backward-looking. Trevor-Roper writes:

> ... behind the vague term 'fascism' there lie, in fact, two distinct social and political systems which the opportunism of politicians and the muddled thinking of journalists have constantly confused. These two systems are both ideologically based. Both are authoritarian, opposed to parliamentary liberalism. But they are different... They can be conveniently described as 'clerical conservatism' and 'dynamic fascism'. Almost every fascist movement has been compounded of both these elements, but in varying proportions; ....[15]

The relevance of these distinctions to the contemporary extreme right is essentially geographic. As the accounts in this volume provided by Henry Carey, Taras Kuzio, Thomas Szayna and Vera Tolz suggest, right-wing extremism in Eastern Europe and Russia seems very much different from its counterpart in Western Europe and the United States. Perhaps such terms as 'clerical conservatism' or 'regime' do not fit perfectly. For one thing, the Catholic church is now a strong advocate of parliamentary democracy. Nonetheless, there is some sense in thinking of the various movements as belonging to an earlier stage of European development, when a combination of anti-capitalism, anti-communism, populist ultra-nationalism, hostility to ethnic minorities and religious orthodoxy could be forged into a cohesive political force.[16] In the case of the new Russian Republic we should add some dynamic and potentially very dangerous elements to this mixture: the anger caused by the experience of national humiliation and the emergence of movements aimed at the resurrection of the national community under authoritarian auspices and the reconquest of lost territories by the threat of military force.[17]

The situation in the West is substantially different. We are dealing with countries that are among the most prosperous on earth. To the extent that fascism was 'dynamic' and a 'movement' which offered a particular solution to the problems of production and industrial growth, its relevance to the current post-industrial circumstances is hard to fathom. Further, as Mattei Dogan and other observers of West European politics have noted, there has been a long-term decline in nationalist sentiment among the various populations. Using Eurobarometer survey evidence, Dogan reports that, in general, there has been a decline in feelings of national pride, confidence in one's national army and in willingness to fight for one's country in the event of war. At the same time, the level of trust in national neighbours, for example, French for

Germans and vice versa, has increased as have feelings of belonging to the European Community.[18] Therefore to the degree that fascism in the West, dynamic or otherwise, exploited popular nationalist longings, 'mutilated victory' and so on, its contemporary popular appeal or potential electoral space is quite limited.

The sort of right-wing extremism presently manifesting itself in the advanced industrial democracies of Western Europe is a political force whose discourses are addressed to the present day concerns of many citizens. Among other things, these concerns have to do with the presence of large numbers of immigrants from outside the European Union, people from Algeria, Turkey, South Asia and the West Indies especially, who are often perceived as threatening to the economic status and cultural primacy of the indigenous inhabitants. In some cases the rightists depict themselves as defenders of European civilization now threatened by Ottoman or Moorish invaders. Not uncommonly these extreme rightists use the United States as a negative reference point. It is precisely America's evolving multiculturalism they wish to avoid for their own countries.

There is a certain irony here because other themes, the new right-wing extremists stress, have been borrowed from their counterparts on the other side of the Atlantic. While inter-war fascists celebrated the 'strong state' (totalitarian was a term coined by Mussolini after all), encouraged the subordination of the individual to this entity, and often condemned the market-place as a source of economic and social chaos, the new rightists have been attracted to the views of American conservatives. On balance, the new rightists have found the achievements and views of Ronald Reagan more compelling than those of Julius Evola or the Strasser brothers.[19] The opposition many rightists now voice about Maastricht and the prospect of rule by unresponsive 'eurocrats' from Brussels sounds remarkably like the condemnations of Washington bureaucrats and 'inside the beltway' decision-makers uttered by spokespersons for the American right-wing.

There are fringe groups in Western Europe which express nostalgia for the old fascist regimes, and if pressed LePen, Haider and Schönhuber can be induced to say a few words of sympathy for Hitler and his various imitators, but unlike the inter-war fascists, leaders of the new extreme-right parties do not condemn democratic institutions *per se*. Rather like the right-wing advocates of Proposition 187 in California in 1994, they seek to manipulate these institutions for their own usually xenophobic ends.

Finally, there is the matter of value change, a subject to which Peter Merkl, Michael Minkenberg and Piero Ignazi pay particular attention in this volume. Right-wing extremism in the advanced industrial democracies has been able to exploit what Ignazi has referred to as a 'silent counter-revolution'.[20] (The reference is to Ronald Inglehart's well-known formulation that the growth of 'post-materialist' values constitutes a silent revolution in Western Europe.) More specifically, the changes in outlook that we associate with the 1960s, feminist, environmental, aesthetic, egalitarian, third worldist, pacifist, and so on, stimulated the formation of a host of new social movements and other political organizations – the green parties, for example. These developments have now produced a backlash of significant proportions. In some cases the 'silent counter-revolution' has taken the form of new-right intellectual activity, as Michael Minkenberg points out, while in many other cases the reaction has produced an array of parties and other political groupings, as Merkl and Ignazi have called to our attention. In Western Europe the cultural backlash has been conducted, by and large, without benefit of religious fervour. In the United States, on the other hand, fundamentalist religious groups have often taken the lead in these matters. Despite this difference, the silent counter-revolution is an important source of right-wing extremist sentiment on both sides of the Atlantic.

Notes

1. See for example, D. Bell (ed.), *The Radical Right* (New York: Doubleday, 1963).
2. See for example, A. J. Gregor, *Interpretations of Fascism* (Morristown, NJ: General Learning Press, 1974) pp. 128–70.
3. See for example, A. J. Gregor, *Italian Fascism and Developmental Dictatorship* (Princeton,NJ: Princeton University Press, 1979).
4. For an account of fascist-like movements at work in the Third World see, A. J. Gregor, *The Fascist Persuasion in Radical Politics* (Princeton, NJ: Princeton University Press, 1974); and A. Joes, *Fascism in The Contemporary World* (Boulder, CO: Westview Press,1978).
5. See for example, R. de Felice, *Fascism:An Informal Introduction to Its Theory and Practice* (New Brunswick, NJ: Transaction,1976), pp.97–103; H.R. Trevor-Roper, 'The Phenomenon of Fascism', in S.J. Woolf (ed.), *European Fascism* (New York: Vintage Books,1969), pp. 18–38.
6. See for example, W. Laqueur, *Black Hundred: The Rise of the Extreme Right in Russia* (New York: Harper Collins, 1993), pp. 72–85.
7. J. Linz, 'Some Notes Toward a Comparative Study of Fascism in Sociological Historical Perspective', in W. Laqueur (ed.), *Fascism: A Reader's Guide* (Berkeley and Los Angeles: University of California Press, 1976), pp. 89–91.
8. P. Ignazi, *L'Estrema Destra in Europa* (Bologna: Il Mulino, 1994) pp. 243–5.
9. S. Lipset and E. Raab, *The Politics of Unreason* (New York: Harper & Row, 1970), p. 170.
10. 'The Populist Party: The Politics of Right-Wing Extremism', *ADL FACTS* 30:2 (1985).
11. D. King, *Lyndon LaRouche and the New American Fascism* (New York: Doubleday, 1989) pp.98–9.

12. Expectations that antisemitic sentiments in the new East European democracies would reach inter-war levels do not appear to have been met either. See, R. Cohen and J. Golub, *Attitudes Toward Jews in Poland, Hungary and Czechoslovakia:A Comparative Survey* (New York: The American Jewish Committee, 1991), pp. 1–8.
13. See, for example, R. Block, 'Killers' *The New York Review of Books* (18 Nov., 1993), pp. 9–10.
14. de Felice and Trevor-Roper, *op. cit.*
15. *Ibid.*, p. 25
16. The reader might peruse the essays in P. Sugar (ed.),*Native Fascism in the Successor States* (Santa Barbara, CA: ABC–Clio, 1971).
17. This is the amalgamation of ideas with which Roger Griffin associates 'generic fascism'. R. Griffin, *The Nature of Fascism* (London and New York: Routledge, 1991), pp. 32–50.
18. M. Dogan, 'Comparing the Decline of Nationalisms in Western Europe', *International Social Science Journal*, 136 (1993), pp. 177–98.
19. H.-G. Betz,*Radical Right-Wing Populism* (New York: St. Martin's Press, 1994), pp. 1–17.
20. For an elaboration on this theme see, P. Ignazi, 'The Silent Counter-Revolution', *European Journal of Political Research*, 22:1 (1992), pp. 3–34.

Index

abortion rights 35, 42n
Afrikaner Volksfront (AVF) 267–8
Afrikaner Weerstandsbeweging 257, 264–9
alcohol abuse, and violence 37–40
American Nazi Party 239
anti-Americanism 72, 74, 190
anti-capitalism 120–1, 129, 139, 281
anti-Caucasus nations prejudice (Russian) 224
anti-communism 11–12, 48, 93, 106
  in Belarus 204, 224
  in northern tier states 113, 117, 126, 137–9, 146, 280n
  in US 234
anti-Czech resentment 129, 131–3
anti-democratic sentiment 19–20, 49, 54, 60, 110
  in Eastern Europe 113, 190
  of New Right 68, 72
  political authoritarianism 93, 100, 110
anti-foreign prejudice 17, 109
  against asylum seekers 27–9, 70, 109
  of communists 8
  and German resettlers 29–30
  and migrants from non-EU contries 276
  in northern tier states 106, 120
  and violence 2, 32, 44n
anti-German attitudes 119–20, 124, 126–31
anti-Hungarian prejudice 131–5, 151, 156, 159, 163–5
anti-modernism 66
anti-Muslim prejudice 224
anti-Russian sentiment 7, 208
  in Poland 117–19
  in Ukraine 223–4
anti-Semitism 21, 98–9, 143, 281n
  correlates of 102–4, 113
  in Czech Republic 124–5
  in France 72
  in Germany 59

in Hungary 7, 74, 138–40
in Poland 116–21, 145n
in Romania 160–5, 175n
in Russia 177–80, 188
in Slovakia 129–31
in Ukraine 224
in US 11, 234–6, 240–3
Antonescu, Ion 150, 176n
apartheid 13, 256–63
asylum seekers 1, 6
  in Canada 33
  German policies on 13, 17, 26–32, 40n, 43n, 70, 81
  German prejudice against 28
  in France 33, 70
  in Italy 33
  Republikaner and 29
  in US 31, 33
Austria
  anti-Semitism in 103
  asylum seekers in 33
  FPÖ vote in 1
  Hapsburg 24–6
  homophobia in 105
  inter-war years of 9–10, 24–5, 280
  and Russian right 190
  and Ukraine right 213
  see also Freedom Party of Austria (FPÖ)
authoritarianism 92–3, 98–102, 106, 110, 113, 116

Baltic countries 4, 8, 25, 213, 227n
Barkashov, Aleksandr 186, 194, 200n
Belarus 9, 120, 184, 203–6, 276
Belgium 1, 96, 103–5, 109–10, 280
Black Hundreds 179, 182–5
Blanche, Eugene Terre 257–8
Bosnia 4, 281
Britain 1, 2, 105, 109–10